AF712011

# Religion and Law in Germany

# Religion and Law in Germany

**Third Edition**

**Gerhard Robbers**

This book was originally published as a monograph in the International Encyclopaedia of Laws/Religion Law.

Founding Editor: Roger Blanpain
General Editor: Frank Hendrickx
Volume Editor: Wouter Druwé

Wolters Kluwer

*Published by:*
Kluwer Law International B.V.
PO Box 316
2400 AH Alphen aan den Rijn
The Netherlands
E-mail: lrs-sales@wolterskluwer.com
Website: www.wolterskluwer.com/en/solutions/kluwerlawinternational

*Sold and distributed by:*
Wolters Kluwer Legal & Regulatory U.S.
920 Links Avenue
Landisville, PA 17538
United States of America
E-mail: customer.service@wolterskluwer.com

DISCLAIMER: The material in this volume is in the nature of general comment only. It is not offered as advice on any particular matter and should not be taken as such. The editor and the contributing authors expressly disclaim all liability to any person with regard to anything done or omitted to be done, and with respect to the consequences of anything done or omitted to be done wholly or partly in reliance upon the whole or any part of the contents of this volume. No reader should act or refrain from acting on the basis of any matter contained in this volume without first obtaining professional advice regarding the particular facts and circumstances at issue. Any and all opinions expressed herein are those of the particular author and are not necessarily those of the editor or publisher of this volume.

ISBN 978-94-035-3948-5

e-Book: ISBN 978-94-035-3958-4
web-PDF: ISBN 978-94-035-3968-3

© 2024 Kluwer Law International BV, The Netherlands

All rights reserved. No part of this publication may be reproduced, stored in a retrieval system, or transmitted in any form or by any means, electronic, mechanical, photocopying, recording, or otherwise, without the prior written permission of the publisher.

Permission to use this content must be obtained from the copyright owner. More information can be found at: www.wolterskluwer.com/en/solutions/legal-regulatory/permissions-reprints-and-licensing

# The Author

Gerhard Robbers is a Professor Emeritus of Public Law at the University of Trier, Germany. He has also served as a judge at the Constitutional Court of Rhineland-Palatinate. From 2014 to 2016, he was Minister of Justice and for Consumer Protection of Rhineland-Palatinate.

Born in Germany in 1950, he received his doctoral degree in law in 1978 and his final law degree in 1980 in Freiburg. From 1982 to 1984, he served as a law clerk to the president of the German Federal Constitutional Court. In 1986, he obtained his habilitation in law. From 1988 to 1989, he was professor of law at the University of Heidelberg. Gerhard Robbers was president of the European Consortium for Church and State Research, of which he is a member. He was also a member of the Advisory Council for Freedom of Religion or Belief at ODHIR/OSCE. Professor Robbers has taught as a guest professor at many universities around the world.

A selection of the author's publications includes: *Encyclopedia of World Constitutions* (ed.), 3 volumes, New York 2006; An Introduction to German Law, 8th edition, Baden-Baden 2023 (also in German: 8th edition, Baden-Baden 2023); Encyclopedia of Law and Religion (ed. together with Cole Durham), 5 volumes, Leiden 2016; *State and Church in the European Union* (ed.), 3rd edition, Baden-Baden 2019, 2nd edition, Baden-Baden 2005 (also in German, French, Greek, Polish, Russian, Georgian and Chinese), 1st edition, Baden-Baden 1997 (also in German, French, Italian, Spanish, Hungarian and Czech); *Religion and Law in Germany*, 2nd edition, Alphen aan den Rijn 2013; *Migration Law in Germany*, Alphen aan den Rijn 2020. Further publications cover public law, European Union law, constitutional history, ecclesiastical law and legal philosophy.

## The Author

# Table of Contents

The Author 3

List of Abbreviations 17

Preface 21

General Introduction 23

§1. General Background of the Country 23
I. Basic Structures 23
II. General Legal System 24

§2. Social Facts about Religion 26
I. Religious Affiliation 26
II. Religious Practice 28

§3. Historical Background 28
I. Impact of History 28
II. The Middle Ages 29
III. The Reformation and Its Effects 30
IV. The Nineteenth Century 33
V. The Twentieth Century until Today 35

Part I. Legal Framework and Sources 39

Chapter 1. Constitutional Position of Religion 39

§1. Basic Law 39
I. The Preamble 39
II. Freedom of Religion or Belief 40
III. Institutional Guarantees 40
IV. Religious Instruction in Public Schools 41
V. Equal Treatment 42
VI. Oath of Office 43

§2. Constitutional Provisions of the *Länder* 43
I. Religion in the Preambles 43
II. Individual Freedom of Religion or Belief 44

III. Institutional Guarantees 44
IV. Education 46
V. Treaty Law and Various Issues 47

Chapter 2. Other Legislation with Regard to Religion 48

§1. Range of Legislation 48

§2. Treaty Law 48

§3. Basic Structures of Legislation 49

Chapter 3. Typology of the System 50

§1. Separation and Cooperation 50

§2. Neutrality 50

§3. Tolerance 51

§4. Parity 52

§5. Pluralism 52

§6. Institutionalism 52

§7. Openness Towards Religion 52

§8. Freedom of Religion or Belief 53

Part II. Religious Freedom in General 55

Chapter 1. Individual Religious Freedom 55

§1. Normative Structures 55

§2. Functions 56

§3. Scope of Individual Guarantee 58
I. Nationality 58
II. Religious Maturity 58
A. Role of Parents and Legal Guardians 58
B. Federal Act on the Religious Upbringing of Children 59
C. Bavaria and the Saarland 60
D. Practical Implications of Religious Maturity 60

§4. Forum Internum and Manifestations of Religion or Belief 62

§5. The Right Not to Believe 62

§6. Definitions of Religion and Belief 63

§7. Protected Manifestations 64
I. General Scope of Guarantee 64
II. Specific Issues 65
A. Proselytism 65
B. Conscientious Objection 66
1. Dress Requirements 66
2. Co-educative Physical Education 66
3. Work on Religious Holidays 67
4. Conscientious Objection to Medical Treatment 67
5. Conscientious Objection to Take an Oath 68
6. Conscientious Objection and Military Service 68
7. Conscientious Objection in the Judiciary 70
C. Parental Care 70
D. Ritual Slaughter and Other Religious Food Requirements 70
1. Ritual Slaughter 70
2. Religious Food Requirements in Public Institutions 72

§8. Horizontal Application 72

§9. Limitations to Freedom of Religion or Belief 72
I. General Principles of Limitation 72
A. Special Importance of Freedom of Religion or Belief 72
B. The Variety of Limitations 73
C. System of Limitation Clauses 73
II. Specific Limitations to Freedom of Religion or Belief 75
A. Scope of limitations 75
B. A Minority View: Article 136 Section 1 WRV in Conjunction with Article 140 GG 75
C. Structural Limitations 76
D. State of Defence or Emergency: No Valid Reason for Limitation 76
III. Limitations of Limitations 76

§10. Examples of Case Law on Limitations to Freedom of Religion or Belief 78
I. Criteria of Selection 78
II. Cases 78
A. The Tobacco Case 78
B. Conscientious Objection, Alternative Service, and Total Objection 79
C. Governmental Warnings Against Religious Communities 80

D. The Headscarf Issue 80
E. Muslim Ritual Prayer in Public Schools 84
F. Church Bells and Muezzin-Call 84

Chapter 2. Collective Religious Freedom 86

§1. Basic Principles 86

Chapter 3. Organizational Religious Freedom 87

§1. Basic Principles 87
I. Corporative Freedom 87
II. Freedom to Form Religious Communities 87
III. Fundamental Rights of Legal Persons 87
A. Scope of Legal Persons 87
B. Domestic Legal Persons 88
C. Religious Communities as Corporations under Public Law 88
D. Nature of Rights 89
E. Notion of Religious Community 89

§2. Case Law 90

Chapter 4. Religious Freedom and Equality 92

§1. Constitutional Guarantees 92

§2. General Non-discrimination 92

§3. Non-discrimination in Public Office 93

§4. Institutional Equality 94

§5. Equal Treatment of Non-religious, Philosophical Communities 94

Part III. Legal Status of Religious Communities 97

Chapter 1. Formal Status of Religious Communities 97

§1. Religious Communities as Private Law Corporations 97
I. Basic Principles 97
II. Non-profit Associations 98
A. Idealistic Aim 98
B. Registration Requirements 98
C. Special Treatment of Religious Communities: The Bahá'í Case 99

D. Termination of Non-profit Associations 99

§2. Religious Communities as Public Law Corporations 101
I. General Principles 101
II. Special Rights and Duties of Religious Communities as Public Law Corporations 104
III. Range of Religious Communities with Public Law Status 114
IV. Termination of Status of Public Law Corporations 120
V. Specific Issues of Organization 120

Chapter 2. Autonomy of Religious Communities 123

§1. General Principles 123

§2. Limitations of the Right to Self-Determination 124

§3. Religious Communities and State Court System 127

Chapter 3. Fundamental Rights and Religious Communities 131

Chapter 4. Contractual Religious Freedom 134

§1. Basic Principles and Terminology 134

§2. Historical Development 134

§3. Right and Duty to Conclude Treaties 135

§4. Nature of Treaties 137

§5. Treaties and General State Law 137

§6. The Power to Conclude Treaties 138

§7. Interpretation of Treaty Law 139

§8. Termination of Treaties 140

§9. Legal Enforcement 141

§10. The *Reichskonkordat* 141

§11. Other Concordats 149

§12. Protestant Treaty with Lower Saxony and Further Treaties 151

§13. Treaties with Non-religious, Philosophical Communities 153

§14. Treaties with the Jewish Communities 155

§15. Treaties with Muslim Associations 160

Part IV. International, Transnational and Regional Effects on Religious Communities 161

Chapter 1. International Law Effects on Religious Communities 161

§1. Public International Law 161
I. Basic Principles 161
II. The European Convention on Human Rights 163
A. General Relevance 163
B. Case Law 163
C. The Right to Self-Determination and the European Court of Human Rights 164
III. Other International Instruments 168

§2. European Union Law 168
I. Basic Principles 168
II. Freedom of Religion or Belief in Primary European Union Law 169
III. Religion in Secondary European Union Law 172
A. Provisions 172
B. European Union Law and the German General Anti-discrimination Act 173
IV. The European Court of Justice 174

Chapter 2. Transnational Law Effects on Religious Communities 175

Chapter 3. Regional Law Effects on Religious Communities 176

Part V. Religion and Politics 177

Chapter 1. Religious Influence in Politics 178

§1. Constitutional Law Foundations 178

§2. Religions in Politics Based on Treaty Law 179

§3. Media and Religions 180

§4. Religions and State Political Institutions 181

§5. Religions and Political Parties 181

§6. Political Representation of Religions 182

§7. Political Impact of Religious Communities 184

§8. Religious Communities and Election Campaigns 185

Chapter 2. Political Influence in Religions 186

Chapter 3. Interaction Between Religions and State on a Political and Legal Level 188

Part VI. Labour Law Within Religious Communities 191

Chapter 1. Scope of Application of Labour Law 191

§1. Factual Situation 191

§2. Individual Labour Law 192
I. General Principles 192
II. Secular Labour Law and Its Application on Religious Communities 194
III. Individual Churches 198
A. The Evangelical Church 198
B. The Catholic Church 200

§3. Collective Labour Law 201

§4. The Social Security System 204
I. General Principles 204
II. Employment Promotion 204
III. Health Insurance 204
IV. Pensions Insurance 205
V. Accident Insurance 207

Chapter 2. Religious Ministers and Labour Law 208

Chapter 3. Other Church Employees and Labour Law 209

Part VII. Religious Communities and Protections of the Individual 211

Chapter 1. Protection of Privacy 212

§1. General Principles 212

§2. Data Protection 212

Chapter 2. Freedom to Marry 213

Chapter 3. Freedom of Expression 215

Chapter 4. Due Process Norms and Religious Groups 216

Chapter 5. Professional Secrecy 217

Chapter 6. Medical Deontology 219

Chapter 7. Non-discrimination 221

Chapter 8. Penal Law and Religion 222

§1. Religious Peace 222

§2. Religious Property 224

§3. Religious Titles, Garments and Emblems 225

§4. Confessional Secret 226

§5. Position of Religious Communities 226

§6. Special Duties of Religious Office Holders 227

§7. Administrative Misdemeanours 228

§8. Crimes Against International Law 228

§9. CCAIL Genocide 229

§10. CCAIL Crimes Against Humanity 229

§11. CCAIL War Crimes Consisting of the Use of Prohibited Methods of Warfare 230

Part VIII. Church Financing 231

Chapter 1. Direct Financing of Religious Communities 231

§1. PROTECTION OF PROPERTY 231

§2. STATE SUBSIDIES IN GENERAL 231

§3. CHURCH TAX 232
I. Basic Facts 232
II. Taxable Persons 232
III. Objection to Church Tax 233
IV. Tax Rate 233
V. Administration of the Church Tax 233
VI. Example: North Rhine-Westphalia 233
VII. Church Due 237
VIII. Case Law 237

§4. STATE SUBSIDIES 239

§5. EXAMPLES OF FACTS AND FIGURES 240

Chapter 2. Indirect Financing of Religious Communities 242

Part IX. Education 243

Chapter 1. Religious Education in Public and Private Schools 243

§1. RELIGIOUS EDUCATION IN PUBLIC SCHOOLS 243
I. General Principles of Public Education 243
II. Religious Instruction in Public Schools 247

§2. RELIGIOUS INSTRUCTION IN PRIVATE SCHOOLS 255

Chapter 2. Religious Schools 257

Chapter 3. Theological Faculties and Religious Universities 259

Part X. Matrimonial and Family Law 267

Chapter 1. Legal Position of Religious Marriage 267

Chapter 2. Legal Position of Religious Family Law 268

Part XI. Religion and Culture 269

Chapter 1. Religion and Art 269

§1. Religious Monuments 269

§2. Religion in the Arts 270

Chapter 2. Religion and Media 272

Chapter 3. Religion and Civil Society 275

Chapter 4. Religion and Public Debate 276

Part XII. Religious Assistance in Public Institutions 277

Chapter 1. General Principles 277

Chapter 2. Institutions 278

§1. Cure of Souls in Hospitals 278

§2. Cure of Souls in the Police Forces 278

§3. Cure of Souls in Prisons 278

§4. Military Chaplaincy 279

§5. Special Questions 281

Part XIII. Religions in the Social Field 283

Chapter 1. Basic Principles and Activities 283

Chapter 2. Kindergartens 287

Part XIV. Sunday and Religious Holiday Protection 289

Part XV. The Burial System 293

Part XVI. Data Law 295

Chapter 1. Registration of Residents 295

Chapter 2. Census and Religious Affiliation 298

Part XVII. The Law on Aliens 299

Part XVIII. The Law on Foundations 301

Selected Bibliography 303

Index 305

Table of Contents

# List of Abbreviations

| Abbreviation | German | English |
|---|---|---|
| § | Paragraph | German equivalent of 'section' |
| ArbG | *Arbeitsgericht* | Labour Court |
| ARD | *Arbeitsgemeinschaft der öffentlich-rechtlichen Rundfunkanstalten der Bundesrepublik Deutschland* | Consortium of public-law broadcasting institutions of the Federal Republic of Germany |
| BAG | *Bundesarbeitsgericht* | Federal Labour Court |
| BAGE | *Entscheidungen des Bundesarbeitsgerichts* | Decisions of the Federal Labour Court |
| BAMF | *Bundesamt für Migration und Flüchtlinge* | Federal Agency for Migration and Refugees |
| BaWü | *Baden-Württemberg* | Baden-Wuerttemberg |
| BayObLG | *Bayerisches Oberstes Landesgericht* | Bavarian Highest Regional Court |
| BB | *Brandenburg* | Brandenburg |
| Bbg | *Brandenburg* | Brandenburg |
| BGBl. | *Bundesgesetzblatt* | Federal Law Gazette |
| BGH | *Bundesgerichtshof* | Federal Court of Justice |
| BGHZ | *Entscheidungen des Bundesgerichtshofs in Zivilsachen* | Decisions relating to private law of the Federal Court of Justice |
| BRE | *Bremen* | Bremen |
| Brem | *Bremen* | Bremen |
| BT-Drs. | *Bundestag-Drucksache* | Official Records of the German Parliament (Bundestag) |
| BVerfG | *Bundesverfassungsgericht* | Federal Constitutional Court |

List of Abbreviations

| Abbreviation | German | English |
|---|---|---|
| BVerfG (K) | *BVerfG Kammer* | Chamber of the Federal Constitutional Court |
| BVerfGE | *Entscheidungen des Bundesverfassungsgerichts* | Decisions of the Federal Constitutional Court |
| BVerfGK | *Kammerentscheidung des BVerfG* | Decision of a Chamber of the Federal Constitutional Court |
| BVerwG | *Bundesverwaltungsgericht* | Federal Administrative Court |
| BVerwGE | *Entscheidungen des Bundesverwaltungsgerichts* | Decisions of the Federal Administrative Court |
| BW | *Baden-Württemberg* | Baden-Wuerttemberg |
| BY | *Bayern* | Bavaria |
| CDU | *Christlich Demokratische Union Deutschlands* | Christian Democratic Union of Germany |
| CSU | *Christlich-Soziale Union in Bayern e. V.* | Christian Social Union in Bavaria |
| dB(A) | *Schalldruckpegel A-Bewertung* | A-weighted decibels |
| DDR | *Deutsche Demokratische Republik* | German Democratic Republic |
| DITIB | *Türkisch-Islamische Union der Anstalt für Religion* | Turkish-Islamic Union of the Institute for Religion |
| ECHR | *Europäische Menschenrechtskonvention* | European Convention on Human Rights |
| ECJ | *Europäischer Gerichtshof (EuGH)* | European Court of Justice |
| ECR | *Sammlung der Rechtsprechung des Gerichtshofes und des Gerichts Erster Instanz* | Records of the European Court of Justice |
| EKD | *Evangelische Kirche in Deutschland* | Evangelical Church in Germany |
| GBl. | *Gesetzblatt* | Law Gazette |
| GVBl. | *Gesetz- und Verordnungsblatt* | Law and Ordinance Gazette |
| GVOBl. | *Gesetz- und Verordnungsblatt* | Law and Ordinance Gazette |
| HB | *Bremen* | Bremen |
| HE | *Hessen* | Hesse |
| HessStGH | *Hessischer Staatsgerichtshof* | Constitutional Court of Hesse |

| Abbreviation | German | English |
|---|---|---|
| HfJS | *Hochschule für Jüdische Studien* | College of Jewish Studies |
| HH | *Hamburg* | Hamburg |
| Hmb | *Hamburg* | Hamburg |
| KirchE | *Entscheidungen in Kirchensachen seit 1946* | Decisions in Church Matters (since 1946) |
| KRM | *Koordinationsrat der Muslime in Deutschland* | Coordination Council of the Muslims in Germany |
| KSchG | *Kündigungsschutzgesetz* | Protection Against Unfair Dismissal Act |
| LER | *Lebensgestaltung, Ethik, Religionskunde* | Life Shaping, Ethics, Religious Knowledge |
| LG | *Landgericht* | Regional Court |
| LSA | *Land Sachsen-Anhalt* | *Land* Saxony-Anhalt |
| MCC | *Basisgemeinde Hamburg – Die Kirche (nicht nur) für Lesben und Schwule* | Basis Congregation Hamburg-The Church (not only) for Lesbians and Gays |
| MV | *Mecklenburg-Vorpommern* | Mecklenburg-Western Pomerania |
| M-V | *Mecklenburg-Vorpommern* | Mecklenburg-Western Pommerania |
| NDS, Nds | *Niedersachsen* | Lower Saxony |
| NRW | *Nordrhein-Westfalen* | North Rhine-Westphalia |
| OLG | *Oberlandesgericht* | Higher Regional Court |
| OLGR | *Oberlandesgerichtsreport* | Reports of Higher Regional Courts |
| OVG | *Oberverwaltungsgericht* | Administrative Court of Appeals |
| RLP | *Rheinland-Pfalz* | Rhineland-Palatinate |
| RlPf | *Rheinland-Pfalz* | Rhineland-Palatinate |
| RP | *Rheinland-Pfalz* | Rhineland-Palatinate |
| Schl.-H. | *Schleswig-Holstein* | Schleswig-Holstein |
| SH | *Schleswig-Holstein* | Schleswig-Holstein |
| SL | *Saarland* | Saarland |
| SN | *Sachsen* | Saxony |
| StGH | *Staatsgerichtshof* | Constitutional Court |
| TH | *Thüringen* | Thuringia |

**List of Abbreviations**

| Abbreviation | German | English |
|---|---|---|
| Verf. | *Verfassung* | Constitution |
| VerfGH | *Verfassungsgerichtshof* | Constitutional Court |
| VG | *Verwaltungsgericht* | Administrative Court |
| VGH | *Verwaltungsgerichtshof* | Administrative Court of Appeals |
| VIKZ | *Verband der Islamischen Kulturzentren e. V.* | Association of Islamic Cultural Centres |
| ZDF | *Zweites Deutsches Fernsehen* | German Television Channel II |
| ZMD | *Zentralrat der Muslime in Deutschland* | Central Council of the Muslims in Germany |

# Preface

The law and religion are closely intertwined. The law provides structures and normative conditions in which religion exists. Religion, however, determines the law by the values and convictions of the people. Religion and its counterpart, anti-religious ideas, are fundamentals on which the law grows.

Religion has always had a significant impact on the public sphere in Germany. The German law mirrors this public relevance of religion, and it provides specific structures for the manifestations of religion. Freedom of religion, as well as institutional guarantees, forms the basis on which religious life can develop.

For a long period, religion had seemed to be on the retreat, but recent years have shown a renaissance of religion also in Germany. Religious pluralism and diversity are growing. Religions that are relatively new in the country, especially Islam, have gained importance in German culture, which is still largely coined by Christianity. Jewish life remains a specific factor of moral and historic responsibility of the German people. Non-religious beliefs, as well as widespread disinterest in religion, provide a further feature to which the law on religion has to respond.

This outline of the law on religion in Germany is based on the factual developments in religious demography that are challenging a system that has grown over centuries. The major features of this long-grown system seem to be still valid in practice and able to accommodate new developments, not the least also by gradually changing where necessary. The description of this law emphasizes the long-standing traditions and basic principles of the German law on religion, but it also gives an account of its details and characteristic solutions. The federal structure of Germany demands to be careful about differences between its sixteen federal states. These differences may sometimes seem to be of minor importance at first sight, but they can amount to basic divergences when seen together. The federal level, again, has a major impact on the overall picture and needs careful attention. Many details, however, have found very similar solutions throughout the various federal states and the federation itself; fundamental principles are the same. Where appropriate, a detailed description refers to one of the federal states or the federal level as an example and provides references for further material. European Union law exercises growing influence also in the field of law and religion in Germany.

In describing the German law on religion, the basic structure developed by the editor has been followed. This will make it easier for the reader to compare the German system with others. It must be kept in mind, however, that this approach does not always fit into the usual German legal doctrine and its structures. Yet, the advantages of this common structure seem to prevail over doctrinal purism. Some general information beyond the mere law on religion is also given in order to support the understanding of this specific field of law when this depends on such background data.

I am greatly indebted to the editor of this collection, Prof. Rik Torfs, and to those who have rendered the most valuable help in finalizing this survey in its first two editions: Felix Bode, Katharina Böhme, Christine Brentrup, Ursula Gerbaulet, Dr iur. Angelika Günzel, Dr iur. Bärbel Junk, Ingrid Kehrer, Linda Kern, Claudia Lehnen, Hanno Merten, Annabelle Mertes, Björn Müller, Anika Natus, Moritz Reger, Dr iur. Robert Schiller, Jana Schollmeier, Gerhild Scholzen-Wiedmann, Oliver Windgätter and Oliver Wolf, LLM. This third edition still rests on their contributions but adds new developments and highlights additional aspects and approaches.

# General Introduction

## §1. General Background of the Country

### I. Basic Structures

*1.* Germany is a federal state made up of the federation as such and sixteen federal states, called *Länder*. Each individual *Land* is a state on its own and has its own constitution. Federalism implies important differences between the various *Länder*; it is highly significant for the legal structures of the country and for day-to-day life. Notwithstanding this, federalism in Germany is of a unifying character; that is, the federal level has the competences to govern many important fields of life and law, the states often take to similar solutions for matters that they are competent for, and fundamental rights, as well as basic principles guaranteed by the federal constitution, lead to far-reaching similarities among the *Länder*. Roughly speaking, the *Länder* in the German federal republic have predominant competencies in the fields of culture, education, police, administration, and the non-federal judiciary. Religion, thus, often deals with the *Länder* when the secular issues of religion are at stake.

*2.* The German population was 84,400,000 in 2022.[1] Some 13.4 million, i.e., about 15.88%, of the inhabitants are non-German with a wide range of national backgrounds.[2] Germany has become a country of immigration; the largest group of immigrants is of Turkish origin.

*3.* Of considerable political and social importance, but also with significant impact on the religious situation, is the reunification of Germany in 1990 when the formerly Communist-ruled German Democratic Republic (*Deutsche Demokratische Republik* (DDR)) joined the Federal Republic of Germany. Both parts of Germany are still growing together, and differences between the two eastern and western parts in economic, political, and religious perspectives remain visible.

*4.* The complete moral breakdown of Germany under National Socialism between 1933 and 1945, which led to the murder of millions of Jews and other

1. Statistisches Bundesamt, https://www.destatis.de/DE/Home/_inhalt.html, 9 Nov. 2023.
2. https://de.statista.com/statistik/daten/studie/1221/umfrage/anzahl-der-auslaender-in-deutschland-nach-herkunftsland/, 9 Nov. 2023.

people, still provides a background for many fields of law and the practice of religion. The legal, political and social status of the Jewish population in Germany is largely based on this experience.

*5.* Human rights provide the basis of the entire legal and political system. They are widely respected, and an independent judiciary is a stronghold when individual cases of violations of human rights occur. German law is characterized by the idea of fitting in, coordinating, and balancing competing and, often, colliding interests into a system of law. The legal system is based on the idea that the law should constitute a well-functioning system to accommodate all legitimate interests adequately. The law is not primarily regarded as a weapon but a structure, a system accommodating interests and balancing them. The law provides for structures in which everybody can live as freely as possible. It is not regarded as a means or instrument to enforce only one's own interests. Limits to any fundamental right, such as limitations on religious freedom, must always be interpreted in light of the importance of the right limited. All legitimate interests, the interest of religious freedom, as well as the interest limiting religious freedom, must be given adequate space. This balancing of interests approach is a predominant feature of German law.

## II. General Legal System

*6.* The German constitution of 23 May 1949, called Basic Law (*Grundgesetz für die Bundesrepublik Deutschland* (GG)), contains the most important provisions about religion in German law. In addition to that, each constitution of the sixteen *Länder* also contains specific norms concerning freedom of religion and the relationship between the state and religious communities. Although these provisions differ in some details from each other and from the Basic Law, there is no difference in substance. In any case, the constitutions of the *Länder* are inferior in rank in relation to the Basic Law and have to be interpreted according to the federal constitution.

*7.* Within the system of federal law – and similarly within the framework of the law of the states – the hierarchy of norms begins at its top with the constitution. The constitution is the highest-ranking norm with which all other legal provisions must conform.

*8.* There is some debate whether there is something like natural law or 'superpositive' law following from the nature of human beings, the will of God or perhaps from human culture that has binding force even for the constitution itself. In a very early decision, the Federal Constitution Court ruled that even if any such super-positive law existed, its practical legal relevance would depend on a positive decision by the Constitution to include any of such rules into the framework of positive, binding constitutional law.[3]

3. *See* BVerfG 18 Dec. 1953, BVerfGE 3, 225, 237.

*9.* In extraordinary cases, when the positive law fails to meet generally existing standards of human rights, as expressed in the international human rights treaties, these general standards apply and take precedence over the failing positive law, as occurred under National Socialism and also in the DDR.

*10.* European Union Law takes precedence over German law, including constitutional law, in the individual cases of application according to the principle of primacy of application of Union law.

*11.* On the level directly below the federal constitution, rank the general rules of international law that take precedence over the ordinary laws and directly create rights and duties for the inhabitants of the federal territory. Only a few general rules of international law have been identified explicitly by the Federal Constitutional Court to form part of this level of the law, among them the prohibition of torture.[4]

*12.* The next level is formed by ordinary laws passed by the legislature. This level also encompasses international law that is not qualified as 'general rules' of international law: mostly international treaties and international customary law. Thus, the European Convention on Human Rights (ECHR) has the rank of ordinary law; however, the Federal Constitutional Court has ruled that it exercises important influence on the interpretation of the Basic Law and its fundamental rights guarantees. The rulings of the European Court of Human Rights, therefore, influence the impact of religious rights.

*13.* Below ordinary law are statutory instruments issued by the federal government, a federal minister or the *Länder* governments according to Article 80 GG. This type of instrument can only be used if authorized by law, and the content, purpose, and scope of the authority confirmed must be specified in that law. Each statutory instrument must contain a statement of its legal basis.

*14.* On the same level as the statutory instruments, there are by-laws or regulations of municipalities or other entities that have the right of self-government according to the laws. Municipalities are part of the administrative structure of the respective *Land* in which they exist. Municipalities have the right to regulate all local affairs on their own responsibility, within the limits prescribed by the laws (Article 28 section 2 GG). This predominant municipal autonomy entails the right to create binding by-laws or regulations.

*15.* Statutory instruments, by-laws or regulations may limit fundamental rights only if an ordinary law entitles them to do so. Any limitation of any fundamental right must be based on ordinary law.

*16.* Federal law of whichever level takes precedence over the law of the *Länder* (as is stated in Article 31 GG). On the level of the *Länder*, there is again first the constitution of the *Land*, then ordinary laws, and finally the statutory instruments.

4. BVerfG 8 Apr. 2004, *Strafverteidiger* 24 (2004), 440, 441.

*17.* According to Article 30 GG, the exercise of state powers and the discharge of state functions is a matter for the *Länder* except as otherwise provided or permitted by the Basic Law. Since large parts of the issues concerning religion and religious communities are not assigned to the Federal Republic, the *Länder* have widespread competencies regarding religion and religious communities. Since Article 31 GG states that 'federal law shall take precedence over *Land* law', any federal law breaks contradicting law of a *Land*. Ordinary federal laws would thus – within the scope of federal competencies – take precedence also over the constitutions of the *Länder*. A special provision deals with the hierarchy of fundamental rights in the federation: According to Article 142 GG provisions of *Land* constitutions remain in force insofar as they guarantee basic rights in conformity with Articles 1–18 of the Basic Law. This means that basic rights as stated in the *Land* constitution remain in force as long as they are identical to the fundamental rights guaranteed in the federal constitution; when basic rights of the *Land* constitution guarantee less far-reaching rights than the Basic Law, the rights guaranteed by the Basic Law prevail; in as far as basic rights of the *Land* constitution guarantee more far-reaching rights than the Basic Law these basic rights of the *Land* constitution have priority over the less far-reaching basic rights of the federal constitution.

*18.* The constitutions of the sixteen *Länder* provide for freedom of religion as a human right.[5] They do so by explicitly stating such a right or by referring to the fundamental rights provisions of the Basic Law of the Federal Republic.[6]

## §2. Social Facts about Religion

### I. Religious Affiliation

*19.* The religious affiliation of the population differs among the various *Länder*. The north of Germany is predominantly Protestant, while the southern part is predominantly Roman Catholic; in some parts of Germany, these two Christian confessions equal each other in numbers and importance. Again, in some parts of Germany, a majority of people do not have any religious affiliation. This especially is the case for the eastern part of Germany, which – from 1949 to 1990 – was the Communist-ruled DDR; taking into account the rule of National Socialism, these parts of Germany have experienced a total of fifty-seven years of decidedly anti-religious government since 1933.

*20.* Within Germany and its population of about 84.4 million people, there are two major churches, which are nearly equal in size and social importance, a great variety of other religious communities, and many non-believers. Islam has become

5. Article 107 Constitution of the Free State of Bavaria (BayVerf); Art. 29 Constitution of Berlin (VvB); Art. 13 Constitution of Brandenburg (BBgVerf); Art. 4 Constitution of the Free Hanseatic City of Bremen (BremVerf); Art. 9 Constitution of Hesse (HessVerf); Art. 8 Constitution of Rhineland-Palatine (RLPVerf).
6. For the latter *see* Art. 3, s. 2 Constitution of Lower Saxony (Verf LSA); Art. 4 Constitution of North Rhine-Westphalia (NRWVerf).

strong within the last fifty years. More detailed statistics about population and religious adherence can be found at the German *Statistisches Bundesamt*.[7]

*21.* In 2022, the Roman Catholic Church had about 20,937,600 members, while the Protestant Church had about 19,100,000 members.[8] The Catholic Church is structured in twenty dioceses and seven archdioceses. There are numerous orders and congregations and independent order provinces.

*22.* The Protestant Church consists of several separate territorially based *Landeskirchen* (*Land* churches), each of these churches being an independent unit. Together, they form the Protestant Church in Germany (*Evangelische Kirche in Deutschland* (EKD)) with its 19,100,000 members.[9] There are also a number of smaller Protestant churches that have chosen to stay outside this federation; they are known as the *Freikirchen* (Free Churches). The Protestant churches are either Lutheran or Reformed (Calvinist) churches; some follow a unified confession, shaped in various ways from these two creeds.

*23.* The Jewish communities consisted of about 90,885 members in 2022.[10] Jewish immigration from East Europe, especially from the former Soviet Union states, has been strong in recent years.

*24.* There are about 5.3 to 5.6 million Muslims in Germany, of which 2.2 to 2.6 million are of German nationality. These figures (2020) are based on rough estimates since there is no register. The numbers are calculated primarily from immigration from Muslim countries such as Turkey, former Yugoslavia, Iran, Morocco, Afghanistan, Iraq, Lebanon, Pakistan, and Syria.[11] The Muslim population is spread over all of Germany, but in some major cities such as Berlin, Cologne, Hamburg, Stuttgart, Munich, and others, there are substantial Muslim concentrations. While there has been a small Muslim presence throughout the centuries, immigration of large numbers of Muslims as 'guest workers' began in the 1960s. Initially expected to return home after finishing work, many of them have stayed in Germany.

*25.* Orthodox Christians amount to almost 1.7 million, belonging to a variety of different churches.[12]

---

7. Destatis, https://www.destatis.de/DE/Home/_inhalt.html, 9 Nov. 2023; *see also* Religionswissenschaftlicher Medien- und Informationsdienst (Remid), https://www.remid.de/, 9 Nov. 2023.
8. https://fowid.de/meldung/religionszugehoerigkeiten-2022, 9 Nov. 2023.
9. *Ibid.*
10. https://de.statista.com/statistik/daten/studie/1232/umfrage/anzahl-der-juden-in-deutschland-seit-dem-jahr-2003/, 9 Nov. 2023.
11. Bundesamt für Migration und Flüchtlinge (ed.), *Muslimisches Leben in Deutschland 2020*, https://www.bamf.de/SharedDocs/Pressemitteilungen/DE/2021/20210428-studie-mld-2020.html?nn=282772, 9 Nov. 2023.
12. Religionswissenschaftlicher Medien- und Informationsdienst (ed.), 'Mitgliederzahlen: Orthodoxe, Orientalische und Unierte Kirchen', https://www.remid.de/info_zahlen/orthodoxie/, 9 Nov. 2023.

*26.* There are also many smaller religions in the country, some having a long-established tradition in Germany, others having been in Germany for only a short while. Their membership is estimated at about 1.6 million persons.

*27.* There are an estimated 37 million inhabitants of Germany who profess themselves to be without any confession.[13] The confessional viewpoints in Germany tend to change rapidly as a result of immigration and other social shifts, so estimates remain uncertain and tentative.

## II. Religious Practice

*28.* In the big churches, service attendance is not strong. For a considerable number of years, many members of those churches have been leaving their churches; these churches are still losing more members than they gain. Secularism, atheism, agnosticism, and probably even more, the sheer lack of interest in religion are widespread. The scandal of sexual child abuse in the Catholic Church, but also in the Protestant Churches, has led to great waves of leaving the church; it has also led to a more critical view towards the churches. This has also stopped a former tendency of growing interest in religious questions and ideas that had become apparent in the previous couple of years.[14] This had not only led to the growth of new, smaller or esoteric religions, but had also brought about a new turning to the traditional religions in Germany. The media have taken up the subject of religion and report broadly. The special situation of immigrants has contributed to a visible and intensive Muslim religious life.

# §3. Historical Background

## I. Impact of History

*29.* The history of religions in Germany still has a coining influence on the religious situation of the country.[15] The Christian heritage is a major basis of contemporary life. The split between the Catholic and the Protestant Churches has an impact that can hardly be overestimated. A persistent historical structure has been and remains to be the situation of the Jewish part of the population.

---

13. https://fowid.de/meldung/religionszugehoerigkeiten-2022, 9 Nov. 2023.
14. Cf. Bertelsmann Stiftung (ed.), 'Religionsmonitor 2008', Gütersloh: Gütersloher Verlagshaus, 2007; short report of the results: Stefan Huber & Constantin Klein, 'Kurzbericht zu ersten Ergebnissen des Religionsmonitor der Bertelsmann-Stiftung (Befragung in Deutschland)', www.bertelsmann-stiftung.de/cps/rde/xbcr/SID-96313B36-B810DC0C/bst/xcms_bst_dms_23407_23408_2.pdf, 6 Jul. 2010.
15. *See* Christoph Link, *Kirchliche Rechtsgeschichte* (Munich: C.H. Beck, 2008).

## II. The Middle Ages

*30.* The relationship between the church and the secular power in the Middle Ages was strongly influenced by the theory of the two swords, which relates to the Gospel of Luke 22:38. According to this theory, which was formulated in classical words by Pope Gelasius I (492–496), the world is governed by two swords: the authority of the church and the power of the king. In the medieval empires, the influence of the secular powers over the church became strong. An expression of that was the system of proprietary church. From the eighth and ninth centuries onwards, church buildings were regarded as part of the real estate that was not property of the church. The secular nobility thus had certain rights over the church, such as the power to decide over the property related to that specific church building and the right to appoint the priest. Bishops and abbots were, from the early medieval times, entrusted with secular political powers. When Germany emerged as a specific political entity from the tenth century onwards to become known as the Holy Roman Empire, the first German emperors, such as Otto the Great (936–973), gave many secular rights to bishops and abbots in order to weaken the powers of the secular nobility of the German tribes. Indirectly, this strengthened the central power of the emperor. Dioceses and abbeys received powers such as the right to issue coins, toll rights, market rights, etc., and they were given large territories. During the course of time, the spiritual principalities developed. Trier, Cologne, and Mainz became the most important of these spiritual principalities, forming prince-electorships that had – together with the four and finally nine secular prince-electorships – the right to elect the king and emperor of the Holy Roman Empire. The emperor claimed supremacy over the church in the empire, appointed the bishops and thought it to be his right to name the Pope. This provoked the reform movement of the tenth to the twelfth centuries with a centre in the Abbey of Cluny (the reform of Cluny), which tried to achieve a stricter distinction between the spiritual and the secular powers. It developed the theory of co-existence of Emperor and Pope into a theory of supremacy of the spiritual over the secular power. The conflict between Pope and Emperor culminated in the investiture controversy of the eleventh century when Pope Gregory VII ex-communicated Emperor Henry IV, and Henry IV backed down in his famous Walk to Canossa in 1077. While the struggle continued for several decades, papal rights were acknowledged in the Concordat of Worms in 1122. The Holy Roman Emperor was recognized as having the right to invest bishops with secular authority in the territories they governed but not with religious authority. The Pope emerged as a figure above and out of the direct control of the Holy Roman Emperor. Pope Boniface VIII (1294–1303) proclaimed in his bull *Unam sanctam* (1302) complete supremacy of the papacy: While the Pope governed by the spiritual sword directly, the secular princes had to govern by the secular sword according to the directives given by the church. However, by this time, the factual power of the papacy had already declined. In 1338, the Declaration of Rhense (*Kurverein zu Rhense*) proclaimed the independence of the election of the king and emperor of the Holy Roman Empire from the Pope. This was confirmed by the Golden Bull in 1356, one of the foremost fundamental laws of the Holy Roman Empire. Papal powers continued to decline in the Holy Roman Empire.

Regional princes and cities seized the administration of the church in their territories, deciding over the income of the church and the appointment to offices therein.

## III. The Reformation and Its Effects

*31.* The religious situation in Germany, even today, is strongly influenced by the Reformation of 1517 led by Martin Luther. The relationship between the Lutheran Reformation and the territorial sovereignty and activities of the local princes led to the existence of the protestant regional churches, the *Landeskirchen* of today, for the secular local sovereigns themselves often held the position of the supreme bishops of such churches. They worked out a close relationship between the Throne and the Altar that existed until 1919.

*32.* The Protestant Reformation is probably the most important historical event that coined the relationships between the religious and the secular sphere in Germany. It caused the permanent existence – and in fact co-existence – of two equally strong and often hostile religious denominations, the Catholic and the Protestant Churches. Taken together with the special status of the Jews in Germany, this amounts to some basic features of a pluralistic system of religious co-existence. For centuries, Germans have lived in a situation in which different denominations have lived together in close neighbourhoods.

*33.* A first nucleus of a somewhat hidden but powerful freedom of religion in a German constitutional document was created as early as 1555. In the Religious Peace of Augsburg of 25 September 1555,[16] the Lutheran and Catholic confessions were recognized as essentially equal. After Martin Luther had initiated the Reformation in Germany in 1517, Germany was soon split into those territories adhering to the Catholic faith and those territories following the Lutheran denomination. In the Lutheran territories, the secular monarchs took up the office of bishop of their churches, being the so-called *summus episcopus*. The 1555 Religious Peace of Augsburg granted the princes and monarchs in their territories the power to decide for all their subjects on which confession to follow (*cuius regio, eius religio*).[17] This was often said to be based on the *ius reformandi*, the right to Church reform of the princes. There were two important exceptions to that rule: in the free and imperial cities (*Freie und Reichstädte*),[18] which all had adopted the new Lutheran church regiment, the status quo for the minorities that had remained Roman Catholic was guaranteed in respect of the manifestation of their religion and in respect of the

16. Axel Gotthard, *Der Augsburger Religionsfrieden* (Münster: Aschendorff, 2004); text in Arno Buschmann, *Kaiser und Reich* (Munich: Deutscher Taschenbuch-Verlag, 1984), 215 et seq.
17. Roughly translated: He who rules the land decides on the religion (whose realm, his religion).
18. Free and imperial cities (*Freie und Reichsstädte*) were those towns that did not belong to a territory and thus had no lord over them but the Empire itself. They were formally ruled by the emperor only, while the majority of cities in the Empire belonged to a territory and so were governed by one of the many princes of the Empire. Free cities also had independent representation in the Reichstag of the Holy Roman Empire. The biggest such cities were Augsburg, Nuremberg, Hamburg, Bremen, Frankfurt, Cologne and Lübeck.

church property. Full freedom to follow their own Catholic or Lutheran belief was thus granted to the inhabitants of the free and imperial cities, that is, cities directly subject to the emperor, such as Nuremberg, Augsburg, and many others. The second exception was that the Roman Catholic-ruled territories directly subordinate to the Empire had to remain Roman Catholic (*reservatum ecclesiasticum*). This applied especially to the spiritual prince-electorships Trier, Cologne, and Mainz and to the territories governed by prince-bishops. Those prince-elector bishops and prince-bishops who turned to the Protestant faith thus lost not only their church office but also their territory; the people in those territories had to remain Roman Catholic.

*34.* One of the most important achievements of the 1555 Religious Peace of Augsburg was that those subjects who disagreed with the Catholic or Lutheran confession established by their lords were granted the right to emigrate (*ius emigrandi*). This right was explicitly limited to the Catholic and the Lutheran faith, whilst the Jewish minorities remained in their special position.[19] Other denominations were excluded from this right to emigrate, and it certainly was only the very first step in granting freedom of religion. However, this right to emigrate for religious reasons opened the door for the idea that no one may be forced against his or her will to follow or not to follow a religion, in fact. The Religious Peace of Augsburg also laid the ground for the religious neutrality of the state in that two competing confessions were accommodated in the Empire and equal treatment on the level of the Empire was granted to them in the end.

*35.* The Religious Peace of Augsburg did not manage to put an end to the rivalry between the religious parties, who also were conflicting about the powers of the individual territories against the central Empire, the emerging nation-states in Europe, and dynastic aspirations. These conflicts culminated in the devastating Thirty Years' War of 1618–1648. At the end of that war, both religious parties emerged without victory. The peace treaty, the 1648 Peace of Westphalia,[20] reaffirmed and developed the Religious Peace of Augsburg. It explicitly mentioned and guaranteed '*conscientie libertate*', the freedom of conscience.[21] It was again limited basically to Catholics and Lutherans, Jews and others being to various extents tolerated. The denominational status of the territories, being either Roman Catholic or Protestant, was fixed according to the status they had had on 1 January 1624, the so-called *Normaljahr* (Normal Year). This in fact brought an end to the principle of

---

19. There is some lack of research regarding the specific law on religion for Jews in German history; cf. Michael Toch, *Die Juden im Mittelalterlichen Reich* (Munich: Oldenbourg, 2002), 43; Reinhard Rürup, *Emanzipation und Antisemitismus* (Göttingen: Vandenhoeck & Ruprecht, 1975); Landesarchivverwaltung Rheinland-Pfalz (ed.), *Dokumentation zur Geschichte der jüdischen Bevölkerung in Rheinland-Pfalz und im Saarland von 1800 bis 1945* (Koblenz: Landesarchivverwaltung Rheinland-Pfalz, 1974).
20. Text in Arno Buschmann, *Kaiser und Reich* (Munich: Deutscher Taschenbuch-Verlag 1984), 285 et seq.
21. 1648 Peace of Westphalia, Art. VII Instrumentum Pacis Osnabrugensis. For a short history of freedom of religion in Germany, *see* Martin Heckel, 'Religionsfreiheit', in *Staatslexikon*, Görres-Gesellschaft ed., vol. 4, 7th edn (Freiburg: Herder, 1988), c. 820–825.

'*cuius regio eius religio*' and limited the *ius reformandi* of the princes. The followers of either creed who lived in the territory of the other creed were allowed to exercise their religion in private. The principle of the Normal Year was, however, not extended to the Habsburg Austrian territories and the Upper-Palatinate part of Bavaria, which subsequently were brought back to or remained in the Roman Catholic denomination. Freedom of religion was also extended to the 'reformed' denomination, that is, basically, the Calvinists. Even today, the territorial distribution of religious congregations in Germany is enduringly marked by these events.

*36.* Another important result of the conflicts was that the princes gained supremacy over the churches in their territories. This was, based on a variety of theological and legal doctrines, in fact, equally the case for the Protestant as well as for the Catholic territories. For the Habsburg territories, this culminated in the system called 'Josephinism', named after Emperor Joseph II (1780–1790), who diminished the influence of the Pope by interrupting direct communication between the Pope and bishops and by prohibiting travels of members of religious orders to Rome. Joseph II also abolished in his territories the papal rights to appoint clergy, he established dioceses by his own assumed right and appointed the bishops, contemplative religious orders were abolished, and other orders were restructured.

*37.* While state supremacy over church affairs grew, individual religious freedom grew also. An important step in widening the range of religious freedom was taken by the Edict of Potsdam of 1685, by which the monarch of Prussia, Prince Elector Frederick William, called the Calvinists (Huguenots) from France into Prussia, granting them full religious freedom. The impact of that step is still visible at the Berlin square called *Gendarmenmarkt*, where the Lutheran 'German Dome' and the Calvinist 'French Dome' were erected as two churches equal in size and significance.

*38.* The Common Law of the *Land* for the Prussian States (*Allgemeines Landrecht für die Preußischen Staaten* (PrALR)) of 1794 provided that the ideas of any inhabitant of the state concerning God and godly issues, their beliefs and internal religious service cannot be a matter of compelling laws. Each inhabitant of the state must be granted complete freedom of belief and conscience.[22] Limitations were obvious. Religious service of any creed at home could be installed by the 'house father'. Any group could form a church association as long as they taught reverence to God, obedience to the law, loyalty to the state and kept good morals. The law distinguished between publicly accepted church associations and tolerated church associations.

*39.* Certainly, it must be kept in mind that throughout history and in many places, one has to be aware of the divide between what the law tells and what life offers. All too often, the legal guarantee of freedom is nothing more than an empty promise. On the other hand, promises may serve as a key to improvement by providing a benchmark to live up to.

22. Part II, Title 11, §§1 and 2 PrALR.

## IV. The Nineteenth Century

*40.* A major shift in state-church relations came with the '*Reichsdeputationshauptschluss*' (Principal Conclusion of the Extraordinary Imperial Delegation) of 1803. Following the French Revolution in 1789, France had conquered and annexed the German territories west of the river Rhine. This was recognized by the Empire in the 1801 Peace of Lunéville. A sort of recovery of damages was made by the major secular lords of the 'right of the Rhine' for their 'left of the Rhine' losses to France. In the process, the worldly sovereignty of the ecclesiastical princes was, for the most part, abrogated, and the majority of their territory was reallocated to the neighbouring secular princes as part of the so-called German Mediatisation. The property of the Catholic Church was, for the most part, secularized and seized by the secular lords so that not much more remained for the church than the property belonging to local parishes. However, the states now had to pay for the religious needs and to guarantee the religious use of the churches. They were obliged to make regular payments to the churches so that those could continue to function. Many of these dotations still persist today and are guaranteed by constitutional law. However, these dotations are currently undergoing a process of negotiations between the state and the relevant Churches with the aim of ending these payments.

*41.* The declarations of fundamental rights in the early constitutions of the German *Länder* (1818 Constitution of Bavaria, 1818 Constitution of Baden, 1819 Constitution of Wuerttemberg), which were now forming a loose Union in the '*Deutscher Bund*' (German Confederation), granted religious freedom in a fairly elaborate way. The same was true for the following constitutions throughout the nineteenth century. In general, these constitutions guaranteed equal rights to the three Christian denominations (i.e., the Catholic, Lutheran, and Reformed Churches) and their followers. In Bavaria, this was extended to the Greek Church.[23] Members of other religious communities were granted rights in specific laws and regulations. It is noteworthy that all inhabitants were granted full freedom of conscience. This means, again, in general, that everybody was allowed to have a simple service at home regardless of which religion he or she belonged.[24] However, religious services in public were restricted to privileged religious communities.

*42.* The 1812 Emancipation Edict about the Jews in Prussia granted the same civil rights and freedoms for Prussian Jews as were enjoyed by the Prussians of the Christian faith.[25]

---

23. Cf. Edict über die äußeren Rechtsverhältnisse der Einwohner des Königreichs Baiern, in Beziehung auf Religion und kirchliche Gesellschaften, 2nd addendum to the Verfassungsurkunde für das Königreich Bayern of 26 May 1918 2nd addendum (GBl., 101) as amended on 1 Jul. 1834 (GBl., 149).
24. Cf. Ch. 1, §9 'Verfassungsurkunde für das Königreich Bayern vom 26. Mai 1818', in *Deutsche Verfassungsdokumente 1803–1850*, vol. 1 of *Dokumente zur deutschen Verfassungsgeschichte*, Ernst Rudolf Huber ed. (Stuttgart: Kohlhammer, 1978), 162.
25. 'Edikt betreffend die bürgerlichen Verhältnisse der Juden mit dem Preußischen Staate vom 11. März 1812', in *Deutsche Verfassungsdokumente 1803–1850*, vol. 1 of *Dokumente zur deutschen Verfassungsgeschichte*, Ernst Rudolf Huber ed. (Stuttgart: Kohlhammer, 1978), 49.

*43.* The revolutionary German Constitution of 1848–1849 provided in its Articles 144 and 145 full freedoms of belief and conscience. Every German was free to perform religious rites at home and in public. Article 147 of the German Constitution provided that each religious association shall regulate and administer its affairs independently but remain subject to the general laws of the state. No religious community should have any privileges, and there was no state church. New religious communities could be freely established, and no recognition of their faith by the government was needed.[26] The revolution, however, failed, and the German Constitution was formally repealed in 1851.

*44.* Throughout the nineteenth century, the ties between the state and the Protestant Church were gradually loosened while the position of the monarchs as *summus episcopus* of their *Land* church remained intact until the revolution of 1918. Increasing autonomy of the Protestant *Land* churches was achieved by a step-by-step restructuring of the monarch's administration of the church. In Prussia, a ministry for clerics, education, and medicine was created in 1817, which took care of the royal rights in respect of the two great denominations, but internal church matters were entrusted to royal consistories; in 1850, the Evangelical Higher Church Council (*Evangelischer Oberkirchenrat*) was established as the governing body in the Protestant Church, which put an end to the supervision by the Ministry of Culture over church institutions. From all this follows that the history of religious freedom and its limitations in Germany can be seen as a process of gradual, step-by-step widening of the range of freedom of religion or belief. Limitations were reduced step-by-step. Evolution, not revolution, created freedom of religion or belief.

*45.* For the Roman Catholic Church, the abrogation of the church's secular sovereign powers in the *1803 Reichsdeputationshauptschluss* and through the end of the Holy Roman Empire of the German Nation in 1806 brought the chance of restructuring and a new focus on the spiritual tasks. As was the case for the Protestant churches, the overall political development took the direction of increasing church autonomy from state interference, though at different speeds and steps in the various German states.

*46.* The autonomy of the Roman Catholic Church in Germany was also finally strengthened by the result of the '*Kulturkampf*' (Cultural Struggle). This conflict between the newly founded German Empire of 1870–1871 and the Roman Catholic Church was, in part, also an attempt of the predominantly Protestant Prussia in the north of Germany to dominate the predominantly Roman Catholic south of the Empire. It also aimed at suppressing Polish national sentiments in the eastern part of the Empire. Under Chancellor Bismarck, a number of laws were passed with the aim of reducing the influence of the Catholic Church. Among them was the introduction of paragraph 130a into the German Criminal Code (*Strafgesetzbuch*), which

26. Cf. 'Verfassung des Deutschen Reichs vom 28. März 1848', in *Deutsche Verfassungsdokumente 1803–1850*, vol. 1 of *Dokumente zur deutschen Verfassungsgeschichte*, Ernst Rudolf Huber ed. (Stuttgart: Kohlhammer, 1978), 391.

threatened clergy who discussed politics from the pulpit with two years of prison.[27] Religious schools were forced to undergo intense government inspection, and religious teachers were banned from government schools. In 1872, the Jesuits were banned (and remained banned until 1917), and the German government broke off diplomatic relations with the Holy See. The state began to monitor the education of clergy closely, created a secular court for cases involving the clergy, and required notification of all clergy employment. In 1875, religious orders were abolished, state subsidies to the Catholic Church stopped, and religious protections were removed from the Prussian constitution. Civil marriage became mandatory. Catholic resistance against this suppression was so great, however, that Bismarck finally sought a peaceful settlement of these issues; the laws were repealed or voluntarily accepted by the Vatican in the concordats to come. The struggle led, not in the least, to increased support for the Catholic political party, the *Zentrum*, in the population.

## V. The Twentieth Century until Today

*47.* The 1918 revolution at the end of World War I put an end to the remaining state supremacy over the churches. The 1919 Constitution of the Weimar Republic (WRV) guaranteed in its Article 135 full freedom of religion or belief and declared that, nevertheless, the general laws of the state remained unaffected. The institutional guarantees of Articles 136–141 WRV provided religious freedom and freedom of manifestation of religion or belief for all individuals as well as for every religious and non-confessional philosophical community. Their self-determination was only limited by the 'laws valid for all'. It was soon argued that the term 'laws valid for all' means only those laws that are indispensable for the nation's very existence and well-being.[28] The 1919 Weimar Constitution resulted in the establishment of a separation of church and state, nevertheless recognizing and allowing for cooperation in matters such as religious instruction in the public school system, the church tax and military chaplaincy.

*48.* It was the complete moral and legal breakdown under National Socialism in Germany that brought an end to freedom and to the very physical existence of millions of Jews and other people. The Nazi rulers tried to take over power also over the churches. The struggle that arose from this is known as the '*Kirchenkampf*' (Church Struggle). Within the Protestant Church of Germany, a Nazi bishop was appointed. Here, it was the small yet important minority called '*Bekennende Kirche*' (Confessing Church) that maintained resistance against Nazi rule over the Protestant Church. In 1934, the Barmen Declaration of the Confessing Church reaffirmed that the German Church was not an 'organ of the state' for the purpose of strengthening the Nazi agendum but only subject to Christ and his mission. The

27. This is called the *Kanzelparagraph* – from the German term '*Kanzel*' (pulpit).
28. Johannes Heckel, 'Das staatskirchenrechtliche Schrifttum der Jahre 1930 und 1931', *Verwaltungsarchiv* 37 (1932): 280 et seq.; for an overview of the discussion cf. Konrad Hesse, 'Das Selbstbestimmungsrecht der Kirchen und Religionsgemeinschaften', in *Handbuch des Staatskirchenrechts I*, Joseph Listl ed., 2nd edn (Berlin: Duncker & Humblot, 1994), 544.

Roman Catholic Church, in many parts, lived in confrontation with the Nazi regime. Many believers were killed because of their resistance against National Socialism, including the Protestant Dietrich Bonhoeffer. However, one must not forget that probably a majority of Protestants and Catholics did follow the Nazi regime. Jewish resistance against the Nazi murderers was important, as was shown in the revolt in the Warsaw ghetto in 1943. Resistance was also important among other religious groups, such as Jehovah's Witnesses or the Seventh Day Adventists. The resistance group '*Weiße Rose*' (White Rose) had a Christian basis.

*49.* After the liberation that came with the end of the Second World War in 1945, religious freedom took a foremost place in the new constitutional order. It can be argued that the suffering of the Jewish people (regardless of their individual beliefs), the relatively strong moral positions of the Catholic Church and of parts of the Protestant churches, and the fundamentally anti-religious policy of the National-Socialist regime were reasons for the far-reaching guarantee of freedom of religion and belief in the new constitution. Taking responsibility for the murder of millions of European Jews by Nazi Germany in the 1940s has led Germany to give the Jewish religious communities, though still small in numbers, the space for a very visible role in society.

*50.* While the 1949 (in its Articles 41–48) and the 1968–1974 (in its Article 39) constitutions of the DDR promised freedom of religion, the state was explicitly atheist, discriminated against religion, and often persecuted individual believers. Yet, the Communist state accepted the existence of religious communities. Opposition against the regime could gather under the umbrella of the churches. The Protestant and Roman Catholic churches were a political factor of the utmost importance during German reunification at the end of the 1980s. Throughout the existence of the DDR, from 1949 to 1990, the churches remained a counterpart to the ruling system. They maintained their independence in spite of manifold, and often successful, attempts by the regime to place its own people in church offices as unofficial collaborators of the Secret Service. The regime accepted the churches and other religious communities as existing and somewhat autonomous institutions. Their property was not expropriated and was generally regarded as public property. Contacts between church institutions in East and West Germany remained largely intact. These contacts were often used to secretly transfer money and to pay for letting people emigrate into the West who had been arrested for attempted escape from the Republic. During that time, the Protestant Church came largely to accept a description of their existence as a 'church in socialism', to be distinguished from a possible 'church for socialism' or a 'church against socialism'. The Protestant Church, historically far stronger in the country than the Roman Catholic Church, then protected people who opposed the regime in the late 1980s. In substance, this development was closely linked to the events in Poland that were supported by the Roman Catholic Church. The famous 'Monday Demonstrations' that contributed to the final breakdown of the Communist regime started from the Protestant church St. Nikolai in Leipzig on 4 September 1989. They followed the 'prayers for peace' that were led by the pastors Christian Führer and Christoph Wonneberger starting in 1982. During the demonstrations, hundreds of thousands of citizens of the DDR gathered to protest the regime and to demand full freedom of travel. Many of the demonstrators were not church members and were often non-believers, but they found a place to meet, discuss, and demonstrate in a space that had been created by religious communities.

# Part I. Legal Framework and Sources

## Chapter 1. Constitutional Position of Religion

### §1. Basic Law

#### I. The Preamble

*51.* The German constitution starts with the first sentence of its preamble stating: 'Conscious of their responsibility before God and man, inspired by the determination to promote world peace as an equal partner in a united Europe, the German people, in the exercise of their constituent power, have adopted this Basic Law.'

*52.* This *invocatio dei* makes reference to the idea of God; it is not an *advocatio dei*, which would directly place the constitution under the will of God, as is the case in many other countries' constitutions, such as the Irish constitution or the one of Greece or Switzerland.

*53.* The preamble does not restrict its reference to the Christian idea of God. It would be a thought unthinkable that in 1949, after the murder of the Jews by the Germans, and in the attempt to reconnect Germany with its pre-Nazi and anti-Nazi good traditions, the new German constitution would exclude the Jewish idea of God. It is generally understood that the preamble of the Basic Law does not refer to any specific idea of teachings of God, such as the Christian, the Jewish, the Muslim or any other specific concept of God.

*54.* Instead, the reference to God is a reference to religion as such. The preamble of the German constitution, by making reference to God, acknowledges the existence of transcendence, of the idea that there is more than the visible world, that there is something beyond. By this reference to the responsibility before God, the preamble of the Basic Law accepts that there is something more and other than the state and its constitution, something that goes beyond what is made by humankind. It is thus acknowledging that the state the constitution creates and structures is not all-encompassing; that is, the state is not total. The reference to God in the German constitution is anti-total and is thus anti-totalitarian.

## II. Freedom of Religion or Belief

*55.* The constitution of the Federal Republic of Germany guarantees freedom of religion in its Article 4, thus in a very predominant place. Article 4 of the Federal Constitution reads:

> Article 4 [Freedom of faith, conscience, and creed]
>
> (1) Freedom of faith and of conscience, and freedom to profess a religious or philosophical creed, shall be inviolable.
> (2) The undisturbed practice of religion shall be guaranteed.
> (3) No person shall be compelled against his conscience to render military service involving the use of arms. Details shall be regulated by a federal law.

## III. Institutional Guarantees

*56.* The relationship between the state and religious communities is further specified in Article 140 Basic Law. This provision incorporates Articles 136–139 and 141 WRV, promulgated on 11 August 1919, into the present Basic Law. These provisions of the Weimar Constitution form an integral part of the Basic Law. They create a general structure of guarantees, which in German legal terminology is called an 'institutional guarantee'. Article 140 Basic Law and Articles 136–139 and 141 Weimar Constitution read:[29]

> **Article 140 Basic Law [Provisions respecting religious societies]**
> The provisions of Articles 136, 137, 138, 139, and 141 of the German Constitution of August 11, 1919 shall be an integral part of this Basic Law.
>
> **Article 136 (Weimar Constitution)**
>
> (1) Civil and political rights and duties shall be neither dependent upon nor restricted by the exercise of religious freedom.
> (2) Enjoyment of civil and political rights and eligibility for public office shall be independent of religious affiliation.
> (3) No person shall be required to disclose his religious convictions. The authorities shall have the right to inquire into a person's membership in a religious society only to the extent that rights or duties depend upon it or that a statistical survey mandated by a law so requires.
> (4) No person may be compelled to perform any religious act or ceremony, to participate in religious exercises, or to take a religious form of oath.
>
> **Article 137 (Weimar Constitution)**
>
> (1) There shall be no state church.

29. *See* Constitution of the Weimar Republic (Weimarer Reichsverfassung – WRV), officially known as Constitution of the German *Reich* (Verfassung des Deutschen Reichs).

(2) The freedom to form religious societies shall be guaranteed. The union of religious societies within the territory of the *Reich* shall be subject to no restrictions.
(3) Religious societies shall regulate and administer their affairs independently within the limits of the law that applies to all. They shall confer their offices without the participation of the state or the civil community.
(4) Religious societies shall acquire legal capacity according to the general provisions of civil law.
(5) Religious societies shall remain corporations under public law insofar as they have enjoyed that status in the past. Other religious societies shall be granted the same rights upon application, if their constitution and the number of their members give assurance of their permanency. If two or more religious societies established under public law unite into a single organization, it too shall be a corporation under public law.
(6) Religious societies that are corporations under public law shall be entitled to levy taxes on the basis of the civil taxation lists in accordance with *Land* law.
(7) Associations whose purpose is to foster a philosophical creed shall have the same status as religious societies.
(8) Such further regulation as may be required for the implementation of these provisions shall be a matter for *Land* legislation.

**Article 138 (Weimar Constitution)**

(1) Rights of religious societies to public subsidies on the basis of a law, contract, or special grant shall be redeemed by legislation of the *Länder*. The principles governing such redemption shall be established by the *Reich*.
(2) Property rights and other rights of religious societies or associations in their institutions, foundations, and other assets intended for purposes of worship, education, or charity shall be guaranteed.

**Article 139 (Weimar Constitution)**

Sunday and holidays recognized by the state shall remain protected by law as days of rest from work and of spiritual improvement.

**Article 141 (Weimar Constitution)**

To the extent that a need exists for religious services and pastoral work in the army, in hospitals, in prisons, or in other public institutions, religious societies shall be permitted to provide them, but without compulsion of any kind.

## IV. Religious Instruction in Public Schools

*57.* The Basic Law specifically provides for religious education in public schools. The relevant Article 7 sections 2 and 3 GG reads:

(2) Parents and guardians shall have the right to decide whether children shall receive religious instruction.
(3) Religious instruction shall form part of the regular curriculum in state schools, with the exception of non-denominational schools. Without prejudice to the state's right of supervision, religious instruction shall be given in accordance with the tenets of the religious community concerned. Teachers may not be obliged against their will to give religious instruction.

*58.* Concerning religious education, Article 141 GG provides special rules for historically based special cases that apply especially to Berlin and Bremen. Article 141 Basic Law reads:

> The first clause of section 3 of Article 7 shall not apply in any *Land* in which *Land* law otherwise provided on 1 January 1949.

## V. Equal Treatment

*59.* The Basic Law also provides explicit rules on equal treatment in relation to religions in Article 3 section 3 and Article 33 section 3 GG:

Article 3 section 3 Basic Law reads:

(3) No person shall be favoured or disfavoured because of sex, parentage, race, language, homeland and origin, faith, or religious or political opinions. No person shall be disfavoured because of disability.

Article 33 section 3 Basic Law reads:

(3) Neither the enjoyment of civil and political rights, nor eligibility for public office, nor rights acquired in the public service shall be dependent upon religious affiliation. No one may be disadvantaged by reason of adherence or non-adherence to a particular religious denomination or philosophical creed.

Furthermore, as mentioned above, Article 136 WRV provides:

(1) Civil and political rights and duties shall be neither dependent upon nor restricted by the exercise of religious freedom.
(2) Enjoyment of civil and political rights and eligibility for public office shall be independent of religious affiliation.

## VI. Oath of Office

*60.* The president of the Republic takes an oath of office that refers to God, as stated in Article 56 GG. According to Article 64 section 2 GG, the federal chancellor and the federal ministers take the same oath of office. Article 56 GG states:

> On assuming his office, the Federal President shall take the following oath before the assembled Members of the *Bundestag* and the *Bundesrat*:
> I swear that I will dedicate my efforts to the well-being of the German people, promote their welfare, protect them from harm, uphold and defend the Basic Law and the laws of the Federation, perform my duties conscientiously, and do justice to all. So help me God.

The oath may also be taken without religious affirmation.

*61.* While it is an expression of freedom of religion or belief that the oath can be taken without religious affirmation, it is of significance that the Constitution has religious affirmation as the standard way of taking the oath. This is different from the 1919 Constitution of the Weimar Republic, which in its Article 42 held for an oath of office of the president without religious affirmation while allowing for a religious formula as the exception when the person taking the oath should so wish. This development is a significant signal for the increased openness of German constitutional law to religion after the experience of National Socialism.

# §2. Constitutional Provisions of the *Länder*

## I. Religion in the Preambles

*62.* Some constitutions of the *Länder* also have references to God in their preambles, while others, such as Brandenburg, do not. This and other differences in approach to religious issues are not the least due to differences between East and West Germany and to the time in history in which the constitutions were framed. The preamble of the 1946 constitution of Bavaria begins with the words: 'In view of the expanse of rubble to which an order of state and society without God, without conscience, and without respect for the dignity of the human being has led the survivors of the Second World War.'

*63.* Initiated by a referendum, the constitution of Lower Saxony was amended in 1994 to include a preamble: 'Conscious of their responsibility before God and humankind, the people of Lower Saxony through their *Land* parliament have adopted this constitution.'[30]

30. *See also* preamble of the Constitution of Saxony-Anhalt (Verf LSA).

## II. Individual Freedom of Religion or Belief

*64.* As an example of the guarantee of freedom of religion or belief in a *Land* constitution, the constitution of Bavaria states in its Article 107:

> (1) Freedom of belief and conscience is guaranteed. (2) The undisturbed practice of religion is under the protection of the state. (3) The enjoyment of civil and political rights shall be neither dependent upon nor restricted by the religious affiliation. It may not diminish the political duties. (4) Eligibility for public office shall be independent from the religious affiliation. (5) No person shall be required to disclose his religious convictions. The authorities shall have the right to inquire into a person's membership in a religious society only to the extent that rights or duties depend upon it or that a statistical survey mandated by a law so requires. (6) No person may be compelled to perform a religious act or to participate in any religious exercises or ceremonies, or to take a religious form of oath.

*65.* Another example of religious freedom guaranteed in a *Land* constitution is Article 13 of the constitution of Brandenburg:

> Freedom of conscience, belief and confession. (1) Freedom of conscience, faith, and to profess a religious or philosophical creed shall be inviolable; the undisturbed practice thereof shall be guaranteed. (2) No person shall be required to disclose his religious or philosophical convictions. The authorities shall have the right to inquire into a person's membership in a religious community only to the extent that rights or duties depend upon it. (3) No person may be compelled to participate in a religious or philosophical act or to take a religious form of oath. (4) If a citizen cannot fulfil civic duties because they contradict his conscience, the *Land* should offer him if possible alternative, equally burdensome duties. This does not apply to financial duties.

## III. Institutional Guarantees

*66.* Constitutions of the *Länder* also contain provisions about the institutional status of religious communities.

*67.* In Bavaria, these institutional guarantees are:

**Article 142**

(1) There shall be no state church.
(2) The freedom of association to common home service, to public cult activity, and to religious communities as well as their union within Bavaria shall within the generally valid laws not be subject to limitations.
(3) Churches and recognized religious communities as well as those philosophical communities the aims of which do not contradict the generally

valid laws shall be free from patronizing by the state. They shall regulate and administer their affairs independently within the limits of the law that applies to all. They shall confer their offices without the participation of the state or the civil community.

**Article 143**

(1) Religious communities and philosophical communities shall acquire legal capacity according to the general provisions of civil law.
(2) Churches and recognized religious communities shall remain corporations under public law insofar as they have enjoyed that status in the past. Other recognized religious communities and those philosophical communities the aims of which do not contradict the generally valid laws shall after an existence of five years be granted the same rights upon application.
(3) Churches and religious communities as well as philosophical communities that are corporations under public law may levy taxes on the basis of the civil taxation lists.

**Article 144**

(1) In the fulfilment of their official duties clergymen shall enjoy the protection of the state.
(2) Any public maligning of religion, its institutions, of clerics and members of religious orders in their capacity as religious official shall be prohibited and punishable.
(3) Clerics shall not be obliged to report before courts and other authorities what has been confided to them in their capacity as spiritual advisers.

**Article 145**

(1) Rights of religious communities to subsidies by the state or the municipalities on the basis of a law, contract, or special grant shall be guaranteed.
(2) New voluntary subsidies of the state, municipalities or associations of municipalities to a religious community are raised as a supplement to the public taxes and payments by the members of that religious community.

**Article 146**

Property rights and other rights of religious communities, religious associations, orders, congregations, philosophical communities in their institutions, foundations, and other assets intended for purposes of worship, education, or charity shall be guaranteed.

**Article 147**

The Sundays and holidays recognized by the state shall remain protected by law as days of spiritual improvement and of rest from work.

**Article 148**

To the extent that a need exists for religious services and pastoral work in hospitals, in prisons, or in other public institutions, religious communities shall be permitted to provide them, but without compulsion of any kind.

**Article 149**

(1) The municipalities shall have the duty to care that each deceased person can be properly buried. The religious communities shall decide by themselves about their cooperation.
(2) In cemeteries that are assigned to only specific religious communities the burial of persons of different creed has to be allowed in the forms that are customary to them and without isolation when another suitable burial place is not available.
(3) Notwithstanding this, the simultaneous use of churches and cemeteries shall be governed by the law previously in force as far as no changes are provided for by law.

**Article 150**

(1) The churches shall have the right to educate and provide further training to their clerics in their own ecclesiastical colleges.
(2) The theological faculties at the universities shall be preserved.

*68.* These provisions deviate only in nuances from the guarantees provided for by the Basic Law. They also entail norms about theological faculties at state universities, education of clergy, and cemeteries, as these matters lie within the competencies of the *Länder* and not of the Federal Republic. The constitutions of the other *Länder* are very much like the Bavarian provisions, although some variations in detail do exist that often take up regional characteristics in religious demography and history. This is strikingly visible in the new constitutions of the *Länder* in the East of Germany after the 1990 German reunification, which, in general, mirror a more distant relationship between state and religion.

## IV. Education

*69.* Constitutions of the *Länder* provide for the specific structure of the school system, often in regard to religion. The constitution of North Rhine-Westphalia states in its Article 12 section 6:

> In Community Schools, children shall be educated and brought up in community on the basis of Christian educational and cultural values in openness for the Christian confessions and for other religious and philosophical convictions. In Confessional Schools, children of the Catholic or the Evangelical belief or of another religious community shall be educated and brought up according to the principles of the respective denomination. In Philosophical

Schools to which belong also the Non-confessional Schools, children shall be educated and brought up according to the principles of the respective philosophy.

*70.* A number of *Länder* have adopted provisions in their constitutions concerning aims of education of the young generation and the organization of the school system. Article 28 of the constitution of Rhineland-Palatinate guarantees that the churches and religious communities contribute to education. Public schools are organized as Christian Community Schools (Article 29). Article 30 of the Rhineland-Palatinate constitution determines that schools shall educate the youth to fear of God and brotherly love as well as to other aims such as respect and tolerance or responsibility to nature and environment, doing this in a free democratic spirit.[31] Again, the constitutions of other *Länder,* such as Brandenburg, do not have such an explicit reference to God when they deal with the aims of education.

*71.* Constitutions of the *Länder* also provide for religious instruction in public schools in various ways, as does Article 14 constitution of North Rhine-Westphalia. Again, Brandenburg does not do so nor does Mecklenburg-Western Pomerania.

## V. Treaty Law and Various Issues

*72.* Some *Land* constitutions explicitly provide for the possibility to conclude treaties between the *Land* and religious communities (Article 9 section 2 constitution of Mecklenburg-Western Pomerania, Article 32 section 4 constitution of Saxony-Anhalt) or they explicitly protect the charitable activities of religious communities (Article 19 section 2 constitution of Mecklenburg-Western Pomerania, Article 32 section 2 constitution of Saxony-Anhalt). Mecklenburg-Western Pomerania includes Articles 136–139 and 141 of the Weimar Constitution into its own constitution (in Article 9 section 1) as it is done by the Basic Law of the Federal Republic.[32]

---

31. *See also* Art. 7, s. 1 NRWVerf.
32. *See also* Art. 32, s. 5 Verf LSA.

# Chapter 2. Other Legislation with Regard to Religion

## §1. Range of Legislation

*73.* The detailed arrangements of the constitutional foundation for a church-state system are further elaborated and specified in numerous regulations in the legal provisions ranking below the Basic Law. The provisions regulating issues of religion and religious communities are spread throughout the entire legal system of the Federal Republic of Germany and its *Länder*.

*74.* There is no specific law on the relationship between the state and religious communities in Germany in the sense of a comprehensive act relating to these issues. The status of religious communities is regulated within the various contexts at stake. This means that the general laws on taxation also contain provisions on taxation concerning religious communities, the school laws contain provisions on religious communities and schools, the laws on universities contain provisions on religious communities and universities, etc. Looking into the relationship between the state and religion in Germany requires looking at the legal order in its entirety. Many provisions also relate to religion without reference to any specific religious community, such as conscientious objection to military service, regulations on oaths, etc.

## §2. Treaty Law

*75.* The Federal Republic of Germany and its *Länder* have also concluded numerous treaties with religious communities.[33] There are many concordats (treaties with the Holy See) and treaties with religious communities, including many churches, the Jewish faith communities and also non-religious, philosophical communities called *Weltanschauungsgemeinschaften*. In relation to the Catholic Church, the *Reichskonkordat* of 1933 is an essential basis that is recognized as a treaty under international law. Church-state treaties with the Protestant churches and those made with Catholic dioceses are sui generis but are treated as being in a category similar to that of international treaties. The subject matter of such church-state treaties includes the cooperation between the state and the religious communities, religious freedom, guarantees and arrangements for religious instruction in public schools, theological faculties in public universities, military chaplaincy, the position of the religious community in the public sphere, and also the financing of religious communities.

33. For a first, though in parts outdated, impression *see* Joseph Listl (ed.), *Konkordate und Kirchenverträge in der Bundesrepublik Deutschland*, 2 vols (Berlin: Duncker & Humblot, 1987).

## §3. Basic Structures of Legislation

*76.* Concepts that have been developed in religions appear in contexts beyond the specific status of religious communities or specific beliefs of individuals. German law is deeply influenced by concepts of religion, primarily by Christian traditions. Jewish ideas have intensely contributed, and – to a much lesser extent – concepts exist that have grown in Muslim contexts, the latter being visible, for example, in the payment by cheque. It is obvious that Muslim concepts are rare, but they are visible in specific matters.

*77.* The predominantly Christian influence on the law can be seen throughout the legal order in ideas such as freedom and equality, subsidiarity, rule of law, democracy or solidarity. It is quite obvious in the idea of human dignity and human rights as well as in the idea of separation between state and religious communities. Further examples include the idea and structure of public office, representation or in the field of procedural law the principle of *in dubio pro reo* and the inquisition procedure. It can well be argued that the concept of the law as such is an idea developed primarily in the religious sphere. German law cannot be understood in depth without taking into consideration the manifold religious influences.

# Chapter 3. Typology of the System

## §1. Separation and Cooperation

*78.* Under the church-state systems of Europe, Germany takes a middle-of-the-road approach. The Basic Law lays down a system under which there is a separation of religious communities and the state while, at the same time, a constitutionally secured form of cooperation exists between the two spheres. This is done in order to care cooperatively for the needs of the people. Cooperation presupposes separation of state and religious as well as ideological communities. Cooperation is only possible among partners who are not identical. In fact, separation of the state and religious and ideological communities is strict and specific in the sense that the state and the communities respect the self-stance and the independence of the partner. This enables cooperation on the basis of equal standing and respect for the other's field of exclusive competence. It has to be noted, however, that most scholars in legal doctrine describe the system as not advocating a strict separation;[34] this view is based on the assumption that strict separation would mean a hostile attitude towards religion or at least exclude any interaction between the state and religion.

*79.* Freedom of religion or belief is the very basis of the legal system of cooperation between secular and religious institutions in Germany. The legal basis of the German system of state-religion relationship is structured by several basic principles of which neutrality, tolerance, parity, and pluralism may be regarded as the most prevalent ones from a legal point of view. Openness to religion is a predominant feature of the system.

## §2. Neutrality

*80.* Neutrality requires the state not to identify with a church; there is to be no Established Church (Article 137 section 1 WRV in conjunction with Article 140 GG).[35] The state is not allowed to have any special inclination to a particular religious community or to judge such an organization's particular merits or ideologies to be true. Ideological institutions are to be on equal footing with religious institutions; this deals with organizations that have a humanistic ideology or a position without reference to the question of a God or gods; they might also be called world-view communities. However, religious institutions must not be placed in a more disadvantageous position than societal groups; anti-religious state policies would be incompatible with a neutral approach because these would discriminate against religion. This prohibits a decision in favour of state atheism. Neutrality, furthermore, means non-intervention; that is, the state is not allowed to take decisive action in the affairs of religious communities. This is made particularly clear in Article 137

34. Juliane Kokott in *Grundgesetz. Kommentar*, Michael Sachs ed., 9th edn (Munich: C.H. Beck, 2021), Art. 4, n. 7; *see also* BVerfG 24 Sep. 2003, BVerfGE 108, 282, 300.
35. Cf. also Art. 136 WRV in conjunction with Art. 140, s. 4 and Art. 33, s. 3 GG.

section 3 WRV in conjunction with Article 140 GG: 'Every religious community regulates and administers its own affairs independently within the framework of the general law that applies to all.' This right of self-determination is valid, regardless of the legal status of the religious congregation.

*81.* Neutrality does not mean neutrality in respect of specific values. It is quite clear that the Basic Law and, with it, the entire legal system is based on strong values such as human dignity, freedom, and equality. However, neutrality means not to identify with a specific religious or philosophical concept, teaching or institution. State neutrality is not violated when the state takes up values and concepts that have been developed in the religious sphere.

*82.* Neutrality also means positive neutrality. This concept obligates the state to actively support religion and to provide for the space religion needs to flourish. This makes it possible and requires, for example, for the state to include religious needs in planning law: State authorities have to provide for real estate in their urban development plans on which religious communities can construct places of worship according to the needs of the population. This concept of positive neutrality is predominant in the official discourses and not only in the law. It is actively supported and implemented by the courts and state authorities. Some scholars, however, argue that the state should have a more distant stance towards religion. Some people feel that separation of state and religious communities is not intense enough.[36] A still new challenge is visible with respect to the integration of the Muslim population with their specific needs.

## §3. Tolerance

*83.* The principle of tolerance obliges all state authorities to respect the various religious and non-religious creeds. While neutrality refers predominantly to the organizations of religion and belief, tolerance focuses more on the individual. In doing so, tolerance means a positive tolerance of not merely enduring different views but the duty to actively create an atmosphere of tolerance in society. This has been underscored by the Federal Constitutional Court in its early decisions on prayer in the public school system: While it is legal for the public school to offer prayers and religious services for the pupils, attendance must be completely optional; those who want to opt out must be free to do so. If any individual is looked at or treated by his or her fellow pupils in a discriminatory way because of opting out or participating, the school staff must do everything possible in order to create a general atmosphere of tolerance among the pupils.[37] Today, this principle has gained new importance, especially in view of Muslim pupils and their religious needs.

---

36. Gerhard Czermak, *Religions- und Weltanschauungsrecht. Eine Einführung* (Berlin/Heidelberg: Springer, 2008), 85 et seq.
37. BVerfG 16 Oct. 1979, BVerfGE 52, 223 et seq.; HessStGH 27 Oct. 1965, KirchE 7, 275 et seq.; BVerwG 30 Nov. 1973, BVerwGE 44, 196.

## §4. Parity

*84.* Parity means the obligation to treat all religious communities equally. Equal treatment of religions is a key feature of the law on religion. Equal treatment does not require identical treatment but means to treat equally what is equal and to treat unequally what is not equal according to the extent of the differences. This means that through a constitutional differentiation of legal status, a sort of graded parity exists that has to provide an adequate basis for dealing with the various social phenomena in the field of religious communities. This parity is a specific, group-orientated shaping of the idea of equal treatment that finds its historical roots in the equality of confessions – the result of the religious wars of the sixteenth and seventeenth centuries.

## §5. Pluralism

*85.* Pluralism is another basic feature of the German system of the law on religion. There is a great variety of religions, confessions, and non-confessional concepts of life. Everyone has full freedom of religion or belief. No preferences may be made by the state and state authorities regarding specific religions. The adherence to a specific religion must not be and in general is not a reason for any favouring or disfavouring state action.

## §6. Institutionalism

*86.* Religious institutions may also rely on the freedom of faith, which exists as a corporative right. It is important to note that the German law on religion presupposes that in general religions form religious communities. Believers traditionally form groups and associations. Regardless of their specific legal structure, these groups, associations, etc., form religious communities that can acquire legal entity status. Thus, the Catholic Church, the Protestant churches, the Jewish faith communities, Jehovah's Witnesses, etc., form religious communities that enjoy legal personality in their own right. This way of organization has its traditional roots in Roman law and Christian tradition. This approach is based on the assumption and expectation that the state would find representatives of religions to deal with, cooperate with them, and establish long-term structures. It is one of the basic challenges of contemporary German law when a religion, especially Islam, does not form such entities. However, Muslims in Germany have formed associations that take care of the religious needs of their members. These associations may well be recognized as religious communities by the state administrative authorities and the courts.

## §7. Openness Towards Religion

*87.* A basic feature of the system is its openness to religion. Religion is regarded as something positive and a phenomenon that also forms part of the public sphere.

German law does not refer to laicism or secularism. Laicism and secularism are not legal concepts in German law. 'Laicism' and also 'laicity' are widely regarded as terms that represent a basically hostile stance of the state towards religion and religious communities. These are therefore used rarely and, if so, by those who prefer a fundamental change of the system.[38]

*88.* However, legal and philosophical theory has taken up the concept of the 'secular state', which has to accommodate religion and which lives on the basis of preconditions that the secular state cannot guarantee by means of legal enforcement.[39] In this concept, religions appear as providers of values and ideas on which the state relies. A constant and intense debate is going on concerning the relationship between the state and religion, religion and culture, and the basic foundations of the German legal and political system in Christianity and its links with Judaism and other religions.

## §8. Freedom of Religion or Belief

*89.* The basic principles of the law on religion and the debate about them are also to be seen in the setting of the freedom of religion or belief according to Article 4 GG. It is here that one finds the requirement of a positive stance towards religion. Freedom of faith is guaranteed in order to give every individual the right to believe what he or she wills. Also included is the freedom of faith in a negative aspect; this is the right not to have a creed and/or the right not to belong to a particular religious faith. Religious freedom also guarantees the right to act according to one's beliefs. As a result, conscientious beliefs present a problem in certain criminal cases: a woman was critically ill but refused medical treatment on the basis of her faith. Her husband, of the same faith, respected her wishes; the woman died as a result. The Federal Constitutional Court quashed his conviction for neglect of a duty to help because the man could not be held responsible; truly acting in accordance with one's faith and conscience can result in an absence of criminal liability for those who break the law.[40]

*90.* Freedom of faith in the sense of positive tolerance also allows for the possibility of the state offering in public schools the opportunity for interdenominational school prayer, so long as participation is a part of the existing social attitude and, as such, is completely voluntary. The state must make sure that it

38. *See also* Stefan Mückl, 'Trennung und Kooperation – das gegenwärtige Staat-Kirche-Verhältnis in der Bundesrepublik Deutschland', zum Thema Staat und Kirche, vol. 40 (Münster: Aschendorff, 2007), 41–83.
39. Ernst-Wolfgang Böckenförde, 'Die Entstehung des Staates als Vorgang der Säkularisation', in *Staat, Gesellschaft, Freiheit. Studien zur Staatstheorie und zum Verfassungsrecht*, Ernst-Wolfgang Böckenförde ed. (Frankfurt: Suhrkamp 1976), 42–64.
40. Cf. BVerfG 19 Oct. 1971, BVerfGE 32, 98.

provides an atmosphere of tolerance. In situations creating a certain degree of control over an individual's surroundings, the state is required to provide for the religious needs of this person, such as when one is obliged to attend school.[41] This applies equally to the National Defence Force and penal institutions.

41. Cf. BVerfG 16 Oct. 1979, BVerfGE 52, 223.

# Part II. Religious Freedom in General

## Chapter 1. Individual Religious Freedom

### §1. Normative Structures

*91.* Individual freedom of religion or belief in Germany is guaranteed on the federal level in Article 4 GG. According to Article 4 GG, freedom of faith and of conscience, and freedom to profess a religious or philosophical creed, shall be inviolable; the undisturbed practice of religion shall be guaranteed; and no person shall be compelled against his conscience to render military service involving the use of arms, details thereof shall be regulated by federal law.

*92.* The close connection between freedom of religion or belief and freedom of conscience in Article 4 of the federal constitution shows the importance that the constitution attributes to deep individual convictions. It also shows the respect that the legal order pays to those personal convictions. It may further also be explained by the assumption that historically, the individual conscience very often was seen to be formed by religious beliefs. However, today, it is common doctrine and court practice that the conscience can well be based on non-religious and also in non-philosophical convictions. Conscientious objection to military service is not dependent on religious or philosophical creed.

*93.* Section 1 of Article 4 GG guarantees the freedom of faith and conscience as well as the freedom of religious or ideological creed.[42] Section 2 of Article 4 GG guarantees the undisturbed practice of religion.[43] Both sections of Article 4 GG are understood as one whole and undivided fundamental right.[44] The guarantees of Article 4 GG are seen to be especially important expressions of personality rights and human dignity.[45] They are a basis of state neutrality in matters of religion and philosophy.

---

42. *See* Art. 4, s. 1 GG.
43. *See* Art. 4, s. 2 GG.
44. *See* BVerfG 16 Oct. 1968, BVerfGE 24, 236, 245 et seq.; BVerfG 19 Oct. 1971, BVerfGE 32, 98, 106; BVerfG 8 Feb. 1977, BVerfGE 44, 37, 49; BVerfG 5 Feb. 1991, BVerfGE 83, 341, 354.
45. BVerfG 17 Jul. 1973, BVerfGE 35, 366, 376; Juliane Kokott in *Grundgesetz. Kommentar*, Michael Sachs ed., 9th edn (Munich: C.H. Beck, 2021), Art. 4, n. 3.

§2. FUNCTIONS

*94.* Article 4 GG is regarded as an individual guarantee. It protects freedom of religion or belief for individual persons and – as far as applicable – for legal entities.

*95.* Including freedom of religion or belief, but going beyond that and encompassing all fundamental rights, fundamental rights are indeed the centre and axis on which all legal thinking turns. The functions that are ascribed to them are correspondingly numerous. This is also the case for freedom of religion or belief. Fundamental rights are, first of all, seen to be defensive rights. Particular emphasis has been placed on this function since the nineteenth century. This means that the state may not interfere with the legal position of the individual unless there is a special reason to do so. Unjustified interferences can be blocked by the individual. This means that he or she has legal remedies against unjustified detention, against the confiscation of his or her property, or against the banning of a particular point of view. Apart from their defensive function, fundamental rights also traditionally involve the right to participate in the democratic political process. Particularly in the case of rights such as freedom of assembly, freedom of the press and of opinion, and the right to vote, this aspect is prominent. It also applies to religiously based activities and views: Religious or belief convictions must not be a reason to allow or prohibit a person's or organization's participation in the public democratic process. To a very carefully limited extent, a certain positive dimension entitling to services from the state is also recognized as a function of fundamental rights. Insofar as this is practical, the state has a duty to ensure that circumstances conducive to the exercise of fundamental rights are created. For example, the right to freely choose one's career and the associated course of education obliges the state to make available a number of places in educational institutions insofar as such a course of studies is a legal requirement for the exercise of the profession or trade in question. The right to freedom of religion or belief does, however, not convey a right that the state should provide or guarantee the material basis for the manifestation of religion; there is no right to be provided with certain rooms or other means for religious purposes.[46] Closely related to this positive dimension, basically entitling to services are the fundamental rights as a protective duty of the state to act. Thus, the state is not only required to respect the right to life and physical integrity in its negative defensive sense by not infringing on this right itself. It is also obliged to actively intervene to protect these rights against infringements by third parties or other sources of danger. The Federal Constitutional Court has stated this duty explicitly also to apply in respect of freedom of religion or belief.[47] Lastly, the fundamental rights are also a guarantee of organization and procedure. The state must provide appropriate organizational and procedural structures to ensure the prompt and effective protection of fundamental rights. Thus, for example, administrative officials planning a road-building operation must accord reasonable consideration to

46. BVerfG 28 Feb. 1992, *Neue Juristische Wochenschrift* 45 (1992): 2812 et seq.
47. BVerfG (K) 26 Mar. 2001, *Deutsches Verwaltungblatt* 116 (2001): 984 et seq.; BVerfG 19 Dec. 2000, BVerfGE 102, 370 et seq.

the rights of owners of neighbouring property by informing them properly and giving them an opportunity to give their views on the subject.

*96.* These five functions, which the fundamental rights are recognized as having, make clear the two dimensions of these rights. First, they are the subjective rights of the individual and of legal entities. However, they simultaneously form a sphere of the objective law. In doing so, fundamental rights are a guarantee for what is called in legal doctrine 'institutions': fundamental rights are not only guarantees for individual rights and, as such, individual guarantees, but they also are 'institutional guarantees'. Thus, for example, the free, democratic political process as such is protected and not only the right of the individuals to participate in it. Fundamental rights also often guarantee specific legal institutions: marriage (Article 6 section 1 GG), property (Article 14 GG), contract (Article 2 section 1 GG), a free press (Article 5 section 1 GG), the structures for regulating industrial disputes (Article 9 section 3 GG). This objective dimension of fundamental rights serves to reinforce the rights of individuals but is independent of any attempt by a specific individual to enforce rights in a specific instance. Particularly here, the state appears in its role as the guarantor of freedom by creating legal structures in which freedom can flourish.

*97.* The fundamental right to freedom of religion or belief is a guarantee against undue state intrusion into the person's freedoms. However, this right – as do other fundamental rights – also obliges the state to provide the necessary space for the person to positively live a life in accordance with his or her religion.

*98.* Freedom of religion or belief shares with other fundamental freedoms the function of obliging the state to protect the individual in exercising his or her freedoms. State authorities must actively provide the necessary and reasonable protection against infringements by other people into these rights. The legal system must provide appropriate instruments of protection. This can be relevant in extreme cases, such as the call to kill a dissenter or public assaults against places of worship. It also can be relevant when a member of a religious community is kept against his or her will in this community by the other members. Since another generally accepted function of fundamental rights is the duty of the state to provide legal structures of organization and procedure, the state must care for the possibility of every member of a religious community to end his or her membership in that community without burdensome procedures.

*99.* The right to freedom of religion or belief also has an institutional meaning. It guarantees the institution of neutrality of the state in matters of religion or belief. This institutional meaning of basically individual freedom has the function of intensifying and further protecting that individual freedom. As such, it forms part of an 'objective level' of constitutional guarantee strengthening the 'subjective rights' of the individuals. The state has to provide a system of law by which everyone can freely live his or her religion or belief, in which religious and philosophical communities and associations can flourish, and in which pluralism, tolerance, and equality form basic structures of actual life. As has been stated by the Federal Constitutional Court:

> The Basic Law obliges the state through Article 4 section 1, Article 3, Article 33 section 3 as well as through Article 136 section 1 and section 4 and Article 137 section 1 WRV in conjunction with Article 140 GG to religious and philosophical neutrality. It prohibits introducing legal institutions that would have the character of a state church, and it also prohibits privileging specific denominations.[48]

## §3. Scope of Individual Guarantee

### I. Nationality

*100.* Freedom of religion or belief is a human right. It does not depend on the nationality of individual persons.

### II. Religious Maturity

#### *A. Role of Parents and Legal Guardians*

*101.* Children also enjoy the freedom of religion or belief. While, in general, persons reach full legal capacity when they become 18 years old, religion is regarded as being so important to the identity of a person that religious maturity is reached at an earlier age. Until minors have reached religious maturity, it is up to their parents or legal guardians to act on behalf of their children in matters of religion or belief. At the same time, parents enjoy their own individual right to raise and educate their children as is guaranteed in Article 6 section 1 GG in combination with Article 4 GG. Personal decisions of minors in religious matters relate to parental care. While Article 6 section 2 GG provides that 'the care and upbringing of children is the natural right of parents and a duty primarily incumbent upon them', children have the fundamental right of religious freedom as a personal right. Article 6 section 2 GG also stipulates in relation to parental care that the state shall watch over the parents in the performance of their duty. Germany is a signatory state of the 1990 Convention on the Rights of the Child, which provides in its Article 14 that States Parties shall respect the right of the child to freedom of thought, conscience, and religion and that States Parties shall respect the rights and duties of the parents and, when applicable, legal guardians, to provide direction to the child in the exercise of his or her right in a manner consistent with the evolving capacities of the child.

48. BVerfG 14 Dec. 1965, BVerfGE 19, 206, 216.

*B. Federal Act on the Religious Upbringing of Children*

*102.* Religious maturity is legally structured in the Act on the Religious Upbringing of the Child of 15 July 1921 (RelKErzG).

*103.* The two parents decide by way of free agreement with each other about the religious upbringing of the child as far as they have the right and the duty of parental care for the child. The agreement can be revoked at any time and ends with the death of one of the spouses (§1 RelKErzG).

*104.* If such an agreement does not exist or has been revoked, the general rules of civil law about parental care also apply to the religious upbringing of the child (§2 RelKErzG). However, as long as matrimony exists, no spouse can decide without the consent of the other spouse that the child should be raised in another confession than that which was the common confession at the time of marriage or in another confession than before or that the child should be withdrawn from religious instruction at school. In the case that consent is not given, it is possible to apply for a mediation or decision of the family court. The court will usually hear the spouses and, if necessary, also relatives and teachers of the child if this is reasonably possible. When the child is over 10 years of age, the child will also be heard by the court.

*105.* In the case that the father or mother and a legal guardian have the common care for the child, the decision of the father or mother about the religious upbringing of the child prevails over the decision of the legal guardian unless the father or the mother has lost the right to care for the religious upbringing of the child according to the civil code (§3 section 1 RelKErzG).

*106.* If the legal guardian has exclusive care for the child, he or she also has to decide about the religious upbringing of the child. The approval of the guardianship court is needed for the decision. Before a decision is taken, parents, relatives and teachers of the child have to be heard if this is reasonably possible. The child also has to be heard if he or she is over 10 years of age. The legal guardian cannot change a decision about the religious upbringing that has already been taken (§3 section 2 RelKErzG).

*107.* Treaties about the religious upbringing of a child have no civil law effect (§4 RelKErzG). Thus, an agreement of spouses who belong to different denominations to raise their child in one of those denominations – which is often done when a Roman Catholic marries a Protestant – cannot be enforced as such before a state court. The family court, if applied to, would have to decide according to the general rules.

*108.* When having reached the age of 14, the child can freely decide about his or her religious confession (§5 RelKErzG). From the age of 12 years onwards, the religious confession of the child cannot be changed against his or her will (§5 RelKErzG).

*109.* All these rules apply also to non-religious beliefs (§6 RelKErzG).

### C. Bavaria and the Saarland

*110.* Special rules apply to the *Länder* of Bavaria and the Saarland. According to Article 137 section 1 of the 1946 Bavarian Constitution, the pupil decides about his or her participation in religious instruction and in church activities and ceremonies from the age of 18 years onwards. Similarly, Article 29 of the 1947 Constitution of the Saarland states that the young person can opt out of religious instruction when he or she has reached the age of 18. These provisions remain in force according to Article 125 number 2 GG because they amended the law of the former German Empire in the time between 8 May 1945 and 23 May 1949; they formed so-called partial federal law. It is a general legal opinion that these provisions, although formally related only to religious instruction at school and – in Bavaria – to religious ceremonies and activities at school, apply to religious maturity in general.[49]

### D. Practical Implications of Religious Maturity

*111.* These rules apply to all matters of religion or belief. Thus, it is up to the parents or legal guardians to have the child baptized; to decide on the participation in religious ceremonies and worship, religious holidays, and prayers; to send it to a kindergarten of religious or belief character or to a school run by a religious or belief community. Since religious maturity in general, except for the states of Bavaria and the Saarland, is reached by the child earlier than legal maturity, the religious maturity of the child and the right of parents to raise and educate their children run parallel for some time. It thus is assumed that before they reach legal maturity at the age of 18, children cannot decide against the will of their parents or legal guardians to stay away from school for religious reasons, travel to distant objects of religious adoration, or enter into religious housing communities.[50]

*112.* In matters of medical treatment influenced by religious or belief convictions – such as blood transfusion – the same age limits apply.[51] General aspects of the limitations to parental care also have to be taken into account: The family court can, pursuant to §1666 BGB, substitute a statement of the parents when the well-being of the child is endangered. The general court practice in these cases is that the court will allow the necessary medical treatment, such as a blood transfusion, on

49. Christoph Link, 'Religionsunterricht', in *Handbuch des Staatskirchenrechts*, Joseph Listl & Dietrich Pirson eds, vol. 2, 2nd edn (Berlin: Duncker & Humblot, 1995), 478.
50. Juliane Kokott in *Grundgesetz. Kommentar*, Michael Sachs ed., 9th edn (Munich: C.H. Beck, 2021), Art. 4, n. 9.
51. Claus Dieter Classen, *Religionsrecht*, 3rd ed. (Tübingen: Mohr Siebeck, 2021), 175.

application of the medical doctor or another third person.[52] The minor's statement in such cases is legally relevant to the extent of his or her individual intellectual and ethical maturity: There is a general consensus that persons under 14 years of age, usually referred to as children, are not able to consent to medical treatment for lack of legal capacity in this matter. Juveniles who are close to 18 years old – i.e., almost majors – will generally be able to consent to medical treatment. For the problematic cases of patients between 14 and close to 18 years of age, the concrete medical treatment which is to be performed is decisive. Notably, the severity and the urgency of the procedure, as well as the dangers an operation entails and the possibility of permanent consequences, will be taken into account when assessing whether a juvenile has the capacity to consent to medical treatment. Generally, one can say that if routine examinations or completely safe treatments are at stake, juvenile will have the legal capacity to consent to that examination or treatment. If the treatment is not entirely safe, as is the case with operations, the courts will usually negate the juvenile's legal capacity to consent to the treatment.

*113.* A decision of the Regional Court (*Landgericht* (LG)) Köln, a lower criminal court, stating that male circumcision of minors is a criminal offence and not justifiable for religious reasons, has triggered an intense public debate. While religious male circumcision of minors had always been legal before, the court held that the Muslim doctor, who had circumcised a 4-year-old Muslim boy at the request of his parents, had committed a bodily injury not justified by the right of the parents to the religious upbringing of their child. Nevertheless, the court acquitted the accused, as he had not been able to know about the illegality of his action since circumcision of minors had not been regarded as a crime before. An amendment to the Civil Code, the introduction of a new paragraph (§1631d Civil Code), was brought on its way to legalize consented male circumcision of minors for non-medical reasons. The new provision, tabled by the Federal Government and enacted in December 2012, reads as follows:

> §1631d BGB Circumcision of the male child
>
> (1) Personal care also includes the right to consent to a medically unnecessary circumcision of the male child who is not capable of understanding and judgment, if this is to be carried out in accordance with the rules of medical art. This does not apply if circumcision endangers the child's best interests, even taking into account its purpose.
> (2) In the first six months after the birth of the child, persons designated for this purpose by a religious society may also perform circumcisions in accordance with subsection (1) if they are specially trained for this purpose and, without being doctors, are comparably qualified to perform circumcision.

52. OLG Celle, *Neue Juristische Wochenschrift* 1995, 792; Uwe Diederichsen in *Palandt. Bürgerliches Gesetzbuch*, Otto Palandt ed., 68th edn (Munich: C.H. Beck, 2009), §1666, n. 25.

## §4. Forum Internum and Manifestations of Religion or Belief

*114.* The fundamental right in Article 4 GG provides first for the inner freedom to believe and whatever to believe. This '*forum internum*' of the individual person is completely free. The first section of Article 4 section 1 GG also guarantees the external freedom to make one's belief known and to spread it.[53] Moreover, it provides for the right of the individual to relate his or her whole activity to the teaching of his or her belief and to act according to his or her internal convictions and beliefs. This is related to imperative teachings as well as to those religious convictions that give advice on the best way of handling a situation in life.[54]

## §5. The Right Not to Believe

*115.* The Constitution also protects the right not to believe and not to confess any belief in its Article 4 GG. This is further made explicit for a specified context in Article 136 section 4 WRV in conjunction with Article 140 GG: 'No person may be compelled to perform any religious act or ceremony, to participate in religious exercises, or to take a religious form of oath.' The right not to believe is usually called a 'negative freedom' without any pejorative intention. The 'negative' right to freedom of religion or belief also protects against having to participate in religious activities or ceremonies of whatever kind and in whatever context. An example of that is the right of pupils as well as of teachers to opt out of confessional religious instruction in public schools, as is also explicitly stated in Article 7 sections 2 and 3 GG. No one can be forced to participate in a religious ceremony or a prayer in a public school. The 'negative' right to freedom of religion also prohibits enforcing contributions to manifestations of religion other than those of one's own religion; therefore, only members of the qualified religious community and no one else can be obliged to pay church tax. There are possible conflicts between the 'positive' and the 'negative' right to freedom of religion or belief. The negative right would support not to be confronted with religious ideas or symbols whereas the positive right to freedom of religion would support the right to exhibit such symbols or to live in a context where such symbols are being exhibited. Such conflicts have to be solved in a way of tolerance.[55] There is no right that the public sphere should be free of any religious manifestations; thus no one can claim the absence of Christmas and its manifestations in the German public, which has a Christian tradition. Likewise, no one has a right that the traditional cross situated on the top of mountains should be removed.

53. BVerfG 24 Sep. 2003, BVerfGE 108, 282 et seq. (judgment of the Constitutional Court regarding a Muslim woman teacher wearing a headscarf during lessons).
54. BVerfG 11 Apr. 1972, BVerfGE 33, 23, 28; BVerfG 17 Dec. 1975, BVerfGE 41, 29, 49.
55. BVerfG 17 Dec. 1975, BVerfGE 41, 29 et seq.; *see also* BVerfG 16 May 1995, BVerfGE 93, 1, 16.

## §6. Definitions of Religion and Belief

*116.* Although there are several attempts to define religion – and consequently belief – there is no definite answer in German law about what religion is. Courts are hesitant to define religion. The Federal Constitutional Court has said that religion and belief determine the goals of the human being, touch the human being in his or her core, and explain in an all-encompassing way the meaning of the world and of human life.[56]

*117.* It is generally said that religion is characterized by a reference to transcendence, the idea that the human being is integrated into a larger context, a 'beyond' that the individual can share in prayer or other respective activities.[57] In contrast, philosophical, non-religious belief (*Weltanschauung*), which is explicitly equally protected by Article 4 GG as is religion and faith, is characterized by a concept of the human being as being integrated into a larger context without a 'beyond', without a transcendence, regarding the world as a whole by immanent and not transcendent categories. A definition by the Federal Administrative Court says: 'A religion or a philosophical creed … is a certainty linked with the human person about certain statements on the world as a whole and on the origin and ends of human life.'[58] Since religion and philosophical creed are protected in the same way under the German constitution, it is not important to find a clear-cut distinction between the two; anyway, in practice, they will very often overlap.

*118.* The legal terms 'faith', 'belief', and 'religion' have to be understood in a broad sense. In this context, religion is the broadest notion, encompassing belief and faith. While some have argued that religion and faith should be defined in a Eurocentric and predominantly Christian understanding,[59] the Federal Constitutional Court, as well as the general opinion in legal doctrine, has a broad understanding of religion, which also covers minority religions. However, not each and every conviction that declares to be religious is accepted as a religion. What is claiming to be a religion must be one in fact based on its spiritual contents and its outer appearance. Sufficient plausibility is required.[60] It is up to the state authorities and finally to the state courts to decide on the matter, because the terms of the constitution are part of the state legal order.[61] In deciding on the matter by the state authorities, the

---

56. BVerfG 26 Jun. 2002, BVerfGE 105, 279, 293; cf. also BVerwG 27 Mar. 1992, BVerwGE 90, 112, 115; BAG 22 Mar. 1995, BAGE 79, 319, 338.
57. Juliane Kokott in *Grundgesetz. Kommentar*, Michael Sachs ed., 9th edn (Munich: C.H. Beck, 2021), Art. 4, n. 22.
58. BVerfG 27 Mar. 1992, BVerwGE 90, 112 et seq.
59. Josef Isensee, '*Diskussionsbeitrag*', Essener Gespräche zum Thema Staat und Kirche, vol. 19 (Münster: Aschendorff, 1985), 144; Walter Hamel, 'Glauben- und Gewissensfreiheit', in *Die Grundrechte*, Karl A. Bettermann, Hans C. Nipperdey & Ulrich Scheuner eds, vol. IV/1, 2nd edn (Berlin: Duncker & Humblot, 1972), 79.
60. BVerfG 24 Sep. 2003, BVerfGE 108, 282, 299.
61. BVerfG 5 Feb. 1991, BVerfGE 83, 341; Juliane Kokott in *Grundgesetz. Kommentar*, Michael Sachs ed., 9th edn (Munich: C.H. Beck, 2021), Art. 4, n. 20.

self-understanding of the one who makes the claim is of special importance.[62] The Federal Constitutional Court has ruled that in making any statement about what a religion is, courts have to include the self-understanding of the believer as one important factor in deciding the meaning of 'religion'.[63] The person concerned and his or her self-understanding about freedom of religion thus becomes part of the legal process of defining the content of this specific freedom. The believer is not confronted with the definition of religion by the authorities but is included as an active party in developing an adequate understanding of freedom. We can call this 'law by dialogue'. All this does not prevent the courts from finally deciding on the issue. In their decision, however, they have to take into account the self-understanding of the believer as an important factor in decision-making.

*119.* The Church of Scientology has been accepted as representing a religious faith in some court decisions,[64] in others not.[65] The community is still under surveillance by the Constitution Protection Offices;[66] no evidence as to substantive violations of the law has surfaced, however. In the *Land* Saarland, the judiciary has prohibited the surveillance for lack of proportionality,[67] while the Administrative Court of Appeals of North Rhine-Westphalia has upheld the surveillance in its *Land*.[68]

## §7. PROTECTED MANIFESTATIONS

### I. General Scope of Guarantee

*120.* The freedom to profess a religious or philosophical creed, as guaranteed in Article 4 section 1 GG, provides for the freedom to make one's convictions known to other people. This can have the form of words, spoken or in writing, but also any other form of communication such as painting, sculpture, religious garment, beards, or hair dressing. Violence or threats, however, are not protected because this is not seen to be a form of mental communication.[69]

*121.* It is clear that freedom of religion also includes the right to change one's religion. Article 4 GG provides for full freedom of religion or belief without especially highlighting specific forms of this freedom. This line is followed in order not

62. BVerfG 11 Apr. 1972, BVerfGE 33, 23; BVerfG 16 Oct. 1968, BVerfGE 24, 236, 247; BVerfG 5 Apr. 1991, BVerfGE 83, 341, 353.
63. Cf. BVerfG 5 Apr. 1991, BVerfGE 83, 341, 353.
64. VG Berlin 12 Oct. 1988, *Neue Juristische Wochenschrift* 42 (1989): 2559; VG Frankfurt 4 Sep. 1990, *Neue Zeitschrift für Verwaltungsrecht* 10 (1991):196; BGH 25 Sep. 1980, 78, 274 et seq.
65. BAG 22 Mar. 1995, *Neue Zeitschrift für Arbeitsrecht* 12 (1995): 823 et seq.
66. Cf. Verfassungsschutzbericht des Landes Nordrhein-Westfalen 2022, 277 et seq., https://www.im.nrw/system/files/media/document/file/verfassungsschutzbericht_nrw_2022.pdf, 9 Nov. 2023.
67. OVG Saarland 2 R 14/03 of 27 Apr. 2005.
68. OVG North Rhine-Westphalia 5A 130/05 of 12 Feb. 2008.
69. BVerfG 8 Nov. 1960, BVerfGE 12, 1, 4 et seq.; BVerwG 14 Nov. 1980, BVerwGE 61, 152, 161.

to provoke the impression that by mentioning specific forms of freedom or its manifestations, other forms might be excluded from the range of freedom.

*122.* Freedom of religion or belief provides full freedom for undisturbed practice of religion. Although Article 4 section 2 GG only speaks of religion and not explicitly of philosophical creed, it is generally accepted that the practice of philosophical creed is also equally protected.[70] Practice of religion is conceived in a very broad meaning. Practice of religion does not only cover cultic activities and the exercise and respect of religious customs such as religious services, religious collections, prayers, applying and receiving of sacraments, processions, exhibition of church flags, or bell ringing, but also religious education, free-religious and atheist festivals as well as other manifestations of religious or belief life.[71] In fact, practice of religion means to follow religious convictions in all aspects of one's life and to act accordingly.[72] Thus, the construction of a church and other religious buildings is practising a religion; accordingly, the provisions governing urban planning law must be interpreted and applied in a manner that takes adequate account of those religious needs.[73] Advice centres run by religious communities that give advice with respect to abortion represent practice of religion.[74] The same is true for following religious dress rules or rules of nourishment. Collecting rags to sell them for religious purposes is a practice of religion.[75] The visit of a foreign founder of a religion to Germany is practising a religion; strong reasons for public safety are needed to justify prohibition of entry.[76] The Federal Administrative Court has left undecided whether joint smoking of Hashish can be a practice of religion;[77] since possession and consumption of small quantities of such drugs for personal use is not punishable, the question is only of minor practical impact.

## II. Specific Issues

### A. *Proselytism*

*123.* Proselytism is not prohibited and is clearly a legal and legitimate practice of religion. Advertising a religion on public streets is legal, as it forms part of the so-called communicative general use to which public streets are dedicated. Other users of the public street should not be disturbed beyond what can be regarded as appropriate. Thus, loud shouting or playing music would be illegal also if performed for religious purposes; silent offering of scriptures is legal. However, when using the street entails selling religious products, it is regarded not as general public

70. BVerfG 16 Oct. 1968, BVerfGE 24, 236, 246.
71. *Ibid.*
72. BVerfG 19 Oct. 1971, BVerfGE 32, 98, 106; BVerfG 17 Dec. 1975, BVerfGE 41, 29, 49.
73. OVG Berlin-Brandenburg 30 Mar. 2007, *Deutsches Verwaltungsblatt* 122 (2007): 645 et seq.
74. BayVerfGH 25 Jan. 2006, *Neue Juristische Wochenschrift* 59 (2006): 1050, 1052.
75. BVerfG 16 Oct. 1968, BVerfGE 24, 236, 247.
76. BVerfG (K) 24 Oct. 2006, BVerfGK 9, 371 et seq.
77. BVerwG 21 Dec. 2000, BVerwGE 112, 314 et seq.; *see also* subsequently OVG Lower Saxony 15 Mar. 2004, *Neue Zeitschrift für Verwaltungsrecht – Rechtsprechungsreport* 17 (2004), 884 et seq.

use of the street but as a special use that needs permission from the authorities (and usually involves paying a fee), as does any other economic activity in public streets. Authorities appropriately – that means favourably – have to take into account the religious background of the activity in making their decision.[78] The legitimate needs and interests of other users of the street also have to be taken into account when deciding whether to allow such special use.[79]

*124.* However, the Federal Constitutional Court has also held that there may be something like improper proselytism that can result in legal sanctions.[80] The courts have rejected the application of a prisoner for early release from prison because he had tried to induce his fellow prisoners to leave their church by offering them tobacco. The Federal Constitutional Court has upheld this rejection. While it is a legitimate manifestation of freedom of religion or belief to move someone to leave his or her religious community, it amounts to improper and unfair action to exploit situations of need of fellow prisoners to achieve such a goal.

### *B. Conscientious Objection*

#### 1. Dress Requirements

*125.* Freedom of religion might allow to reject wearing a Muslim headscarf: Iranian passport rules require Iranian women to wear a headscarf on their passport photograph. An Iranian woman expelled to Iran from Germany on grounds of alien law needed a passport in order to enter Iran. She refused to wear a headscarf for the passport photograph on the grounds of freedom of religion, so she could not travel. The Bavarian Administrative Court of Appeals ruled in a much-criticized judgment that the official order to produce such a photograph in order to comply with Iranian passport requirements does not have any religious significance in German law. But it might infringe the right of Article 4 section 1 GG if a contrary religious conviction was explicitly claimed and set forth by the individual. There was no final court decision on this question because the Iranian woman finally left Germany by travelling to the United States.[81]

#### 2. Co-educative Physical Education

*126.* Objection to participate in co-educative physical education classes is possible when based on religious convictions such as religious dress rules. A Muslim

78. BVerwG 4 Jul. 1996, *Neue Juristische Wochenschrift* 50 (1997): 406, 407.
79. BVerwG 4 Jul. 1996, *Neue Juristische Wochenschrift* 50 (1997): 406, 407.
80. BVerfG 8 Nov. 1960, BVerfGE 12, 1 et seq.
81. VGH Bavaria 23 Mar. 2000, *Neue Zeitschrift für Verwaltungsrecht* 19 (2000): 952; this decision was much criticized by legal scholars; *see*, e.g., Hans Michael Heinig & Martin Morlok, 'Von Schafen und Kopftüchern', *JuristenZeitung* 58 (2003): 777 et seq.

girl can opt out of co-educative physical education courses.[82] Freedom of religion or belief has to be balanced with the public aims of education. Some courts have been reluctant to give preference to freedom of religion or belief in this context.[83]

### 3. Work on Religious Holidays

*127.* Objection to work on religious days of rest is part of freedom of religion. While in such cases the needs and interests of the employer have to be balanced with the religious needs of the employee, the state must not draw negative consequences from such objection: When a person loses his or her job because of religious objection to perform work on specific days contrary to general working hours, public social aid may not be cut by the authorities.[84]

### 4. Conscientious Objection to Medical Treatment

*128.* Objection for religious reasons to medical treatment is part of freedom of religion. In any way, it is a general crime to treat someone against his or her will. However, it is also a crime not to help a person who is in need because of an accident or general hazard when that is possible.[85] In 1971, the Federal Constitutional Court decided a case concerning a woman who had objected to a blood transfusion and died. The woman was a member of a religious community called the Evangelical Brethren Association. In giving birth to her fourth child at home, complications occurred. The medical doctor whom her spouse had called urged him to bring her to the hospital and to give her a blood transfusion. The woman objected to that and insisted on calling a priest to pray for her – believing that this would help. In full agreement with his spouse, her husband prayed for her but did not call for medical assistance. He continued to do so even when his spouse had lost consciousness. While the lower courts first convicted the husband for manslaughter by inactivity and then (only) for failure to render assistance in an emergency, the Federal Constitutional Court held that because of the husband's religious motives, he was not to be punished.[86] Today, this case would probably be decided with the same outcome but on the grounds of the patient's general right to individual self-determination (Article 2 section 1 GG).

---

82. BVerwG 25 Aug. 1993, BVerwGE 94, 82 et seq.
83. OVG North Rhine-Westphalia 5 Sep. 2007, *Nordrhein-Westfälische Verwaltungsblätter* 22 (2008): 154; VG Düsseldorf 30 May 2005, *Nordrhein-Westfälische Verwaltungsblätter* 20 (2006): 68 et seq.; VG Düsseldorf 18 K 301/08 of 7 May 2008.
84. Juliane Kokott in *Grundgesetz. Kommentar*, Michael Sachs ed., 9th edn (Munich: C.H. Beck, 2021), Art. 4, n. 81.
85. §323c Criminal Code (StGB).
86. BVerfG 19 Oct. 1971, BVerfGE 32, 98 et seq.

5. Conscientious Objection to Take an Oath

*129.* Objection for religious reasons to take an oath is protected. No one may be obliged to take an oath with a religious formula; he or she can take the oath without such religious words. Moreover, if someone objects to take any oath at all for religious reasons, an alternative way of affirmation must be and is provided.[87]

6. Conscientious Objection and Military Service

*130.* Objection to military service is a fundamental right made explicit in Article 4 section 3 sentence 1 GG: 'No person shall be compelled against his conscience to render military service involving the use of arms.' Details are regulated by a federal law, the federal Act on Refusal to Render Military Service involving the Use of Arms on Grounds of Conscience (KDVG). Religion and belief can constitute reasons of conscience that allow objection to compulsory military service. Conscientious objection is not limited to conscripts but is also open to career soldiers. It can be lodged at any time before, during, and after the service. Conscientious objectors to military service who still are under duty to serve have to perform an alternative civilian service. As of 31 June 2011, general conscription has been suspended in Germany. Accordingly, there is also no longer an obligation to render an alternative civilian service. The following deliberations therefore pertain to the legal situation before the suspension of both services. They would also be relevant in the event that general conscription and alternative civilian service were to be reintroduced.

*131.* It is a punishable crime not to perform compulsory military or civilian service if conscribed. This has led to considerable problems in cases in which people have objected to both the military and the civilian service. This has occurred especially in cases of Jehovah's Witnesses who were so-called total objectors. While the courts have initially punished them for every single objection, the Federal Constitutional Court has held that a conscientious objector to all services can only be sentenced once if the objection was based on only one conscientious decision that would cover all future refusals to enter the service.[88] It would then count as one act only, and the same act may be punished only once, as is provided in Article 103 section 2 GG. Since 1969, moreover, §15a of the Act on Civilian Service for Conscientious Objectors (ZDG) now states that persons who cannot accept civilian service are not drafted if they take up voluntary civil employment with normal working hours in a hospital or other social institution; the employment has to last eight months longer than the civilian service. After all, Jehovah's Witnesses have accepted to perform civilian service since 1996.[89]

87. BVerfG 11 Apr. 1972, BVerfGE 33, 23 et seq.
88. BVerfG 4 Oct. 1965, BVerfGE 19, 135, 138; BVerfG 5 Mar. 1968, BVerfGE 23, 127, 132.
89. Wikipedia (ed.), 'Kriegsdienstverweigerung der Zeugen Jehovas', https://de.wikipedia.org/wiki/Kriegsdienstverweigerung_der_Zeugen_Jehovas#Deutschland, 26 Apr. 2024.

*132.* Churches and religious communities that are corporations under public law are permitted to represent applicants for conscientious objection against military service in the hearing before the recognition committee free of charge (§8 KDVG).

*133.* An advisory council for the civilian service is formed at the Federal Ministry for Family Affairs, Senior Citizens, Women and Youth. The advisory council advises the Federal Ministry for Family Affairs, Senior Citizens, Women and Youth in matters concerned with civilian service, including the question of what tasks the civilian service conscripts (persons liable for civilian service) are to be allocated to outside the social field. This advisory council consists of representatives from a broad range of groups, including one representative each of the Protestant and Catholic churches (§2a ZDG).

*134.* The federal Act on Compulsory Military Service (WPflG) provides for exemptions from compulsory military service for certain religious personnel. These persons do not have to actively object to military service on reasons of conscience but are by law exempt from compulsory service. This applies to ordained clerics of the Protestant confession, clerics of the Roman Catholic confession who have been ordained to the deaconship, and full-time clerics of other confessions whose office corresponds to that of an ordained cleric of the Protestant or of a cleric of the Roman Catholic confession who has been ordained to the deaconship; the Federal Constitutional Court has held this requirement of equivalence constitutional.[90] Furthermore, according to §12 WPflG, conscripts who are preparing for spiritual office are postponed from military service on request. §13 WPflG provides for further exemptions in case of indispensability: to compensate for the need for staff for the tasks of the Federal Armed Forces and for other tasks, a conscript may be regarded as indispensable for military service in the public interest if and as long as the work that he carries out cannot be foregone; the replacement military authority decides on indispensability at the suggestion of the competent administrative authority and the churches and religious communities also have the right of proposal for their employees if they are corporations under public law. The same rules of exemptions for religious reasons apply to the compulsory alternative service that conscientious objectors to military service have to perform (§§10–12, 16 ZDG).

*135.* The conscripts of civilian service as well as soldiers have a right to undisturbed religious exercise; participation in religious services is voluntary.[91]

*136.* Every soldier has to be appointed and employed according to his or her aptitude, qualifications and professional achievements, irrespective of his or her faith, belief, or religious convictions (§3 SG). While the career soldier's oath of office begins with the words 'I swear' and provides for the religious formula 'so help me God', the oath can be taken without the religious formula (§10 SG). Federal law can allow members of religious communities to use other words instead of 'I swear'.

---

90. BVerfG (K) 11 Apr. 1990, *Neue Zeitschrift für Verwaltungsrecht* 9 (1990): 1064 et seq.
91. §38 ZDG; §36 Act on the Legal Position of Soldiers (SG).

### 7. Conscientious Objection in the Judiciary

*137.* Religious servants and members of such religious associations whose statutes oblige them to reside together will not be appointed to the office of lay judge.[92] Clerics and religious servants may decline the appointment to the office of an honorary judge in the administrative courts.[93]

*138.* Professional as well as lay judges may refuse to sign a decision of their court for reasons of conscience. These cases are extremely rare.[94]

*139.* While the cross is exhibited in some but not all courtrooms in Germany, any party in a court proceeding can object on religious reasons to participate in a court hearing when the cross is exhibited.[95] The hearing must be held in another room either without a cross or the cross must be taken away. The Federal Constitutional Court had decided a case in the year 1973 in which a Jewish lawyer, admitted at the Higher Regional Court of Düsseldorf, living in London, of British and formerly German citizenship, representing a case of indemnification for wrongs perpetrated under National Socialism, had objected to the cross in the courtroom where the hearing was held. While the lower courts rejected the claim, the Federal Constitutional Court held that freedom of religion or belief gives a right to act in a courtroom without a cross.

## *C. Parental Care*

*140.* The mere membership of parents in a small, not mainstream religious community – what some people call a 'sect' – is not a legitimate reason to suspend their right of custody over their child or, as such, a reason not to attribute the right of custody to one of the parents in case of divorce.

## *D. Ritual Slaughter and Other Religious Food Requirements*

### 1. Ritual Slaughter

*141.* Ritual slaughter is allowed as a consequence of freedom of religion. In general, however, the federal Animal Protection Act (*Tierschutzgesetz*) prohibits slaughtering without previous stunning for reasons of animal protection. According to §4a Animal Protection Act (*Tierschutzgesetz* – TierSchG), a warm-blooded animal may only be slaughtered if it has been anaesthetized prior to the removal of blood. Article 20a GG provides that the state has to protect animals. Yet, there are

92. §34, s. 1, no. 6 Courts Constitution Act (GVG).
93. §23 Procedural Code for the Administrative Courts (VwGO).
94. Hans Lisken, 'Zur Gewissensfreiheit des Schöffen', *Neue Juristische Wochenschrift* 50 (1997): 34 et seq.
95. BVerfG 17 Jul. 1973, BVerfGE 35, 366 et seq.

a number of exceptions to the general requirements of slaughtering; §4a section 2 number 2 of the Animal Protection Act allows for such exceptions. The state authority can give permission to slaughter an animal without previous stunning 'if that is necessary to meet the needs of members of a specific religious community within the range of the law who are compelled by binding rules of their religious community to ritual slaughter or to refrain from the consumption of meat of non-ritually slaughtered animals'. The Federal Constitutional Court has held this provision to be in conformity with the federal constitution.[96] It has been argued that ritual slaughtering performed by a Muslim butcher to enable his customers to consume meat in conformity with their religious convictions has to be seen in the light of freedom of religion or belief. This means that the exception norm of the Animal Protection Act must be interpreted and applied in a way that allows Muslim butchers to receive an exemption permit. State authorities still and increasingly tend to be reluctant to give such permission.[97] However, in practice, ritual slaughter is possible and practised.

*142.* In 2009, the Federal Constitutional Court had to decide again about Muslim ritual slaughtering by the same butcher who had been the plaintiff in the case leading to the 2002 decision. After the Federal Constitutional Court had decided in 2002 that the state administration had violated the fundamental rights of the plaintiff by prohibiting ritual slaughtering, he had been allowed by preliminary permit to slaughter according to Muslim rules. Litigation, however, went on before the administrative courts about details of the case. Finally, the state administrative authorities granted permission for a time-limited until the end of 2008 to ritually slaughter five hundred sheep and two hundred cattle in 2008. The application for ritual slaughter in 2009 was not decided on by the state administrative authorities. The administrative court allowed the slaughtering by way of provisional order under the condition that the butcher cared for the presence of a public veterinary officer during the slaughter procedure; the administrative Court of Appeals repealed that decision and dismissed the claim of the butcher. The Federal Constitutional Court held that the decisions violated the fundamental rights of the plaintiff to effective legal remedy: the condition established by the administrative court to care for the constant presence of a public veterinary officer in the ritual slaughter procedure needed the cooperation of the state administrative authorities and was not within the powers of the plaintiff to achieve. It also declared that the handling of the matter by the administrative and court authorities would bring about the danger that the plaintiff could not ritually slaughter at all in 2009, even if he had the right to do so. The Federal Constitutional Court made no explicit statements about the question of what kind of consequences the 2002 constitutional amendment introducing the protection of animals as a constitutionally established task would have on the fundamental right of a believing Muslim butcher to supply his customers with ritually slaughtered meat in accordance with their religious beliefs. The case shows the stern reluctance of some administrative authorities and courts to follow the direction that the Federal

96. BVerfG 15 Jan. 2002, BVerfGE 104, 337 et seq.
97. VGH Hesse 24 Nov. 2004, ESVGH 55, 129 et seq.; BVerwG 23 Nov. 2006, BVerwGE 127, 183, 186.

Constitutional Court had shown in the matter of ritual slaughter. The animal protection clause in the Basic Law remains an undecided issue in the field.

### 2. Religious Food Requirements in Public Institutions

*143.* Religious food requirements are respected in public institutions. Prison authorities have to ensure that prisoners can follow their religious communities' nourishment rules as stated in §86 Act on Execution of Sentences (StVollzG). Similar rules apply to the military. Hospitals also respect these needs.

## §8. Horizontal Application

*144.* The relationships among private individuals and entities are governed by the freedom of religion or belief in general structures of horizontal application of fundamental rights: The general law has to be interpreted and applied in a way compatible with the values expressed in the fundamental rights guaranteed by the constitution. The conflicting interests of private persons have to be balanced so that both conflicting parties can exercise as much of their rights as possible. This is of considerable importance in the field of labour law, but also in many other fields of life. For example, a Muslim female salesperson in a perfume shop must be allowed by her employer to wear a headscarf for religious reasons.[98] Another example of practical impact is the need for believers to pray during working hours or observe religious holidays during general working time. Here, again, the religious freedom of the believer has to be balanced with the legitimate interests of the employer; usually, a reasonable solution is found, and many companies have organized prayer rooms for Muslim employees, and working processes are being structured in a way that believers can follow their religious rules.

## §9. Limitations to Freedom of Religion or Belief

### I. General Principles of Limitation

#### A. *Special Importance of Freedom of Religion or Belief*

*145.* The German constitution guarantees the freedom of religion or belief in its Article 4 without providing for any specific, explicit limitations. This does not mean that no limitations exist. It does mean, however, that freedom of religion or belief holds a foremost place in human rights and is considered by the Constitution to be of utmost importance. In guaranteeing freedom of religion or belief without any explicit limitations, the framers of the constitution went a step further beyond the guarantee provided by the preceding German constitution, the 1919 Constitution of

98. BAG 10 Oct. 2002, *Neue Juristische Wochenschrift* 56 (2003): 1685, 1686 et seq.; BVerfG (K) 30 Jul. 2003, *Neue Juristische Wochenschrift* 56 (2003): 2815.

the Weimar Republic. Article 135 WRV guaranteed full freedom of belief and conscience while stating that the general laws of the state remained unaffected.[99] Today's constitution regards freedom of religion or belief as so high-ranking and important that it does not add any provision stating this freedom can be limited by law or by decisions based upon law.

## *B. The Variety of Limitations*

*146.* There is no general law on limitations of fundamental rights in Germany. The federal Basic Law also does not provide for a general rule on limitations. For each fundamental right guaranteed in the constitution, the Basic Law has special limitation rules. Each fundamental right faces its own specific limitation clause, if any. The result of this is a rather heterogeneous, complicated panorama of many limitation clauses. The idea behind this is that each fundamental right should face only those limitations strictly necessary in view of its own specific impact. Highly important rights have few limitations, rights regarded by the constitution as of somewhat lesser importance can be limited more easily as can be highly important rights with far-reaching impacts on the rights of others or public needs. To some extent, a somewhat hierarchical system of fundamental rights can be followed from the individual limitation clauses. Notwithstanding this, one should note that all fundamental rights share the same constitutional validity, but whenever one fundamental right has to be balanced against another fundamental right, the limitation clauses attached to those rights can give a hint as to the weight and relevance of each fundamental right.

*147.* Since there is no law or basic document on freedom of religion as such in Germany, provisions relating to religious freedom are spread throughout the legal system. Thus, statutes related to religious freedom or limits thereof are very numerous.

## *C. System of Limitation Clauses*

*148.* Despite the heterogeneous picture of the manifold limitation clauses, it is possible to find something like a system of limitation clauses. German legal doctrine basically distinguishes three levels of limitations to fundamental rights: (1) limitations according to the range of protection; (2) reservations by law, general or qualified; and (3) limitations inherent to the Constitution.

*149.* (1) Limitations according to the range of protection are limitations inherent to the fundamental right itself. Fundamental rights carry their limitations by the very

99. This was interpreted as providing a limitations clause indicating that freedom of religion was limited by all laws of the state: State law prevailed before religious commandment if the state law is a general law; cf. Gerhard Anschütz, *Die Verfassung des Deutschen Reichs*, 14th edn (Berlin: Stilke, 1933), 621.

scope of their applicability: Accordingly, freedom to assemble peacefully and without weapons, as guaranteed in Article 8 of the German Constitution, does not allow to assemble performing violence or carrying weapons, and freedom of religion protects religion but not profession, which is protected by a specific separate fundamental right in Article 12 of the constitution. Thus, limitations to certain fundamental rights are established by the range and interpretation of what exactly they protect. All fundamental rights are subject to such limitations.

*150.* (2) Certain fundamental rights are guaranteed only with reservations by law. For example, as to the right of freedom of assembly, Article 8 section 2 GG states: 'In the case of outdoor assemblies, this right may be restricted by or pursuant to a law.' This reservation is called a general reservation by law since any law conforming to the Constitution and carrying any interest that does not contradict the Constitution can limit the freedom of outdoor assemblies. In other cases, the reservation by law is specified; this is called a qualified reservation by law. When, therefore, the law limiting the fundamental right must fulfil certain conditions established by the constitution, it is a qualified law. For example, all Germans have the right to move freely throughout the federal territory according to Article 11 GG; however, Article 11 section 2 GG provides:

> This right may be restricted only by or pursuant to a law, and only in cases in which the absence of adequate means of support would result in a particular burden for the community, or in which such restriction is necessary to avert an imminent danger to the existence or the free democratic basic order of the Federation or of a *Land*, to combat the danger of an epidemic, to respond to a grave accident or natural disaster, to protect young persons from serious neglect, or to prevent a crime.

*151.* (3) Limitations inherent in the constitution cover those cases in which the fundamental right is guaranteed without any explicit or specified limitation clause. This applies, for example, to indoor assemblies as guaranteed by Article 8 section 1 GG and to the protection of marriage and the family by Article 6 section 1 GG. It also applies to the freedom of religion or belief as guaranteed in Article 4 sections 1 and 2 GG. In these cases, the legislature is not free to restrict the fundamental right by any well-founded interest. This does not mean, however, that these fundamental rights are guaranteed without any limits at all. Here, also, the principle of unity of the constitution applies. Fundamental rights are guaranteed only within the frame of the Constitution. Competing or contradicting constitutional interests can and do limit any other constitutional interest. This is the case, for example, in respect of the freedom of indoor assemblies: This freedom can be limited by the needs of a well-functioning prison system. Prisoners in state prisons certainly enjoy the fundamental right of free indoor assembly also for worship reasons, but this can be restricted by prison laws to prevent disturbances of prison routine – assemblies can, for example, be banned at night or when they become too big or a threat to prison safety. The constitution explicitly calls for a well-functioning prison system in Article 28 section 1 GG, establishing the rule of law and in Article 74 section 1 number 1 GG in giving legislative competencies to the Federation for criminal law and corrections. One has to see that almost all relevant legitimate interests do find a basis in the Constitution. There was, however, some discussion until recently regarding animal protection. Animal protection became an explicit constitutional aim guaranteed in Article 20a GG only in 2002. Before that, it was somewhat unclear whether ordinary law could ban the cruel treatment of animals in religious ceremonies.

## II. Specific Limitations to Freedom of Religion or Belief

### *A. Scope of limitations*

*152.* Since freedom of religion or belief is guaranteed by Article 4 GG without providing for any specific, explicit limitations, only those limitations apply that are inherent to the constitution. Thus, prisoners in state prisons can definitively make use of the fundamental right to free indoor assembly for reasons of worship. However, this right can be restricted by prison laws to protect the legitimate interests of criminal law and corrections as provided for by the Basic Law. Fundamental rights of other persons and general constitutional law principles are the foremost limitations to freedom of religion. Many legitimate interests are inherent in the constitution and can limit freedom of religion or belief; freedom of religion or belief is not a danger to proper societal interests.

*153.* Limits to the freedom of religion or belief as freedom without limitation clause also need a sufficiently concrete provision in a law.[100] Community values based on the Constitution therefore must be sufficiently concrete and in general be based on a parliamentary law. This prohibits general interests, such as those interests based on morals or ethics only, to serve as sufficient reasons to limit freedom of religion or belief.

### *B. A Minority View: Article 136 Section 1 WRV in Conjunction with Article 140 GG*

*154.* There is a minority opinion holding that religious freedom can be limited by ordinary law according to Article 136 section 1 WRV.[101] Article 136 section 1 WRV, in conjunction with Article 140 GG, says: 'Civil and political rights and duties shall be neither dependent upon nor restricted by the exercise of religious freedom.' The Federal Constitutional Court and the majority opinion have rejected this, mostly saying that this provision is not a limitation clause to freedom of religion or belief but serves as a guarantee for religious equality.[102]

100. *See* BVerfG 27 Nov. 1990, BVerfGE 83, 130, 142.
101. *See* Dirk Ehlers in *Grundgesetz. Kommentar*, Michael Sachs ed., 9th edn (Munich: C.H. Beck, 2021), Art. 140, n. 4.
102. *See* BVerfG 11 Apr. 1972, BVerfGE 33, 23, 30; Juliane Kokott in *Grundgesetz. Kommentar*, Michael Sachs ed., 9th edn (Munich: C.H. Beck, 2021), Art. 4, nn. 132 et seq.

### *C. Structural Limitations*

*155.* Structural limitations on religion or belief are such limitations that do not specifically limit the freedom of religion or belief but follow from the structures of the legal system. They are not identified as such within the German legal system. However, such a structural limitation can be seen in the protection of days of rest that have their historical, cultural, and traditional basis in Christian convictions. Article 140 GG, in conjunction with Article 139 WRV, states that Sundays and holidays recognized by the state remain protected by law as days of rest from work and of spiritual improvement. It is thus the Sunday (and Christmas, Easter, and other Christian holidays) that are, by law and the Constitution, protected as days of rest. Although holidays of other religions and creeds are also protected by law in specific ways, Christian holidays prevail and enjoy more intense protection. For example, Muslims, Jews, non-believers or other shopkeepers cannot opt out of Sunday shop closing if they want to close their individual shop on a Friday or Saturday according to the rules of their religion.

*156.* Another structural limitation can be seen in the way that certain rights are attributed to religious groups. These groups can enjoy rights only when they are organized in the structures provided for by the legal system. This requires representation, offices, and specific legal structures. Not all religions can easily organize alongside these requirements for theological reasons. It is a substantial challenge to the system to develop solutions that can accommodate all religions with their specific and legitimate structural needs.

### *D. State of Defence or Emergency: No Valid Reason for Limitation*

*157.* The state of defence as such would not fit to limit religious freedom. The constitution does not allow any specific limitations to fundamental rights merely because of the state of defence. There are only minor exceptions to this rule. For instance, Article 115c section 2 number 2 GG extends terms of imprisonment without access to an independent judge from a maximum of forty-eight hours to ninety-six hours, and Article 115c section 2 number 1 GG makes possible expropriation for military reasons with only later law of compensation. These exceptions prove the validity of the rule.

*158.* No specific limitations to any fundamental right, including freedom of religion or belief, are allowed in a state of emergency, a special state the constitution provides for in case of a natural catastrophe or a very heavy accident (Article 35 GG) or in case of riots (Article 87a section 4, Article 91 GG).

## III. Limitations of Limitations

*159.* All laws providing for limitations of fundamental rights must themselves meet further constitutional requirements; they themselves are limited. In German constitutional doctrine, this is called 'limitations on limitations'. There is no closed list of these requirements; they simply follow from the constitution. However, the most important ones of these 'limitations on limitations' are listed in the following.

*160.* The law must be clear and definite. The scope of the limitation must follow clearly and with certainty from the wording of the law. This also applies to limits to the fundamental rights guaranteed by the Basic Law without limitation clause; they also need a sufficiently concrete provision in a law. It is not enough that the reasons for those limitations are based on provisions inherent in the document of the constitution; they must also be concrete and foreseeable.

*161.* Insofar as a fundamental right may be restricted by or pursuant to a law, such law must apply generally and not merely to a single case (Article 19 section 1 clause 1 GG).

*162.* Notwithstanding certain exceptions,[103] the limiting law must specify the basic right affected and the article in which it appears (Article 19 section 1 clause 2 GG).

*163.* In no case may the essence of a fundamental right be affected (Article 19 section 2 GG).

*164.* The law limiting the fundamental right must be proportionate, as must be the limitation in the individual case based on that law. This principle of proportionality is, in practice, perhaps the most important condition any limitation of a fundamental right must comply with. It is part of the balancing process that is a striking feature of German law in general. Proportionality is a basically three-tiered structure that beforehand requires a legitimate interest, a goal to pursue that is in line with the Constitution: Limitations to any fundamental right must be: (1) suitable to achieve the legitimate goal they are meant for; (2) necessary, which means that there is no other equally suitable means to achieve the goal that is less burdensome for the one whose freedom is limited; and (3) proportionate, which means that the burden caused by the limitation of the freedom must not exceed the positive effect for the community interest caused by the limitation.

*165.* It is of utmost importance that all limitations to fundamental rights must be interpreted in a way that respects the importance of the fundamental right that is limited. Thus, the limitation is itself limited. This follows from the basic principle of proportionality: all limitations must be proportionate in view of the rights they are limiting.

---

103. For an account of such exceptions, *see* Hans Dieter Jarass in *Grundgesetz für die Bundesrepublik Deutschland*, Hans Dieter Jarass & Bodo Pieroth eds, 17th edn (Munich: C.H. Beck, 2022), Art. 19, nn. 4 et seq.

## §10. Examples of Case Law on Limitations to Freedom of Religion or Belief

### I. Criteria of Selection

*166.* The limitations on freedom of religion or belief have been elaborated in a substantial amount of case law concerning the freedom of religion or belief. The cases discussed in the following sections can only be examples of the multitude of cases concerning freedom of religion or belief. They mirror the public debate as well as the general legal situation. Only those cases are discussed in the following that are of significance to the structure of the system or that are representative of what may be called the 'legal atmosphere' in the country. Other cases may well be of high individual relevance. It must be noted that the legal atmosphere which influences court rulings does develop over time; former decisions may thus be outdated when public opinion changes. Many cases not reported here are discussed below in the framework of specific fields of law related to freedom of religion or belief and the institutional status of religious communities.

### II. Cases

#### A. *The Tobacco Case*

*167.* The basic structure of limitations on freedom of religion or belief in Germany has perhaps become particularly clear in an early case, decided by the Federal Constitutional Court on 8 November 1960, that has been already referred to above.[104] A prisoner in a state prison propagated among his fellow prisoners to secession from the church. In a number of cases, he did so by promising individual prisoners to give them tobacco if they left the church. Because of this – and other reasons – his application to be released from prison on probation was rejected. The Federal Constitutional Court upheld this decision. The prisoner certainly had the right to propagate secession from the church. He had, however, gone too far by prompting his co-prisoners by promising tobacco. In the specific situation of a prison, the gift of tobacco, which as such has nothing to do with religion, has a far-reaching impact on the decisions of co-prisoners. One can say that promising tobacco in prison is an unfair means of convincing someone to leave his or her religious community. It is important to see the specific circumstances of the case. While the explicit legal reasoning behind the decision is not based on this fact, one may note that this specific prisoner had been a very active National-Socialist and a high-ranking member of the SS during the Nazi regime in Germany. During this time, he had been especially active in persecuting Freemasons, Jews, and Christians. The prisoner was a follower of the 'Union for Knowledge of God (Ludendorff) Registered Association' (Bund für Gotteserkenntnis (Ludendorff) e. V.) and a former

104. BVerfG 8 Nov. 1960, BVerfGE 12, 1 et seq.

member of an anti-masonry, anti-Judaistic, anti-Christian association; he had joined the Nazi SS because of its anti-Christian attitude. During the Second World War, he had trained French collaborators for their secret agent activities in France, and after the war, he was convicted and imprisoned for spy activities for the Communist DDR. While it is a legitimate manifestation of freedom of religion or belief to move someone to leave his or her religious community, it is regarded to be improper and unfair action to exploit situations of need of fellow prisoners to achieve such a goal.

### *B. Conscientious Objection, Alternative Service, and Total Objection*

*168.* An interest based on the constitution providing limitations for religion or belief is compulsory military or alternative service. Article 4 section 3 GG provides that no person may be compelled against his conscience to render military service involving the use of arms. Article 12a section 2 GG provides that any person who, on the grounds of conscience, refuses to render military service involving the use of arms may be required to perform alternative service. The duration of alternative service must not exceed that of military service.

*169.* As stated above in paragraph 131, a Jehovah's Witness refused not only to perform military service but also refused to perform alternative service. Alternative service is social service in hospitals, homes for the elderly, etc. The Jehovah's Witness argued that his religion prohibits any participation in such state-run services. The courts gave him a six-month suspended sentence. After that, he was again called to alternative service, which he rejected again. The criminal court then revoked the probation. The Federal Constitutional Court, in its 1988 decision, held that the revocation was unconstitutional.[105] It argued that the Jehovah's Witness could trust the courts to respect the once and for all decision to object also to the alternative service. Before that, the Federal Constitutional Court had decided in 1968 that the objection of a Jehovah's Witness to any state service was based on one basic decision covering all future drafts to equivalent state service.[106] Therefore, any future refusal to perform alternative service amounts to one single act because it was based on the one decision taken once and for all. Therefore, this is only one act, and no one may be punished twice for the same act (Article 103 section 3 GG). Although the decision of the Federal Constitutional Court did help the Jehovah's Witness the basic fact remains that the duty of alternative service in case of conscientious objection does provide a constitutionally based limitation on the freedom of religion or belief. Today, these cases of total conscientious objection against all state-run services, including alternative social service, have in practice lost their significance because Jehovah's Witnesses do not object to social service anymore, and the law has, anyway, introduced in §15a of the Act on Civilian Service for Conscientious Objectors the possibility to perform service by contracting into private institutions. Currently, the problem of total conscientious objection has

105. BVerfG 30 Jun. 1988, BVerfGE 78, 391.
106. BVerfG 7 Mar. 1968, BVerfGE 23, 191.

lost all of its practical relevance because the alternative social service has, as a consequence of the suspension of general conscription, likewise been suspended since 31 June 2011.

## *C. Governmental Warnings Against Religious Communities*

*170.* A somewhat more restrictive approach was taken by the Federal Constitutional Court in a case of state warning against a specific religious community. The government had publicly warned against the Osho movement, a new religious movement in Germany, formerly known as the Shree Rajneesh or Bhagwan movement. The government authorities had called it a sect since 1979 and declared that especially young people could come under the influence of that movement and that this could lead to consequences that at the time were a matter of public concern. The government had furthermore called the Osho movement 'destructive' and 'pseudo-religious'. The religious community instituted legal proceedings before the competent administrative court in 1984. In its ruling of 2002, the Federal Constitutional Court held that calling the Osho movement 'destructive' and 'pseudo-religious' was unconstitutional.[107] It infringed upon the freedom of religion of that movement and was contrary to the neutrality of the state. However, the Federal Constitutional Court also held that calling the movement a 'sect' and warning the public against possible consequences of public concern was in fact constitutional. The government has a right and an obligation to inform the public and to warn against possible dangers, regardless of whether they originate from religious groups or from any other source. In this case, the Federal Constitutional Court even held that a specific law on which such governmental warning and information activity could be based was not necessary; the right to informative action followed directly from the Constitution. The ECHR held that the German authorities had not violated Article 9 ECHR because the warnings were based on a law, pursued a legitimate aim, namely the protection of public safety and public order and the protection of the rights and freedom of others, and were also justified in principle and proportionate to the aim pursued. However, the European Court of Human Rights held that Germany had violated Article 6 ECHR because the length of the proceedings before the domestic courts had been excessive and failed to meet the 'reasonable time' requirement.[108]

## *D. The Headscarf Issue*

*171.* The Federal Constitutional Court held it a violation of equal treatment in conjunction with freedom of religion or belief when a judge consistently prohibited the wearing of a Muslim headscarf by women in the public audience of court hearings without establishing whether this in fact disturbed the court proceedings.[109]

107. BVerfG 26 Jun. 2002, BVerfGE 105, 279.
108. ECHR, *Leela-Förderkreis et al. v. Deutschland*, 6 Nov. 2008, appl. no. 58911/00.
109. BVerfG (K) 27 Jun. 2006, *Neue Juristische Wochenschrift* 60 (2007): 56 et seq.

*172.* In a 2003 decision following a judgment by the Federal Labour Court, the Federal Constitutional Court affirmed that the freedom of religion of a department store saleswoman who changed her religious belief to that she felt obliged to wear a Muslim headscarf at work may prevail over the shopkeeper's freedom of trade, guaranteed by Article 12 GG.[110] The shopkeeper had only claimed that the employee's religious dress was not compatible with the store's distinctive reputation and would bring down sales. The court implied that there could be reasons in which the employer's interest might be so important as to restrict the dress code of his or her employees, but this would have to be profoundly established if it is to restrict the freedom of religion. In this specific case, the religious interests of the employee prevailed over the business interests of the employer.

*173.* There are no specific rules on religious scarves or other religious symbols for students in German state schools or universities. There is no case law on the subject. Pupils and students can freely wear headscarves and do so. Total coverage of the face by a burka would run contrary to the educational requirements of the school and could therefore be prohibited. A case in a Berlin school involved three young Muslim girl pupils wearing the hijab during school lessons. After some discussions with the headmaster, the girls no longer insisted on wearing the garment and came to school without the burka.

*174.* A decision of the Federal Constitutional Court – the so-called *Ludin* Case – relates to a Muslim woman teacher wearing a headscarf while teaching in a public school.[111] Debate and reaction by the legislature mirror new underlying and general developments in the approach to freedom of religion and belief in Germany, especially in view of immigration.

*175.* School laws of the *Länder,* as well as laws on public officials of the *Länder* and the Federation, require public officials and, thus, teachers in state schools to be religiously neutral. They do not deprive teachers of their fundamental rights while performing his or her functions, though, thus neither of their religious freedom. Until some time ago, there were no problems with Muslim women teachers insisting on wearing a headscarf. There are no known cases with respect to orthodox Jewish teachers wearing a kipa or traditional style of hair.

*176.* In the *Land* Baden-Württemberg, Ms Ludin, a Muslim woman teacher in a public school and German national with an Afghan background, insisted on wearing a headscarf while teaching. The state authorities dismissed Ms Ludin; the decision was upheld by the administrative courts. The Federal Constitutional Court has ruled in this case that the prohibition of wearing a headscarf for religious reasons would at least need a special law entitling the authorities to such kind of prohibition. For lack of such a special legal provision, it was declared unconstitutional not to employ this specific woman teacher. The Constitutional Court argued that the

---

110. BAG, 10 Oct. 2002, BAGE 103, 111, 112 et seq.; BVerfG (K), 30 Jul. 2003, *Neue Juristische Wochenschrift* 2003: 2815.
111. BVerfG 24 Sep. 2003, BVerfGE 108, 282 et seq.

headscarf is not necessarily a politically aggressive or religiously compelling sign (in which case the woman teacher would have acted against her obligation to neutrality). Headscarves, the Court argued, can also be a symbol for emancipation of women, of sexual self-determination, or cultural identity.[112] After an amendment of the school law in Baden-Württemberg, Ms Ludin was again dismissed and lost her case before the administrative courts. She did not take the constitutional complaint to the Federal Constitutional Court but left the school service.

*177.* A number of *Länder* (Baden-Württemberg, Hesse, Bremen, Berlin, Lower Saxony, Bavaria, North Rhine-Westphalia, and the Saarland) have subsequently introduced specific laws in order to meet the requirements they see in the decision of the Federal Constitutional Court. In the other *Länder* (Rhineland-Palatinate, Brandenburg, Mecklenburg-Western Pomerania, Schleswig-Holstein, Hamburg, Saxony, Saxony-Anhalt, Thuringia), no such specific prohibitions exist, while political demands to introduce similar provision are an ongoing part of public debate. Because they mirror some of the religious-political controversies and give an insight into the atmosphere of underlying developments that are not the least due to immigration, some of the relevant provisions are outlined below in more detail; they also stand as an example of the diversity of approaches to religious issues that are taken in the federal system of Germany.

*178.* The law of Baden-Württemberg provides that teachers at public schools are not allowed to exercise political, religious, ideological or similar manifestations that may endanger or disturb the neutrality of the state towards pupils or parents or the political, religious, or ideological peace of the school. Particularly illegitimate is a behaviour that can appear to pupils and parents to be a teacher's demonstration against human dignity, non-discrimination, the rights of freedom, or the free and democratic order of the constitution. Exercising the task of education according to the *Land's* constitutional provisions – and the respective exhibition of Christian and occidental educational and cultural values or traditions – does not contradict the duty of behaviour according to the School Act. The duty of religious neutrality does not apply within the religious instruction provided in accordance with Article 18 sentence 1 of the constitution of the *Land* Baden-Württemberg.[113]

*179.* Baden-Württemberg has extended these principles also to state-maintained kindergartens:[114]

> In institutions to which this law applies and which are held by the *Land*, an administration district, a municipality, a public administrative community or a special administrative union of local or regional authorities skilled persons … and other staff in charge of taking care or educating are not allowed to exercise political, religious, ideological or similar manifestations that may endanger or disturb the responsible body's neutrality towards children and parents or the

112. *Ibid.*
113. §38, s. 1, sentence 4 Schooling Act of Baden-Württemberg (Schulgesetz für Baden-Württemberg).
114. §7 Child Daycare Act Baden-Württemberg (KiTaG BW).

> political, religious or ideological peace of those institutions which this section applies to. Particularly illegitimate is a behaviour that can appear to children or parents to be a skilled person's or other educating or caretaking staff's demonstration against human dignity, non-discrimination according to Article 3 Basic Law, the rights of freedom or the free and democratic order of the constitution. The exercise of the task of Article 12 section 1 of the constitution of the *Land* Baden-Württemberg, which is to educate the youth in the spirit of Christian love and fraternity among mankind and the respective exhibition of such traditions does not contradict the duty of behaviour according to clause 1.

*180.* A number of *Länder* have extended the scope of prohibition of religious garments beyond teachers in public schools and staff of kindergartens and applied it to further fields of public service.

*181.* In Berlin, the Act concerning Article 29 Berlin Constitution (Article 29-G Berlin) provides in its §1:

> Public servants on duty that work within the field of justice administration, penal law enforcement or police are not allowed to wear any visible religious or ideological symbols that signal the spectator an affiliation to a specific religious or ideological group and any noticeably religious or ideologically imbued garments. In the area of justice administration this only applies to public servants that exercise governmental functions.

*182.* Furthermore, §2 of this Act states:

> Teachers and other employees with pedagogical tasks on duty at public schools according to the Public School Act are not allowed to wear any visible religious or ideological symbols that demonstrate the spectator an affiliation to a specific religious or ideological community and any noticeably religious or ideologically imbued garments. This does not apply to religious or ideological instruction at school.

*183.* However, the Federal Labour Court decided in 2020 that the law discriminates against Muslim teachers because of their religion and thus is unconstitutional. The Federal Constitutional Court upheld the ruling.[115] The Senate of Berlin now does not prohibit Muslim teachers from wearing the headscarf while teaching unless the school peace is endangered.[116]

*184.* The Federal Administrative Court has ruled that all laws prohibiting religious garments in public schools must be interpreted in a way that treats all religions equally while respecting the German cultural tradition.[117] However, it seems

115. BVerfG 17 Jan. 2023, Az. 1 BVR 1661/21.
116. https://www.rbb24.de/politik/beitrag/2023/03/berlin-kopftuch-lehrerinnen-schulen-neutralitaetsgesetz.html, 9 Nov. 2023.
117. *See also* BVerfG 24 Sep. 2003, BVerfGE 108, 282 et seq.

that this issue remains a challenge for an adequate coordination of religious freedom for Muslims and limitations to that right.

### E. *Muslim Ritual Prayer in Public Schools*

*185.* A Muslim pupil wished to pray the Muslim ritual prayer 'as-salat' out of class times but on the school grounds of a Berlin public school if the timeframe allocated for this prayer fell into school time. Together with other Muslim pupils, he performed the Muslim ritual prayer in the school hallway while other pupils watched. The headmistress of the school forbade Muslim prayer because religious statements of this nature were not allowed at the school. The Muslim pupil insisted on his right to pray at school outside of class times and brought the question to court. The Federal Administrative Court held that as pupils cannot simply leave the school grounds, even during break times, the school cannot refer them to prayer places and times out-of-school grounds and times because the school administration has provided all rooms for other purposes only.[118] The pupils' fundamental right to religious freedom thus, in principle, entitles them to pray on the school grounds. However, this freedom is limited by the requirement of keeping the school peace, of which religious peace is an element of utmost importance. Because performing the Muslim prayer in the school hallway would intensify an already existing concrete danger to school peace, the Federal Administrative Court held that the Muslim pupil was not allowed to perform the Muslim prayer in public at school. As a milder measure to prohibit prayer at school, the school must examine whether it is possible to provide a prayer room. In the Berlin case, a prayer room that had already been opened had to be closed again after religious strife among the pupils occurred. Since the school did not have the organizational means to provide a prayer room and keep the peace between all religious convictions involved, it did not have to provide a prayer room at all. It is likely that the Federal Constitutional Court would have overturned this decision and allowed the public Muslim prayer, obliging the school to more actively enhance religious tolerance in the school. However, the pupil did not lodge a constitutional complaint and the decision of the Federal Administrative Court has become final.

### F. *Church Bells and Muezzin-Call*

*186.* Church bell ringing for liturgical reasons in general does not amount to considerable molestation in the legal sense; it is rather considered to be a reasonable, socially appropriate activity. Ringing each hour to indicate the time during the night (10 pm until 6 am) is subject to the ordinary laws on protection against emissions, which means that noise of more than 60dB(A) is in general not allowed in residential areas at night. Individual court rulings have allowed for some more than

118. BVerwG 30 Nov. 2011, *Neue Juristische Wochenschrift* 2012, 162 et seq.

that.[119] The Muezzin-call is allowed and can be transmitted via loudspeaker. The needs 'of neighbours and the general public not to be inappropriately disturbed' must be respected.[120]

119. BVerwG 2 Sep. 1996, *Baurecht* 1996, 819 et seq.; BVerwG 30 Apr. 1992, *Neue Juristische Wochenschrift* 1992, 2779; BVerwG 27 Feb. 1992, *Neue Juristische Wochenschrift* 1992, 2170 et seq.; OVG Saarland 16 May 1991, *Neue Zeitschrift für Verwaltungsrecht* 1992, 72.
120. OVG Rhineland-Palatinate 20 Nov. 2000, *Neue Zeitschrift für Verwaltungsrecht* 2001, 933 et seq.

# Chapter 2. Collective Religious Freedom

## §1. Basic Principles

*187.* Collective religious freedom in German legal doctrine means that everybody has the right to exercise his or her freedoms in community with others. While doing so, the specific rights keep their character as being individual rights of each of the persons involved. One could say that individual rights are exercised in parallel. An association would, in this case, be regarded as an expression of the individual rights of each of the members to assemble freely. The association as such would not have a right on its own if only collective freedom was involved. The association could, however, exercise the individual rights of its members in representing them. By that, the religious community would represent the freedom of religion of its members. This approach does not have much significance in German legal practice or doctrine. Significant, however, is the notion of a 'corporative fundamental right' by which an organization as such can have rights.

# Chapter 3. Organizational Religious Freedom

## §1. Basic Principles

### I. Corporative Freedom

*188.* Organizational religious freedom in German legal doctrine and practice is known as 'corporative freedom of religion or belief' as opposed to collective religious freedom. Organizations such as religious communities enjoy the freedom of religion or belief in their own right. Organizations do not only represent the rights of their members but also have their own proper rights. The fundamental rights also apply to domestic legal persons to the extent permitted by the nature of such rights.

### II. Freedom to Form Religious Communities

*189.* Everyone has the right to freely associate to form a religious organization. This is guaranteed in Article 4 sections 1 and 2 GG as a manifestation of freedom of religion or belief. This right is further specified by Article 137 section 2 WRV in conjunction with Article 140 GG: 'The freedom to form religious societies shall be guaranteed. The union of religious societies within the territory of the *Reich* shall be subject to no restrictions.' Due to the constitutional changes in the past and the renaming of Germany, the name '*Reich*' in Article 137 section 2 WRV now has to be read as 'Federal Republic of Germany'. The guarantee in Article 137 section 2 WRV in conjunction with Article 140 GG is part of the freedom of religion as guaranteed in Article 4 GG;[121] it is not a special norm with the effect that the general provision of Article 4 GG would be excluded.[122] The right to freely associate for religious reasons is a human right and not dependent on citizenship or the quality of being a German as specified in Article 116 GG. It forms part of the general freedom of religion clause of Article 4 GG. While the general guarantee to associate in Article 9 section 1 GG is restricted to Germans, the right to associate as part of religious freedom is not thus limited and as the more specific norm prevails over Article 9 section 1 GG.

### III. Fundamental Rights of Legal Persons

#### A. *Scope of Legal Persons*

*190.* As Article 19 section 3 GG provides, 'the fundamental rights shall also apply to domestic legal persons to the extent that the nature of such rights permits'. Legal persons in the meaning of Article 19 section 3 GG are all those associations that have a minimum of internal organizational structures so that they can act as an

---

121. BVerfG 5 Feb. 1991, BVerfGE 83, 341, 354, 363 et seq.
122. *See*, however, Dirk Ehlers in *Grundgesetz. Kommentar*, Michael Sachs ed., 9th edn (Munich: C.H. Beck, 2021), Art. 140 GG/Art. 137 WRV, n. 3.

organization. This applies to all legal persons of civil law with full legal capacity, such as foundations, registered associations, and companies. It also applies to associations with limited civil legal capacity, such as non-registered associations. Moreover, legal persons in the meaning of Article 19 section 3 GG are all those groupings that are associations protected by the freedom of association in Article 9 section 1 GG; this guarantee protects the entire spectrum of organization from the loosely formed citizens' action group to the highly structured economic entity.[123] Thus, all forms of religious associations and organizations as such enjoy freedom of religion or belief in their own right.[124] This guarantee must be interpreted and applied in a broad and encompassing way. Should there be any aspect of activity not covered by the association's right, the individual right to freedom of religion or belief would apply; no practical issue has surfaced in that respect insofar as yet.

### *B. Domestic Legal Persons*

*191.* The protection of Article 19 section 3 GG applies only to domestic legal persons. Foreign legal persons do not, as such, enjoy fundamental rights in general.[125] This can be of relevance for foreign religious communities that operate in Germany. An association is a foreign legal person when its seat, that is, the actual centre of its activity, is located abroad. A branch of that foreign association that is founded and operating in Germany is a domestic legal person.[126] Certain fundamental rights, such as the right to the legally provided judge (Article 101 GG),[127] the right to have a court hearing (Article 103 GG),[128] but also the right to petition (Article 17 GG), and the right to access a court against state action (Article 19 section 4) are also guaranteed for foreign legal persons and thus for foreign religious organizations.[129]

### *C. Religious Communities as Corporations under Public Law*

*192.* Religious communities that have the status of public law corporations also fully enjoy fundamental rights in the scope of Article 19 section 3 GG. In contrast, those public law entities that are part of the state generally do not have fundamental rights, as fundamental rights are meant to protect against the state, not to protect the state. The status of public law corporations of religious communities, however, does not incorporate these religious communities into the state structures. There is no

123. BVerfG 18 Dec. 1974, BVerfGE 38, 281, 303.
124. *See* BVerfG 5 Feb. 1991, BVerfGE 83, 341, 351.
125. Hans Dieter Jarass in *Grundgesetz für die Bundesrepublik Deutschland*, Hans Dieter Jarass & Bodo Pieroth eds, 17th edn (Munich: C.H. Beck, 2022), Art. 19, n. 26.
126. *Ibid.*, Art. 19, n. 27.
127. BVerfG 12 Apr. 1983, BVerfGE 64, 1, 11.
128. *Ibid.*
129. Hans Dieter Jarass in *Grundgesetz für die Bundesrepublik Deutschland*, Hans Dieter Jarass & Bodo Pieroth eds, 17th edn (Munich: C.H. Beck, 2022), Art. 19, n. 26.

state church (Article 136 section 1 WRV in conjunction with Article 140 GG). Religious communities are not created by the state but are – on the contrary – rooted in the non-state area; within their own field, they do not administer state tasks nor exercise state powers.[130] The status of religious communities as public law corporations is a status sui generis.

## *D. Nature of Rights*

*193.* As Article 19 section 3 provides, legal persons only enjoy fundamental rights 'to the extent that the nature of such rights permits'. Thus, not all the rights guaranteed by the lot of fundamental rights also apply to religious communities. As an example, freedom of conscience, as provided for by Article 4 section 1 GG, presupposes an individual human person since conscience is a purely individual phenomenon; no legal entity can have a conscience. Another example is the human dignity that Article 1 section 1 GG declares to be inviolable: human dignity is inseparably attributed to individual human beings. However, religious communities do enjoy the freedom of religion or belief as guaranteed in Article 4 sections 1 and 2 GG.[131] Religion and belief is a matter that usually is experienced and lived in community with others. Legal persons rooted in a religious or philosophical ethos therefore enjoy those freedoms. Other legal entities, such as normal business companies, do not enjoy the freedom of religion or belief.[132]

## *E. Notion of Religious Community*

*194.* The meaning of the term 'religious community' is very broad. It primarily covers the religious community as an organization of faith and its organs, such as – in a Christian context – bishops and synods, a clerical hierarchy, etc., the so-called constituted church. However, reaching beyond that, it encompasses all organizations and institutions that are related to the religious community in specific ways if they are meant to achieve a part of the tasks and aims of the religious community in the world according to the self-understanding of the religious community.[133] The term 'religious community' therefore entails also the hospitals, kindergartens, homes for the elderly, support offices for drug addicts, offices for marriage counselling, abortion advice offices, even banks and breweries of the religious communities if they are specifically linked to the organized (constituted) religious community.

---

130. BVerfG 2 May 1967, BVerfGE 21, 362, 374; BVerfG 21 Sep. 1976, BVerfGE, 42, 312 et seq.; 61, 82, 102.
131. BVerfG 16 Oct. 1968, BVerfGE 24, 236, 246 et seq.
132. BVerfG (K) 18 Oct. 1989, *Europäische Grundrechte Zeitschrift* 17 (1990): 195, 196; BVerwG 14 Nov. 1980, BVerwGE 61, 152, 160.
133. BVerfG 11 Oct. 1977, BVerfGE 46, 73 et seq.

§2. CASE LAW

*195.* Religious communities do not need special legal authorization to make public statements about other competing religious communities; the Basic Law does not limit their activities to the teachings of their own religious ideas. The right to freedom of religion or belief does not give a right to religious communities or to their members that the state should protect them against critical, even sharply critical statements by other religious communities. In one case heard by the Federal Constitutional Court, the so-called sect-commissioner of the Evangelical Church in Bavaria, a Protestant *Land* church with the status of a public law corporation, had publicly warned against a certain new religious movement. Such offices in charge of monitoring small and new religious movements regarded as dangerous are run by several of the larger churches in Germany. The Federal Constitutional Court has held that the general protection of personal honour against insults or slanderous statements in civil and criminal law provides sufficient protection.[134]

*196.* Sometimes, the names of religious communities have caused conflicts when one religious community insists on having the same or a similar name as another religious community. Here, the general law on names applies in substance. §12 BGB protects the right to one's name that may not be violated by somebody else tortuously using the same name or a name that can lead to confusion with the original bearer in the public sphere. The Federal Constitutional Court has decided in a case in which the names 'Catholic' and 'Roman Catholic' were used by a community of the followers of Archbishop Lefebvre who established a split-off from the Roman Catholic Church, the then so-called Society of St. Pius X (SSPX).[135] The German Courts had prohibited the use of the terms 'Catholic' and 'Roman Catholic' by that community for its institutions and events upon application of the Roman Catholic Church. The Federal Constitutional Court upheld these prohibitions because the right to freedom of religion or belief of the split-off community found its limitations in the same right to freedom of religion or belief of the Roman Catholic Church. In this situation, the general principle of priority of name prevailed.

*197.* Calling from the pulpit to support the collection of rags by a religious youth organization is protected by freedom of religion or belief; it does not constitute unfair advertising practice. The Federal Constitutional Court has held this in a case in which a professional rag-picker had filed a suit against the religious community, stating that the collection by the religious youth organization diminished his income.[136] This decision is also important in that it explicitly states that freedom of religion or belief does not only cover acts of worship and teaching but also protects acting freely according to one's beliefs, even when such activities can also be performed by others for purely secular, economic reasons.

134. BVerfG (K) 13 Jul. 1992, *Deutsches Verwaltungsblatt* 108 (1993): 1204.
135. BVerfG (K) 31 Mar. 1994, *Neue Juristische Wochenschrift* 47 (1994): 2346 et seq.
136. BVerfG 16 Oct. 1968, BVerfGE 24, 236 et seq.

*198.* A religious community does not have a right based on freedom of religion or belief to break a legally valid private law contract on electricity supply because it objects to receiving energy produced in nuclear power plants.[137]

137. BVerfG 29 Sep. 1982, *Neue Juristische Wochenschrift* 36 (1983): 32.

# Chapter 4. Religious Freedom and Equality

## §1. Constitutional Guarantees

*199.* Religious equality is made explicit in several special provisions of the Basic Law. While the general equal treatment clause in Article 3 section 1 GG also covers matters that relate to religion, further special equal treatment provisions focus on questions of religion. The general non-discrimination norm of Article 3 section 3 GG stipulates that no person shall be favoured or disfavoured because of faith or religious opinions. Article 33 section 3 GG is a specific non-discrimination norm and provides that neither the enjoyment of civil and political rights, eligibility for public office, nor rights acquired in the public service shall be dependent upon religious affiliation. The norm further states that no one may be disadvantaged by reason of adherence or non-adherence to a particular religious denomination or philosophical creed. This is again stated in Article 136 sections 1 and 2 WRV in conjunction with Article 140 GG: '(1) Civil and political rights and duties shall be neither dependent upon nor restricted by the exercise of religious freedom. (2) Enjoyment of civil and political rights and eligibility for public office shall be independent of religious affiliation.' Basic structures as to equal treatment are laid out by Article 137 sections 1 and 3 WRV in conjunction with Article 140 GG in providing that there is no state church and that all religious communities govern their affairs independently. A special norm of equal treatment guarantee puts communities of philosophical creed (belief communities) on the same legal level as religious communities: Article 137 section 7 WRV, in conjunction with Article 140 GG, provides: 'Associations whose purpose is to foster a philosophical creed shall have the same status as religious societies.' This forms part of the more general principle of 'parity' that governs the equal treatment of religious communities and equivalent bodies. Similar equal treatment guarantees are held by the constitutions of the *Länder*. These equal treatment clauses form a part of the general principle of state neutrality in religious matters.

## §2. General Non-discrimination

*200.* Article 3 section 3 GG provides that no person shall be favoured or disfavoured because of faith or religious opinions. The terms 'faith' and 'religious opinions' in Article 3 section 3 GG also cover non-religious as well as anti-religious convictions. The provision also prohibits discrimination because of the expression of such opinions because the guarantee would be useless and without practical application if it only covered the *forum internum*.[138] The Federal Constitutional Court has insisted that it could violate Article 3 section 3 GG if a Jewish applicant were excluded from general compensation for persecution under National

138. Angelika Nußberger in *Grundgesetz. Kommentar*, Michael Sachs ed., 7th edn (Munich: C.H. Beck, 2018), Art. 3, nn. 305 et seq.

Socialism because he or she might also turn to the Jewish Claims Conference or other Jewish compensation funds and receive compensation through those organizations.[139]

## §3. Non-discrimination in Public Office

*201.* As was noted above, Article 33 section 3 GG provides that no one may be disadvantaged for the reason of adherence or non-adherence to a particular religious denomination or philosophical creed. Article 33 section 3 GG can be seen as an explicit reaction to the historical experience of discrimination in connection with religious affiliation. The provision puts an end to appointments to office in denominational proportion, which was a common feature in history in order to treat the Catholic and the Protestant denominations equally; while this denominational group equality contributed to the pacification of the religious struggles from the sixteenth century onwards, it obviously leads to discrimination of individuals. It has been held a violation of Article 33 section 3 GG to take into account the religious affiliation of teachers in public non-denominational schools.[140] However, the Federal Constitutional Court has decided that it does not violate Article 33 section 3 GG when the pupils' denominational adherence in a public school is taken as a relevant reason for appointing teachers according to their religion;[141] this decision may well be outdated today. Article 33 section 3 GG does not prevent taking into account religious affiliations in cases of public offices that are destined to serve religious interests, such as teachers of religious instruction or clerics for military or other institutional chaplaincy.[142] Foreign law marriage impediments due to differences in religion are incompatible with Article 33 section 3 GG and may therefore not be recognized by German authorities.[143] It is a violation of Article 33 section 2 GG to exclude someone from a public municipal office because he or she objects to taking the oath of office for religious reasons.[144] The Federal Constitutional Court has held it a violation of Article 33 section 3 GG to prohibit a Muslim woman teacher in a public school from wearing a Muslim headscarf if there is no legal basis in a specific formal law for this prohibition;[145] if the legislature of a *Land* decides in favour of a prohibition, all religions must be treated equally.[146]

139. BVerfG 13 Jun. 1958, BVerfGE 8, 38, 41.
140. BVerwG 24 Nov. 1988, BVerwGE 81, 22, 24.
141. BVerfG 17 Dec. 1975, BVerfGE 41, 29, 60; BVerfG 14 Dec. 1975, BVerfGE 41, 65, 87.
142. Ulrich Battis in *Grundgesetz. Kommentar*, Michael Sachs ed., 7th edn (Munich: C.H. Beck, 2018), Art. 33, n. 44.
143. BGH 12 May 1971, BGHZ 56, 180, 191.
144. BVerfG 25 Oct. 1988, BVerfGE 79, 69, 75.
145. BVerfG 24 Sep. 2003, BVerfGE 108, 282 et seq.
146. BVerwG 24 Jun. 2004, BVerwGE 121, 140 et seq.

## §4. Institutional Equality

*202.* Equality of religious communities follows from Article 137 section 1 WRV prohibiting any kind of state church and from Article 137 section 3 WRV protecting the self-determination of all religious communities. It further follows from Article 3 section 3 GG, according to which no person shall be favoured or disfavoured because of faith or religious opinions. This is further elaborated in Article 33 section 3 GG. Equal treatment of religious communities as well as of philosophical communities requires treating equally what is equal and treating unequally what is unequal according to the degree of their differences. Equal treatment in legal practice and doctrine is not identical treatment, but more sophisticatedly a treatment in accordance to the specificities of the issues at stake. This is a general rule throughout the legal system and is not only related to religious communities and religion. Any unequal treatment must be legitimized by appropriate reasons. The treatment must be proportionate in relation to the differences between the issues concerned and to the aims pursued by the treatment.

*203.* A special expression of the rule of equal treatment in religious matters is the principle of parity. This parity principle has evolved historically as a response to the factual existence of generally two equally strong Christian denominations within the Holy Roman Empire of the German Nation. It can be seen as a former group right for these two denominations that guaranteed equal number of representation, for example, in the Supreme Court of the Empire, the '*Reichskammergericht*'. Today, parity has developed into a general right of equal treatment of religions.

*204.* It is generally accepted that the difference in status between religious communities that have the status of corporations under public law and those religious communities with a normal civil law status does not contradict the right to equal treatment. In any case, the two categories of status are directly and explicitly part of constitutional law. As such, they determine what is required by equal treatment according to the Constitution because all provisions of the Constitution have the same rank, and the Constitution must be seen as one entity. The difference in status draws its legitimacy from the social impact and relevance that the various religions and denominations have; it also meets differences in approach and self-understanding of the religions and denominations. Rights that are attached to each status match duties that follow from the status. Either status can be obtained when the individual religious community meets minimum requirements.

## §5. Equal Treatment of Non-religious, Philosophical Communities

*205.* Non-religious, philosophical communities (*Weltanschauungsgemeinschaften,* belief communities) have the very same status in law as religious communities. This is made explicit in Article 137 section 7 WRV in conjunction with Article 140 GG: 'Associations whose purpose is to foster a philosophical creed shall have the same status as religious societies.' This applies, for example, to the Humanist organizations. Equal status was assigned to these communities in the

1919 German constitution as a result of developments at the end of the nineteenth century and the beginning of the twentieth century when socialist and atheist groups emerged. In Part III below, non-religious, philosophical communities (belief communities) are not always mentioned alongside religious communities. This is done for reasons of style only, in order to avoid lengthy and over-complicated language.

# Part III. Legal Status of Religious Communities

## Chapter 1. Formal Status of Religious Communities

*206.* There are two different forms of status that religious communities can acquire. Every group of people organizing for religious reasons has access to legal status as an organization under conditions that are usually very easy to meet. The two different forms of status are organizing under civil law and organizing under public law. The system, thus is a two-tier system. In addition to that, it is clear from freedom of religion or belief that every religious group is free to function without having legal entity status; registration is not a required condition to function.

### §1. Religious Communities as Private Law Corporations

#### I. Basic Principles

*207.* The civil law status of religious communities is governed by Article 137 section 4 WRV in conjunction with Article 140 GG: 'Religious societies shall acquire legal capacity according to the general provisions of civil law.' Religious organizations can organize by making use of the forms established by civil law. They have the right to organize and to take part in general legal life.[147] Article 137 section 4 WRV does not guarantee the right to a specific form of legal entity; this is left to the specific provisions of civil law.

*208.* The most common means to set up a religious community as a legal entity is to make use of the civil law institution of a registered non-profit association (*eingetragener Verein*). The registered non-profit association is a form of legal entity for all sorts of purposes not specific to religious associations. The underlying concept is that a registered non-profit association would be created with a non-profit aim, such as tennis clubs, scientific associations, or others. Registration takes place at the local ordinary courts. The registered non-profit association is based on §21 of the Civil Code (BGB). Other forms, such as a company, a cooperative, a foundation or others, are also possible.

---

147. BVerfG 5 Feb. 1991, BVerfGE 83, 341, 355.

*209.* Membership in religious communities that are organized as private law associations is acquired by a membership declaration; resignation is effected in the same way. This declaration is made to the association itself. The same rules apply as for any secular association.

## II. Non-profit Associations

### A. *Idealistic Aim*

*210.* Organizations that want to be registered as a non-profit association must have idealistic (i.e., non-economic) aims. They may perform economic activities as a subordinate aim in order to support their non-economic primary aims. When economic activity becomes predominant, the non-profit association loses this status and has to register as a for-profit organization.

### B. *Registration Requirements*

*211.* Religious entities, like any other entity wishing to be registered as a non-profit association, would have to meet the formal requirements of §§55–79a Civil Code, the most important of which are:

- A minimum of seven founding members (no matter which nationality); the association will be legally dissolved if the number of members drops below three.
- The deposit of a statute of the association with a minimal content of: aim, name, seat of the association, and the request to be registered (signed by the founding members), date of creation. The statute should have provisions about joining and leaving the association, financial contributions of the members, creation of the governing body, members' meetings (§§57–59 BGB).
- The name of the association should differ significantly from the names of other associations that are registered in the same local community (§57 section 2 BGB).
- Changes in the statute have to be registered with the state authorities in order to come into force (§71 BGB).

*212.* Religious communities – as other legal entities – that are not registered as an association or as any other specific form of a legal entity have the status of non-registered associations (§54 BGB). This kind of association enjoys partial legal capacity; in practice, the courts widely make use of analogies to the provisions for the registered associations.

*213.* Since there is no special registration required for religious communities as such, and registration as a legal entity takes place according to general provisions, and furthermore, because registration takes place before the local ordinary courts, there is no comprehensive list of religious communities registered as civil law associations. Most small religious communities in Germany likely have made use of this way of forming a legal entity.

### *C. Special Treatment of Religious Communities: The Bahá'í Case*

*214.* It is noteworthy that religious freedom of religious communities requires the civil law on associations to adapt to the special needs of religious associations in the specific case. This is based on Article 4 GG and especially on the right to self-determination of religious communities guaranteed by Article 137 section 3 WRV in conjunction with Article 140 GG. Civil law has to be interpreted so that it matches the specific religious needs of these entities, if this is at all possible. This has been made very clear by the Federal Constitutional Court in the Bahá'í-Case:[148] according to this decision, the theological teaching of Bahá'í requires that the National Council of the Bahá'í has hierarchical powers over the local councils. However, German general association law holds the principle of autonomy of associations, which means that an entity can be registered as an association on its own only when it is legally independent of other associations. The Federal Constitutional Court has ruled in favour of the special religious needs of the Bahá'í: A local Council of the Bahá'í in Germany had to be allowed to register as an (independent) association, notwithstanding that it was not independent of the National Council of the Bahá'í in Germany contrary to the general legal principle of autonomy of associations from others.

### *D. Termination of Non-profit Associations*

*215.* Termination of religious communities as legal entities under private law will be effected by dissolution of the association by decision of its members according to its statutes. The association will be legally dissolved if the number of members drops below three (§73 BGB).

*216.* The association can lose legal entity status by decision of the authorities when it endangers the common good by a decision of its members' meeting or by illegal activity of its board. This is also the case when a non-profit association takes up making profit as its predominant aim (§43 BGB).

*217.* The prohibition of religious communities is governed by Article 9 section 2 GG: 'Associations whose aims or activities contravene the criminal laws, or that are directed against the constitutional order or the concept of international understanding, are prohibited.'[149] This applies to all associations. Detailed provisions can be found in §3, §14, and §15 Association Act (VereinsG). The Federal Constitutional Court held in 2003 that the great significance of freedom of religion or belief

148. *Ibid.*, 341 et seq.
149. BVerwG 23 Mar. 1971, BVerwGE 37, 344, 365; BVerwG 26 Jun. 1997, BVerwGE 105, 117, 121.

has to be taken into due account when prohibiting a religious community. In general, a prohibition of a religious community is possible when it tries to combat the fundamental constitutional principles protected in Article 79 section 3 GG in an actively aggressive manner, including the use of violence if necessary.[150] Article 79 section 3 GG protects the division of the Federation into *Länder*, their participation on principle in the legislative process, and the principles laid down in Articles 1 and 20, which are human dignity, human rights, democracy, rule of law, republic, social state, and federal state.

*218.* According to §3 Association Act, an association can only be treated as prohibited (Article 9 section 2 GG) after it has been established by a decree of the prohibiting authority that its aims or activities contravene criminal laws or are directed against the constitutional order or the concept of international understanding; the decree shall declare the dissolution of the association. The prohibition usually includes seizure and confiscation of the property. The competent authorities are those of the *Länder* for associations whose activities are restricted to the territory of one *Land*. The Federal Minister of the Interior has the power to prohibit associations that are active in more than one *Land*. The authorities can base the prohibition on activities of individual members of the association when there is a connection with the activities within the association or with its aims when these activities are based on an organized will and when it can be assumed that the activities are tolerated by the association.

*219.* Associations of foreigners can be prohibited based on §14 VereinsG. This can be of relevance for religious communities formed by non-Germans. Associations of foreigners are such whose members or leaders are all or predominantly foreigners unless these are citizens of a Member State of the European Union (EU). Associations of foreigners can also be prohibited when their aims or activities impair or endanger the forming of the political will in the Federal Republic of Germany or the peaceful co-existence of Germans and foreigners or of different groups of foreigners on federal territory, public safety, or other important interests of the Federal Republic of Germany. They can also be prohibited when their aims or activities contradict the international commitments of the Federal Republic of Germany or support activities outside the Federal Republic of Germany that have aims or means incompatible with fundamental values of a state order that respects human dignity. Furthermore, an association of foreigners can also be prohibited when its aims or activities are directed at endorsing, supporting, or provoking the use of violence as a means to achieve political, religious, or other aims or that support organizations within or outside federal territory that induce, support, or threaten with attacks on persons or things.

*220.* Foreign associations, that is, those having their seat abroad and organization or activity extending over domestic territory, can be prohibited under the conditions stated in §14 VereinsG pursuant to §15 VereinsG. This can apply to foreign religious communities that are active within Germany. The prohibition lies within

150. BVerfG 2 Oct. 2003, *Neue Juristische Wochenschrift* 57 (2004): 47 et seq.

the competence of the Federal Minister of the Interior. When the members and leaders of a foreign association are all or predominantly Germans or citizens of other EU Member States, however, the association can only be prohibited if the requirements of Article 9 section 2 GG are met.

*221.* Based on §3 and §14 VereinsG, the Federal Minister of the Interior has prohibited a number of Muslim organizations such as the '*Kalifatstaat*'. This organization, led by Metin Kaplan, was said to aim at establishing a state within Germany that should be based on Sharia law. Metin Kaplan reportedly had called to murder a rival who, in fact, was assassinated in 1997. The '*Kalifatstaat*' and a number of related organizations were prohibited in 2001.[151] Metin Kaplan was extradited to Turkey and condemned there to lifetime imprisonment. Several other Muslim organizations have been prohibited, but also non-Muslim religious groups.

## §2. Religious Communities as Public Law Corporations

### I. General Principles

*222.* Religious and belief communities can have the special status of a corporation under public law. According to Article 137 section 5 WRV in conjunction with Article 140 GG:

> Religious societies shall remain corporations under public law insofar as they have enjoyed that status in the past. Other religious societies shall be granted the same rights upon application, if their constitution and number of members give assurance of their permanency. If two or more religious societies established under public law unite into a single organization, it too shall be a corporation under public law.

*223.* This status as a public law corporation is the second tier in the two-tier system of legal entity statuses of religious communities.

*224.* Status under public law today means public acceptance of the religious factor in public life. It signifies the public and public law role of religion. The public law status declares religion to be a good and important part of public life. It does not incorporate the religious bodies concerned into government organizations. On the contrary, the Federal Constitutional Court has held that this status stresses the very independence and autonomy of the religious bodies concerned.[152] There is no state church (Article 137 section 1 WRV). Unlike most other public law corporations, religious communities with this status are not integrated into the state structure. They retain their complete independence, even as public corporations. Under this legal norm, no particular identification of religious communities with the state

151. *Ibid.*, BVerwG 27 Nov. 2002, *Neue Zeitschrift für Verwaltungsrecht* 22 (2003): 986 et seq., 990 et seq.
152. Per toto: BVerfGE 31 Mar. 1971, BVerfGE 30, 415, 428.

(or vice versa) is intended. Quite to the contrary, by providing the status of a public law corporation, the state acknowledges that religious communities form a part of good, public life. Even more so, the public law status of religious communities signifies that the state does not monopolize the public law domain; the state has to share that field. This legal structure is an expression of the idea that the state is not total and is not all-encompassing, even in the field of public law. These structures are therefore anti-total and, in fact, anti-totalitarian.

*225.* It may be worth noting that there are other institutions that have the status of public law entities but are not religious communities or state organizations. This, for example, is the case for the Bavarian Red Cross, which is a corporation of public law.[153] Many other organizations have been conferred the status of public law entities in order to provide them with sometimes far-reaching independence from state structures, while they may be regarded as remaining in some special relation to the state. This applies, for example, to public media in order to remain independent from government interference; it also applies to public pension and health insurance institutions.

*226.* Membership in a religious community that is a corporation under public law is acquired by the act prescribed by the religious community. This means that in case of Christian churches, baptism or re-entry after having left the community before is the basic relevant act; the religious community keeps its membership register and informs the state authorities if necessary.

*227.* Leaving a religious community that is a corporation under public law is governed by the law of the *Länder* as far as effects in state law are concerned. An example is the Act Governing Resignation from the Churches, Religious Communities and Ideological Communities under Public Law of North Rhine-Westphalia (KiAustrG NRW). Pursuant to its §1, resignation from a church or another religious or ideological community under public law with effect for the sphere of the state is effected by making a declaration to the Local Court in whose area the declarer has his or her residence or lacking a residence, habitual place of residence.

*228.* According to §2 KiAustrG NRW, resignation may be declared by the person resigning if he or she has reached the age of 14 and is not incapable of entering into legal transactions. For children aged below 14 and for those who are incapable of entering into legal transactions, the legal representative with personal custody can declare the resignation. If the legal representative is a guardian or curator, he or she must acquire the Family Court's approval therefore. If a child has reached the age of 12, his or her resignation may only be declared with his or her consent.

*229.* As §3 KiAustrG NRW provides, the declaration of resignation may be given orally or in writing. The church, religious or belief community from which

153. 'Satzung of 21 July 2001', as amended on 4 Dec. 2021, available at Bayerisches Rotes Kreuz (ed.), https://www.brk.de/fileadmin/user_upload/2023-10-Satzung-Schiedsordnung-Wahlordnung.pdf, 26 Apr. 2024.

the declarer wishes to resign must be clearly designated. Proof of affiliation shall not be required. The declaration of resignation must state last name, first name, date and place of birth, residence, and marital status. In order to avoid confusion with religious and theological questions, the declaration of resignation may not contain reservations, conditions, or supplements. The oral declaration must be made for the record of the registrar of the competent Local Court. The written declaration must be submitted as an individual declaration in publicly certified form. A declaration of resignation by an empowered representative is inadmissible. As to the effects of the declaration, §4 KiAustrG NRW provides that with the effectiveness of the declaration of resignation for the area of state law, all and any rights and duties based on personal affiliation to the church, religious or ideological community shall be ceased. The declaration of resignation becomes effective on the expiry of the day on which the record of the declaration of resignation has been signed or on which the written declaration is received by the Local Court. The end of the duty to pay church tax as a consequence of resignation from the church is governed by the Act on Collection of Church Taxes in the *Land* North Rhine-Westphalia (KiStG NRW). Legal duties not based on personal affiliation to the church, religious or ideological community, in particular burdens for which particular plots of land are liable by reason of a specific legal title, remain unaffected by the declaration of resignation. Pursuant to §5 KiAustrG NRW, the Local Court issues the person resigning with a resignation certificate without delay after submission of the declaration of resignation. The certificate states when the declaration of resignation became effective. The Local Court also informs the church, religious or belief community without delay by sending a certified copy of the declaration of resignation. It communicates resignation to the registration authority competent for the residence of the person resigning and the registrar keeping the family book, or if no family book or life-partnership book is set up, the registrar who certifies the conclusion of marriage or the conclusion of a life partnership. A fee is taken by the state authorities in North Rhine-Westphalia, but not in all *Länder*, for the administrative act; the Federal Constitutional Court has held this to be in conformity with the Basic Law, especially with freedom of religion or belief.[154]

*230.* The Federal Constitutional Court held in 1980 that it violates freedom of religion or belief if a period of one month is prescribed before the declaration of resignation takes effect.[155] Such a period had been provided in order to give the resigning member some time to think about his or her decision and also to give the religious community a chance to speak with the resigning member about his or her motives. Today, no such time period exists, and the declaration of resignation becomes effective immediately. For reasons of administrative practicability, any existing duty to pay church tax ends with the end of the month that follows the month in which the declaration has been filed.[156]

---

154. BVerfG 2 Jul. 2008, *Neue Juristische Wochenschrift* 61 (2008): 2978 et seq.
155. BVerfG 7 Oct. 1980, BVerfGE 55, 32 et seq.; *see also* BVerfG 8 Feb. 1977, BVerfGE 44, 37 et seq.; BVerfG 8 Feb. 1977, BVerfGE 44, 59 et seq.
156. BVerfG 8 Feb. 1977, BVerfGE 44, 37 et seq.: BVerfG 8 Feb. 1977, BVerfGE 44, 59 et seq.

## II. Special Rights and Duties of Religious Communities as Public Law Corporations

*231.* Religious communities, as public law corporations, enjoy a number of specific rights to which specific duties correlate. The most important of these rights are explained in the following. This list is not completely exhaustive because a number of additional smaller and less significant rights are spread, often in hidden places, across various fields of law, especially in the *Länder* due to the developments of legal history.

*232.* The right to tax their own members: According to the explicit rule in Article 137 section 6 WRV in conjunction with Article 140 GG, those religious societies that are public law corporations are entitled to levy taxes on the basis of the civil taxation lists in accordance with *Land* law. Religious communities that have the status of a public law corporation can enforce the payment of the taxes due by way of public administrative action.[157]

*233.* The right to have civil servants: Religious communities that have the status of public law corporations can structure the management of their services in a way similar to the state with regard to their staff. While they can well have employees like a private entity, they can also have a specific civil service. When a religious community that is a public law corporation makes use of this right to have civil servants, they have to conform to the basic principles of that institution.[158] The German public service is still moulded by the concept of the '*Beamte*', the career civil servant for life, with whom the state has a special reciprocal relationship of loyalty. This relationship is structured on the basis of the traditional principles of the professional civil service, which have constitutionally binding character (Article 33 section 5 GG). These civil service relationships are not subject to the general labour law and labour insurance systems but follow special rules and principles. One of the traditional principles of the professional civil service is that of strict party-political and factual neutrality. This does not exclude civil servants from being members of a political party. Another traditional principle of professional civil service is the principle of financial maintenance. The public law corporation has a duty to provide an adequate salary and to provide equivalent support once a civil servant retires. Appointment and promotion must be decided on the basis of performance, ability, and suitability. Another principle is that of life-long employment: as a general rule, the relationship between the civil servant and the state is presumed to be for life, while in exceptional cases, it is also possible to have time-limited civil servant relationships. Once the age limit is reached, civil servants go into retirement and are entitled to receive a pension. They are therefore not required to make contributions to pension schemes or unemployment insurance. Because of the principle of life-long employment, civil servants can only be dismissed in exceptional circumstances, such as serious misconduct or when dismissal is at the request of the

157. BVerfG 14 Dec. 1965, BVerfGE 19, 206, 217.
158. Axel Freiherr von Campenhausen & Heinrich de Wall, *Religionsverfassungsrecht*, 5th edn (Munich: C.H. Beck, 2022), 309 et seq.

person affected. Dismissal brings with it the loss of all rights arising out of the civil-servant relationship, particularly the right to a pension. The aim of the principle of life-long employment is to insulate the professional civil service against party-political pressure, allowing it to remain objective in its decision-making. This objectivity is not affected by the hierarchical principle, in terms of which the civil servants have a duty to follow instructions from their superiors. However, the civil servant bears full personal liability for the legality of acts performed in the course of duty. Further duties flow from the duty of loyalty of the civil servant. Examples are the duty not to disclose information acquired in the course of duty, the requirement that permission be obtained before the civil servant may become involved in additional employment, and not becoming too involved in political activities. However, the public corporation has a duty to care for the civil servant, for example, if he or she falls ill. This means that civil servants have a right to assistance in paying medical expenses and only have to pay for partial medical insurance themselves. The relationship between the public law corporation and its civil servants is not based on a treaty but on an administrative act issued by the public law corporation.[159]

*234.* Clergy and civil servants of religious communities that are public law corporations and members of religious orders are free from compulsory membership in the public health insurance system (§6 section 1 numbers 2, 4, 7 Social Code V – Statutory Health Insurance (SGB V)).

*235.* The right to take disciplinary measures towards their officials: These sanctions can take various forms, such as warnings, cuts in salary, transfer to another post as a matter of sanction, or administrative fines. These disciplinary measures also have consequences for the state because the state authorities have to render administrative assistance to the religious community that has the status of a public law corporation.[160]

*236.* The right to take oaths from their officials.[161] This is primarily relevant for internal civil servant law reasons: a public servant has to take an oath when taking up his or her service promising that he or she will fulfil the duties of the office as provided for by the law and to the best of ability; not taking the oath is a reason to dismiss the public servant.

*237.* The right to create public property in a specific sense (*res sacrae* and others):[162] in general public law, public property entails goods that are specifically assigned for public use. This classification includes such diverse things as streets

159. *Ibid.*, 306.
160. *Ibid.*, 257.
161. Paul Kirchhof, 'Die Kirchen als Körperschaften des öffentlichen Rechts', in *Handbuch des Staatskirchenrechts der Bundesrepublik Deutschland*, Joseph Listl & Dietrich Pirson eds, vol. 1, 2nd edn (Berlin: Duncker & Humblot, 1994), 671.
162. Axel Freiherr von Campenhausen & Heinrich de Wall, *Religionsverfassungsrecht*, 5th edn (Munich: C.H. Beck, 2022), 315 et seq.

and parks, the office furniture of public authorities, public buildings, exhibits in public museums, and the service weapons of the police and the armed forces. Such goods are generally owned by the responsible public authority, such as the Federal Republic, a *Land*, or a local community. However, it is also perfectly possible for such things to be privately owned. The private property then continues to exist, but the owner has to tolerate public use. For example, a piece of land over which a public way runs may be private property, but the owner has to tolerate that his or her land is used in a public way. The status of public property is conferred by a specific allocation that also determines the specific details of how and for what purpose the good should be used. The consequence of allocation is that public use then takes precedence over private use of the property in question. Thus, a road may be allocated for use by public traffic, or a book may be allocated to the collection of a public library. The terms of the allocation also provide more detailed indications of how the thing may be used. Public allocation of public property takes precedence over civil law use and transactions. While the object can be sold, the new owner has to tolerate the public use of it as long as the public allocation is not withdrawn. For religious communities, this is especially relevant for their real estate. Additional legal aspects apply to the '*res sacrae*' (the 'holy things'). These *res sacrae* are objects that are specifically used for religious worship purposes such as church bells, the Thora roll or the prayer carpet, but also the cemetery of a religious community and the places of worship. They are protected by the general freedom of religion or belief because of their specifically religious use; this protection is enjoyed not only by those religious communities that are public law corporations but also by religious communities of civil law.[163] However, the whole issue of public property, public property of religious communities, and the range of protection of *res sacrae* is disputed, and many details remain unclear.[164]

*238.* The right of access to public-registration files of inhabitants: Religious communities that are public law corporations are integrated into the public-registration system. They are informed by the state-registration authorities about changes of residence of their members.[165]

*239.* In the field of the military, §13 Act on Compulsory Military Service provides for exemptions in case of indispensability: To compensate for the need for staff for the tasks of the Federal Armed Forces and other tasks, a conscript may be regarded as indispensable for military service in the public interest if and as long as the work he carries out cannot be foregone; while the replacement military authority decides on indispensability at the suggestion of the competent administrative authority, the churches and religious communities that are corporations under public law also have the right of proposal for their employees. §13 Act on Compulsory Military Service is still valid law, but due to the suspension of compulsory military

163. *Ibid.*, 316 et seq.
164. OLG Munich 12 Apr. 1979, KirchE 17, 217 et seq.; BVerwG 15 Nov. 1990, BVerwGE 87, 115 et seq.; BVerfG 13 Oct. 1998, BVerfGE 99, 100 et seq. BVerwG 19 Aug. 2008, *Neue Zeitschrift für Verwaltungsrecht* 27 (2008): 1357 et seq.
165. *See*, e.g., §§32, 10 Registration Act of Rhineland-Palatinate (MG RLP).

service, it is only applicable in a state of tension regarding military defence (*Spannungsfall*) or state of defence (*Verteidigungsfall*), *see* §2 Act on Compulsory Military Service. The same rules of exemptions from military service for religious reasons apply to the compulsory alternative service that conscientious objectors to military service have to perform.[166] These provisions, however, are only relevant if an alternative service has to be rendered, which currently is not the case because compulsory military service has been suspended.

*240.* Churches and religious communities that are corporations under public law are permitted to represent free-of-charge applicants for conscientious objection against military service in the hearing before the recognition committee.[167]

*241.* The protection of §132a of the Criminal Code (StGB) against misuse of titles, professional designations, and insignia also applies to religious communities that are public law corporations.

*242.* §133 Criminal Code protects public law religious communities against breach of official custody.

*243.* §132 Criminal Code also protects religious communities as public corporations against unlawful assumption of public office when they perform public activities such as issuing certificates or entries into church books because their offices, while not state offices, are public offices.[168]

*244.* §126 section 1 number 2 of the Administrative Offences Act (OWiG) makes it an administrative offence if someone who is unauthorized wears official costumes or insignia of a religious association recognized by a church or another religious community under public law.

*245.* Representation of religious interests in urban planning law: when the state authorities establish urban development plans, they are obliged to take into account those needs of religious worship and spiritual care that have been established by the churches and religious communities that are public law corporations (§1 section 6 number 6 Town and Country Planning Code (BauGB)).

*246.* Exemption from the general law of insolvency: Religious communities that are public law corporations are not subject to the general law on insolvency. Thus, in terms of law, these religious communities cannot go bankrupt. That does not mean that they will always be able to pay their debts. It does mean, however, that religious communities that are public law corporations do not have to pay fees to the general insolvency insurance system that covers payments to employees in case

166. §§10–12, 16 Act on Civilian Service for Conscientious Objectors (ZDG).
167. §8 Act on Refusal to Render Military Service Involving the Use of Arms on Grounds of Conscience (KDVG).
168. *See*, however, BGH 9 Oct. 1990, *Neue Juristische Wochenschrift* 1991, 367.

of the employer's insolvency.[169] The Federal Constitutional Court has argued that, in the case of an insolvency, an administrator in insolvency proceedings is appointed by the state courts, and the adjudicated bankrupt may not dispose of his or her assets. This would violate the right of self-determination of religious communities and make impossible the use of its assets for worship or other religious aims. Religious communities that are corporations under public law usually have, according to the ruling of the Federal Constitutional Court, a great enough number of members so that it can be assumed that the debts of these religious communities can be covered. The Federal Constitutional Court has left open whether the same principles also apply to institutions belonging to public law-incorporated religious communities that operate under private law; it has also left open whether the same principles apply to religious communities under private law.

*247.* The right to create public documents: Religious communities that have the status of a public law corporation have the right to authenticate documents within the range of their competencies. Public documents have a certain relevance in general procedural law; documents created or authenticated by religious public law corporations have the same status as documents created or authenticated by state authorities.

*248.* The right to form their legal structures independently: This right is sometimes called 'autonomy' as a special case of self-determination.[170] While civil law religious communities have to use the private law forms of associations and other legal entities, this right provides freedom to arrange the internal legal structures of the religious public law corporation independently and in the forms of public law and with binding effects on state authorities as well as for any third person.[171] Since the Federal Constitutional Court has held that also private law structures such as those of the law of associations have to be interpreted and applied in a way that accommodates religious needs of hierarchy and structure appropriately,[172] this specific 'autonomy' right does not make much difference in practice.

*249.* The right to create public law corporations: This is called the 'organizing power'. According to Article 137 section 5 clause 3 WRV in conjunction with Article 140 GG, religious communities that are public law corporations can independently unite and form a new public law corporation: 'If two or more religious societies established under public law unite into a single organization, it too shall

169. BVerfG 13 Dec. 1983, BVerfGE 66, 1, 18 et seq.

170. Axel Freiherr von Campenhausen & Heinrich de Wall, *Religionsverfassungsrecht*, 5th edn (Munich: C.H. Beck, 2022), 321 et seq.

171. Paul Kirchhof, 'Die Kirchen als Körperschaften des öffentlichen Rechts', in *Handbuch des Staatskirchenrechts der Bundesrepublik Deutschland*, Joseph Listl & Dietrich Pirson eds, vol. 1, 2nd edn (Berlin: Duncker & Humblot, 1994), 671.

172. BVerfG 5 Feb. 1991, BVerfGE 83, 341, 357 et seq.

be a corporation under public law.' Moreover, when a religious public law corporation creates a sub-unit, such as a foundation or a corporation, for a specific religious purpose, it can confer the public law status also to these new entities. Likewise, it can change and end this status independently.[173]

*250.* Official liability: while this is debated in legal practice and doctrine, religious communities that are public law corporations are liable in cases of torts in the same way as state public authorities. They are subject to the law of public liability.[174] In general public law, one of the most important bases for claims against the state is §839 BGB, which deals with official liability. This provision states: 'If a civil servant deliberately or negligently breaches his or her official duties to a third party, then he or she is liable to compensate the third party for any harm which results.' This provision is applicable not only to career civil servants in the strict sense but also to any person who acts in the exercise of a public office. According to the literal sense of this rule, the official is personally liable to the third party. Article 34 GG transfers the liability of the official to the public authority for which the civil servant was acting. If, in the exercise of official duties that have been entrusted to the civil servant, the official breaches his or her duties to a third party, then as a general rule, liability is to be borne by the state or the public body in whose service the official stands. The affected party thus has a claim to have his or her entire loss made good by the public administration. However, this liability only exists if the office bearer has acted wrongfully and culpably (in breach of a duty). These principles also apply to religious communities that have the status of public law corporations. They have become practical in the course of the sexual child abuse scandal when the church was held responsible for not having done enough to protect children from being sexually abused by church officials.[175]

*251.* The 'parochial right' (*Parochialrecht*): Members of religious communities that are public law corporations who move their residence within the Federal Republic of Germany automatically become members of the parish of his or her new place of residence.[176] They do not have to register with the new parish. This explains the integration of religious public law corporations into the general public registration system.

*252.* Religious communities that are public law corporations may establish and maintain cemeteries as is provided for, with some differences in details in the burial laws of the *Länder,* of which §14 Burials Act of Mecklenburg-Western Pomerania (BestattG M-V) is an example.[177]

173. Axel Freiherr von Campenhausen & Heinrich de Wall, *Religionsverfassungsrecht*, 5th edn (Munich: C.H. Beck, 2022), 311 et seq.
174. BGH 20 Feb. 2003, BGHZ 154, 54 et seq.; different opinion: OLG Düsseldorf 26 Oct. 2000, *Neue Zeitschrift für Verwaltungsrecht* 20 (2001): 1449 et seq.
175. LG Köln (5. Zivilkammer), Urteil vom 13 Jun. 2023 – 5 0 197/22.
176. Paul Kirchhof, 'Die Kirchen als Körperschaften des öffentlichen Rechts', in *Handbuch des Staatskirchenrechts der Bundesrepublik Deutschland*, Joseph Listl & Dietrich Pirson eds, vol. 1, 2nd edn (Berlin: Duncker & Humblot, 1994), 671 et seq.
177. *See also* Art. 8, s. 4 Burial Act of Bavaria (BestG Bayern); §§1, s. 2 Burial Act North Rhine-Westphalia (BestG NRW).

*253.* Religious communities that are public law corporations enjoy special treatment in tax law. According to a generally applicable definition in §54 section 1 Fiscal Code (AO), a corporation pursues ecclesiastical purposes if its activities aim to selflessly promote a religious community that is a corporation under public law. These purposes include in particular the establishment, equipment, and maintenance of houses of God and church community buildings, holding religious services, training of clerics, giving religious instruction, burial and care for the remembrance of the dead, as well as the administration of church assets, payment of clerics, church civil servants and church servants, old age and disabled pensions for these persons, and pensions for their widows and orphans. While religious purposes of religious communities that are civil law corporations enjoy a very similar protection by general provisions, this special mentioning of public law corporations intensifies the status of those public law corporations.

*254.* As is stated in §3 section 1 numbers 4, 5, and 6 Act on Real Property Tax (GrStG), religious communities under public law and all Jewish faith communities are in general exempt from real property tax.

*255.* Religious communities that are public law corporations are exempt from Corporate Gains Tax according to §5 section 1 number 9 Corporate Gains Tax Act (KStG).

*256.* Pursuant to §4 numbers 18 and 27 Turnover Tax Act (UStG), specific services of religious communities that are public law corporations are exempt from turnover tax, while §4a section 1 Turnover Tax Act grants upon request a tax refund to compensate for the tax levied on them in respect of received delivery of certain items and under specific conditions.

*257.* According to §3 number 6 Trade Tax Act (GewStG), religious communities that are public law corporations are, to a certain extent, exempt from trade tax: corporations, associations of persons, and estates which, in accordance with their statutes, the act of foundation or other constitution, and in accordance with the actual management of business exclusively and directly pursue ecclesiastical ends, are exempt from trade tax. This does not apply to the extent that they operate an economic business establishment – with the exception of agriculture and forestry.

*258.* Legacies to domestic religious societies under public law or domestic Jewish faith communities are exempt from inheritance tax as is provided for in §13 section 1 number 16 Act on Inheritance Tax and Gifts Tax (ErbStG). This applies to Jewish faith communities regardless of their public or private law status; other private law religious communities are exempt from inheritance tax under special provisions.

*259.* According to the Laws on Administrative Fees, religious communities that are public law corporations do not have to pay administrative fees for state official acts when these acts serve directly those church aims (functions) stipulated in §54 AO (§8 section 1 number 5 Act on Administrative Fees of North Rhine-Westphalia (GebG NRW)).

*260.* Forestry management is regulated by the laws of the *Länder*. Special provisions apply for forests owned by public law corporations such as local communities. These special rules, however, do not apply to religious communities that are public law corporations and which sometimes still are the owners of some amount of forest (e.g., §38 *Land* Forest Act North Rhine-Westphalia (FoG NRW)).

*261.* While in general the sale of agricultural and forestry real property requires permission by the state authorities, this is, pursuant to §4 number 2 Real Property Transactions Act (GrdstVG), not needed when the buyer is a religious community with the rights of a public law corporation; however, the permission remains necessary when an agricultural or forestry undertaking is concerned.

*262.* Religious communities that are public law corporations enjoy a special status equivalent to the state in matters of a judicial execution of a pecuniary claim, as stated in §882a Code of Civil Procedure (ZPO). Unless rights in rem are pursued, coercive execution against corporations, institutes and foundations under public law in respect of money receivable may not start until four weeks after the creditor has communicated his or her intention to pursue coercive execution. Coercive execution is not permissible against items that are indispensable for carrying out the public tasks of the debtor or the sale of which is opposed by a public interest. In the context of religious communities, this is not limited to *res sacrae* but includes all chattel indispensable for their welfare duties.[178]

*263.* Religious communities that are public law corporations enjoy a special status equivalent to state bodies in administrative execution pursuant to §17 Administrative Execution Act (VwVG).[179] Coercive means that administrative matters are not permissible against authorities and legal entities under public law unless otherwise stipulated.

*264.* Religious communities that are public law corporations enjoy autonomy in the law on foundations. While this is a matter of the law of the *Länder*, these religious communities are in general not subject to state supervision in managing the foundation. An example of this is given in §20 Foundation Act of Lower Saxony (NStiftG).[180]

*265.* When state subsidies are given to a legal person of public law, the receiving legal person is in general subject to an auditing of accounts by the Federal Audit

---

178. BVerfG 13 Dec. 1983, BVerfGE 66, 1, 23.
179. *See also* §22 LVwVG BW; Art. 29, s. 4 VwZVG Bay; §36 VwVG Bbg.; §73 HessVwVG; §85 SOG M-V; §76 VwVG NRW; §7 LVwVG RlPf; §17 SVwVG Saarl; §234 LVwG S H; §44, s. 3 ThürVwZVG; §21 NVwVG.
180. *See also* §13 Foundation Act North Rhine-Westphalia (StiftG NRW).

Office. Religious communities that are public law corporations are exempt from such auditing, as are the Federal Republic, the *Länder* and the local communities, as is stated in §55 section 1 Budgetary Principles Act (HGrG).

*266.* Persons who work on an honorary basis for religious communities that are public law corporations are by law insured in the accident insurance system (§2 section 1 number 10 Social Code VII – Statutory Accident Insurance (SGB VII)).

*267.* Religious communities that are public law corporations are by law recognized associations of private youth welfare work (§75 section 3 Social Code VIII – Children and Youth Welfare (SGB VIII)). This status gives them a special standing in working within the general public system of youth welfare. Recognition is not a condition for providing youth welfare services but offers advantages such as priority over state-run institutions (§4 section 2 SGB VIII) and participation in public planning for provision of youth welfare (§80 section 3 SGB VIII). It also entails a right to suggest members of the youth protection boards,[181] and it provides the chance to receive permanent subsidies for youth care activities.[182]

*268.* Jewish faith communities and other religious communities that are public law corporations can send representatives to the board that decides on youth-endangering publications. According to the Law on Protection of the Youth (JuSchG),[183] those publications and specific other forms of media that can endanger the good morals of children and young people will be listed and must not be offered, handed out, or made accessible to them. There is an exception for parents and legal guardians in the private sphere lest the provision of such items should severely violate parental duties.[184] Publications will be listed when they are immoral, especially when they stimulate violence, crime, racial hatred, or glorify war. A board that includes representatives of literature, arts, and youth-protecting institutions decides on the listing. According to §19 section 2 number 8 JuSchG, representatives nominated by Jewish faith communities and other religious communities that are public law corporations will also be appointed to this board.

*269.* State authorities of social aid have to cooperate with religious communities that are public law corporations in the field of social aid; the status of those religious communities as associations of private welfare work with their specific social aims has to be respected and must not be prejudiced (§5 Social Code XII – Social Welfare (SGB XII)).

*270.* According to §4 section 2 number 4 Federal Supply Law (BLG), religious communities that are public law corporations and their unions enjoy exemption from certain duties related to defence purposes. In contrast to other people and institutions, they cannot be obliged to supply the state authorities with goods and rights

181. §71, s. 1, nos 2, 4 SGB VIII.
182. §74, s. 1, cl. 2 SGB VIII.
183. §12, s. 3, cl. 1 JuSchG.
184. §28, s. 4, cl. 2 JuSchG; §184, s. 2, cl. 1 StGB.

needed for defence purposes when these goods serve ecclesiastical purposes or are indispensable for their administrative activities.

*271.* The federal Framework Act on Registration (MRRG) allows in its §19 state-registration authorities to communicate to religious communities that are public law corporations certain data of their members such as names, dates of birth, children, residence, and citizenship of their members. To a more limited extent, data of certain relatives of their members can also be communicated. The *Länder* have adopted equivalent provisions in their laws on registration.

*272.* Former provisions of the Federal Data Protection Law (BDSG) related to data protection norms of religious communities with the status of public law corporations have been substituted by the more general and comprehensive EU General Data Protection Regulation, which is directly applicable in the EU Member States.[185] Article 91 of the EU General Data Protection Regulation gives prevalence to existing data protection rules of churches and religious associations. Where in a Member State, churches and religious associations or communities apply, at the time of entry into force of this Regulation, comprehensive rules relating to the protection of natural persons with regard to processing, such rules may continue to apply, provided that they are brought into line with this Regulation. Churches and religious associations which apply comprehensive rules in accordance with paragraph 1 of that Article are subject to the supervision of an independent supervisory authority, which may be specific, provided that it fulfils the conditions laid down in Chapter VI of the Regulation.

*273.* Some other provisions that are sometimes said to be part of the special rights of public law religious communities in fact protect all religions regardless of their legal status. This applies, for example, to §7 clause 2 Act on Limitations of Real Estate for Reasons of Military Defence (SchBerG), by which the use of land can be restricted for military defence purposes; religious needs must be taken into account when applying the law.

*274.* In some other cases, special rights are attributed to specific religious communities regardless of their status as public law corporations. An example is §8 section 3 Act on the West-German Broadcasting Organization Cologne (WDRG NRW). The law states that appropriate broadcasting times have to be granted to the Protestant Church, the Catholic Church and the Jewish Faith Communities to broadcast worship services and ceremonies and other religious programmes. While these religious communities in fact are public law corporations, other religious communities with the same status do not enjoy these rights. These rights are not specifically attached to the public law status.

*275.* While certain rights are explicitly granted to religious communities that are public law corporations, other religious communities enjoy similar rights by way of general provisions. This is the case in the field of tax benefits: Some of those are

185. Regulation (EU) 2016/679 of 27 Apr. 2016.

explicitly granted to religious communities that have the status of public law corporations; the other religious communities enjoy equivalent benefits as far as they pursue general charity or religious ends. Such a situation exists in §3 number 6 Trade Tax Act; §13 section 1 number 16 Act on Inheritance Tax and Gifts Tax; §5 section 1 number 9 Corporate Gains Tax Act; §4 numbers 18 and 27, and §4a section 1 Turnover Tax Act. The advantage for religious communities with the status of a public law corporation is that they benefit based on their general status, while for other religious communities, the benefit depends on the decision in the individual case.

### III. Range of Religious Communities with Public Law Status

*276.* There are religious communities that have the status of public law corporations by constitutional law (the 'old-incorporated religious communities'); the status can also be acquired on application (the 'newly incorporated religious communities').

*277.* Religious communities that had the status of public law corporations at the time when the Weimar Constitution came into force on 14 August 1919 (the old-incorporated religious communities) remain within this status as is explicitly stated in Article 139 section 5 WRV in conjunction with Article 140 GG. This is the case for the big Christian churches such as the Protestant Church and the Roman Catholic Church, but also for the Jewish faith communities.

*278.* Special laws have taken care of the situation of the Jewish population that had survived the murderous times of Nazi rule. These laws have structured the legal status of the Jewish faith communities, confirming their status as public law corporations as far as these communities wanted to have this status. For example, according to §4 *Land* Act on the Jewish cult communities in Rhineland-Palatinate (JüdKGemG RLP), the Jewish cult associations that had their seat before 1 January 1938 on the territory of today's *Land* Rhineland-Palatinate and that were recognized as corporations under public law were legally dissolved with the taking effect of that Act. The rights and obligations of those cult communities have, at the same time, passed by way of law to the Jewish cult communities that are enumerated in that Act.

*279.* Religious communities that are not already public law corporations have the right to be granted the same rights upon application if their constitution and the number of their members give assurance of their permanency, as is stated in Article 137 section 5 WRV in conjunction with Article 140 GG. There has to be sufficient reason for the prognostic assumption that the religious community will also exist in the future.[186] This requirement draws its legitimacy from the rights and duties that are attached to this public law status; especially some of those duties cannot be fulfilled if the permanent existence of the religious community cannot be assumed.

186. BVerfG 19 Dec. 2000, BVerfGE 102, 370, 384 et seq.

*280.* In order to apply equal standards when granting the status of a public law corporation to a religious or belief community, the *Länder* have agreed to an informal 'Guideline on Awarding the Rights of Corporations to Religious and Belief Communities' of 16 February 2017.[187]

*281.* To be constituted as a religious corporation under public law, the association has to be a religious one or a body of ideological creed (*Weltanschauungsgemeinschaft*, belief community).

*282.* The association has to have its organizational seat within Germany. There is no requirement as to the nationality of the members or governors of the association.

*283.* There has to be an application by the religious community. The status of a public law corporation cannot be attributed to a religious community against its own will. The application is made to the Ministry of Culture of the Federal *Land* where the association wants to become a public law corporation.

*284.* In some *Länder*, the public law corporation is established by ordinance, again in others – and most – lands by administrative act. There is no registration file.

*285.* The applicant has to have a constitution. In the context of Article 137 section 5 WRV, in conjunction with Article 140 GG, the term 'constitution' does not only mean a written statute but also the factual and secure general state of the community – a status of quality.[188] It is the factual general state of the religious community that can reasonably provide a basis on which to judge the probability that the community will also exist in the future. This notion of quality was also meant by the National Assembly of Weimar when it made the 1919 Weimar Constitution that focused not on a mere formal requirement but on 'the deeper element of the content of the constitution'.[189]

*286.* A sufficient legal organization is a necessary but not a sufficient condition to be the basis for expecting a permanence of the association. Also necessary is sufficient financial means to meet the manifold financial requirements that are linked with the status of a public law corporation.[190] The religious community that applies for the status of a public law corporation needs sufficient financial resources

---

187. https://recht.nrw.de/lmi/owa/br_bes_text?anw_nr=1&gld_nr=2&ugl_nr=222&bes_id=36407&val=36407&ver=7&sg=&aufgehoben=N&menu=1, 9 Nov. 2023.

188. *Ibid.*; Dirk Ehlers in *Grundgesetz. Kommentar*, Michael Sachs ed., 9th edn (Munich: C.H. Beck, 2021), Art. 140/Art. 137 WRV, n. 28.

189. Deutsche Nationalversammlung (ed.), *Verhandlungen der Verfassunggebenden Deutschen Nationalversammlung*, vol. 329 (Berlin: Druck und Verlag der Norddeutschen Buchdruckerei, 1920), 2159.

190. BVerfG 19 Dec. 2000, BVerfGE 102, 370, 384 et seq.; BVerfG 13 Dec. 1983, BVerfGE 66, 1, 24.

because, otherwise, it will not be able to exist for a reasonable amount of time. Furthermore, the courts require some intensity of the religious life of the community in the absence of which continuity of the organization as a religious one would be endangered.[191]

*287.* The religious community has to have a certain number of members. Because the number alone does not provide a sufficiently reliable indication of the future existence of the community, further detailed criteria have to be applied. These are, for example, the age of the members, the development of the number of memberships, and the social structure of the members.

*288.* Since religious communities with the status of a public law corporation have specific public law rights and duties, religious communities can obtain this status only when it can reasonably be expected that they will be able to continuously meet the requirements that follow from this status.[192] Such public law rights and duties exist towards the members of the religious communities, such as the right to levy church taxes, but they also exist in view of the general public, such as the right to create public things. The decision about awarding the status of a public law corporation to a religious community thus also entails reasons for protection of third persons.

*289.* The applicant has to have an ordinary administration by which the religious community can meet the demands that go with this special status.[193]

*290.* According to a general opinion in legal doctrine and court practice following the Federal Constitutional Court's decision on Jehovah's Witnesses,[194] it is also required that the religious association be loyal to the law.

*291.* Furthermore, a certain time of existence is necessary because a newly founded association in general does not offer the assurance of permanency.[195] The courts have required in general a time of thirty to forty years of existence, which is equivalent to one change of generation.[196] Some demand the existence of two generations or two changes of generations.[197]

191. BVerfG 19 Dec. 2000, BVerfGE 102, 370, 384 et seq.; BVerfG 13 Dec. 1983, BVerfGE 66, 1, 24.
192. BVerfGE 102, 370, 388.
193. Guideline on Awarding the Rights of Corporations to Religious and Belief Communities' of 16 Feb. 2017, https://recht.nrw.de/lmi/owa/br_bes_text?anw_nr=1&gld_nr=2&ugl_nr=222&bes_id=36407&val=36407&ver=7&sg=&aufgehoben=N&menu=1, 9 Nov. 2023.
194. BVerfG 19 Dec. 2000, BVerfGE 102, 370 et seq.
195. *Ibid.*, BVerfGE 102, 370, 384 et seq.; BVerfG 13 Dec. 1983, BVerfGE 66, 1, 24.
196. BVerfG 19 Dec. 2000, BVerfGE 102, 370 et seq.
197. Axel Freiherr von Campenhausen & Heinrich de Wall, *Staatskirchenrecht*, 4th edn (Munich: C.H. Beck, 2006), 135, fn. 66.

*292.* Assurance of permanency is not given when the ratio of old people in the community is so high that there is a persistent danger that the community will soon cease to exist.[198]

*293.* All these criteria have to be applied in view of the individual case. Each one of them only indicates the existence or non-existence of the permanency of the religious community. A merely formal or automatic application of these criteria would be wrong and would not meet the intentions of the law. What is required is a general assessment of the chances of the religious community to permanently exist. In performing this general assessment, the state authorities must not turn to criteria that are beyond the evaluation competence of the religiously and philosophically neutral state.[199] The religiously neutral state must not evaluate the religious ideas and convictions of a religious community.

*294.* The religious communities with large memberships in Germany, and also a considerable number of the smaller religious communities, have the status of public law corporations. The same applies to belief communities. The question of whether the Bahá'í community in Germany can be recognized as a public law corporation was recently decided by the courts; the Administrative Court of Appeals of Hesse held that the Bahá'í community does fulfil the requirements necessary for recognition as a public law corporation.[200] The *Land* Hesse appealed the case to the Federal Administrative Court, which upheld the decision.[201]

*Table 1 Religions and Belief Communities with Public Law Status*[202]

| **1. Evangelische Kirche** | **1. Protestant Church** |
|---|---|
| Evangelische Landeskirchen | Protestant *Land* churches |
| Evangelische Kirche in Deutschland (EKD) | Evangelical Church in Germany (EKD) |
| Evangelisch-Reformierte Kirche | Protestant-Reformed Church |
| Kirchengemeinden und die aus ihnen gebildeten Verbände | Parishes and their associations |
| Vereinigte Evangelisch-Lutherische Kirche in Deutschland (VELKD) | United Evangelical Lutheran Church in Germany (VELKD) |

198. Guideline on Awarding the Rights of Corporations to Religious and Belief Communities' of 16 Feb. 2017, https://recht.nrw.de/lmi/owa/br_bes_text?anw_nr=1&gld_nr=2&ugl_nr=222&bes_id=36407&val=36407&ver=7&sg=&aufgehoben=N&menu=1, 9 Nov. 2023.; OVG Berlin-Brandenburg 17 Apr. 1969, OVG Berlin AS 10, 105, 111.
199. BVerfG 19 Dec. 2000, BVerfGE 102, 370, 384 et seq.
200. VGH Hesse 22 Sep. 2011, *Neue Zeitschrift für Verwaltungsrecht* 30 (2011): 1513 et seq.
201. BVerwG 28 Nov. 2012, 6 C 8.12.
202. Enlarged rough list by the Federal Ministry of the Interior, https://www.bmi.bund.de/DE/themen/heimat-integration/gesellschaftlicher-zusammenhalt/staat-und-religion/koerperschaftsstatus/koerperschaftsstatus-node.html, 9 Nov. 2023,. Translation of names by the author.

| | |
|---|---|
| Union Evangelischer Kirchen in der Evangelischen Kirche in Deutschland (UEK) | Union of Evangelical Churches (UEK) |
| **2. Katholische Kirche** | **2. Catholic Church** |
| (Erz-)Bistümer bzw. (Erz-)Diözesen der römisch-katholischen Kirche | (Arch-)Bishoprics and (Arch-) Dioceses of the Roman Catholic Church |
| Verband der Diözesen Deutschlands (Zusammenschluss der Erzdiözesen und Diözesen zur Wahrnehmung von Aufgaben im rechtlichen und wirtschaftlichen Bereich) | Union of the Dioceses of Germany (Union of Roman Catholic (Arch-) dioceses for Legal and Economic Matters) |
| Kirchengemeinden und die aus ihnen gebildeten Verbände | Parishes and their associations |
| Diverse Ordensgemeinschaften bzw. Einzelklöster | Several religious orders and monastic communities |
| **3. Alt-Katholiken** | **3. Old-Catholics** |
| Katholisches Bistum der Alt-Katholiken | Catholic Diocese of the Old-Catholics |
| **4. Evangelische Freikirchen** | **4. Protestant Free Churches** |
| Bund Evangelisch-Freikirchlicher Gemeinden in Deutschland (BEFG) (Baptisten) | Baptists |
| Bund Freier evangelischer Gemeinden in Deutschland | Federation of Free Protestant Communities in Germany |
| Evangelisch-methodistische Kirche | Protestant Methodist Church |
| Selbständige Evangelisch-Lutherische Kirche (SELK) | Independent Protestant-Lutheran Church |
| Evangelisch-Lutherische (altlutherische) Kirche (in ehemals preußischen Gebieten) | Protestant-Lutheran (old-Lutheran) Church (in former Prussian areas) |
| Evangelische Brüder-Unität (Herrnhuter Brüdergemeine) | Protestant Brethren Unity |
| Mennoniten | Mennonites |
| Bund Freikirchlicher Pfingstgemeinden | Federation of Free Church Pentecostal Community |
| Die Heilsarmee in Deutschland | The Salvation Army in Germany |
| **5. Orthodoxe Kirchen** | **5. Orthodox Churches** |
| Griechisch-Orthodoxe Metropolie in Deutschland | Greek-Orthodox Metropolitan in Germany |

| | |
|---|---|
| Russisch-Orthodoxe Kirche im Ausland | Russian-Orthodox Church Abroad |
| Russisch-Orthodoxe Kirche (Moskauer Patriarchat) | Russian-Orthodox Church (Patriarchate of Moscow) |
| **6. Jüdische Gemeinschaft** | **6. Jewish Community** |
| Zentralrat der Juden in Deutschland | Central Council of the Jews in Germany |
| Jüdische Landesverbände | Jewish Land Associations |
| Jüdische Gemeinden/Israelitische Kultusgemeinden | Jewish Communities/Israelite Cult Community |
| **7. Sonstige** | **7. Others** |
| Neuapostolische Kirche | New Apostolic Church |
| Gemeinschaft der Siebenten-Tags-Adventisten (STA) | Community of Seventh Day Adventists |
| Apostelamt Jesu Christi | Apostle Office Jesus Christ |
| Gemeinde Gottes | Community of God |
| Christengemeinschaft | Christian Community |
| Johannische Kirche | Church of John |
| (Erste) Kirche Christi, Wissenschaftler (Christian Science) | Christian Science |
| Bund Freireligiöser Gemeinden Deutschlands | Federation of Free Church Communities of Germany |
| Freireligiöse Landesgemeinschaften/ Landesgemeinden bzw. Bund Freireligiöser Gemeinden Deutschlands | Free-Religious Communities and their Federations |
| Freie Religionsgemeinschaften (Humanistische Gemeinde Freier Protestanten) | Humanists |
| Unitarische Freie Religionsgemeinde | Unitarians |
| Kirche Jesu Christi der Heiligen der letzten Tagen (Mormonen) | Church of Jesus Christ of Latter Day Saints (Mormons) |
| Bund für Geistesfreiheit Bayern | Union for Freedom of Thought Bavaria |
| Zeugen Jehovahs in Deutschland | Jehovah's Witnesses in Germany |
| Ahmadiyya Muslim Jamaat Deutschland | Ahmadiyya Muslim Jamaat Germany |
| Hindu-Tempelverein | Hindu Temple-Association |

## IV. Termination of Status of Public Law Corporations

*295.* The question under what circumstances and conditions the status of a religious community as a public law corporation is terminated is a matter of debate. One can probably say that the status of a religious community as a corporation of public law ends when it loses its members, when it applies for dissolution, or when the status of a corporation of public law is revoked.[203] The status is revoked when the religious community has to be prohibited according to Article 9 section 2 GG and §§3, 14, 15 Association Act, when the recognition as a public law corporation was illegal or when the requirements stated by Article 137 section 5 clause 2 WRV in conjunction with Article 140 GG have ceased to exist.[204] Deprivation of the status is only possible by or on the basis of a formal law; such laws have been adopted in Bavaria and North Rhine-Westphalia.

*296.* The status of the old-incorporated religious communities can be terminated only by constitutional amendment because, in this case, the status is guaranteed by the Constitution itself. There are no specific law provisions on how such termination of the status or the curtailment of specific rights attached to that status could be accomplished. The Federal Constitutional Court held in 2001 that this does not contradict the duty of the state to protect the rights of third persons: An institution of a religious community with the status of a public law corporation had publicly warned against the religious community 'Universal Life', and the association 'Universal Life' had tried to obligate state authorities to deprive that religious community of its public law status. 'Universal Life' argued that the other religious community had violated its duty of loyalty to the law, which is a precondition to be granted public law status. The Federal Constitutional Court argued that the state while having to protect the rights and freedoms of everybody, enjoyed a margin of discretion as to how best to achieve this goal; there are numerous legal remedies against any possible illegal actions on the side of the public law corporations.[205]

*297.* To the number of old-incorporated religious communities belong the Protestant Churches, the Roman Catholic Church, some Jewish communities, the Old-Catholics, the Old-Lutherans, Baptists, and Mennonites.[206]

## V. Specific Issues of Organization

*298.* Muslim organizations are mostly structured as registered associations according to general association law. It is a matter of controversy whether these

---

203. Dirk Ehlers in *Grundgesetz. Kommentar*, Michael Sachs ed., 9th edn (Munich: C.H. Beck, 2021), Art. 140/Art. 137 WRV, n. 31.

204. *Ibid.*, VG Berlin 10 Oct. 1994, *Neue Zeitschrift für Verwaltungsrecht* 14 (1995): 513 et seq.; Gottfried Held, *Die kleinen öffentlich-rechtlichen Religionsgemeinschaften im Staatskirchenrecht der Bundesrepublik* (Munich: Claudius, 1974), 146; BVerwG 15 Oct. 1997, BVerwGE 105, 255 et seq. (continuation of the Synagogue Adass Jisroel).

205. BVerfG (K) 26 Mar. 2001, *Deutsches Verwaltungsblatt* 116 (2001): 984 et seq.

206. https://www.bmi.bund.de/DE/themen/heimat-integration/gesellschaftlicher-zusammenhalt/staat-und-religion/koerperschaftsstatus/koerperschaftsstatus-node.html, 9 Nov. 2023.

associations are religious communities in the sense of constitutional law, which is a precondition to having a confessional religious instruction at public schools. In 1998, the High Administrative Court of Berlin established that the Islam Federation in Berlin (*Islamische Föderation Berlin*) is a religious community. Similarly, the Alevi Community in North Rhine-Westphalia has been recognized as a religious community. Various other court cases are pending. Hamburg has concluded two treaties with Muslim organizations, one with the Turkish-Islamic Union of the Institute for Religion (*Türkisch-Islamische Union der Anstalt für Religion* (DITIB)) Land Association Hamburg (*DTIB Landesverband Hamburg*), SCHURA – the Council of Islamic Communities in Hamburg (*SCHURA – Rat der Islamischen Gemeinschaften in Hamburg*) and the Organization of Islamic Culture Centres (*Verband der Islamischen Kulturzentren*),[207] the other with the Alevi Community in Germany (*Alevitische Gemeinde Deutschland e.V.*).[208] These treaties acknowledge the respective Muslim organizations as religious communities. Both treaties cover a number of subjects and contain, in particular, provisions concerning religious holidays, religious education and burial practices. In addition to the *Land* Hamburg, the *Land* Bremen has also concluded a treaty with Muslim religious communities, which came into force in January 2013.[209] In the *Land* Hessen, public schools offer religious instruction classes for Muslim pupils. North Rhine-Westphalia has been offering Islamic studies for Muslim pupils in schools as a part of the classes for their languages of origin since 1986; Islamic studies in German have been offered as part of a school pilot project since 1999.[210] Since the school year 2012–2013, primary schools which have the necessary organization and teachers may provide Muslim religious education; from the school year 2013–2014 onwards, the same applies to secondary schools.[211] The state cooperates with Muslim organizations – which do not have to be religious communities – on the basis of treaties concluded with them. An advisory body composed of Muslim representatives who are qualified in theology, religious education or Islamic studies oversees the implementation and content of the religious education classes for Muslim pupils.[212] In Hamburg, common

207. Freie und Hansestadt Hamburg (ed.), 'Vertrag zwischen der Freien und Hansestadt Hamburg, dem DITIB-Landesverband Hamburg, SCHURA – Rat der Islamischen Gemeinschaften in Hamburg und dem Verband der Islamischen Kulturzentren', https://schurahamburg.de/uber-uns/staatsvertrag-muslimischen-verbaenden/, 9 Nov. 2023.
208. Freie und Hansestadt Hamburg (ed.), 'Vertrag zwischen der Freien und Hansestadt Hamburg und der Alevitischen Gemeinde Deutschland e.V.', https://www.buergerschaft-hh.de/ParlDok/dokument/38534/1-vertrag-zwischen-der-freien-und-hansestadt-hamburg-dem-ditib-landesverband-hamburg-schura-%E2%80%93-rat-der-islamischen-gemeinschaften-in-hamburg.pdf, 9 Nov. 2023.
209. Land Bremen (ed.), 'Vertrag zwischen der Freien Hansestadt Bremen und den Islamischen Religionsgemeinschaften im Lande Bremen', http://www.bremische-buergerschaft.de/drs_abo/Drs-18-727_be4.pdf, 9 Nov. 2023.
210. Schulministerium NRW (ed.), 'Islamkunde (Islamische Unterweisung)', https://www.schulministerium.nrw/islamkunde-islamische-unterweisung, 9 Nov. 2023.
211. Schulministerium NRW (ed.), 'Islamischer Religionsunterricht', https://www.schulministerium.nrw/islamischer-religionsunterricht, 9 Nov. 2023.
212. §132a School Act for the Land North Rhine-Westphalia (Schulgesetz für das Land Nordrhein-Westfalen) of 15 Feb. 2005 as amended on 23 Feb. 2022 (GV. NRW. 2022 p. 250).

religious instruction is offered for pupils of all religions.[213] As of 2020, about 60,000 pupils take part in Muslim religious instruction classes in about 900 schools.[214] Alevite religious instruction is offered in eight *Länder*.[215]

*299.* The local mosque community is the smallest organizational unit. These are usually structured as associations in private law. Up to now, most mosques are formed by members of the same national background. The majority of mosque associations are members of associations that are active on a national level. There are more than a dozen such associations.

*300.* Some of these associations have united into umbrella organizations. In some of the sixteen *Länder*, alliances of Muslim organizations have been formed. The largest umbrella organizations on the federal level are: the DITIB, under the guidance and supervision of the Turkish Presidency for Religious Affairs (*Diyanet*);[216] Central Council of the Muslims in Germany (*Zentralrat der Muslime in Deutschland* (ZMD)), predominantly non-Turkish Muslims;[217] Islam-Council for the Federal Republic of Germany;[218] Union of the Islam-Albanian Centres in Germany (ZRMD);[219] Zentralrat der Marokkaner in Deutschland (ZRMD);[220] The Association of Islamic Cultural Centres (VIKZ), Sunni.[221]

*301.* Five of these organizations are members of the Coordination Council of the Muslims in Germany (*Koordinationsrat der Muslime in Deutschland* (KRM)), which is developing into an interlocutor with the German public.[222] The Union of the Islam Cultural Centres left the Coordination Council of Muslims in Germany in October 2023. The various organizations often compete with one another but also cooperate in questions of common interest, such as Muslim religious instruction in public schools.

*302.* As has been referred to above, several Muslim organizations have been prohibited because of anti-constitutional activities. Among them are the *Kalifatstaat*, *Al-Aqsa e.V.*, *Hizb ut-Tahrir al-Islami*, *YATIM-Kinderhilfe e.V.*, and *Yeni Akit GmbH*.

---

213. Mediendienst Integration, Religion an Schulen Islamischer Religionsunterricht in Deutschland, https://mediendienst-integration.de/fileadmin/Dateien/MDI_Informationspapier_Islamischer_Religionsunterricht_Mai_2020.pdf, 9 Nov. 2023.
214. *Ibid.*
215. *Ibid.*
216. Türkisch-Islamische Union der Anstalt für Religion e. V. (DITIB) (ed.), www.ditib.de.
217. Zentralrat der Muslime in Deutschland e. V. (ZMD) (ed.), http://zentralrat.de, 9 Nov. 2023.
218. Islamrat für die Bundesrepublik Deutschland (ed.), www.islamrat.de, 9 Nov. 2023.
219. Union der Islamisch-Albanischen Zentren in der Bundesrepublik Deutschland (UIAZD) (ed.), https://www.uiazd.de/kreu/, 9 Nov. 2023.
220. Zentralrat der Marokkaner in Deutschland (ZRMD) (ed.), https://ikwev.org/zrmd-zentralrat-der-marokkaner-in-deutschland/, 9 Nov. 2023.
221. Verband der Islamischen Kulturzentren e. V. (VIKZ) (ed.), www.vikz.de, 9 Nov. 2023.
222. Koordinationsrat der Muslime in Deutschland (KRM) (ed.), http://koordinationsrat.de/, 9 Nov. 2023.

# Chapter 2. Autonomy of Religious Communities

## §1. General Principles

*303.* The right to self-determination (Article 137 section 3 WRV in conjunction with Article 140 GG) may be considered to be the central reference point for the legal and social existence of religious communities in the Federal Republic of Germany. The right to self-determination or religious autonomy has a far-reaching impact in many fields of law. Every religious community independently regulates and administers its own affairs within the limits of the law that applies to all. Every religious community may then, regardless of its legal status, manage its own affairs independently. The right of self-determination covers such things as religious dogma and teaching, making official appointments, religious services, and organizing charitable activities. It also applies to matters concerning important parts of the relationship between church employers and employees, and data protection. The list of possible examples should not mislead one into supposing that the right of self-determination is not all-encompassing, nor should it be taken to suggest that the operating spheres of the churches are to be restricted into certain defined areas. There is, however, an ongoing debate on which matters belong to religious autonomy and where its limits are.

*304.* Self-determination of religious communities in Germany is equivalent to church autonomy in international human rights law. However, German legal doctrine draws a distinction between self-determination and autonomy. 'Autonomy' is used as a technical legal term to describe the competence of state institutions to govern their affairs in a way that is independent of superior state institutions; yet, the transfer of autonomy is dependent on the will of the state. In this meaning, there is autonomy of local communities in governing local affairs, while these local communities remain a part of the state. Likewise, state universities enjoy autonomy in governing research and teaching affairs while they remain state institutions. However, religious self-determination, and in this sense, autonomy of religious communities, means independence from state interference. There is no state church, and there is no state religious community or state philosophical community. Religious self-determination is not conferred on the religious community by the state but is acknowledged by the state as a pre-existing feature of a religious community's own pre-state right. That is, in terms of human rights doctrine, the self-determination of religious communities is an aspect of the fundamental understanding that human rights (and, in this case, the rights of religious communities) are inherent and innate in human beings, not conferred by the state.

*305.* Self-determination of religious communities, as has been stated above, is enjoyed by all religious communities in Germany, regardless of their legal status. Religious communities with civil law status, as well as religious communities with the status of public law corporations, enjoy self-determination. According to legal doctrine, religious communities with the status of public law corporations have a special right to form their legal structures independently. This right is sometimes called 'autonomy' as a special case of self-determination.[223] The Federal Constitutional Court has held that private law structures such as those of the law of associations also have to be applied in a way that accommodates religious needs appropriately;[224] this autonomy right does not make much difference in practice.

*306.* The range of religious autonomy is rather large. The service rendered by religious communities is understood by state law to be a single whole. The right of self-determination is therefore not merely attributed to a religious community itself as a distinct entity but instead is something common to all institutions, which are connected in some way or another with the religious community, regardless of the legal form taken by those links. This is true so long as, according to their self-identity, their goals or duties are suitably carried out and are held to be true mandates of the religious community.[225] The term 'religious community' in Article 137 section 3 WRV, in conjunction with Article 140 GG, is thus interpreted in a wide sense. Religious autonomy is not only enjoyed by the religious community as a defined legal institution, that is, the core religious institution, but also by all institutions that are attached to this core, that is, the official religious community (to the 'constituted' religious community).[226] This means that hospitals, schools, kindergartens, homes for the elderly, etc., that are run by a religious community also enjoy this religious autonomy. There only needs to be a general link with the 'main' religious community: The institution may be defined in its statutes as Protestant or Roman Catholic and accepted as such by the main church; a bishop or other religious leader may hold a seat in the board of that institution. Because the big religious communities run social, health, and cultural institutions to a large extent and even own banks, this right to self-determination is of considerable social, legal, and political impact.

## §2. Limitations of the Right to Self-Determination

*307.* Self-determination of religious communities does not exist without limitations. These limitations provide protection for the rights and interests of others, of society and of the state. In German legal practice, it must be decided on a case-by-case basis where the limitations to the self-determination of religious communities exactly lie. These limitations result from an interpretation of the 'law that applies to all' as stated in Article 137 section 3 WRV in conjunction with Article 140 GG.

*308.* The 'law that applies to all' in the sense of Article 137 section 3 WRV in conjunction with Article 140 GG is not identical to a law of general application or a general law in the sense of other fundamental rights provisions of the German constitution. It has a special meaning. It is generally accepted to say that a law that

223. Axel Freiherr von Campenhausen & Heinrich de Wall, *Religionsverfassungsrecht*, 5th edn (Munich: C.H. Beck, 2022), 321.

224. BVerfG 5 Feb. 1991, BVerfGE 83, 341, 356; BVerfG 25 Mar. 1980, BVerfGE 53, 366, 401.

225. BVerfG 25 Mar. 1980, BVerfGE 53, 366 et seq.; BVerfG 4 Jun. 1985, BVerfGE 70, 138, 162 with further references.

226. BVerfG 11 Oct. 1977, BVerfGE 46, 73 et seq.

applies to all is only such a law that provides for the pressing needs of society as a whole. The right to self-determination cannot prevail against a general law that represents a provision of particular importance to the common weal.[227] Furthermore, a law that limits self-determination must again be interpreted narrowly in light of the high importance of religious self-determination.[228]

*309.* A 'law that applies to all' has been defined in German legal doctrine as a law that serves compelling requirements of a peaceful co-existence of state and church in a religiously neutral political community.[229] In this understanding, the limitations relevant to the self-determination of religious communities in German constitutional law and practice are sometimes regarded as being no different than the limitations set to the freedom of religion in Article 9 section 2 of the ECHR.[230]

*310.* German legal doctrine and court practice view the limitation clause of Article 137 section 3 WRV in conjunction with Article 140 GG in relation to the freedom protected: The guarantee of religious freedom has to be coordinated and balanced with the guarantee of other legal values that likewise belong to the order of the whole community as structured by the constitution and are important for it.[231] A fair balance has to be struck between the self-determination of religious communities and the other interests protected by the Constitution in the specific case.[232] This, in fact, is equivalent to what is required by the limitation clauses of Articles 8 and 9 of the ECHR.

*311.* The meaning and formulation of limitations of the right of self-determination is not uncontroversial. The case law of the Federal Constitutional Court has also produced some further interpretations of the concept of a 'law that applies to all' as a limitation to the self-determination of religious communities. The Federal Constitutional Court has distinguished between matters of religious communities that have no direct legal implications for the secular field and those matters that do have implications for the secular legal and societal field. In the first sphere, self-determination of religious communities faces no law that applies to all and thus faces no limitation whatsoever. In the other sphere, any general law would limit the self-determination of the religious communities.[233] However, it is almost impossible to draw a clear line between such spheres. Drawing such a line by a secular court would easily interfere with the right of religious communities to independently determine which of its activities are religious and which are not. A secular court would inevitably have to make decisions about the proximity of activities

227. BVerfG 21 Sep. 1976, BVerfGE 42, 312, 334; BVerfG 13 Dec. 1983, BVerfGE 66, 1, 20.
228. BVerfG 25 Mar. 1980, BverfGE 53, 366, 404; BVerfG 4 Jun. 1985, BverfGE 70, 138, 167; BVerfG 14 May 1986, BVerfGE 72, 278, 289.
229. Axel Freiherr von Campenhausen & Heinrich de Wall, *Religionsverfassungsrecht*, 5th edn (Munich: C.H. Beck, 2022), 134.
230. *Ibid.*
231. *Ibid.*, 135.
232. BVerfG 25 Mar. 1980, BVerfGE 53, 366, 400 et seq.; BVerfG 13 Dec. 1983, BVerfGE 66, 1, 22; BVerfG 4 Jun. 1985, BVerfGE 70, 138, 167; BVerfG 14 May 1986, BVerfGE 72, 278, 289.
233. BVerfG 17 Feb. 1965, BVerfGE 18, 385, 387 et seq.

to the teaching of the specific religious community, a task that is beyond the competencies of a secular court because it involves decisions in religious matters. Also, what constitutes a core issue of religious activity for one religious community need not be a core religious issue for another religious community.

*312.* Another interpretation taken up by the case law of the Federal Constitutional Court defines the law that applies to all as a law that has the same meaning for the religious communities as for everybody else, which therefore does not impose substantially greater burdens on religious communities than on anyone else.[234] Subject to that, a law breaches a community's right of self-determination when the religious community itself is not affected to the same extent as everyone else, but rather, within its special qualities as a religious community, its self-identity and in particular its spiritual-religious duty, is subject to particular disadvantages. However, this interpretation also leads to problems and ambiguities. There are laws that affect exclusively religious communities and in fact are meant to do that, while their legitimacy as a law limiting the autonomy rights of religious communities is beyond doubt. An example is given by the laws on the church tax; these laws provide limitations only for the activities of religious communities but clearly are necessary to protect the rights and interests of the church taxpayers. These laws put a burden only on religious communities with public law status and thus impose a substantially greater burden on them than on anyone else; yet within the system of the church tax, they are as such clearly in accordance with the constitution.

*313.* It is important for the understanding of this matter to note that the Federal Constitutional Court attributes major importance to the religious community's self-identity: What is meant by the community's own affairs is determined particularly by how the religious community itself views its own affairs. However, the competence to make a final decision based on the Basic Law is still reserved for the state courts. The central relevance of the right of self-determination of a religious community must furthermore be considered when defining the boundaries of this right.

*314.* A religious community's right to self-determination is not restricted to a narrowly drawn field of specifically 'ecclesiastical' activities. The idea of freedom of religious practice extends to preserve the right of self-determination in other areas that are also based on religious objectives, such as the running of hospitals, kindergartens, retirement homes, private schools, and universities.

*315.* In very substantial ways, the large churches in Germany provide social services, particularly in the form of the Caritas of the Catholic Church and the Diaconical Works of the Evangelical Church. Without these services, the guarantees of a social state in Article 20 section 1, Article 23 section 1, and Article 28 section 1 GG would be mere empty platitudes. All these activities are part of what, for many religious communities, religion is really about.

234. BVerfG 21 Sep. 1976, BVerfGE 42, 312, 334.

*316.* Also, taking into account the status of a public corporation, this approach has led the Federal Constitutional Court to regard religious hospitals as not falling under the state's insolvency laws, even when, according to the hospitals' statutes, they are only loosely associated with the particular organized church. It would not be compatible with the idea of the right of self-determination that a judicially ordered administrative receiver should act within the particular structure or organization of a religious establishment.[235]

## §3. Religious Communities and State Court System

*317.* The space that the framework of the right of self-determination offers to religious communities has been used by the large churches in Germany to work out their own detailed and voluminous internal legal systems with their own peculiarities and particular church emphases, which operate in parallel with state law. Within the framework of the right of self-determination, there is also a jurisdictional system belonging to the respective religious community. So far as the right of self-determination applies, the jurisdiction of the religious community is exclusively the community's own affair and religious matters settled internally are not reviewed by public courts. In detail, however, there is still much that is a matter of debate. New developments indicate that state courts are becoming more ready to interfere in matters of religious communities, but they give ample space to the right of self-determination in assessing each individual case.

*318.* There is, for example, considerable debate about the powers of state courts to decide on internal matters of religious communities, such as the status of priests. The Federal Constitutional Court and the Federal Administrative Court have insisted on far-reaching exemption of religious communities from state jurisdiction: Complaints to state courts against internal decisions of religious communities are inadmissible. The Federal Supreme Court (*Bundesgerichtshof*), however, and some other courts have held that such complaints are admissible, but the state court must respect the religious community's right to self-determination in its material decision on the matter. Although the decisions of the Federal Constitutional Court have binding power on all state authorities, including other courts (§31 section 1 Federal Constitutional Court Act (BVerfGG)), this rule applies only when the relevant legal questions at stake are the same; deviations in substance therefore remain possible between the court practice of the Federal Constitutional Court and other courts. The whole issue of the right to self-determination of religious communities and the state court powers remains in flux. However, when the religious community makes use of secular law, such as labour law, the recourse to the state courts is admissible; state courts then must respect the religious community's right to self-determination and bring it into a fair balance with other rights and interests.

---

235. BVerfG 13 Dec. 1983, BVerfGE 66, 1 et seq.

*319.* The Federal Constitutional Court has declared a constitutional complaint against a decision of a church court inadmissible.[236] A pastor of the Protestant Church in the Rhineland had been transferred by the church authorities into the so-called waiting status because the parish community and the pastor had come into severe disagreement. This waiting status means not only a cut in pay but also the chance to look for another appointment within the church; if no other post can be found, the pastor will be compulsorily retired. The church court had upheld that decision and the pastor had appealed against the church court decision to the Federal Constitutional Court. The Federal Constitutional Court held that constitutional complaints are admissible only against violations of fundamental rights by public authorities; public authorities, in this meaning, are only actions by state authorities and the effects that emerge from that. Purely internal actions of religious communities are thus not subject to constitutional complaint.[237] The Federal Constitutional Court reiterated that, according to the Basic Law, each religious community governs and administers its affairs independently within the limitations provided by the law that applies to all. By virtue of this, the state recognizes the right to self-determination of the religious communities, which by their nature are independent of the state and do not have their powers deriving from the state. The consequence of this is that the state must not interfere with their internal affairs.[238]

*320.* The Federal Constitutional Court also reiterated that the independence of religious communities is not put into question when they have the status of a public law corporation. In view of the religious and denominational neutrality of the state enshrined in the Basic Law, this summarizing description of the status of religious communities does not mean an equation with other public law corporations that are organizations integrated into the state. This status for religious communities only means the attribution of a public status that puts them into a special position in relation to religious communities with private law status but does not subject them to any special church supremacy of the state or increased state supervision. Following from this public law status and from the public role of the religious communities that they draw from their special assignment and by which they differ from other entities of society, the powers of the religious communities are not state powers. Only insofar as religious communities exercise powers that have been conferred upon them by the state or that reach over into the sphere of the state, the religious communities also indirectly exercise state powers with the consequence that their self-determination is subjected to a justified limitation.[239]

*321.* If state courts decided about the affairs of religious communities, they would influence these affairs even if trying to respect the independence of the religious community. It is a matter of experience that whenever state courts deal concretely with conflicting interests and rights in an individual case, this can lead to a

236. BVerfG (K) 9 Dec. 2008, *Neue Juristische Wochenschrift* 62 (2009): 1195 et seq.
237. *See also* BVerfG 17 Feb. 1965, BVerfGE 18, 385, 386; consistent practice: BVerfG 21 Sep. 1976, BVerfGE 42, 312, 334 et seq.; BVerfG 13 Dec. 1983, BVerfGE 66, 1, 20; BVerfG 14 May 1986, BVerfGE 72, 278, 289; BVerfG 27 Jan. 2004, BVerfGE 111, 1, 5.
238. *See also* BVerfG 17 May 1965, BVerfGE 18, 385, 386.
239. *See also ibid.*, 387.

gradual increase in the intensity of judicial control and thus is in danger of disregarding the religious legitimacy of religious norms and in consequence, violates the neutrality of the state in religious matters. This, however, would be especially problematic in the sensitive field of religious offices, the self-determination of which is expressly guaranteed in Article 137 section 3 clause 2 WRV. The status of a pastor within the Protestant Church is a matter that has not been transferred to the church by the state but is a genuine part of its self-determined internal affairs.

*322.* Although the Federal Constitutional Court thus denied its own competence to decide in the matter of the parish pastor case, it nevertheless made ample statements regarding the merits of the case in substance.[240] It seems that the Federal Constitutional Court felt that it should give its own opinion about the legitimacy of the norms and actions of the church in the case, perhaps in order to contribute to legal peace and convince the pastor that he had not been ill-treated, even though a decision in the matter was beyond the competence of the Federal Constitutional Court. The Federal Constitutional Court held that Article 33 section 5 GG, which provides for certain structures in state civil service, does not apply to internal matters of religious communities even when they have the status of public law corporations. Also, sub-constitutional state provisions about the civil service do not apply to the civil service of religious communities. The Federal Constitutional Court also held that the religious authorities had not violated the general prohibition of arbitrary action. Because all these statements of the Federal Constitutional Court concerning the substantive law are merely obiter dicta, this does not mean that the general prohibition of arbitrary action should apply within religious communities. What exactly 'arbitrary' means depends on different reasons in the secular and the religious fields; what can be arbitrary in secular matters can be well-founded in religious ones.

*323.* The Federal Supreme Court decided the general question in a different way that tried a new approach as compared to the previous general court practice.[241] Because the Federal Supreme Court did so before the Federal Constitutional Court took its decision on the parish pastor case,[242] this Federal Constitutional Court's decision can be viewed as a direct (and rejecting) answer to the new approach of the Federal Supreme Court. The Federal Supreme Court had to decide about the claim of an officer of the Salvation Army who had been dismissed by the church to be paid a salary by his church. According to the principles of the Salvation Army, an officer is equivalent to a priest in other religious communities; the relationship between the officer and the Salvation Army is explicitly not that of a labour or other secular contract but is a purely spiritual relationship. The Federal Supreme Court has held that there is a right to legal recourse to a state court for a claim of pay by a priest, even when the merits of the case depend on the question of whether the cleric has been effectively dismissed from his or her service. The right to self-determination of a religious community does not limit the duty of the state to give

240. BVerfG (K) 9 Dec. 2008, *Deutsches Verwaltungsblatt* 124 (2009): 238 et seq.
241. BGH 28 Mar. 2003, BGHZ 154, 306 et seq.
242. BVerfG (K) 9 Dec. 2008, *Deutsches Verwaltungsblatt* 124 (2009): 238 et seq.

recourse to a state court, but it does limit the range of review: (1) if there is the possibility of recourse to an internal court of the religious community, there is no legitimate interest to take legal action before the state court before the exhaustion of these internal remedies; (2) an action of the religious community that is based on its autonomous law can be reviewed by a state court only in view of its effectiveness, not in view of its legality; the review concerning the effectiveness of the measure is limited to whether it violates fundamental principles of the legal order as they are expressed in the general prohibition of arbitrariness as enshrined in Article 3 GG, the good morals as protected in §138 Civil Code or in the *ordre public* as provided for in Article 6 Introductory Law of the Civil Code (EGBGB); (3) decisions of courts of religious communities being res judicata also are subject to review as of effectiveness only. The question of whether a cleric has effectively been dismissed from office is a matter of the autonomous decision of the religious community.

*324.* The general question of access to state courts in matters of religious communities remains difficult and is open to further development. The constitutional guarantee of self-determination of religious communities does not mean exclusion from the state legal order in the meaning of legally empty space in the field of access to courts, but it creates, on the contrary, a special status within the state legal order respecting the common manifestation of freedom.[243] This not only follows from Article 4 GG in the meaning of common freedom of religion or belief, but it is also a manifestation of the institutional guarantee of the independence of religious communities from the state as enshrined in Article 137 WRV in conjunction with Article 140 GG.

The German decisions in the parish pastor and Salvation Army cases have been upheld by the European Court of Human Rights,[244] allowing for ample autonomy of religious communities.

243. *Ibid.*

244. ECHR, *Baudler v. Germany*, 6 Dec. 2011, appl. no. 38254/04 (parish pastor); ECHR, *Reuter v. Germany*, 6 Dec. 2012, appl. no. 39775/04 (parish pastor); ECHR, *Müller v. Germany*, 6 Dec. 2012, appl. no. 12986/04 (Salvation Army).

## Chapter 3. Fundamental Rights and Religious Communities

*325.* Religious communities fully enjoy fundamental rights. The only exceptions are those human rights, such as human dignity or freedom of conscience, that by their very nature cannot apply to legal persons but to individual persons only. As has been described above in paragraph 190, Article 19 section 3 GG provides that the fundamental rights also apply to domestic legal persons to the extent that the nature of such rights permits. Because religion and belief are matters that usually are experienced and lived in a community with others, religious communities do enjoy the freedom of religion or belief as guaranteed in Article 4 sections 1 and 2 GG.[245] Thus, all forms of religious associations and organizations as such enjoy freedom of religion or belief in their own right.[246] It has not yet been decided whether foreign religious communities, that are those which have their seat abroad, enjoy full freedom of religion or belief – which of course foreign individual persons do. In any case, the right to the legally provided judge (Article 101 GG),[247] the right to have a court hearing (Article 103 GG),[248] but also the right to petition (Article 17 GG) and the right to access a court against state action (Article 19 section 4) are also guaranteed for foreign religious communities.[249] Furthermore, on the level of ordinary law, foreign religious communities do enjoy the most part of relevant rights. This is more the case for religious communities that have their seat in a Member State of the EU or in a country with which bilateral treaties cover the matter and that consequently must not be discriminated against.[250]

*326.* Religious communities that have the status of public law corporations also fully enjoy fundamental rights in the scope of Article 19 section 3 GG because this status does not incorporate them into the structure of the state (Article 136 section 1 WRV in conjunction with Article 140 GG).[251] The status of religious communities as public law corporations is a status sui generis.

*327.* Religious communities are not, at least not directly, obliged by human rights guarantees of the Basic Law. Regarding the binding force of fundamental rights beyond state entities, the general principles of the horizontal application of fundamental rights apply. Private persons, however, are essentially not bound by fundamental rights – fundamental rights are intended to create rights for the individual, not duties.

*328.* The same principles apply to religious communities that have the status of public law corporations. This status does not integrate them into state structures. It

245. BVerfG 16 Oct. 1968, BVerfGE 24, 236, 246 et seq.
246. *See* BVerfG 5 Feb. 1991, BVerfGE 83, 341, 351.
247. BVerfG 12 Apr. 1983, BVerfGE 64, 1, 11.
248. *Ibid.*
249. Hans Dieter Jarass in *Grundgesetz für die Bundesrepublik Deutschland. Kommentar*, Hans Dieter Jarass & Bodo Pieroth eds, 17th edn (Munich: C.H. Beck, 2022), Art. 19, n. 26.
250. *Ibid.*
251. BVerfG 2 May 1967, BVerfGE 21, 362, 374; BVerfG 21 Sep. 1976, BVerfGE 42, 312, 321 et seq.; BVerfG 8 Jul. 1982, BVerfGE 61, 82, 102.

is a status that supports the freedom of religious communities and does not diminish it. Also, when religious communities are corporations under public law, they enjoy the full range of fundamental rights protection. The only exception to this is when a religious community exercises state-like powers in special cases: Religious communities that are corporations under public law are bound to observe fundamental rights when they make use of sovereign powers transferred to them by the state, such as the right to levy the church tax.[252]

*329.* The only situation in which private persons are directly bound by fundamental rights (so-called direct horizontal effect, in German '*unmittelbare Drittwirkung*') is set out in Article 9 section 3 GG, which guarantees the freedom to form coalitions. (The term 'horizontal application' is in contrast to the 'vertical application' between state and individual.) However, because of their prevailing freedom of religion and the right to self-determination of religious communities, this exception to the general rule does not apply to religious communities. The right to form associations for the protection and promotion of working and economic conditions is guaranteed for every person and for all trades and professions. Agreements that attempt to limit or hamper the exercise of this right are void, and measures with such an object are illegal. This right is particularly relevant to the formation of trade unions and employers' associations, the organization of industrial action, and the conclusion of agreements regulating wages and working conditions. Article 9 section 3 GG thus directly forbids an employer from making it a condition for employment of a worker that the worker belongs to a particular union or that the worker does not belong to a union. Otherwise, there is no direct horizontal application of fundamental rights. At the very most, the prohibition of any action to hamper an attempt to gain election to the federal or state legislatures contained in Article 48 GG can also be considered to fall within this category. Again, however, freedom of religion and the right to self-determination of religious communities prevail and allow them to prevent their officeholders from taking up public office by stating incompatibilities in this respect.[253]

*330.* However, the idea of indirect horizontal application (*mittelbare Drittwirkung*) has been accepted. This is the case also for religious communities. Fundamental rights permeate all areas of the law because they represent a constitutional decision in favour of certain values. In the interpretation and application of ordinary law, in other words, all laws inferior in status to the constitution, the value judgments contained in fundamental rights must be given effect. Human dignity may also not be injured, and freedom and equality must be respected, and this also applies to relations between private individuals. However, in this situation, different fundamental rights that are in principle of equal status usually stand in conflict with one another: for example, the right of the landlord to the protection of his or her property and the right of the tenant to artistic freedom when the tenant wishes to practice his or her trumpet late at night and disturbs the other tenants. Here, the law must find a solution that gives reasonable regard to the rights of all the parties with

252. BVerfG 31 Mar. 1971, BVerfGE 30, 415, 422.
253. BVerfG 21 Sep. 1976, BVerfGE 42, 312 et seq.

reference to the basic value decisions contained in the constitution. This is a balancing process in which an appropriate balance respecting all the relevant fundamental rights at stake in the issue has to be found. All these principles also apply to religious communities. It has to be seen that the practice, at least of the higher courts, attributes high weight and impact to religious rights in the relevant balancing processes.

# Chapter 4. Contractual Religious Freedom

## §1. Basic Principles and Terminology

*331.* Treaties between the state and religious communities are a significant feature of the law on religion. Many parts of the law on religion are dealt with in such treaties. There are very many of them. The legal status of these treaties varies. Many of the treaties' provisions repeat constitutional guarantees. This does not alter the status of these guarantees, but it is also not irrelevant because, by way of including them in treaty law, these guarantees gain a further basis in mutual agreement: When the constitution is changed against the accord in the treaty, the treaty is violated.

*332.* There is no overall accepted legal terminology as to the names of such treaties, but in general, the term 'state-church treaties' (*Staatskirchenverträge*) is used as an overall name that covers concordats and other treaties between the state and religious communities. The term 'state-church treaties' seems to be somewhat outdated in view of the growing religious pluralism in Germany; there are treaties also with non-Christian religious and belief entities such as the Jewish faith communities, with Muslim associations, and with atheist belief communities. However, no new term has yet been coined or found general acceptance. The state can conclude treaties with any kind of religious community; it does not matter whether these are private law or public law entities.

*333.* Concordats are treaties between the state and the Holy See. The perhaps most visible of these is the 1933 *Reichskonkordat*, the concordat concluded between the German *Reich* and the Holy See. Many *Länder*, too, have concluded concordats with the Holy See. There are also many treaties between the state and the individual Roman Catholic dioceses. The name 'concordat' is reserved for those treaties of the state with the Holy See that have a fundamental and encompassing significance. Treaties of similar significance between the state and the Protestant churches are usually called Evangelical Church treaties (*Evangelische Kirchenverträge*); others are called according to their specific contents, such as financial treaties, school treaties, etc. The term 'treaty' is usually taken for those arrangements that need a consenting decision of parliament on the side of the state and in the case of treaties with the Protestant churches by the church synod. Other stipulations are called according to their individual legal meaning, such as agreement or settlement.

## §2. Historical Development

*334.* While treaties between the secular powers and the Roman Catholic Church date back far into history, such as the 1122 Concordat of Worms between Pope Calixtus II and Holy Roman Emperor Henry V or the 1516 Concordat of Bologna between King Francis I of France and Pope Leo X, it is in the nineteenth century that the instrument of church-state treaties assumed significant relevance in structuring the relationship between state and churches in Germany. It can be said that the growing significance of this legal instrument during the nineteenth century is an expression as well as a means for the then-growing tendency towards separation between the state and the churches. The treaty law came to flourish during the period of the Weimar constitution between 1919 and 1933. Numerous state-church treaties were concluded at that time. Many of those treaties are still in force today. Concordats were concluded with Bavaria (29 March 1924), Prussia (14 June 1929), and Baden (12 October 1932). Treaties with the Protestant churches followed: Bavaria (15 November 1924), Prussia (11 May 1931), and Baden (14 November 1932). This connection between Catholic and Protestant treaties can already be seen as an expression of the principle of parity between these churches in the German law on religion.

## §3. Right and Duty to Conclude Treaties

*335.* The German constitutions that are currently in force accept the legitimacy of structuring the relationship between the state and religious communities by way of treaties. While there is no explicit enabling norm to conclude such treaties in the Basic Law, it does accept the possibility of treaties between the state and religious communities in its Article 140 in conjunction with Article 138 section 1 WRV and in Article 123 section 2 GG. Also, in view of the *Reichskonkordat*, Article 123 GG provides that subject to all rights and objections of interested parties, treaties concluded by the German *Reich* concerning matters within the legislative competence of the *Länder* under the Basic Law shall remain in force, provided they are and continue to be valid under general principles of law, until new treaties are concluded by the authorities competent under this Basic Law, or until they are in some other way terminated pursuant to their provisions. Article 138 section 1 WRV guarantees the rights of religious societies to public subsidies on the basis of a law, contract, or special grant until they are redeemed by legislation of the *Länder*. These provisions of the Basic Law refer positively to state-church treaties and do not put their general legitimacy into any question. Also, the constitutions of the *Länder* acknowledge the basic possibility of state-church treaties;[254] the constitution of Hesse explicitly provides that it is the task of 'law or agreement' to clearly delimitate the spheres of the state and churches from each other. While thus the legal possibility of concluding such treaties is beyond doubt, there is no constitutional duty of either side to structure their relationships in the forms of this legal instrument. However, the Federal

254. Article 8, Constitution of Baden-Württemberg (LV BW); Art. 145 Constitution of the Free State of Bavaria (BayVerf); Art. 50, s. 1 Constitution of Berlin (VvB); Art. 91, s. 2 Constitution of Brandenburg (BbgVerf); Art. 103, s. 2 Constitution of Hesse (HessVerf); Art. 35, s. 2 Constitution of Lower Saxony (NdsVerf); Arts 21–23 Constitution of North Rhine-Westphalia (NRWVerf); Art. 101 Constitution of Rhineland-Palatinate (RLPVerf); Art. 35, s. 2 Constitution of Saarland (SLVerf); Art. 109, s. 2 Constitution of the Free State of Saxony (SächsVerf); Art. 32, s. 4 Constitution of Saxony-Anhalt (Verf LSA); Art. 30, s. 2 Constitution of Schleswig-Holstein (SHVerf); Arts 76, 77 Constitution of the Free State of Thuringia (ThürVerf); Art. 47, s. 2 Constitution of Mecklenburg-Western Pomerania (Verf M-V).

Constitutional Court was wrong when it stated in an early decision that it is completely left to the discretion of the state whether and with which religious communities it concludes such treaties.[255] While the Federal Constitutional Court has had no opportunity yet to discharge its practice on the matter, today, it is generally accepted that the constitutional principle of equal treatment and especially parity between the religious communities obliges the state to conclude a treaty with other religious communities in a matter when it has concluded such a treaty with one of them and when the circumstances are the same.[256] The state-church treaties themselves also oblige the state to act in the form of agreement and treaty in cases of amendments to such treaties. Finally, constitutional provisions oblige the state to use the form of agreements in those cases in which the constitution makes an offer to religious communities the acceptance of which it cannot enforce upon them. This is the case, for example, when the state wants to establish theological faculties in state universities: It can do so only with the consent of the relevant religious community. Also, the state cannot enforce the use of the church tax system upon any individual religious community. The introduction of this system depends on the agreement with the respective religious community.

*336.* State neutrality in religious matters is the basic idea in favour of treaty law in respect of the relationship between state and religious communities. The state has no competence in religious matters because the state is a secular institution. Thus, whenever religious matters are at stake, the state can only take measures when the respective religious side agrees, failing which the state would unduly intrude into the religious sphere. One-sided decisions by the state would amount to state supremacy over religious communities, and the state would violate its own identity as a secular body. Furthermore, the instrument of treaty law allows for individual and specific responses to different religious needs of the various and different religious communities. Freedom of religion can thus be served. In any case, treaties between state and non-state institutions are nothing exclusive for religious communities: The state concludes treaties and other agreements with many institutions of civil society and other non-governmental bodies. Finally, it is a well-established phenomenon that the state very often does not enact laws one-sidedly but almost traditionally contacts and involves the people and institutions that are potentially affected by the prospective law in the process of law-making. While in the past, some authors have called state-church treaties questionable from a democratic point

255. BVerfG 28 Apr. 1965, BVerfGE 19, 1, 12.

256. Martin Heckel, 'Die religionsrechtliche Parität', in *Handbuch des Staatskirchenrechts der Bundesrepublik Deutschland*, Joseph Listl & Dietrich Pirson eds, vol. 1, 2nd edn (Berlin: Duncker & Humblot, 1994), 613 et seq.; Stephan Mückl, 'Grundlagen des Staatskirchenrechts', in *Freiheitsrechte*, vol. 7 of *Handbuch des Staatsrechts der Bundesrepublik Deutschland*, Josef Isensee & Paul Kirchhof eds, 3rd edn (Heidelberg: C.F. Müller, 2009), §159, n. 74.

of view,[257] they are, on the contrary, an expression of democratic law-making and respond to the nature of pluralism. They are and must always be based on the democratically founded law and constitution.

## §4. Nature of Treaties

*337.* There is some debate about the general legal nature of state-church treaties. Today, neither the medieval papal privilege theory, whereby concordats are privileges granted to the state which can be freely revoked by the Pope, has any legal relevance anymore, nor the nineteenth-century theory that held concordats to be no more but a legally irrelevant consent of the church to a law given by the state.[258] The current opinion still seems to distinguish between concordats and evangelical state-church treaties.[259] Concordats are seen as normal international public law treaties or at least quasi-international public law treaties to which the principles of general public international law apply. The evangelical state-church treaties are seen to be coordinative treaties that are neither part of state law nor public international law but constitute public law in delimitating the spheres of church and state. Concordats and evangelical state-church treaties in this approach differ only in that the latter do not form part of public international law; there is no other difference in nature or legal rank. This theoretical approach, however, seems to be somewhat outdated in focussing exclusively on treaties that have been concluded with the traditional big churches in Germany; they also concentrate misleadingly on the major and fundamental treaties while not sufficiently taking into account the many smaller agreements on the level of dioceses or (parish) communities. Moreover, the practical relevance of the theoretical dispute is questionable.

## §5. Treaties and General State Law

*338.* Legally important is the question of the relationship between state law and treaties. The more important treaties are incorporated into the state legal system by way of ordinary law. This law makes the treaty applicable within the sphere of the state. In general, the principle of *lex posterior derogat legi priori* (i.e., the later law derogates the preceding law) applies. A subsequent state law takes legal preference over a state-church treaty that has been incorporated into the state legal system by

257. Hermann Weber, *Grundprobleme des Staatskirchenrecht* (Bad Homburg: Gehlen, 1970), 50; Helmut Quaritsch, 'Kirchenvertrag und Staatsgesetz', in *Hamburger Festschrift für Friedrich Schack zu seinem 80. Geburtstag am 1. Oktober 1966*, Friedrich Schack & Hans-Peter Ipsen eds (Hamburg: Metzner, 1966), 125 et seq.

258. For the latter *see* Rudolph Sohm, *Das Verhältnis von Staat und Kirche aus dem Begriff von Staat und Kirche entwickelt* (Tübingen: Laupp, 1873), 53.

259. Dietrich Pirson, 'Vertragsstaatskirchenrecht', in *Evangelisches Staatslexikon*, Roman Herzog ed., vol. 2, 3rd edn (Stuttgart: Kreuz, 1987), c. 3814–3827; for more specific distinctions *see* Alexander Hollerbach, 'Die vertragsrechtlichen Grundlagen des Staatskirchenrechts', in *Handbuch des Staatskirchenrechts der Bundesrepublik Deutschland*, Joseph Listl & Dietrich Pirson eds, vol. 1, 2nd edn (Berlin: Duncker & Humblot, 1994), 273 et seq.

way of a law. Agreements that have not been made applicable by law have a lesser rank than the law anyway and have to give way to the higher-ranking law. Thus, the subsequent law that is in conflict with the treaty obligations of the state remains valid and applicable. This is a consequence of the principle of democratic sovereignty. However, while the state can legally contradict the treaty, it does in fact violate the treaty; the contradicting law is valid but constitutes a violation of the treaty. As is often put in other words: The state can break the treaty, but it must not.

*339.* The rank of the treaty within the hierarchy of norms of the state legal system also has to be seen in the light of some specific provisions. In Baden-Wuerttemberg, the 1953 *Land* constitution provides in its Article 8 that 'rights and duties that follow from treaties with the Protestant and the Catholic Church remain unaffected by this constitution'. This provision does not give state-church treaty law a higher rank than the constitution of Baden-Wuerttemberg, but it determines that in the case of doubt or conflict, the treaty takes precedence by way of constitutional law prevalence. This means that the treaty prevails also over ordinary conflicting law even when this law has been enacted after the treaty. Article 23 section 2 of the constitution of North Rhine-Westphalia states that the consent of the treaty's parties and a law of the *Land* are needed in order to change existing treaties and to conclude new treaties with the Catholic and the Evangelical Church. Similarly, Article 67 clause 2 of the constitution of Hesse provides that no law is valid that is in conflict with the rules of public international law or with a state treaty. These rules, however, apply only within those *Länder* and for the state-church treaties that have been concluded by them.

## §6. The Power to Conclude Treaties

*340.* The distribution of the competencies to conclude treaties with religious subjects of public international law between the Federal Republic of Germany and the *Länder* is somewhat debated. This debate is of practical relevance almost exclusively in view of treaties with the Holy See. Article 32 sections 1 and 3 GG provide that relations with foreign states shall be conducted by the Federation; insofar as the *Länder* have the power to legislate, they may conclude treaties with foreign states with the consent of the federal government. The Federal Constitutional Court and most authors hold that Article 32 GG only applies to secular entities of public international law;[260] relations with the Holy See are not included in that concept. Thus, following the general distribution of competencies laid down in Articles 30 and 70 GG, the right to conclude state-church treaties is subject to the general competency according to the matter at stake. Matters that are in the competency of the *Länder* can be regulated by way of state-church treaties by the *Länder* also in international

260. BVerfG 26 Mar. 1957, BVerfGE 6, 309, 362; Rudolf Streinz in *Grundgesetz. Kommentar*, Michael Sachs ed., 9th edn (Munich: C.H. Beck, 2021), Art. 32 GG, n. 16; for the opposing opinion Albrecht Weber in *Grundgesetz. Mitarbeiterkommentar*, Dieter C. Umbach & Thomas Clemens eds (Heidelberg: C.F. Müller, 2002), Art. 32 GG, n. 15.

relations, while the Federation can conclude church treaties in matters of its competency such as the military chaplaincy or spiritual care in the federal police. The *Länder* do not need the consent of the Federation when concluding public international law state-church treaties, but they have to inform the Federation of such activity, as follows from Article 32 GG and the principle of federal loyalty.

*341.* However, while the *Länder* can conclude public international law treaties in the field of religious matters, they cannot establish diplomatic representations abroad, something that would apply for diplomatic representations at the Holy See; Article 87 section 1 GG prohibits such activity by stating that the foreign service shall be conducted by federal administrative authorities with their own administrative substructures.

*342.* Because neither concordats nor the other state-church treaties are treaties with foreign states in the meaning of Article 59 section 1 clause 2 GG, it is not the federal president who has the formal power to conclude these treaties when the Federation is the partner of the treaty. However, by way of diplomatic courtesy, the federal president is active in this way; this also applies to treaties with the Protestant Church by way of parity.

*343.* The more general and substantive treaties need the consent of parliament. Article 59 section 1 clause 1 GG provides this explicitly for treaties that regulate the political relations of the Federation or relate to subjects of federal legislation; such treaties require the consent or participation, in the form of a federal law, of the bodies responsible in such a case for the enactment of federal law. This certainly applies to treaties with the Holy See; parity requires this also for other equivalent treaties with religious communities, and political practice acts accordingly. Article 23 section 2 of the constitution of North Rhine-Westphalia explicitly requires a formal law for treaties with religious communities. Otherwise, the general provisions on state treaties apply, which require a formal law. In the absence of such provisions, the general principle can be drawn upon that the government needs the consent of parliament when concluding treaties that regulate legislative matters.[261] Agreements of lesser fundamental importance that regulate details are usually concluded in the form of administrative agreements. These do not need parliamentary consent.

## §7. Interpretation of Treaty Law

*344.* In the interpretation of state-church treaties,[262] the general principles of public international law are applied *mutatis mutandis*. State-church treaties also have to be interpreted in a way that keeps them, if at all possible, in conformity with

261. BVerfG 28 Jul. 1955, BVerfGE 4, 250, 276.
262. Cf. Alexander Hollerbach, 'Die vertragsrechtlichen Grundlagen des Staatskirchenrechts', in *Handbuch des Staatskirchenrechts der Bundesrepublik Deutschland*, Joseph Listl & Dietrich Pirson eds, vol. 1, 2nd edn (Berlin: Duncker & Humblot, 1994), 279 et seq.

the state constitution and with the parties' intentions. State-church treaties usually include a clause according to which differences in opinion between the partners of the treaty are to be settled in a friendly way – the friendly settlement clause. This does not exclude the final use of litigation or mediation but stresses the priority of attempts to do without such means; it also is an expression of the fundamental idea that the relationship between the state and religious communities is best structured in trustful and loyal cooperation. Oftentimes, this idea is further elaborated in the treaties by way of structured procedures that require regular contact between the partners of the treaty.[263]

## §8. Termination of Treaties

*345.* Usually, the more fundamental state-church treaties are concluded unlimited in time. Lacking a specific termination clause, such treaties can be terminated in case of mutual consent; they may also consensually declare the treaty or certain of its clauses to be suspended. In the case of a serious change of circumstances, the *clausula rebus sic stantibus* applies; each of the partners can then give notice of termination of the treaty within an appropriate time period. Such one-sided termination presupposes that all means of the friendly settlement clause, which such treaties usually entail, have been unsuccessfully exhausted.

*346.* Changes in the territory of the religious community that can happen by way of changing the circumscription of dioceses or *Land* churches do not affect the validity of the state-church treaty. The same applies in principle in the case of a change of partner on the side of the religious community; this can happen when two or more *Land* churches merge, or a religious community splits; however, in serious cases, the *clausula rebus sic stantibus* clause can take effect. Equivalent principles apply on the side of the state: State practice, especially after the Second World War, has respected that changes in territory on the side of the state do not affect the validity of the state-church treaties; the newly founded state takes over the treaty relationships for its territory as a partner with full rights and obligations. An example of this is the legal situation in the *Land* Rhineland-Palatinate: The *Land* Rhineland-Palatinate was founded after the Second World War on 30 August 1946; the 1929 concordat between the Holy See and Prussia still applies for the formerly Prussian parts of the territory of Rhineland-Palatinate, while the 1924 concordat between the Holy See and Bavaria applies for the formerly Bavarian parts of the *Land* as does the 1933 concordat between the Holy See and the German *Reich*.[264] The legal situation in other German *Länder* is similarly complicated. Finally, for those changes of state territory that have effect in the field of public international law, specific principles apply. When the territory of the state expands, the state-church treaty does

263. For example, Art. 9, s. 1, cl. 1 Concordat between the Holy See and the Land Lower Saxony (NdsKonkordat).

264. Act concerning the concordat of 29 Apr. 1969 between Rhineland-Palatinate and the Holy See amending the concordational clauses in Rhineland-Palatinate of 20 Nov. 1969 (KonkordatErgG RP).

not automatically follow the expansion, as would be the case under general principles of public international law; rather, the expansion of the treaty would need the consent of both partners of the treaty. The diminution of the state territory does not affect the validity of the state-church treaty in the remaining territory, while for the ceded or separated territory, the treaty loses its validity when one of the partners so invokes.

## §9. Legal Enforcement

*347.* The state-church treaties often have specific clauses on arbitration and litigation. Apart from that, disagreements on individual rights and obligations can be solved under normal court procedures, mostly before the administrative courts, but also by way of constitutional complaints by the religious community. A special provision is Article 130 section 1 clause 2 Constitution of Rhineland-Palatinate, whereby every corporation under public law that believes its rights to be violated can seek redress from the *Land* Constitutional Court against a (*Land*) law or action of a state constitutional organ. Also, European law, such as the ECHR and the protections offered by the EU court system, can provide legal protection against the violation of state-church treaties.

## §10. The *Reichskonkordat*

*348.* The *Reichskonkordat*, that is, the 1933 concordat between the Holy See and the German *Reich*,[265] is still in force today. It was signed on 20 July 1933 by Eugenio Cardinal Pacelli and Franz von Papen on behalf of Pope Pius XI and President Paul von Hindenburg, respectively. The ratification documents were exchanged on 10 September 1933. Negotiations about a concordat for the whole of the German *Reich* between the German government and the Holy See had started as early as 1919, and various steps were taken to proceed with the issue; however, these negotiations were difficult and overshadowed by divergent priorities on both sides. It was only when Adolf Hitler was appointed Chancellor of the German *Reich* on 30 January 1933 that the negotiations were revived again. Adolf Hitler saw his interest in the concordat in order to stabilize the rule of National Socialism in Germany, to counteract international mistrust, and to eliminate 'Political Catholicism' within Germany. In fact, the German Nazi government made far-reaching concessions to the Holy See that had not been offered by previous governments of the Weimar Republic; the only substantial concession on the side of the Holy See was the 'depoliticization clause' of Article 32 and also of Article 31 *Reichskonkordat*. By these provisions, the Holy See promised to issue provisions for the exclusion of clerics and members of religious orders from membership in political parties, and from

265. *See* Rudolf Morsey & Alexander Hollerbach, 'Reichskonkordat', in *Staatslexikon*, Görres-Gesellschaft, vol. 4, 7th edn (Freiburg: Herder, 1988), c. 787–792; Stewart A. Stehlin ed., *Weimar and the Vatican 1919–1933* (Princeton: Princeton University Press, 1983).

engaging in work on their behalf. The Holy See thus accepted the factual development and policy of the Nazi government towards the prohibition of other political parties; this development had found an expression on the Catholic side by the self-dissolution of the Catholic Centre-Party (*Deutsche Zentrumspartei*) on 5 July 1933 that had forestalled the party's forcible dissolution by the Nazi government. However, while the Nazi government did violate many of the provisions of the concordat on many occasions during the course of its rule – as had been foreseen by the Catholic Church – the *Reichskonkordat* did provide the Catholic Church with some substantial protection against Nazi arbitrary action. When the Nazi government violated the concordat, bishops and the papacy protested against these violations; protests culminated in the 1937 papal encyclical '*Mit brennender Sorge*' (With Burning Concern) of Pope Pius XI. For the Nazi government, the *Reichskonkordat* was the third international agreement that it was able to conclude, and it provided an international reputation. The *Reichskonkordat*, after all that, does in fact suffer from this initial history and from the initial meaning of some of its provisions. However, its individual provisions, which are still in force today and interpreted correctly, are in harmony with the contemporary democratic order and the rule of law.

*349.* Today's binding force of the *Reichskonkordat* and the scope thereof is subject to some debate and uncertainty. When the *Land* Lower Saxony adopted a new school law after the Second World War, the Holy See complained that it violated the terms of the concordat. The federal government called upon the Federal Constitutional Court for clarification. In its ruling of 26 March 1957,[266] the Federal Constitutional Court decided that the circumstances surrounding the conclusion of the concordat did not invalidate it. Considering that the Basic Law grants authority in school matters to the *Länder*, it ruled that the federal government has no authority to intervene in these matters, and the *Länder* had no obligation against the Federation to observe the concordat. The Federal Constitutional Court has not decided with binding effect on an obligation of the *Länder* to observe the concordat directly vis-à-vis the Holy See. While the binding force of the *Reichskonkordat* vis-à-vis the German *Länder* remains disputed, solutions have been found in most matters of practical importance. The new concordats between the Holy See and the new *Länder* after the German reunification in 1990 use language that has followed the path of pacification and friendly settlement. The preamble of the concordat between the Holy See and the Free State of Thuringia (THHlgStStV) can serve as an example of this and also of the equivalent issue of the ongoing validity of the 1929 Prussian concordat: This preamble expresses the common goal to develop the legal status of the Catholic Church in the Free State of Thuringia 'taking into account the concordat between the Holy See and the German *Reich* of 20 July 1933, which is in force, as far as it is binding upon the Free State, and in consideration of the treaty of the Free State of Prussia with the Holy See of 14 June 1929'.

*350.* According to Article 2 of the *Reichskonkordat*, the concordats concluded with Bavaria (1924), Prussia (1929) and Baden (1932) remain in force, and the rights and liberties of the Catholic Church recognized therein are secured

266. BVerfG 26 Mar. 1957, BVerfGE 6, 309 et seq.

unchanged within the territories of the states concerned; thus, these three concordats take preference before the *Reichskonkordat* even today.

*351.* Several provisions of the *Reichskonkordat* reassure and specify general rights that are guaranteed by the federal constitution. This applies to Article 1 *Reichskonkordat*, whereby the German *Reich* guarantees freedom of confession and public exercise of the Catholic Religion. It recognizes the right of the Catholic Church, within the limits of those laws that are applicable to all, to regulate and manage her own affairs independently and, within the framework of her own competence, to issue laws and orders binding on her members. Also, Article 4 provides that in its communication and correspondence with the bishops, clerics and other members of the Catholic Church in Germany, the Holy See enjoys full freedom. The same applies to the bishops and other diocesan authorities in their communication with the faithful in all matters belonging to their pastorate. The status as a corporation under public law is guaranteed by Article 13:

> Catholic parishes, parish and diocesan associations, Episcopal sees, bishoprics and chapters, religious orders and brotherhoods, as well as institutions, foundations and property of the Catholic Church which are under the administration of ecclesiastical organs, shall retain or acquire, respectively, legal capacity in the sphere of the state according to the general provisions of law. They shall remain corporations under public law in so far as they have been such hitherto; similar rights may be granted to the remainder in accordance with those provisions of the law which are applicable to all.

*352.* The Final Protocol *in re* Article 13 reassures that it is understood that the church's right to levy taxes remains ensured. The constitutional guarantees of property protection are reiterated by Article 17. Equivalent protection is promised in view of the state subsidies to the church by Article 18:

> If the public subsidies towards the church, based on law, contract or special legal title, should be detached, the Holy See and the *Reich* will bring about an amicable accord in due time prior to the elaboration of the principles to be established for the redemption. Also, the convention establishing a right is to be considered as special legal title. The redemption must grant suitable compensation of the claimant for the loss of the state benefits.

*353.* Furthermore, the right to establish and exclusively maintain training institutions is reiterated by Article 20; Catholic religious instruction in public schools is guaranteed by Articles 21 and 22 in conformity with today's Article 7 GG: Catholic religious instruction in elementary, intermediate, secondary, and vocational schools constitutes a part of the regular curriculum, and is to be taught in compliance with the principles of the Catholic Church. In religious instruction, the education to patriotic, civic, and social conscientiousness in the spirit of Christian faith and the moral code will be cultivated with special emphasis, as is done in the complete remainder of instruction; these provisions, of course, have to be interpreted today in light of the aims of education provided for by the Basic Law. The subjects taught and the selection of textbooks for religious instruction will be determined in accordance with the higher ecclesiastical authorities. The higher ecclesiastical authorities, in accordance with the education authority, will have the opportunity to investigate whether pupils are receiving religious instruction in compliance with the doctrine and demands of the church. Article 22 stipulates in addition to this:

> With regard to the appointment of teachers of Catholic Religion, communication will take place on the part of the bishop and the *Land* government. Teachers declared by the bishop unfit for the further exercise of their teaching functions, either on grounds of their teachings or by reason of their moral conduct may not be employed as teachers of religion so long as that obstacle exists.

*354.* The right to establish and maintain private Catholic schools is guaranteed by Article 25: Insofar as these schools follow provisions prescribing the curriculum for state schools, those attending them acquire the same qualifications as those attending state schools. The admission of members of religious orders or religious brotherhoods to the teaching profession and their appointment to elementary, intermediate, or secondary schools are subject to the general conditions.

*355.* Spiritual care in public institutions is guaranteed by Article 28 *Reichskonkordat*:

> In hospitals, penal establishments, and similar institutions of public purse, the church is to be permitted for undertaking of pastoral visitation and of religious ceremonies, subject to the general house regulations of the said institutions. If regular cure is established in such institutions, and if clerics have to be appointed as state or other civil servants, such appointments will be made in accordance with the higher ecclesiastical authority.

*356.* Finally, spiritual care in the military is guaranteed by Article 27:

> The German army is granted cure of souls for its Catholic officers, personnel and other officials, as well as for the families of the same exempt from the territorial competent Catholic community. The management of military chaplaincy lies with the Army Bishop. His ecclesiastical appointment is to be made by the Holy See after contact has been made by the latter with the German government in order to appoint a suitable personality in accordance with it. The ecclesiastical appointment of military chaplains and other military clerics will be made after previous consultations with the competent authority of Germany by the Army Bishop. The latter may nominate only such clerics as received permission from their Diocesan Bishop to engage in military chaplaincy. Military clerics have the rights of parish priests with regard to the troops and other army personnel assigned to them.

*357.* The secret part of the concordat (at the time of conclusion) further stipulates the background of the then-existing international treaty limitations to the German military:

> In the case of a transformation of the current German military system entailing the introduction of general compulsory military service, the call up of priests and other members of the clerics of religious orders and of the clergy of the world to render compulsory military service will approximately be regulated in accordance with the Holy See under the terms of the following guiding principles: a) Those studying philosophy and theology in ecclesiastical institutions in preparation for the priesthood are exempt from military service and exercises in preparation thereof, excepting in the event of a general mobilisation; b) In the case of a general mobilisation, those clerics engaged in diocesan administration or cure of souls will be exempted from appearance before the draft board. As such shall be deemed the diocesan authorities, the members of the diocesan authorities, directors of seminaries and ecclesiastical religious residences, professors of the seminaries, parish priests, curators, rectors, coadjutors and those clerics who are in continual charge of a church providing public religious service; c) The remainder of the clerics, provided they will be passed as fit, join the armed forces of the state, in order to provide cure of souls to the troops under the ecclesiastical jurisdiction of the Army Bishop, unless they are called up for medical service; d) The remainder of the clerics *in sacris* or members of religious orders who are not yet priests will serve in the medical service. The same should happen where possible in the case of candidates for the priesthood mentioned at a) who have not yet been ordained to the priesthood.

*358.* Other provisions do not have such close connections with constitutional guarantees that already exist but give relatively independent guarantees. Article 3 *Reichskonkordat* structures the diplomatic relations between the Holy See and Germany: 'In order to foster good relations between the Holy See and Germany, an Apostolic Nuncio will reside in the capital of Germany and an Ambassador of Germany at the Holy See, as heretofore.' The Final Protocol *in re* Article 3 further provides that the Apostolic Nuncio to Germany shall be the Dean of the Diplomatic Corps thereto accredited. Other provisions give detailed guarantees for the status of clerics in secular law, as does Article 5: 'In the exercise of their spiritual activities, the clerics enjoy the protection of the state in the same way as civil servants of the state.' Furthermore, Article 6 provides that clerics and religious are freed from any obligation to succession to public offices and such obligations as, according to the provisions of canon law, are incompatible with the holy or religious orders. This applies particularly to the office of lay judge, juryman, member of the taxation committee or member of the Finance Courts. For the acceptance of an appointment or office in the state or in any corporation under public law dependent on the state, the clerics need – as Article 7 stipulates – the *nihil obstat* of their diocesan ordinary, as well as that of the ordinary at the seat of the corporation under public law. The *nihil obstat* may be withdrawn at any time for important reasons affecting ecclesiastical interests. This is followed by the guarantee in Article 8, whereby the official income of the clerics is exempt from compulsory execution to the same extent as the official remuneration of civil servants of Germany. According to Article 9, the clerics may not be required by judicial and other authorities to give information concerning matters that have been entrusted to them while exercising the cure of souls and which therefore come within the obligation of pastoral secrecy. The wearing of clerical dress or of a habit of an order on the part of lay folk, or of clerics or religious who have been forbidden to wear them by a final and valid injunction made by the competent ecclesiastical authority and officially notified to the state authority, is liable to the same penalty on the part of the state as the abuse of military uniform, as provides Article 10.

*359.* Rules for the circumscription of church territory are given by Article 11: the (then) current diocesan organization and circumscription of the Catholic Church in the German *Reich* shall persist. A new establishment of a bishopric or of a church province appears to be required in future, or other alterations of diocesan circumscriptions, so far as they concern new formations within the boundaries of a German *Land*, remain subject to the understanding with the competent *Land* government. In case of new establishments and alterations that extend beyond the boundaries of a German *Land*, communication with the German government takes place, to whom it shall be left to bring about the consent of the *Land* governments in question. The same applies to new establishments or alterations of church provinces involving several of the German *Länder*. These conditions shall not apply to such shifts of ecclesiastical borders taking place merely in the interests of local cure of souls. In the case of any territorial reorganization within Germany, the German government will get in touch with the Holy See for rearrangement of the diocesan organization and circumscription. This is further elaborated in Article 12:

> Irrespective of the provisions of Article 11, church offices may be established and transformed freely, if no expenditures are claimed from state funds. The state's cooperation in forming and altering parishes shall be carried out according to guidelines to be agreed upon with the diocesan bishops, and for which the German government will endeavour to secure uniform formation as far as possible from the *Länder* governments.

*360.* The provisions regarding the appointment to church offices are of specific significance. Article 14 stipulates as a general rule that the church shall principally have the right to appoint freely to all church offices and benefices without the cooperation of the state or of civil communities, insofar as other provisions have not been made in the 1924 Bavarian, the 1929 Prussian, or the 1932 Baden concordats. These concordats provide for specific procedures and rights of the Cathedral Chapters in the appointment of a bishop. The regulation made for appointment to the Metropolitan See of the Upper Rhine Church Province of Freiburg shall apply *mutatis mutandis* to the two Suffragan Bishoprics of Rottenburg and Mainz, as well as to the Bishopric of Meißen. With regard to Rottenburg and Mainz, the same applies to appointments to the Cathedral Chapter bodies and to the regulation of the right of patronage. Furthermore, Article 14 determines that there is accord on the point that Catholic clerics who hold a religious office or who exercise pastoral or teaching functions in Germany must: 'a) be German citizens, b) have a school leaving certificate entitling them to studies at a German higher educational institution, and c) have studied philosophy and theology for at least three years at a German state university, a German ecclesiastical academic educational institution, or a papal university in Rome.' While these provisions seem to be at least questionable today in view of EU law guaranteeing for free movement of labour, Article 14 allows for exceptions: 'In case of church and state accord, these requirements may be disregarded.'

*361.* Article 14 also contains the provision on the political clause: The Bull nominating Archbishops, bishops, coadjutors *cum jure successionis*, or a *Praelatus Nullius*, will not be issued until the name of the person designated has been communicated to the governor of the *Reich* in the competent *Land* (who now is the *Land* prime Minster or the equivalent state organ), and until it has been ascertained that no objections of a general political nature exist. This does not give the state veto power but a power to raise objections. The Final Protocol *in re* Article 14 section 2 number 2 provides:

> It is understood that when objections of a general political nature exist, they shall be presented within the shortest possible time. If after twenty days such representations have not been made, the Holy See will be entitled to assume that no objections exist to the candidate in question. The names of the personalities in question will be kept completely confidential until the announcement of the appointment. A veto power of the state shall not be derived from this Article.

*362.* Closely connected with this is the loyalty oath pursuant to Article 16: before bishops take possession of their Dioceses, they are to take an oath of loyalty either to the governor of the *Reich* in the competent *Land* (who now is the *Land* prime Minster or the equivalent state organ) or to the President of Germany, according to the following formula:

> Before God and on the Holy Gospels I swear and promise as becomes a bishop, loyalty to the German *Reich* and to the *Land* of ... I swear and promise to respect the in accordance with the constitution legally constituted government and to cause the clerics of my Diocese to respect it. In my dutiful care for the welfare and the interests of the German polity I will, in the performance of the office transferred to me, strive for averting all detrimental acts which might endanger it.

Of course, again, the German *Reich* today is called 'Germany'.

*363.* Article 15 maintains that religious orders and brotherhoods are not subject to any special restrictions on the part of the state as regards their foundation, establishment, number, and – subject to Article 15 section 2 – the qualities of members, their activity concerning the cure of souls, education, sick nursing and charitable work, or as regards the management of their affairs and the administration of their property. Religious superiors whose headquarters are within Germany must be German citizens. Heads of provinces and superiors of religious orders, whose headquarters lie outside the territory of Germany, have the right of visitation to those of their establishments which lie within Germany, even if they are foreign nationals. The Holy See will make sure that the provincial organization of establishments of orders within Germany shall be such that, as far as possible, German establishments do not fall under the jurisdiction of foreign heads of provinces. Exceptions may be made in accordance with the German government, particularly in cases where the small number of establishments makes the formation of a German province impracticable or where special grounds exist for the retention of a provincial organization which is firmly established and has acquired a historic nature. Again, the provision on German citizenship appears questionable in respect of EU law.

*364.* Article 19 guarantees the existence of Catholic theological faculties at state universities: 'Catholic theological faculties in state universities are to be maintained. Their relation to ecclesiastical authorities shall be governed by the provisions laid down in the respective concordats and in the final protocols attached to the same, and with due regard to the ecclesiastical provisions in their regard.'

*365.* The *Reichskonkordat* also contains the general friendly settlement clause in its Article 33 clause 2: 'Should a difference of opinion arise in future regarding the interpretation or execution of any of the provisions of this concordat, the Holy See and Germany will reach a friendly solution by mutual agreement.'

*366.* A number of provisions of the *Reichskonkordat* are regarded to have lost their relevance or have become void for various reasons. This is said to apply to some of the provisions that concern schools, as do Articles 23 and 24, not the least because these now fall under the competence of the *Länder*:[267] the retention of Catholic denominational schools and the establishment of new ones remains ensured. In all communities in which parents or those entitled to bring up their children apply for it, Catholic elementary schools will be established, provided that the number of pupils available appears to be sufficient for a school managed and administered in accordance with the standards prescribed by the state, due regard being given to the local conditions of school organizations. Article 24, which provides that in Catholic elementary schools, only such teachers who are members of the Catholic Church are to be employed, is no longer of relevance today.

*367.* More importantly, the problematic provision on minorities in Article 29, which has the character of a retaliation clause, is out of function today. This provision reads:

> Catholic members of a non-German ethnical minority living within the German *Reich*, in matters concerning the consideration of their mother tongue in church services, religious instruction and the clubs, societies, and associations

267. Rudolf Morsey & Alexander Hollerbach, 'Reichskonkordat', in *Staatslexikon*, Görres-Gesellschaft ed., vol. 4, 7th edn (Freiburg: Herder, 1988), c. 791.

of the church, will be treated no less favourably than as it corresponds to the legal and actual situation of members of German origin and language within the boundaries of the corresponding foreign state.

*368.* Article 26 *Reichskonkordat* has lost its legal relevance only recently. This provision has to be understood on the basis of the formerly compulsory preceding secular conclusion of marriage before concluding a religious marriage; today, everybody is free to conclude a religious marriage before or independently of a secular marriage. The provision reads:

> Subject to a later comprehensive regulation of marriage law, it is understood that, apart from cases of critical illness of one member of an engaged couple which does not permit a postponement, also in cases of severe moral emergency, the presence of which must be confirmed by the competent ecclesiastical authority, the ecclesiastical marriage ceremony may precede the civil ceremony. In such cases, the parish priest is obliged to inform the registrar's office of the matter without delay.

*369.* Obsolete are the de-politicization clauses in Articles 31 and 32 because of the complete change of the political situation and because such political abstinence, as required by the state, would contradict the basic principles of democracy. Finally, the provision of Article 30 has fallen into desuetude: 'On Sundays and the mandatory holidays, a prayer, conforming to the Liturgy, will be inserted following the main religious service for the welfare of the German *Reich* and its people in all Episcopal, parish, subsidiary and conventual churches of the German *Reich*.'

## §11. Other Concordats

*370.* Another example of long-standing concordats in Germany is the 1929 concordat between the Free State of Prussia and the Holy See (PreußKonk), which is still in force in many parts of Germany. Also still in force are the 1932 Concordat between the Holy See and the Free State Baden (BadKonk) and the 1924 Concordat between the Holy See and the State of Bavaria (BayKonk), which has been amended several times since. Within the Federal Republic of Germany, the validity of the concordat with Prussia had been acknowledged after the Second World War by the newly founded *Länder* that had been established on the territories of the former Free State of Prussia; this state having finally been dissolved by the Allied Control Council on 25 February 1947, while the DDR did not recognize the continuation of the concordat. The remaining disagreement about the validity of the Prussian concordat in the new *Länder* after Germany's reunification in 1990 has been overcome by language in the newly concluded concordats: The concordat of the Free State of Thuringia has been concluded as have been other recent concordats with the new *Länder* in consideration of the treaty of the Free State of Prussia with the Holy See of 14 June 1929.[268]

*371.* The concordat with Prussia reiterates the guarantee of freedom of religion for the Catholic Church (Article 1) and specifies the organization, circumscriptions, and existence of the dioceses (Articles 2 and 3).

*372.* Article 6 Prussian concordat determines the procedure of nomination, election, and appointment of bishops, attributing far-reaching rights to the Chapter of the Cathedral:

> (1) After an Archiepiscopal or Episcopal See ended, both the Metropolitan or Chapter of a Cathedral in question, as well as the Diocesan Archbishops and Bishops of Prussia shall submit to the Holy See lists of canonically qualified candidates. Estimating these lists, the Holy See shall nominate to the chapter three persons from whom the latter shall elect the Archbishop or bishop in a free, secret ballot. The Holy See shall not appoint anyone as an Archbishop or bishop unless the chapter after election has determined by enquiring of the Prussian State Government that no reservations of a political nature exist against him. (2) The non-residing canons shall contribute towards setting the list of candidates and in the elections.

*373.* Article 7 Prussian concordat further enlarges the scope of the political clause: 'The Holy See shall not nominate anyone as *Praelatus Nullius* and coadjutor of a diocesan bishop with the right of succession without having determined by enquiring of the Prussian State Government that no reservations of a political nature exist against him.' These limitations of the papal rights, including those stipulated by Article 6 Prussian concordat, apply to many German dioceses such as Cologne, Trier, or Aachen. Equivalent rules apply to the Archdiocese of Freiburg according to Article III of the Baden concordat; these rules have been extended to the dioceses of Dresden-Meissen, Rottenburg-Stuttgart, and Mainz by the *Reichskonkordat*. Greater freedom for the Pope in appointing bishops is guaranteed according to Article 14 §1 Bavarian concordat for the dioceses covered by this concordat such as Munich and Freising, Würzburg, Regensburg, or Augsburg, but also the diocese of Speyer: 'The Holy See can freely choose among the names of suitable candidates on lists provided by the Chapter of the Cathedral, the Bavarian bishops, and Chapters. Before publication of the bull, the Holy See will contact the Bavarian government in order to satisfy itself that no reservations of a political nature exist against the candidate.' New concordats with the new *Länder* after Germany's reunification leave complete freedom of appointment to the Holy See, as does the Brandenburg concordat (Article 3) or Article 15 concordat Mecklenburg-Western Pomerania.[269]

---

268. *See also* the preamble of the concordat between the Holy See and the Free State of Saxony (SächsHlStStV).

269. Concordat between the Holy See and the Land Mecklenburg-Western Pomerania (HeilStV M-V).

*374.* The concordats guarantee the rights of the Catholic Church to establish and maintain clerical training institutions such as seminaries. The Catholic theological faculties in state universities are guaranteed; the teaching staff, especially professors, need the *nihil obstat* by the church authorities.[270] The Bavarian concordat (Article 3), moreover, guarantees in a number of state universities numerous theological, but also general philosophical and pedagogical chairs, the professors of which must conform to the teaching of the Catholic Church, and the Catholic Church enjoys the right to raise relevant objections against the candidate or the professor.

*375.* Concordats also guarantee Catholic religious instruction in public schools in conformity with Article 7 sections 1 and 3 GG where applicable. Where the system of confessional religious instruction in public schools has been challenged, as in Brandenburg, the guarantee is less far-reaching: the Catholic Church enjoys the right to teach Catholic religion in the rooms of the public schools; this language not only gives room for interpretation but also allows conformity with Article 7 section 2 GG.

## §12. Protestant Treaty with Lower Saxony and Further Treaties

*376.* After the Second World War, the 1955 Treaty between the *Land* Lower Saxony and the Protestant *Land* churches in Lower Saxony (*Loccumer Vertrag*) took the lead in re-establishing the treaty relations between the newly democratic state and religious communities; a complementary agreement was concluded in 1965.[271] The 1955 treaty is known as the Loccum Treaty because it was signed in the Protestant monastery of Loccum. This treaty acknowledged in its preamble the 'public assignment' of the churches: The treaty was concluded 'in compliance as to the public assignment of the churches and their independence', which respected and acknowledged the public function of the religious communities in the democratic state. This has to be understood in view of the devastating experience of Nazi terror and meant to assign to the churches a function of moral 'guardians' for democracy. The Loccum treaty, again, guarantees freedom of religion in its Article 1: '(1) The Land of Lower Saxony shall grant statutory protection to the freedom of confession and the exercise of the Protestant faith. (2) The Protestant churches shall regulate and administer their affairs independently within the limits of the law that applies to all. They shall remain corporations under public law; their service shall remain civil service.' Regular dialogue is structured in its Article 2:

> (1) The *Land* Government and the church managements shall strive to have regular meetings to deepen their relations. They will at all times make themselves available to discuss questions concerning their mutual relationship. (2) The churches will enter into close cooperation among themselves in order to

---

270. *See*, e.g., Arts IX and X of Concordat between the Holy See and the Free State of Baden.
271. Complementary Treaty to the Treaty between the Land Lower Saxony and the Protestant Land Churches in Lower Saxony (ErgänzungsV Loccumer Vertrag).

uniformly represent their interests towards the state. They will appoint joint agents and establish an agency at the seat of the *Land* Government.

*377.* The treaty and the complementary treaty, as do many other state-church treaties, also determine details of the levy of the church tax and of state payments to the churches.

*378.* The rights of the Protestant churches in relation to the staff of the Protestant theological faculties at state universities are somewhat less far-reaching than the respective rights of the Catholic Church pursuant to the concordats: 'The relevant Protestant church gives an opinion on the creed and the teaching of the candidate to a professorship.'[272] Such differences can well result from differences in the doctrines of the respective churches; the very purpose of the instrument of state-church treaties is to respect and accommodate these specific differences in the teachings of the religious communities. In contrast to the relevant concordats, neither the Loccum treaty nor the complementary agreement mentions a right of the Protestant Church to prevent a candidate against whom they have reservations; there also is no explicit statement on the possibility and consequences of the churches' objections when a professor of Protestant theology does not keep in conformity with their religious teaching. However, because of the general rules of equal treatment and parity, the same principles have to be applied to cases of the Protestant Church as are effective for the Catholic Church, as long as the Protestant Church so wishes. An example of this is the case of a professor of New Testament at the faculty for Protestant theology of the University of Göttingen who has his status in 1999 because of his teaching. This professor had publicly rejected the idea of the Last Supper, the Last Judgment, the historical truth of the resurrection of Jesus Christ, and any belief in a revelation.[273] On the intervention of the Protestant Church, the state authorities first tried to move this professor, being a state civil servant with his life-long status at the university, to a chair in the faculty of philosophy. When that faculty rejected this move, his chair was renamed into a non-confessional chair for history and literature of the early Christendom, he was no longer allowed to participate in examination of the faculty of Protestant theology, and his classes were announced with the addition that these courses have no relevance for theological training. The professor filed a lawsuit against this solution but lost his case in all court instances; the Federal Constitutional Court rejected his constitutional complaint and, while acknowledging his freedoms of science and teaching, held that these freedoms found their limitations in the freedom of science and teaching of the faculty, its identity as a theological faculty, and the right to self-determination of the religious community.[274]

272. Article 3, s. 2 Loccumer Vertrag; Art. 2 ErgänzungsV Loccumer Vertrag.

273. Gerd Lüdemann, *Der große Betrug. Und was Jesus wirklich sagte und tat.* (Springe: Zu Klampen, 1998).

274. BVerfG 28 Oct. 2008, *Neue Juristische Wochenschrift* 62 (2009): 2190 et seq.

*379.* Similar treaties have been concluded by the new *Länder* after the 1990 German reunification. In its preamble, the Treaty between the Free State of Thuringia and the Protestant churches in Thuringia (ThEvKirchStV) sets the tone referring implicitly to the Loccum treaty:

> The parties conclude the treaty in the intention to preserve and safeguard the independence of the church and the principle of mutual independence of the state and the church, observing the basic right of religious freedom and of the church's public assignment, wishing to reach agreement on the exercise of the church's assignment in a state which is neutral in religious and ideological questions, and thereby to promote in particular the educational and cultural political as well as socio-charitable activities of the churches in the Free State of Thuringia, in consideration of and advancement of historically grown rights and duties, (and) with the aim to put legal relations between the state and the church in a free constitutional system on a comprehensive, new basis and design it as such for the long term.

## §13. Treaties with Non-religious, Philosophical Communities

*380.* Treaties have also been concluded with non-religious, philosophical communities, also called belief communities. One example among several others is the treaty between the *Land* Lower Saxony and the Free-Religious *Land* Community of Lower Saxony (FrRelVtr NDS), which in its English translation is sometimes also called the Non-denominational *Land* Community of Lower Saxony. The legal successor of the Free-Religious *Land* Community of Lower Saxony is the Organization of Free Humanists of Lower Saxony, both being explicitly atheist communities. Such treaties have a very similar structure and equivalent fields of application as have the treaties with religious communities. This is an expression of the equal treatment clause in Article 137 section 7 WRV in conjunction with Article 140 GG, whereby associations whose purpose is to foster a philosophical creed shall have the same status as religious societies. A general freedom clause opens the treaty with the Free-Religious Community in section 1:

> (1) The *Land* shall ensure the Non-denominational Religious Land Community's free activity in the framework of the Basic Law of the Federal Republic of Germany for the free religious humanist care of its members and of other persons not belonging to a religious and ideological community. (2) The Non-denominational Religious Land Community avows itself to the Basic Law of the Federal Republic of Germany and to the Temporary Lower Saxon Constitution. It shall exercise its activities in view of the common public welfare.

*381.* Atheist groups usually have a specific view on the system of religious instruction in public schools, which is expressed in the treaty's sections 2 and 3:

> The *Land* will continue to be deliberate that the instruction in the different religions[275] provided for in section 5 clause 6 of the Lower Saxon Schooling Act (NSchG) at the public schools shall be given with equal rights in addition to religious instruction within the meaning of the Christian confessions. It shall in particular take care that those entitled to bring up the children, if they are concerned, shall be regularly referred to the instruction events coming into question (§2 FrRelVtr NDS).

*382*. The *Land*, in the sphere of universities, shall facilitate academic preparatory training for instruction in different religions. The teaching assignment issued at the Pedagogical University of Lower Saxony, Hanover department, for religious science and didactics of instruction in different religions shall remain (§3 FrRelVtr NDS). Also, the presence of atheist views in the media is taken care of in section 4 of the treaty: 'The *Land* shall, with regard to broadcasting corporations in which it holds a share, continue to be deliberate that the statutes contain provisions in accordance with which the Free-Religious *Land* Community is given suitable on-air times and that it is facilitated a suitable representation of its interests in questions of programming.' Moreover, section 5 of the treaty stipulates in relation to general education issues that the freedom of the Free-Religious *Land* Community to act in adult education shall be ensured. Finally, financial issues are covered: section 6 reassures that the Free-Religious *Land* Community will receive permits to make collections according to general collection law: 'The Free-Religious Land Community and its communities shall be entitled to collect from its members for non-denominational and charitable purposes.' Section 7, lastly, guarantees direct state payments and the relevant procedures:

> (1) The *Land* shall pay to the Free-Religious Land Community from the year 1970 onwards as an annual subsidy towards personnel costs the sum of one hundred thousand Deutsche Mark. The amount of the sum shall be adjusted to the changes in the remuneration of the *Land* civil servants, as in the case of comparable public subsidies. (2) The public subsidy shall be paid on a quarterly basis with one quarter each of the annual amount being paid in advance.

---

275. Knowledge about the different religions is provided in the subject 'Werte und Normen' (ethics) in accordance with the Lower Saxon Schooling Act (NSchG), which is regulated by §128 NSchG as follows (extract):

> §128 Instruction in Values and Norms
>
> (1) Anyone not attending religious instruction shall instead be obliged to attend classes in values and norms if the school offers this subject. To those, whose religious instruction according to their religious community has been introduced as regular subject, the precedent obligation applies only after expiration of one school year during which religious instruction could not be provided. The school shall offer instruction in values and norms as a part of the regular curriculum from the fifth year onwards if at least twelve pupils are obliged to attend. ( … )
>
> (2) Instruction in values and norms provides knowledge about different religions, understanding of moral concepts and norms applicable in society and an approach to philosophical, ideological and religious issues.

(3) The Land Court of Audit shall be entitled to check the use of the financial support *in situ*, to inspect the required documentation and to require information.

## §14. Treaties with the Jewish Communities

*383.* Of very special significance are the treaties that have been concluded with the Jewish communities. The preamble of the 2006 treaty between the *Land* Saxony-Anhalt (LSA) with the Jewish Community in Saxony-Anhalt (VertrJüdGem) makes explicit reference to the historic background of the treaty as having been concluded:

> in responsibility before the history of Germany also shaped by the persecution and destruction of people of the Jewish faith and Jewish origin, in the knowledge of the measures of bare or hidden violence in the time of the Communist tyranny, conscious of the great loss suffered by the *Land* Saxony-Anhalt through the destruction of Jewish life and Jewish culture, (and) in the desire to make it easier for the Jewish Community in Saxony-Anhalt to rebuild a community life.

*384.* Article 1 reassures freedom:

> (1) The *Land* guarantees on the basis of its Constitution and of the Basic Law for the Federal Republic of Germany the unrestricted freedom of the Jewish faith, and grants statutory protection of the practice of religion. (2) The Jewish congregations in the Land Saxony-Anhalt and the Land Association shall regulate and administer their affairs in accordance with Jewish traditions and laws within the limits of the law that applies to all.

*385.* A regular dialogue and cooperation are promised in Article 2:

> (1) The *Land* Government and the Land Association shall regularly and where needed meet to discuss questions that are tangenting their relationship to each other or other questions which are of mutual interest. (2) In intended law-making and manifestos in fields directly concerning the interests of the Jewish Community in Saxony-Anhalt, the *Land* Government shall suitably involve the Land Association. (3) The *Land* will involve the Land Association in particular within the scope of work concerned with memorials where Jewish concerns are affected.

*386.* The Final Protocol *in re* Article 2 section 1 stipulates in this respect that the Jewish Land Association shall inform the *Land* government of vacancies in and new appointments as to the senior offices (e.g., Chairpersons of the Land Association and of the Jewish communities). Special protection for the Jewish is offered in Article 3: 'The *Land* shall ensure the protection of the institutions of the Jewish Community in Saxony-Anhalt and shall promote the maintenance of historical sites.' Article 4 gives recognition to Jewish holidays: 'The *Land* shall ensure the rights of indemnity contained in the Act on Sundays and Holidays (FeiertG LSA) of 22 May 1992 on Jewish holidays.'[276] These holidays are, according to Final Protocol *in re* Article 4: Rosh Hashanah (Jewish New Year) on the 1st and 2nd days, starting on the previous day at 4 p.m.; Yom Kippur (Day of Atonement), starting on the previous day at 4 p.m.; Succot (Feast of Tabernacles) on the 1st and 2nd days, starting on the previous day at 5 p.m.; Shemini Azeret (Eighth Day of Succot), starting on the previous day at 5 p.m.; Simchat Torah (Rejoicing of the Law), starting on the previous day at 5 p.m.; Passover (exodus of the Jewish people from Egypt) on the 1st, 2nd, 7th and 8th days, starting on the previous day at 5 p.m.; Shavuoth (Feast of Weeks) on the 1st and 2nd days, starting on the previous day at 5 p.m. The treaty also protects Jewish property in its Article 5: 'In applying expropriation law provisions, the *Land* and the municipal territorial authorities shall take account of the concerns of the Jewish Community in Saxony-Anhalt and where appropriate shall assist in acquiring indemnity land of equal value.' Article 6 further stipulates:

> (1) The *Land* and the municipal territorial authorities will observe the intangibility of the authorized Jewish burial places that have not been abandoned. (2) Jewish cemeteries shall enjoy the same state protection as municipal cemeteries. The Jewish communities shall have the right to establish new cemeteries within the framework of the legal provisions. When establishing new cemeteries, the *Land* and the local territorial authorities shall examine possibilities for promotion within the framework of the budgetary funds available. (3) Within the framework of agreements between the Federation and the *Länder*, the *Land* shall grant subsidies for the maintenance and care of those Jewish cemeteries or parts thereof which cannot be reoccupied in accordance with the provisions of the community.[277]

*387.* As to Article 7 of the treaty:

> (1) The Jewish Community in Saxony-Anhalt undertakes to maintain and preserve buildings with a value as monuments together with the appurtenant real estates, as well as their works of art and culture where these obligations do not lead in an individual case to unacceptable strains on the Jewish community concerned or on the Land Association. The monument authorities shall, with cultural monuments of the Jewish Community in Saxony-Anhalt which are intended to serve the purposes of religious services or other acts of worship, pay prior regard to the worship and religious concerns to be ascertained by the

276. The wording of §6 FeiertG LSA as follows: §6 Release on Religious Holidays:

(1) Employees and trainees shall be granted uncompensated release on application on religious holidays according to their religious affiliation unless opposed by operational necessities.
(2) In order to celebrate religious holidays according to their church or religious community, pupils shall obtain release from school on application.

277. Note: This refers to the religious provisions of the Jewish communities.

competent board. Prior to the implementation of measures, the authorities shall consult with the competent board. (2) In allocating the *Land* funds for the preservation of monuments, the Jewish Community in Saxony-Anhalt will be suitably taken into consideration with due regard to the regulations of the Monument Protection Act. The *Land* shall advocate that the Jewish Community in Saxony-Anhalt also receives assistance from facilities active at national and international level for the preservation of culture and other monuments.

*388.* Furthermore, according to Article 8, '(1) The Jewish Community in Saxony-Anhalt shall have the right to establish and operate general schools maintained by Jewish organizations on a confessional basis. (2) Detailed regulations of the procedure for governmental approval and recognition of such schools and their co-financing from public funds shall remain reserved to *Land* law.' Finally, special provisions on education, healthcare, and in the social field are laid out in Article 9 in a very general way: 'The Jewish Community in Saxony-Anhalt shall have the right to maintain its own facilities in the educational and social fields, as well as in health care.' Jewish culture is maintained and supported according to Article 10: 'The Contracting Parties shall advocate giving the only remaining synagogue building of this type in Germany in Gröbzig an enduring basis and to make it permanently accessible to the public'; and Article 11 stipulates: '(1) The Contracting Parties shall strive to hold Jewish cultural festivals at intervals of three years preferably, where needed also in cooperation with other facilities and organizations. (2) The *Land* shall support within the bounds of its possibilities the Jewish Community in Saxony-Anhalt in researching Jewish history and in dealing with German-Jewish heritage.' Moreover, the media are taken into account in Article 12 of the treaty: 'The *Land* shall work towards providing suitable on air times by the public broadcasting corporations to the Jewish Community in Saxony-Anhalt for broadcasting religious programmes.' In the supervisory bodies (broadcasting councils, programme committees and comparable bodies), the Jewish Community in Saxony-Anhalt should be represented. Financial subsidies are provided by Article 13:

> (1) The *Land* shall pay to the Land Association a total subsidy (public subsidy). Over and above this public subsidy, further benefits shall only be effected to the Jewish Community in Saxony-Anhalt if they are provided for in this treaty or by the general statutes. (2) The *Land* subsidy amount in the year 2005 to 1,045,592.83 €. (3) If subsequently the remuneration of civil servants in the service of the state changes, the public subsidy shall change *mutatis mutandis* on the basis of the amount agreed for 2005. The starting office for the higher, non-technical, general administrative service shall be taken as a basis, salary group A 13 of the Federal Remuneration Ordinance, 7th grade of seniority, two children. (4) The public subsidy shall be paid monthly in advance to the Land Association in twelfths of the annual amount.

*389.* Financial issues are also covered by Article 14: 'The *Land* shall extend the remission of fees based on *Land* law for the *Land* to the Jewish Community in Saxony-Anhalt and its public-law institutions, foundations, associations and clubs.'

General clauses conclude the provisions. Article 15 revokes a general best treatment clause: 'If the *Land* in treaties with other comparable religious communities should grant rights and benefits over and above those in this treaty, the Contracting Parties will examine together whether amendments to this treaty are required because of the principle of parity.' The traditional friendship clause is found in Article 16: 'The Contracting Parties will settle any difference of opinion occurring between them in future as to interpreting a provision of this treaty in an amicable manner.'

The treaty between the LSA and the Jewish Community in Saxony-Anhalt is typical for so-called full treaties (*Vollverträge*), which contain provisions not only on financial issues but on a range of important topics relating to the practice of religion, such as religious holidays, burial practices and religious education.

*390.* The treaty was the subject of a major court case when the (relatively new) liberal Jewish community wanted to participate in the public subsidies and applied for funding by the Jewish community. It was controversial whether the liberal Jewish community was part of the Jewish community in the meaning of the treaty and whether the state subsidies were also meant to be distributed by the Jewish community to newly founded communities. The Federal Administrative Court decided in favour of the liberal Jewish community.[278] While this result does not seem to be legally questionable, the ruling of the Federal Administrative Court appears to be highly problematic in that it defines by way of state decision who is Jewish and who is not, a step that is hardly acceptable in view of the German history and on the basis of state religious neutrality. The contracting parties of the treaty have reacted to this decision by introducing further provisions on the membership in the Jewish Community in the meaning of the treaty: The Final Protocol *in re* Article 1 section 2 defines:

> The Land Association of Jewish Communities Saxony-Anhalt and the following Cult Communities belong at present to the Jewish Community in the meaning of this treaty: The Synagogue Community at Magdeburg, the Jewish Community at Halle, the Jewish Community at Dessau and the Synagogue Community at Halle. Newly originating Jewish communities belong in the meaning of this treaty to the Jewish Community when they have existed for a period of five years, have at least 50 members, have an orderly statute, have orderly representatives on the basis of valid election rules, a lively religious community life (services, holidays), are registered as an association (the *Land* will decide according to the provisions of law about the granting of the rights of a corporation under public law), are members of the Land Association or are recognized by the groupings ORK (Orthodoxy) or ARK (liberal-progressive-conservative) represented in the German Rabbi Conference.

*391.* By this way of agreement, the decision on who is Jewish and who is not is at least in principle left to the religious community because this side is free to accept the agreement or to reject it. However, German courts should be more reluctant in

278. BVerwG 28 Feb. 2002, BVerwGE 116, 86 et seq.

making decisions on such points. A way to do this while respecting and protecting the rights of newcomers could be to oblige the state to seek additional agreements on such issues with the dissenting religious communities. This perspective may well be the political consequence of a 2009 decision of the Federal Constitutional Court in a case concerning the *Land* Brandenburg that is somewhat similar to the one decided by the Federal Administrative Court for Saxony-Anhalt:[279] Under the terms of the 2005 Agreement between the *Land* Brandenburg and the Land Association of Jewish Communities, the *Land* Brandenburg contributed EUR 200,000 annually to the Jewish Community in Brandenburg for the maintenance of Jewish community life. Article 8.1 of the Agreement provided for the amount to be administered by the Land Association of Jewish Communities, which is a public corporation and is the Jewish religious community in Brandenburg with the most members. It should do so on behalf of all of the *Land's* Jewish communities, irrespective of whether or not they belong to the Land Association. The Land Association was obliged to give a reasonable share of the funds to all Jewish communities. In Brandenburg, there is also a registered association called the Law-Abiding Jewish *Land* Community of Brandenburg (*Verein Gesetzestreue Jüdische Landesgemeinde Brandenburg*), which does not share the religious convictions of the Land Association and therefore does not belong to it. The two religious communities are rivals. The agreement left the decision as to the amount of the funds that it would pass on entirely in the hands of the Land Association. After the agreement was concluded, the Land Association did not initially give the Law-Abiding Jewish *Land* Community a share of the funds provided by the *Land*. The Federal Constitutional Court decided that the provision on the allocation of funds by the Land Association was not compatible with those aspects of the fundamental right to freedom of religion, which affect grants, and the right to participate in grants contained in Article 4 GG in connection with the requirement of impartiality. The Court argued that it must also be taken into account that the Land Association had a strong self-interest in the funds. The fact that the challenged provision places the Law-Abiding Jewish *Land* Community in a position of dependence in relation to the Land Association was also declared to be incompatible with the requirements of state neutrality and of an administrative organization in a state governed by the rule of law. The provision was therefore declared void.

There are two possible reactions to this decision of the Federal Constitutional Court, both of which have been shown by the *Länder*. One is to adhere to the concept of one treaty with all Jewish communities (*Einheitsvertrag*). Such a treaty lays the definition of what a Jewish community is partly into the hands of the state. An example of this type of treaty is the one concluded by the *Land* Hesse and the Jewish Land Association (JüdGemStVtr Hesse).[280] This appears highly problematic in view of religious autonomy. The second way to react is to conclude a treaty with each Jewish community or association of Jewish communities individually. The treaty is then only applicable to that particular Jewish organization and its members. This kind of treaty was concluded between the *Land* Rhineland-Palatinate and

279. BVerfG 12 May 2009, BVerfGE 123, 148 et seq.

280. Treaty between the *Land* Hesse and the Jewish Land Association of 1 Jan. 1986, Hess. GVBl. I, 395 et seq., as amended on 15 Nov. 2011, Hess. GVBl. I, 671 et seq.

the Jewish Land Association of Rhineland-Palatinate on 16 May 2012 (JüdGemStVtr RLP).[281] It is a full treaty and, as such, covers a variety of different subjects in relation to the exercise of religion.

One can observe that in their preambles, all of the new full treaties concluded between the *Länder* and the Jewish Land Associations contain a reference to the time of National-Socialist terror and the complete destruction of the Jewish communities. This impacts the content of the treaties because, at this time, the financial foundation of the Jewish communities in Germany was destroyed, and the treaties served (in part) to help rebuild Jewish life in the country and to preserve the German-Jewish heritage.

*392.* The Federal Republic concluded a treaty with the Central Council of the Jews in Germany in 2003 (ZdJStVG). Its preamble, as do the other treaties with the Jewish communities, refers especially to the Shoah. It states that the treaty has been concluded 'conscious of the special historic responsibility of the German people for the Jewish life in Germany, faced with the immeasurable suffering that the Jewish population had to endure in the years 1933–1945, guided by the desire to support the rebuilding of Jewish life in Germany and to strengthen and to deepen the friendly relationship to the Jewish faith community'. The treaty primarily deals with cooperation issues and support for cultural and social tasks, including the integration of Jewish immigrants in Germany; state financial support for this is provided.

## §15. Treaties with Muslim Associations

*393.* Hamburg, as the first *Land*, has concluded two treaties with Muslim organizations.[282] The treaties, among them also the treaty concluded between the *Land* Bremen and Muslim religious communities at the beginning of the year 2013, cover, *inter alia*, the subjects of religious education in schools, the building of mosques and the operation of kindergartens (*see also* above paragraph 298).

281. GVBl. RP 2012, 157 et seq.

282. Freie und Hansestadt Hamburg (ed.), 'Vertrag zwischen der Freien und Hansestadt Hamburg, dem DITIB-Landesverband Hamburg, SCHURA – Rat der Islamischen Gemeinschaften in Hamburg und dem Verband der Islamischen Kulturzentren', https://www.buergerschaft-hh.de/ParlDok/dokument/38534/1-vertrag-zwischen-der-freien-und-hansestadt-hamburg-dem-ditib-landesverband-hamburg-schura-%E2%80%93-rat-der-islamischen-gemeinschaften-in-hamburg.pdf, 9 Nov. 2023; Freie und Hansestadt Hamburg (ed.), 'Vertrag zwischen der Freien und Hansestadt Hamburg und der Alevitischen Gemeinde Deutschland e.V.', https://www.buergerschaft-hh.de/ParlDok/dokument/38534/1-vertrag-zwischen-der-freien-und-hansestadt-hamburg-dem-ditib-landesverband-hamburg-schura-%E2%80%93-rat-der-islamischen-gemeinschaften-in-hamburg.pdf, 9 Nov. 2023.

# Part IV. International, Transnational and Regional Effects on Religious Communities

## Chapter 1. International Law Effects on Religious Communities

### §1. Public International Law

#### I. Basic Principles

*394.* Germany has signed and ratified all important and relevant international treaties concerning freedom of religion. Many bilateral international public law treaties, including of course the concordats, are part of the corpus of international commitments in the field of religion.

*395.* International law ranks below the Constitution.[283] According to Article 25 of the Constitution, the general rules of public international law have priority before ordinary laws[284] and directly create rights and obligations for all citizens. There are few general rules of public international law that have been explicitly accepted by the Federal Constitutional Court to share in this rank, and none is directly related to religious freedom.[285]

*396.* Public international law, other than general rules and transformed by national laws into the German legal system, has the same rank as ordinary law. This applies in the field of religion or belief, for example, to Article 9 ECHR or Article 18 ICCPR. As these international provisions are regarded as guaranteeing no more than Article 4 GG does, and as they are easily limited by their own limitation clauses, these provisions do not play any major role in German legal doctrine or

283. With the exception of peace-related treaties according to Art. 79, s. 1 GG.
284. Ordinary laws rank below the Basic Law and include formal statutes passed by parliament as well as statutory instruments and by-laws.
285. These are for example: The rules of universal customary international law (BVerfG 14 May 1968, BVerfGE 23, 288, 317; BVerfG 10 Jun. 1997, BVerfGE 96, 68, 86); the generally fundamental rules of public international law (BVerfG 14 May 1968, BVerfGE 23, 288, 316; BVerfG 10 Jun. 1997, BVerfGE 96, 68, 86); among those the principles of territoriality, state immunity, general prohibition of violence, individual access to legal protection by courts.

court practice. From time to time, they are referred to, but the guarantees of religious freedom of Article 4 GG do prevail.

*397.* All courts in Germany apply international human rights law throughout their practice. This is done more implicitly than explicitly because the German Federal Constitution, in most cases, guarantees fundamental rights in a more complete way than international human rights law does or at least in an equivalent way. If, in an individual case, there were an exception to this general rule, any court in Germany would directly and explicitly apply international human rights law.

*398.* The German legislatures conform to international standards and would amend laws accordingly, if necessary. In case of international human rights treaties, these treaties become part of German domestic ordinary law by way of a law of ratification (Article 59 GG). According to the principle of *lex posterior derogat legi priori,* these laws prevail over any ordinary law passed before this ratification law. The legislature also complies with Germany's obligations following from international law. The Federal Constitutional Court has held that the German Constitution entails the principle of 'openness to international law'.[286] According to this principle, all German law has to be interpreted in a way compatible with Germany's international obligations. The rare case of colliding obligations following from the constitution on the one hand and from international law on the other[287] has not had any relevance in respect of freedom of religion or belief. In this case, the constitutional obligations would prevail over the international ones.

*399.* International treaties that regulate the political relations of the Federation or relate to subjects of federal legislation require the consent or participation, in the form of a federal law, of the bodies responsible in such a case for the enactment of federal law. In the case of executive agreements, the provisions concerning the federal administration apply *mutatis mutandis* (Article 59 GG). This means that all international treaties relevant to religious freedom would be enacted by law and thus be applicable in Germany. The general rules of international law are an integral part of federal law. They do not need any transformation by a domestic ordinary law. Whether a norm of international law is directly applicable or self-executing has to be decided in each individual case.[288]

286. Cf. Art. 25 GG; Art. 100, s. 2 GG; Art. 24, s. 3 GG; Art. 9, s. 2 GG; BVerfG 30 Jun. 1964, BVerfGE 18, 112, 121; BVerfG 4 May 1971, BVerfGE 31, 58, 75; BVerfG 31 Mar. 1987, BVerfGE 75, 1, 17; BVerfG 10 Nov. 1981, BVerfGE 59, 63, 89.
287. BVerfG 14 Oct. 2004, BVerfGE 111, 307, 329; BVerfG 31 Jul. 1973, BVerfGE 36, 1, 36; BVerfG 30 Jul. 1952, BVerfGE 1, 396, 411; BVerfG 9 Dec. 1970, BVerfGE 29, 348, 358; BVerfG 29 Oct. 1998, BVerfGE 99, 145, 158.
288. Cf. BVerfG 9 Dec. 1970, BVerfGE 29, 348, 360; BVerfG 20 Nov. 1977, BVerfGE 46, 214, 220; BVerfG 8 Apr. 1987, BVerfGE 75, 223, 244; BVerfG 22 Oct. 1986, BVerfGE 73, 339, 367, 375.

## II. The European Convention on Human Rights

### *A. General Relevance*

*400.* The ECHR has gained growing relevance in internal German court procedures. If the European Court of Human Rights convicts Germany because of a violation of the ECHR by one of Germany's courts, this usually does not only have the result of just satisfaction in money to the applicant pursuant to Article 41 ECHR. A conviction of Germany because of a violation of the ECHR is in general also grounds for a resumption of the case before German courts as is stated in §580 number 8 Code of Civil Procedure (ZPO) or §359 number 6 Code of Criminal Procedure (StPO).

*401.* Article 9 ECHR protects the freedom of religion as a right of the individual and of communities. Churches and religious communities have a right of complaint in their own right before the bodies of the ECHR, which are charged with giving legal redress if they can claim to be injured in their rights under Article 9 ECHR.

*402.* The limitation clause of Article 9 ECHR does not play any significant role in German law, although the ECHR is part of German domestic ordinary law by way of the relevant law of ratification. The limitation clause of Article 9 ECHR is, in its wording, more restrictive to religious freedom than the limitations prescribed under Article 4 of the German Constitution. In theory – or legal doctrine – the limitation clause of Article 9 ECHR has to be interpreted in conformity with the German Constitution according to the principle of the 'constitution conforming interpretation',[289] which means that if a law can be interpreted in several ways, the interpretation which keeps the law in conformity with the constitution prevails. This would, in fact, be possible. The German courts, however, usually just disregard the respective limitation clause of Article 9 ECHR in practice and always directly relate to the German Constitution, which is the higher-ranking norm and guarantees more far-reaching freedom of religion or belief than Article 9 ECHR.

### *B. Case Law*

*403.* The European Court of Human Rights has convicted Germany in the case of the government's warnings against the Osho movement to be a dangerous sect, however not because of the warning, but because of the over-long duration of the court procedures (Article 6 ECHR).[290]

---

289. BVerfG 30 Mar. 1993, BVerfGE 88, 145, 166; BVerfG 24 Apr. 1985, BVerfGE 69, 1, 55; BVerfG 3 Jun. 1992, BVerfGE 86, 288, 320 et seq.; BVerfG 15 Oct. 1996, BVerfGE 95, 64, 81, 93.

290. ECHR, *Leela-Förderkreis et al. v. Germany*, 6 Nov. 2008, appl. no. 58911/00 (warning against the Osho sect).

*404.* In the case of conscientious objection by a Jehovah's Witness against both compulsory military service and substituting compulsory social work, a decision of the Ministerial Committee was issued but no violation of the ECHR has been established.[291]

*405.* One of the most visible cases that involved Germany before the institutions of the ECHR was the case *Rommelfanger v. Federal Republic of Germany*:[292] Rommelfanger was a medical doctor employed in a hospital that was maintained by the Catholic Church. Rommelfanger publicly opposed in newspapers and television media the teaching of the Roman Catholic Church in relation to abortion and pleaded for freedom of abortion. He was therefore given notice by the hospital, an act that was finally upheld by the Federal Constitutional Court and by the European Commission of Human Rights. The ECHR held that the freedom of speech of the applicant, Mr Rommelfanger, had to be appropriately balanced with the right to freedom of speech of the employer and the Roman Catholic Church. Because the actions of Mr Rommelfanger compromised the teaching of the church and the church regarded the exercise of charitable functions as one of its essential tasks, the rights of the church and the employer prevailed. The decision is questionable in that it based the ruling on the freedom of speech of the religious community and not on freedom of religion.

### *C. The Right to Self-Determination and the European Court of Human Rights*

*406.* The right to self-determination of religious communities in German law has come under scrutiny by the ECHR.[293] It has been strongly upheld by the Court. Several basic issues were at stake in these cases. In secular settings, the national law may and must take account of the necessity to secure an employee's freedoms under Articles 8, 9 or 10 ECHR or other pertinent human rights guarantees of the ECHR against unreasonable demands of his or her employer, even if they result from a valid employment contract. However, where the employer is a belief organization (i.e., one based on certain convictions and value judgments that it considers essential for the performance of its functions in society), it is in fact also necessary to protect the freedom of religion of the employer. A similar statement has been made by the European Commission of Human Rights in the *Rommelfanger* case concerning a church's freedom of expression.[294] An employer of this kind cannot effectively exercise its freedom without imposing certain duties of loyalty and/or worthiness on its employees. As regards employers such as a church, the law, in any event, ensures that there is a reasonable relationship between the measures affecting

291. ECHR, *Grandrath v. Germany*, 29 Jun. 1967, appl. no. 2299/64 (conscientious objection and objection against civilian service of a member of Jehovah's Witnesses).
292. ECHR, *Rommelfanger v. Federal Republic of Germany*, 6 Sep. 1989, appl. no. 12242/86; BVerfG 4 Jun. 1985, BVerfGE 70, 138 et seq.
293. *See* ECHR, *Hanna and Peter Müller v. Germany*, appl. no. 12986/04; *Obst v. Germany*, appl. no. 425/03; *Siebenhaar v. Germany*, appl. no. 18136/02.
294. *See* ECHR, *Rommelfanger v. Federal Republic of Germany*, 6 Sep. 1989, appl. no. 12242/86; BVerfG 4 Jun. 1985, BVerfGE 70, 138 et seq.

the freedoms under the ECHR and the nature of the employment, as well as the importance of the issue for the employer. In this way, it protects an employee against compulsion in matters of the freedoms protected by the Convention, which would strike at the very substance of this freedom.[295] Article 8 of the Convention does not impose a positive obligation on the state to provide protection beyond this standard.[296] In addition, one has to see that in cases involving a religious community, the religious freedom of all other individual members of the religious community is at stake. The religious freedom of leaders of religious communities is compromised if they are precluded from effectively guiding the overall activities of the religious community because they are forced to continue the employment of visible leaders who flaunt the religious community's teachings. The general membership of the religious community also suffers because the nature of the institution that represents their beliefs is compromised, as is the clarity of the religious community's position on vital matters of doctrine and practice.

*407.* The European Court of Human Rights has repeatedly made very clear in its settled case law that, as enshrined in Article 9 ECHR, freedom of thought, conscience, and religion is one of the foundations of a 'democratic society' within the meaning of the ECHR. It is, in its religious dimension, one of the most vital elements that make up the identity of believers and their conception of life, but it is also a precious asset for atheists, agnostics, sceptics and the unconcerned. The pluralism indissociable from a democratic society, which has been dearly won over the centuries, depends on it.[297]

*408.* Church autonomy – self-determination – is a foremost and integral part of freedom of religion. Where the organization of the religious community is at issue, Article 9 ECHR must be interpreted in the light of Article 11 ECHR, which safeguards associative life against unjustified state interference. Seen in this perspective, the believers' right to freedom of religion encompasses the expectation that the community will be allowed to function peacefully and free from arbitrary state intervention. Indeed, the autonomous existence of religious communities is indispensable for pluralism in a democratic society and is thus an issue at the very heart of the protection that Article 9 ECHR affords. It directly concerns not only the organization of the community as such but also the effective enjoyment of the right to

---

295. *See* ECHR, *Young, James and Webster v. The United Kingdom*, 13 Aug. 1981, appl. nos 7601/76 and 7806/77, 23 §55.
296. *See also* ECHR, *Rommelfanger v. Federal Republic of Germany*, 6 Sep. 1989, appl. no. 12242/86; BVerfG 4 Jun. 1985, BVerfGE 70, 138 et seq.
297. *See* ECHR, *Religionsgemeinschaft der Zeugen Jehovah's and Others v. Austria*, 31 Jul. 2005, appl. no. 40825/98, §61; ECHR, *Metropolitan Church of Bessarabia and Others v. Moldova*, 31 Dec. 2001, appl. no. 45701/99, §114; ECHR, *Serif v. Greece*, 14 Dec. 1999, appl. no. 38178/97, §49; ECHR, *Kokkinakis v. Greece*, 25 May 1993, appl. no. 14307/88, §§31, 33; ECHR, *Hasan and Chaush v. Bulgaria*, 26 Oct. 2000, appl. no. 30985/96, §60.

freedom of religion by all its active members. If the organizational life of the community is not protected by Article 9 ECHR, all other aspects of the individual's freedom of religion would become vulnerable.[298] If religious autonomy is not preserved, state supremacy would be the outcome. State neutrality would be compromised, as would the undisturbed authenticity of religious life and practice. Separation of state and religious communities would become impossible.

*409.* In the case of *Hasan and Chaush*, the European Court of Human Rights has recalled that religious communities traditionally and universally exist in the form of organized structures. They abide by rules that are often seen by followers as being of a divine origin. Religious ceremonies have their meaning and sacred value for the believers if they have been conducted by ministers empowered for that purpose in compliance with these rules. The personality of the religious ministers is undoubtedly of importance to every member of the community. Participation in the life of the community is thus a manifestation of one's religion, protected by Article 9 ECHR.[299] Similar reasons apply to employees of the religious community. This is a vital and practical reality, whether the employee representing the community holds a high position responsible for representing the community in visible public settings or whether the employee is a normal employee who nonetheless represents the religious community and its values, albeit in a more humble context.

*410.* The first requirement for pluralism is to respect the different identities of religious communities. Without respect for the differences between religious communities from general secular behaviour, pluralism would be an empty word and would lack institutional grounding. Since the autonomous existence of religious communities is indispensable for pluralism in a democratic society, differences between religious communities must be tolerated and respected. This holds true not only for issues of worship and ritual practice but also for matters of religious beliefs about the way the religious community should be structured. The same holds true for differences between a specific religious community and general state law; religious communities have the right to organize their affairs and to establish and enforce behavioural and organizational requirements that are different from patterns of state affairs. Furthermore, the European Court of Human Rights has observed that, in principle, the right to freedom of religion for the purposes of the ECHR excludes assessment by the state of the legitimacy of religious beliefs or the ways in which those beliefs are expressed.[300] This respect must be rendered even if secular law and secular convictions do not agree with such a belief or hold that more lax standards should apply to society at large.

298. *See* ECHR, *Hasan and Chaush v. Bulgaria*, 26 Oct. 2000, appl. no. 30985/96, §62; ECHR, *Metropolitan Church of Bessarabia and Others v. Moldova*, 13 Dec. 2001, appl. no. 45701/99, §118.
299. *See* ECHR, *Metropolitan Church of Bessarabia and Others v. Moldova*, 13 Dec. 2001, appl. no. 45701/99, §118.
300. *See* ECHR, *Moscow Branch of the Salvation Army v. Russia*, 5 Oct. 2006, appl. no. 72881/01, §92; ECHR, *Metropolitan Church of Bessarabia and Others v. Moldova*, 13 Dec. 2001, appl. no. 45701/99, §117.

*411.* Freedom of religion and autonomy of religious communities require that the decision-making about loyalty and worthiness obligations within the religious community are, in principle, left in their entirety to the relevant religious community itself. State authorities or other authorities outside the religious community must not force the religious community to introduce gradations of loyalty obligations into its internal structures and hierarchies. Otherwise, the religious community could feel forced to structure itself according to actual or presumed and uncertain expectations of non-religious authorities. A religious community should not be forced to guess when it is free to require its employees to follow church teachings and when (or with respect to what class of employees) it may be required to compromise those standards.[301] Uncertainty may create pressures that would deter religious groups from asserting the full scope of their right to religious freedom. It is also not within the state's competence to decide on which functions in a religious community are central to its teaching and which are not. As the European Court of Human Rights has stated, the right to freedom of religion for the purposes of the Convention excludes assessment by the state of the legitimacy of religious beliefs or the ways in which those beliefs are expressed.[302] This includes making assessments of what teachings and practices are important to a religious community. Secular courts are not free to substitute their judgment for the religious judgments of a community. Furthermore, the religious life within a religious community is not necessarily or exclusively dependent on the leading – or 'visible' – people. Spiritual experiences can occur anywhere. Sometimes, it may be the cook in the kitchen of a religious institution, the gardener in the churchyard, or anyone else within the religious community who impresses somebody else with his deeds and beliefs – or who compromises the teaching of the religious community. The loyalty and worthiness of such persons to the beliefs of a religious community and its practice have a decisive impact on the very existence of the religious community. If credibility among members and the public is lost, the sensitive interrelationships that bind the members to each other and to the religious community are jeopardized, and its essential nature is compromised. If these sensitive relationships are undermined, the glue that holds the members of the religious community together is lost.

*412.* The need for autonomous decisions about such loyalty obligations is not uniquely linked to religious communities. There are many institutions that are in a comparable situation. Many institutions exist for the sake of a special ideal, a specific morale or a defined interest. Trade unions, political parties, newspapers and other media, and many other such institutions must be able to define their own philosophical identities. They must be able to also define and ensure the relevant conduct of their employees or members. This is generally accepted. It is a precondition for the proper functioning of a democratic society. This being the case for secular organizations with their limited interests, it must be all the more applicable

301. *See* ECHR, *Church of Scientology Moscow v. Russia*, 5 Apr. 2007, appl. no. 18147/02, §91; ECHR, *Moscow Branch of the Salvation Army v. Russia*, 5 Oct. 2006, appl. no. 72881/01, §90 (requiring religious organizations to guess as to standards for registration is impermissible).

302. *See* ECHR, *Metropolitan Church of Bessarabia and Others v. Moldova*, 13 Dec. 2001, appl. no. 45701/99, §117.

to religious communities as a matter of religious freedom since their ethos, their beliefs, and their truth are the very essence of their existence.

## III. Other International Instruments

*413.* Freedom of religion, as well as autonomy of religious communities, has been identified as a foremost right also by international instruments other than the Convention. An example is provided by the commitments within the framework of the OSCE. Principle 16.4 of the Vienna Concluding Document provides that participating states will respect the right of the religious communities not only to organize themselves according to their own hierarchical and institutional structure but also to select, appoint and replace their personnel in accordance with their respective requirements and standards as well as with any freely accepted arrangement between them and their state. It is thus well accepted in international law that religious communities have the freedom to appoint and replace their personnel in accordance with their own requirements and standards. Principle 17 of the Vienna Concluding Document stipulates that participating states recognize that the exercise of this right relating to the freedom of religion or belief may be subject only to such limitations as are provided by law and consistent with their obligations under international law and with their international commitments.

# §2. European Union Law

## I. Basic Principles

*414.* Germany is a founding Member State of the EU. EU law takes precedence over any Member State's law including their constitution in the individual case in which it is applied. Member States' law that contradicts EU law of whichever rank (founding treaties and other primary law, ordinances, directives or other) would not be null and void, but in each individual case in which this contradicting Member State's law would apply, the EU law takes precedence. The Member State's law, including its constitution would in such a case be inapplicable. In Germany, this has not been relevant to freedom of religion so far.

*415.* Because there is a considerable amount of EU law relevant to religious issues, EU law today has a decisive impact on freedom of religion in Germany. Also, the Federal Constitutional Court has repeatedly stated that it will respect this priority of EU law; however, if the EU law should infringe in a gross manner upon fundamental rights guaranteed in the German constitution in an individual case or if it should disrespect those fundamental rights in general, the German Federal Constitutional Court would resume its judicial review and step in.[303]

303. BVerfG 12 Oct. 1993, BVerfGE 89, 155 et seq.

## II. Freedom of Religion or Belief in Primary European Union Law

*416.* Fundamental rights, including freedom of religion or belief, form part of the common constitutional traditions of the Member States of the EU and, as such, also form an integral part of EU law itself.[304]

*417.* Freedom of religion or belief is also guaranteed in Article 10 of the European Charter of Fundamental Rights. The limitation clause in the European Charter of Fundamental Rights relating to religious freedom as well as to other fundamental rights and freedoms will – with respect to Germany – not be stronger or narrower than the German constitutional limitations. Article 53 of the Charter states that the limitation clause of the European Charter of Fundamental Rights will not extend further than Member States' limitation clauses. In addition, the limitation clause of Article 9 ECHR will prevail before the limitation clause of the European Charter of Fundamental Rights with respect to religious freedom, as it does not allow for as strong limitations as the limitation clause of the European Charter of Fundamental Rights.[305] Article 21 European Charter of Fundamental Rights prohibits discrimination on grounds of religion or belief. The EU respects the multitude of cultures, religions, and languages according to Article 22 European Charter of Fundamental Rights.

*418.* Basic structures of European law on religion are evident. It finds its basis in religious freedom as an element of EU law. Further structural principles are the obligation of the EU to remain neutral in questions of religion and belief, to show tolerance towards different religions and beliefs, and to grant equal treatment to religious and belief communities. The safeguard of the cultures of the Member States and their national identity, according to Article 4 section 2 Treaty on European Union (TEU), requires special respect towards traditionally developed institutions of civil ecclesiastical law in the Member States. The principle of EU loyalty in the form of respect for the constitutional structure of Member States prohibits unilateral assimilation of the law where these matters are concerned. Finally, the principle of subsidiarity, according to Article 5 TEU, requires a reticence on the part of the EU with regard to questions of the law on religion.

*419.* The religious communities' right to self-determination finds a means of support in religious freedom. The European Court of Justice (*Europäischer Gerichtshof (EuGH)* (ECJ)) has acknowledged it. According to Article 6 subsection 3 TEU, the EU respects the fundamental rights as they are guaranteed by the ECHR and as they result from the common constitutional traditions of the Member States as a general principle of the EU's law.

---

304. Cf. Art. 6 Treaty on European Union (TEU).
305. Cf. Gerhard Robbers, 'State and Church in the European Union', in *State and Church in the European Union*, Gerhard Robbers ed., 3rd edn (Baden-Baden: Nomos, 2019), 684.

*420.* A restriction on the action of the EU's law in matters of the law of religion in the Member States of the EU is formed in particular by the principle of subsidiarity. Article 5 TEU provides that the EU, according to the principle of subsidiarity, takes action only if and insofar as the goals of the intended measures cannot adequately be achieved at the level of the Member States, and so, because of their scale or their effects, may be achieved better at EU level. In the area of religious matters, better achievement of goals usually means that the needs of historically developed religious beliefs determined by national and regional circumstances, emotional ties and historical experience must be given space. In consequence, the realization of goals in these matters may be achieved at the level of the Member States and their subdivisions, not, however, at the EU level.

*421.* Article 4 section 2 TEU obliges the EU to respect the national identities of its Member States. The variety of the religious circumstances and their legal treatment in the Member States of the EU shows how great the formative influence of the religious communities on the national identities of the Member States is. History, culture and tradition of the Member States are always influenced by the system of the law on religion.

*422.* The idea of common constitutional traditions of the Member States still forms a basis for the development of religious law structures in EU law in other matters apart from those of human rights. Such common constitutional traditions exist to a great extent. Everywhere in the EU, religious freedom is in general recognized and everywhere the religious communities possess institutional independence. That is true even where the system includes a state church, at least for those religious communities in the Member State which are not state churches. It is clear that, for instance, in labour law, the communities' religious conception of themselves as an employer must be taken into consideration. Article 167 Treaty on the Functioning of the European Union (TFEU), confers responsibility for the protection of cultural variety upon the EU. The law on religion is indeed a part of this culture. According to Article 167 TFEU, the EU contributes to the development of the cultures of the Member States while safeguarding their national and regional diversity. In this, the common cultural heritage of Europe is emphasized. This also and especially points to the religious roots and traditions of Europe. Article 167 TFEU is, however, based on a restricted understanding of culture. Cultural competences refer to research and education, general and professional education, artistic and literary creation, to the protection of historic monuments, literature, architecture and the mass media. Competences of the EU may be derived from Article 165 TFEU for the area of professional and general education. In this way, all religiously maintained educational institutions, such as private schools, theological faculties and academies, and not least religious education classes, benefit from support according to EU law.

*423.* According to Article 351 TFEU, the rights and obligations created by treaties concluded between a Member State and a third state before the Treaty came into force are not affected by the Treaty. Insofar as the agreements are not compatible with the EU's law, the Member States are obliged to remedy these incompatibilities, if necessary, by renegotiation. This can and does affect treaty obligations that require a certain nationality of officeholders of religious communities.

*424.* Of particular relevance for the status of churches and religious communities is Article 17 TFEU. It reads:

(1) The Union respects and does not prejudice the status under national law of churches and religious associations or communities in the Member States.
(2) The Union equally respects the status of philosophical and non-confessional organizations.
(3) Recognizing their identity and their specific contribution, the Union shall maintain an open, transparent and regular dialogue with these churches and organizations.

*425.* Article 17 TFEU is an expression of the existing neutrality of the EU in religious and philosophical matters. This neutrality, according to the wording of the provision, relates to the Member States' law on religion; indirectly, this neutrality also relates to churches and religious and philosophical communities.

*426.* The provision acknowledges churches and religious communities as factors within community law. It respects the Member States' competence in the field of religion. Whenever the European institutions exercise their competences, they must respect and not prejudice the Member States' law on religion within the scope of EU law. Because of the principle of unity of the European primary law, institutions are also bound by other provisions of European primary law. For example, this has an impact on freedom of religion, equality, non-discrimination and democracy in this field. Article 17 TFEU also does not perpetuate the law on religion within the Member States. They are completely free to develop these relations. It is the status of churches and religious communities as it stands at the respective time that has to be respected.

*427.* Article 17 section 3 TFEU provides for a dialogue between the EU and all of its institutions with those churches and religious communities. The dialogue will have to be developed in full respect of the identities, special needs, and relevance of religious entities. This includes the possibility of concluding agreements with them. The dialogue must be open, transparent and regular. In acknowledging the special contribution of those churches and communities, the Constitution does in fact acknowledge their spiritual, social, and cultural contribution. However, it also acknowledges openly the impact of Christianity on the existing European law without disregarding the contributions of other religions and philosophies. By explicitly using the term 'churches', special reference is being made to Christianity, this term being an exclusively Christian term. The intense public debate about an explicit reference to Christianity in the preamble thus seems to have been somewhat overexcited. Article 17 TFEU carries interesting parallels and differences in relation to Article 11 TEU. The latter provision relates to an open, transparent, and regular dialogue with the representative institutions of civil society. The dialogue with churches and religious and philosophical communities is based on similar principles, as is the dialogue with institutions of civil society. Churches and similar communities must not be placed in a worse position. By giving them a special place in the treaties, the EU recognizes that those churches and religious and philosophical communities are not a mere part of civil society. On the contrary, the EU acknowledges the special contribution and the specific identities of these churches and religious and philosophical communities. However, as far as these entities or their organizations are in fact also parts of civil society, they also enjoy the rights provided in Article 11 TEU. Much of the cooperative approach of the German law on religion is thus secured also on the level of EU law.

## III. Religion in Secondary European Union Law

### A. *Provisions*

*428.* Of major impact on the religious communities' right to self-determination is Article 4 of the directive concerning equal treatment in employment and occupation (Directive 2000/78/EC). Article 4 provides:

> Occupational requirements
>
> 1. …
> 2. Member States may maintain national legislation in force at the date of adoption of this Directive or provide for future legislation incorporating national practices existing at the date of adoption of this Directive pursuant to which, in the case of occupational activities within churches and other public or private organizations the ethos of which is based on religion or belief, a difference of treatment based on a person's religion or belief shall not constitute discrimination where, by reason of the nature of these activities or of the context in which they are carried out, a person's religion or belief constitutes a genuine, legitimate and justified occupational requirement, having regard to the organization's ethos. This difference of treatment shall be implemented taking account of Member States' constitutional provisions and principles, as well as the general principles of Community law, and should not justify discrimination on another ground.

*429.* Provided that its provisions are otherwise complied with, this Directive shall thus not prejudice the right of churches and other public or private organizations, the ethos of which is based on religion or belief, acting in conformity with national constitutions and laws, to require individuals working for them to act in good faith and with loyalty to the organization's ethos. The autonomy rights of the religious communities are thus secured to a far-reaching extent.

*B. European Union Law and the German General Anti-discrimination Act*

*430.* The 2006 General Anti-Discrimination Act (AGG)[306] is to prevent or to stop discrimination on the grounds of race or ethnic origin, gender, religion or belief, disability, age, or sexual orientation. While according to its §7 section 1 employees shall not be permitted to suffer discrimination on any of these grounds, §8 AGG states that a difference of treatment on any of such grounds shall not constitute discrimination where, by reason of the nature of the particular occupational activities or of the context in which they are carried out, such grounds constitute a genuine and determining occupational requirement, provided that the objective is legitimate and the requirement is proportionate. §9 AGG further stipulates permissible differences of treatment on the grounds of religion or belief:

(1) Notwithstanding §8, a difference of treatment on the grounds of religion or belief of employees of a religious community, facilities affiliated to it (regardless of their legal form) or organizations which have undertaken conjointly to practice a religion or belief, shall not constitute discrimination where such grounds constitute a justified occupational requirement for a particular religion or belief, having regard to the ethos of the religious community or organization in question and by reason of their right to self-determination or by the nature of the particular activity.
(2) The prohibition of different treatment on the grounds of religion or belief shall be without prejudice to the right of the religious community referred to under §1, the facilities assigned to it (regardless of their legal form) or organizations which have undertaken conjointly to practice a religion or belief, to require individuals working for them to act in good faith and with loyalty to the ethos of the organization.

*431.* There is some ongoing debate about the meaning and interpretation of this provision. The provision has to be interpreted in the light of the directive. Therefore, some say the ethos or self-understanding of the religious community must be narrowly interpreted in the light of the directive and cannot constitute a reason for unequal treatment.[307] However, in view of Article 17 TFEU as well as the fundamental rights commitments on freedom of religion or belief, these provisions of the General Anti-Discrimination Act fully conform to the directive in their broad understanding and scope of the religious communities' self-determination within employment issues.

306. Available in English at GBB Aachen & ARIC-NRW e.v. (ed.), 'AGG-Ratgeber', http://agg-ratgeber.de/files/pdf/AGG_en.pdf, 9 Nov. 2023,.
307. ArbG Hamburg 4 Dec. 2007, *Arbeit und Recht* 2008, 109 et seq.

## IV. The European Court of Justice

*432.* The ECJ first acknowledged the fundamental right to religious freedom, at least in its core, in the decision of *Prais v. Council of 1976*,[308] providing for basic respect for religious needs. In other contexts, the ECJ has also had the opportunity to make decisions relevant to religious communities. The *Bhagwan* case of 1988 states that remunerated labour and services in the context of the economic activity of the religious community can form part of economic life within the meaning of the EC.[309] The difficulties European Community law has had in dealing with the special characteristics of church existence became particularly clear in the case of *van Rosmaalen v. Bestuir van de Betrijfsvereinigingen*.[310] Van Rosmaalen, a Premonstratensian priest and missionary in Zaire, had for some decades been maintained by the members of his missionary community rather than by his order, and the ECJ therefore held the priest to be self-employed in the sense intended by Community law, so that he received a pension according to the laws of the Member State. This decision had provided particularly clearly that the categories of Community law for a long time were hardly able to deal adequately with church circumstances, even if the ECJ reached an appropriate decision in the particular case because the notion of 'self-employed' is hardly fit for a Roman Catholic priest in his capacity as a missionary. It has at the same time, however, underlined the need for explicit provisions on religion within the framework of EU law, thus supporting the cause for an open and conscious approach towards the religious sphere.

308. ECJ 27 Oct. 1976, Case 130/75 (*Vivien Prais v. Council of the European Communities*), ECR 1976, 1589 et seq.
309. ECJ 5 Oct. 1988, Case 196/87 (*Steymann v. Staatssecretaris van Justitie*), ECR 1988, 6159 et seq.
310. ECJ 23 Oct. 1986, Case 300/84 (*A. J. M. van Roosmalen v. Bestuur van de Bedrijfsvereniging voor de Gezondheid, Geestelijke en Maatschappelijke Belangen*), ECR 1986, 3097 et seq.

## Chapter 2. Transnational Law Effects on Religious Communities

*433.* Germany, as has been stated above, is a federal state consisting of the Federal Republic and sixteen federal *Länder*. According to Article 31 GG, federal law takes precedence over *Land* law, the law of the *Länder*. This applies to any law of the Federal Republic. Thus, the federal constitution prevails over not only the law of the *Länder* but also any other federal law, statute, or regulation that takes precedence over any law of the *Länder*, including the constitution of a specific *Land*.

*434.* It has to be reiterated and emphasized that special provisions exist in respect of fundamental rights. Notwithstanding Article 31 GG, provisions of *Land* constitutions remain in force insofar as they guarantee basic rights in conformity with Articles 1–18 of the federal constitution (Article 142 GG). This somewhat complicated and puzzling provision is usually interpreted in a way that it upholds fundamental rights guaranteed in a *Land* constitution that might guarantee fundamental rights exceeding those of the federal constitution. An example could be that the constitution of the Saarland guarantees in its Article 11 the right of asylum to everybody who is persecuted in violation of any fundamental right provided for in the constitution of the Saarland and has fled into the Saarland. According to the federal constitution Article 16a, political asylum is guaranteed only to a lesser extent. Although this has never become practical until today, this provision could provide political asylum for those who have been persecuted for religious reasons and might not have obtained political asylum based on federal law. It remains uncertain, however, whether courts would follow such reasoning.

*435.* According to Article 28 section 1 GG, the constitutional order in the *Länder* must conform to the principles of a republican, democratic, and social state governed by the rule of law within the meaning of the federal constitution. Basic principles within this range of republican, democratic, and social state governed by the rule of law that might not by any reasoning follow from the wording of a *Land* constitution would, by virtue of Article 28 section 1 GG, form a direct part of that *Land* constitution. Again, this has not become practical in respect of freedom of religion or belief.

*436.* Because the Federal Republic of Germany is a federal entity, religious communities are affected by federal law in whichever field the numerous powers of the Federation as such apply. In fact, and as has been indicated above, over the course of the decades of its existence and through manifold constitutional amendments, the Federation has gained in competencies, and the powers of the *Länder* have been reduced in scope and impact. While, in view of the general principles, the relation between the state and religious communities remains a matter of the *Länder*, in practice, many powers lie with the Federation today. This is more the case as the fundamental rights and institutional guarantees concerning religious matters that are laid out in the Basic Law do have a unifying force and impact.

## Chapter 3. Regional Law Effects on Religious Communities

*437.* Notwithstanding the general impact of the Federation in religious matters, the general principle remains relevant and important whereby the relations between the state and religious communities are basically matters of the *Länder*, as is expressed in Articles 30 and 70 GG.

*438.* Also, the local communities are of considerable relevance for the practical life of religious communities. The principle of autonomy of local communities is expressed in Article 28 GG: 'Municipalities must be guaranteed the right to regulate all local affairs on their own responsibility, within the limits prescribed by the laws. Within the limits of their functions designated by a law, associations of municipalities shall also have the right of self-government according to the laws.'

*439.* Local communities are linked with religious communities by numerous historic agreements. Still important are those agreements that constitute financial contributions of the municipalities to the maintenance of buildings owned by religious communities because such buildings, at least in history, also served municipal purposes such as fire protection or clocks on church towers that were also of use for the general public. Municipalities are also important partners of religious communities because municipalities have the exclusive power to plan for urban and local development; this includes having regard to the religious and cultural needs of the population as is provided for in §1 section 6 Town and Country Planning Code (BauGB).

# Part V. Religion and Politics

*440.* The religious communities in Germany are free to participate in the democratic process. They have widely accepted that function and take an active part in the democratic system.[311] In general, political influence of religious communities in Germany is regarded as legitimate and necessary. Religions form part of the public democratic process. Religious communities are important institutions in the public debate and have established a number of formalized ways of making their voices heard. The specific German history, especially the complete moral breakdown under Nazi rule, calls for a visible role of religious communities in the public political debate. Religious communities have a 'public assignment'. They usually do not take sides in terms of party politics, and religion is not an important issue in election campaigns. However, in recent years, Muslim immigration and the related issues of religion, such as the wearing of headscarves, have in fact developed some impact on the election campaigns of some political parties. Also, the rise of the right-wing party 'Alternative für Deutschland' (AFD) has caused several religious communities to sharply criticize this party and its anti-Semitic, anti-Muslim, and anti-Christian attitudes.

311. *See* Wolfgang Huber, *Kirche und Öffentlichkeit*, 2nd edn (Munich: Kaiser, 1991).

# Chapter 1. Religious Influence in Politics

## §1. Constitutional Law Foundations

*441.* Political participation of the religious communities is based on a broad understanding of freedom of religion as guaranteed in Article 4 GG. This understanding accepts that religion also teaches how the secular world should best be organized. It is further based on the freedom of speech and freedom of opinion as laid out in Article 5 GG. Religious people and religious communities enjoy these rights in the same way as the non-religious. From this point of view, democracy, as provided for in Article 20 GG and throughout constitutional law, includes the contribution of the religious sphere.

*442.* Seen from a more general perspective, democracy in Germany has, to some, while limited, extent developed into a democracy of associations such as trade unions, employers' associations, or consumer associations that exercise considerable influence on the political process. Religious communities form part of this setting. It would amount to a violation of state neutrality if religious communities were excluded from the political sphere and deprived of their fundamental political rights. Equal treatment, as provided for in Article 3 GG, calls for including the religious communities in the political sphere. Article 140 GG and Article 136 sections 1 and 2 WRV guarantee that civil and political rights neither depend upon nor are restricted by the exercise of religious freedom, and one's enjoyment of civil and political rights and one's eligibility for public office shall be independent of religious affiliation. The right of religious communities to regulate and administer their affairs independently within the limits of the laws that apply to all according to Article 140 GG in conjunction with Article 137 section 3 WRV includes the right to decide upon what are 'their affairs'; affairs of religious communities thus can well be issues relevant in the political sphere, such as the treatment of immigrants and refugees or the structure of the state social services.

*443.* The status of a religious community as a public law corporation does not exclude it from the democratic process; all religious communities, from the legal point of view, take part in the political process in the same way as other non-state organizations. The process of forming the general political will has indeed to go from the people to the state institutions, and not the other way around. However, there is no state church, and religious communities, regardless of their status, are not part of the state. The status of religious communities as public law corporations does not mean that they are incorporated into the state body; they do not become state institutions.

*444.* It may well be difficult – if not impossible – to distinguish clearly between the political and the religious spheres. Both spheres overlap in many cases. Religion is not merely a personal matter (highly personal as religious beliefs and decisions are) but also a public one; it will become part of the public political process. The question of how the political and religious spheres relate to each other has been part of a contemporary debate in Germany regarding the integration of the Muslim population into German society. In general public debate, it is often argued that while Christianity teaches a difference between the secular and the sacred, Islam identifies the two. From this point of view, some fear that Muslims would not be fit to integrate into a constitutional setting in which state neutrality in religious matters is a fundamental assumption. Yet, in this debate, it is often forgotten that in Germany, until the beginning of the twentieth century, state and church were closely intertwined, when the monarchs often were also bishops of the Protestant *Land* churches. One could say that although the institutions of state and religious communities can be separated, religion and politics cannot. The state itself, with its legal system, rests in a general culture shaped not the least by religious convictions, traditions, and experiences. Religious convictions therefore have a function in forming the political will within the constitutional structures. Starting from this point, some argue that the constitutional order itself and the functioning of its institutions depend on cultural preconditions such as a spirit of openness and tolerance or a certain level of education that the state is liable to uphold. Since general culture also depends on religion, this in turn could lead to a state supremacy over religion and to a questioning of the religious neutrality of the state.

*445.* Political influence of religious communities is all too legitimate also seen from a historical perspective. Since the Holocaust, Jewish faith communities have had a special function in the public sphere in Germany. On the federal level, they are represented by the Central Council of Jews in Germany[312] (*Zentralrat der Juden in Deutschland*), which plays an important role in politics by reminding of the special German responsibilities resulting from the crimes committed. As a corporation under public law, the principal task of the Central Council of Jews in Germany is to defend the interests of its members within society as a whole.

*446.* The great Christian churches in Germany acted ambiguously under the Nazi rule. Nevertheless, in the Roman Catholic and Protestant churches, resistance against the Nazi terror was important. It was in these circles that the tone was set for rebuilding the country after the end of the Second World War. Their resistance against the evil of Nazism legitimizes a special acknowledgement of the concept of their public assignment and the public assignment of religious communities in general, which was even sometimes called the 'guardian function' of the religious communities, a concept that has faded away more recently, though.

## §2. Religions in Politics Based on Treaty Law

*447.* The 1955 'Treaty between the Land of Lower Saxony and the Protestant Land Churches in Lower Saxony', also called the Loccum Treaty (*Loccumer Vertrag*), found the most influential words for the political role of religious communities in Germany after the catastrophe of Nazism and Second World War. As has been stated above, in the Loccum Treaty, the *Land* Government of Lower Saxony and the constitutional representatives of the Protestant *Land* churches in Lower Saxony

312. Central Council of Jews in Germany (ed.), http:// www.zentralratdjuden.de, 9 Nov. 2023.

declare that they are conscious of the joint responsibility for the Protestant part of the Lower Saxon population and that they have, in compliance with the public assignment of the churches and their independence, decided to develop the treaty further, with adherence to the rights of the churches within the meaning of true free order. Furthermore, they agree that the *Land* Government and the church managements shall strive to have regular meetings to deepen their relations and that they will at all times make themselves available to discuss questions concerning their mutual relationship. They also agree that the Protestant *Land* churches will enter into close cooperation among themselves in order uniformly to represent their interests towards the state, and that they will appoint joint representatives to the state and establish an agency at the seat of the *Land* Government. The treaty has been a reference point for a number of subsequent treaties between the state and religious communities in shaping the political relationship between them.

*448.* The idea of the 'public assignment', or, as can also be translated, public mission or public task of the religious communities, has been of foremost importance to their political functions. The idea of a public assignment has its original roots in a narrow notion of freedom of religious teaching. Freedom of public teaching had to be fought for against the persecution by the Nazi regime. For example, in 1934, the Theological Declaration of Barmen issued by the Confessional Synod of the German Evangelical Church in opposition to the Hitler Nazi regime stated that it is the assignment of the church to teach the message of the free grace of God through sermon and sacrament to all people. After the moral and material devastation under Nazism, Germans felt that religious communities should be able to have a broad contribution in terms of ethics and politics. Today, the religious communities' public assignment is a centrepiece of their legally described involvement in the political sphere. Several treaties between religious communities and the state have reiterated the notion of a 'public assignment' of the religious community.[313] For example, the 1992 constitution of the *Land* Brandenburg explicitly acknowledges the public assignment of the churches and religious communities in its Article 36 section 3.

## §3. Media and Religions

*449.* The religious communities have a special public mandate that is secured by state-church treaties and that has its foundations in religious freedom. This accordingly allows religious communities to have a say and a right to be informed by the state in matters and affairs of public life. Because of their public mandate, religious institutions have designated time slots on television and radio in the relevant laws of the *Länder*. They are also, as a result, given a representative position on the supervisory boards of public institutions where a particular societal representation is necessary. The religious communities, Christian and Jewish as well as Muslim, send representatives to the broadcasting commissions of public broadcasting corporations such as German Television Channel II (*Zweites Deutsches Fernsehen*

313. Schleswig-Holstein 1957; Hesse 1960; Rhineland-Palatinate 1962.

(ZDF)), Consortium of public-law broadcasting institutions of the Federal Republic of Germany (*Arbeitsgemeinschaft der öffentlich-rechtlichen Rundfunkanstalten der Bundesrepublik Deutschland* (ARD)), and the *Land*-based broadcasting corporations, which are the supervisory commissions for the private television and radio stations, as well as appraisal and classification boards that identify and restrain scripts and films that are deemed harmful to young viewers and listeners. Religious communities also hold seats in the bodies that determine at what age young people should be allowed to view specific movies and whether certain publications are deemed to be pornographic, for example, or otherwise sanctioned.

## §4. Religions and State Political Institutions

*450.* Religious communities are not represented as such in parliament or in any equivalent bodies. Nonetheless, members and personnel of religious communities can run for parliament and similar institutions and exercise political functions like everyone else. There are no legal restrictions on any such activities. Some religious communities have introduced internal restrictions for their personnel concerning political offices, however. The Federal Constitutional Court has declared it constitutional for a religious institution to deny its own officeholders the right to stand for public office while they exercise a religious office.[314] The Catholic Church, for example, does not permit priests to run for public office. Yet, if any particular Catholic priest chooses to do so, the German state will not hinder him.

*451.* According to state law, the right to vote and to be elected is in no way restricted by religious reasons. Any such regulation on incompatibility would not be in harmony with Article 3 section 3 GG, whereby no one is to be disadvantaged or privileged on the basis of his or her religion. Furthermore, Article 33 section 3 GG states that the enjoyment of civil rights, admission to public office, and the rights acquired in the civil service exist independently of one's religious beliefs. No one is to be disadvantaged based on his religious belief. Similar stipulations are found in Article 136 WRV in conjunction with Article 140 GG.

## §5. Religions and Political Parties

*452.* Political parties are in general grounded in basic convictions, ideas, and value systems for which they stand. In many fields, however, political parties overlap. People of all creeds and non-creeds can be found in almost all relevant political parties. In most of the relevant political parties in Germany, religiously oriented members form internal groups in various grades of formal organization. Religious affiliations thus have an influence on the political sphere.

---

314. BVerfG 21 Sep. 1976, BVerfGE 42, 312 et seq.

*453.* There are political parties that explicitly express in their programmes, or even in their names, a basic relation to religious backgrounds. Religious communities do not have specific links with specific political parties, however. Members of political parties can only be natural persons.[315] Religious communities can therefore not directly found a political party. One may nonetheless identify somewhat stronger sympathies for certain political parties in certain religious communities or in parts of them, while such sympathies may change over time and by issue.

*454.* The Christian Democratic Union (*Christlich Demokratische Union* (CDU)) is a Christian, democratic political party that has been a leading political force in Germany since the beginning of the Federal Republic of Germany. On a European level, the CDU is a member of the European People's Party. The party is explicitly based on Christian values but is, however, not organizationally linked with any specific Christian denomination. The CDU has always been open to people from all Christian and non-Christian denominations. Jews, Muslims, and people without a specific religious affiliation have held and are holding offices for the party. When the party was founded, in 1945, the term 'Christian' in its name also stood for overcoming the political antagonisms between Catholic and Protestant parts of the German population. Another major religiously influenced political party in Germany is the Christian Social Union (*Christlich-Soziale Union in Bayern e. V.* (CSU)), a predominantly Christian political party that is based in Bavaria. It is nearly identical to the CDU. On the federal level, CDU and CSU form one single faction in the federal parliament.

*455.* The other politically relevant political parties on the federal level, such as the Social Democratic Party (SPD), the Green Party (*Die Grünen*), the Free Democratic Party (FDP), and also the Left (*Die Linke*), have no explicit and specific religious affiliation, and some are more distant to religions than others. This is also the case for the far-right wing and, at least in great parts Neo-Nazi party AFD.

*456.* Small, religiously influenced political parties in Germany include the *Zentrum* (*Deutsche Zentrumspartei*), the Christian Centre and the Party of Christians Loyal to the Bible (*Partei Bibeltreuer Christen* (PBC)). Each one of them has won considerably less than 1% of the votes cast in federal or *Land* elections.

## §6. Political Representation of Religions

*457.* Political representation of religious communities is often structured by special church institutions. The great churches, such as the Protestant and the Roman Catholic churches in Germany, have established institutions that represent them in the political sphere on the federal level as well as at the level of the *Länder*.

315. §2, s. 1 Act on Political Parties (PartG).

*458.* The Catholic liaison office in Berlin[316] intervenes in political affairs on behalf of the German Bishops' Conference vis-à-vis bodies of the federal government, missions of the *Länder*, political parties, national interest groups, and international institutions. The office is subordinate to the German Bishops' Conference and the Association of German Dioceses. The responsibilities of the liaison office include observing the overall development of the political and social spheres and legislative initiatives of the federal government, supporting the preparation of bills and political decisions, making statements and executing the resolutions passed by the boards of the German Bishops' Conference. The liaison office operates in close cooperation with the boards and commissions of the German Bishops' Conference and the Association of German Dioceses, with the archdioceses and dioceses, with the offices of the German Bishops' Conference, the Central Committee of German Catholics, the Apostolic Nuncio, the Catholic liaison offices at *Land* level, and with the EKD Council Representative to the Federal Government and the EU. Various working groups of experts have been set up to support and consult the liaison office. Working outcomes and statements of long-term significance are published at irregular intervals.

*459.* The EKD has a representative to the federal government and the EU, along with offices in Berlin and Brussels.[317] The representative keeps contact with aspects of politics that are relevant to the Church in very much a similar way to, and very often in close cooperation with, the Catholic Liaison Office. Very similar to its Catholic counterpart, the Protestant representative observes the overall development of the political and social spheres, as well as legislative initiatives of the federal government and supports the preparation of bills and political decisions; of considerable impact is the office's representation in Brussels before the institutions of the EU. Similar to the Catholic Liaison Office, various working groups of experts are set up to support and consult the liaison office; working outcomes and statements of long-term significance are published at irregular intervals.

*460.* The Jewish faith communities, their unions and especially the Central Council of the Jews in Germany are important factors in the political life in Germany. They are vigilant over developments in society and politics, and their word is heard in the political spheres and in the media.

*461.* Muslim associations have begun to play a role in German politics. Many of them take part in the Islam Conference,[318] which was created by the Federal Minister of the Interior. The Conference is a platform to discuss and develop the integration of Muslims into German society and is considered to be the most important forum between the German state and Muslims living in Germany. The Conference is, according to its website, working on concrete, practical projects. It has been

316. Kommissariat der deutschen Bischöfe (ed.), 'Katholisches Büro in Berlin' http://www.dbk.de/ueber-uns/katholisches-buero-berlin/, 9 Nov. 2023.
317. Bevollmächtigter des Rates der EKD (ed.), 'Die Bevollmächtigte des Rates der EKD' https://www.ekd.de/Bevollmaechtigte-10780.htm, 9 Nov. 2023.
318. Bundesamt für Migration und Flüchtlinge (BAMF) (ed.), 'Deutsche Islam Konferenz' https://www.deutsche-islam-konferenz.de/DE/Startseite/startseite_node.html, 9 Nov. 2023.

doing this using flexible structures, alternating event formats and constellations appropriate to the subject areas in question (the 'implementation phase' of the Conference). The Conference involves a broad and diverse range of participants from Muslim national federations, new initiatives outside of traditional mosque structures, individual Muslims, policy-makers and public administration officials as well as representatives from the research community.[319]

## §7. Political Impact of Religious Communities

*462*. The Protestant and Roman Catholic churches have fully accepted the democratic system, as have other religious communities. They regularly contribute to public debate. Their public statements range from views on individual cases to elaborate texts about issues such as stem-cell research, assisted suicide, and the legitimacy of warfare. A recent joint statement by the Roman Catholic Church and the EKD has expressed common views about democracy, especially calling for democratic virtues and active citizen engagement.[320] Although such statements often have little or no impact on public debate, some of these statements have exercised considerable influence on the political process. A prime example of this is the statement on *Ostpolitik* (the policy towards the East) published by the EKD in 1965.[321] The views it expressed were regarded as highly innovative and progressive. The publication called for recognizing the German Eastern border with Poland at the rivers Oder and Neisse because insisting on recovering the formerly German territories would be contrary to peace and harmful to future German reunification. The statement opened up and subsequently supported the new official state policy towards the Eastern Block and helped in the longer run to overcome the post-Second World War East-West confrontation in Germany.

*463*. The Protestant and Roman Catholic churches were, as has been stated above, a political factor of decisive impact during German reunification. They provided a kind of protecting roof for all those who opposed the regime regardless of their religious affiliation; it was from the churches that demonstrations started that finally led to the peaceful end of the DDR and the reunification of Germany.

---

319. https://www.deutsche-islam-konferenz.de/EN/DIK/dik_node.html, 9 Nov. 2023.

320. Evangelische Kirche in Deutschland & Deutsche Bischofskonferenz (eds) 'Demokratie braucht Tugenden. Gemeinsames Wort des Rates der Evangelischen Kirche in Deutschland und der Deutschen Bischofskonferenz zur Zukunft unseres demokratischen Gemeinwesens', http://www.dbk.de/fileadmin/redaktion/veroeffentlichungen/gem-texte/GT_19.pdf, 9 Nov. 2023; Evangelische Kirche in Deutschland (ed.), *Evangelische Kirche und freiheitliche Demokratie: Der Staat des Grundgesetzes als Angebot und Aufgabe* (Kempen: Gütersloher Verlagshaus, 1985), https://www.ekd.de/evangelische-kirche-und-freiheitliche-demokratie-55691.htm, 9 Nov. 2023; John Paul II, 'Centesimus Annus', https://www.vatican.va/content/john-paul-ii/de/encyclicals/documents/hf_jp-ii_enc_01051991_centesimus-annus.html, 9 Nov. 2023.

321. Kurt Scharf, 'Die Lage der Vertriebenen und das Verhältnis des deutschen Volkes zu seinen östlichen Nachbarn: Eine evangelische Denkschrift', https://www.ekd.de/lage_der_vertriebenen_4.htm, 9 Nov. 2023.

## §8. Religious Communities and Election Campaigns

*464.* The Protestant and Roman Catholic churches in Germany no longer take open sides in favour of specific political parties in election campaigns. They usually call for individuals to exercise the right to vote and to take an active part in the democratic process. Interventions in favour of or against a specific political party in elections have been an issue and were controversial some decades ago. The rise of Neo-Nazism and far right-wing attitudes in Germany may well change the situation again and may call for a more explicit approach.

*465.* The Federal Administrative Court decision clearly stated that religious communities have the right to give advice to believers on how to vote.[322] The court did not discuss whether that might have been a violation of freedom of elections had the message been delivered with a threat of sanctions or disadvantages.

*466.* The Federal Constitutional Court has, as stated above, declared it to be constitutional that a religious institution may deny their own church officeholders the right to stand for public office while they exercise a religious office.[323] According to state law, the right to vote and to be elected is in no way restricted, and there are no legal impediments whatsoever as far as religious affiliation is concerned. Such regulation would not be in harmony with Article 3 section 3 GG, whereby no one on the basis of their faith is to be disadvantaged or privileged. Furthermore, Article 33 section 3 GG states that the enjoyment of civil rights and the admission to public office and the rights acquired in the civil service are independent of one's confession. No one as a result of their confession or ideology is to be disadvantaged. Similar stipulations are to be found in Article 138 WRV in conjunction with Article 140 GG. This prohibition against discrimination is, however, independent of the occupation of a religious office.

*467.* The Federal Constitutional Court has held that it is not a valid reason to withhold the status of a public law corporation from a religious community – Jehovah's Witnesses – that teaches abstention from state elections.[324]

322. BVerwG 7 Jan. 1964, *Neue Juristische Wochenschrift* 17 (1964): 1385.
323. BVerfG 21 Sep. 1976, BVerfGE 42, 312 et seq.
324. BVerfG 19 Dec. 2000, BVerfGE 102, 370 et seq.

## Chapter 2. Political Influence in Religions

*468.* The right of religious communities to self-determination prevents unwanted political influence on religious communities. In general, secular political influence on religions is scarce. In some cases, however, political influence from outside is accepted or even welcomed. Political influence can be formal and informal. Formal influence is predominantly based on treaty law between religious communities and the state. Informal political influence is a matter of short-term decisions and long-term traditions.

*469.* A rather visible formal political influence is the political clause in concordats and state-church treaties already referred to above.[325] For example, Article 14 of the *Reichskonkordat* provides that the Bull nominating Archbishops, bishops, coadjutors *cum jure successionis*, or a *Praelatus Nullius*, will not be issued until the name of the person designated has been communicated to the governor of the *Reich* in the competent *Land*, and until it has been ascertained that no objections of a general political nature exist.[326] In some state-church treaties, the term 'objections of a general political nature' has been described as limited to objections by the state of a political nature, whereas church or party-political objections are excluded.[327] This limitation also applies implicitly to the other relevant treaties and concordats. According to Article 14, it is understood that when objections of a general political nature exist, they shall be presented to the Holy See within the shortest possible time. If after twenty days such representations have not been made, the Holy See will be entitled to assume that no objections exist to the candidate in question.[328] The names of the persons in question are kept completely confidential until the announcement of the appointment.[329] The clause also applies to some leading offices in Protestant *Land* churches; it does not take effect when the office is entrusted by a decision of a synod, however.[330] On the whole, this so-called political clause has not been of much relevance in the relationship between the state and religious communities in Germany.

*470.* The *Reichskonkordat* also stipulates that no veto power of the state shall be derived from this provision of the concordat with the *Reich*. Although the concordat concluded with Prussia does provide for such veto powers in its Article 6, prevailing legal opinion is that the denial of a veto power in the *Reichskonkordat* has priority over the Prussian Concordat.[331] The concordat between the Catholic Church

325. Article 14 Reichskonkordat; Art. 14 §1 BayKonk; Art. 3, s. 2 BadKonk; Art. 6, s. 1 PreußKonk; Art. 3, s. 2 Loccumer Vertrag; Art. 29 BayKirchV; Art. 2, s. 2 BadKirchenV.
326. Article 14, no. 2 Reichskonkordat.
327. Article 2, s. 2 BadKirchenV; Art. 7, s. 2 Loccumer Vertrag; Art. 9, s. 2 HessKirchenV.
328. Article 2, no. 4 Reichskonkordat.
329. Article 14, no. 4 Reichskonkordat.
330. Ernst-Lüder Solte, 'Die Ämterhoheit der Kirchen', in *Handbuch des Staatskirchenrechts der Bundesrepublik Deutschland*, Joseph Listl & Dietrich Pirson eds, vol. 1, 2nd edn (Berlin: Duncker & Humblot, 1995), 568.
331. *Ibid.*

and the *Land* Baden expressly stipulates that the Holy See is free to appoint a candidate when no accord is reached in case of state political objections. Special provisions exist for the military bishops; the appointment of the Roman Catholic military bishop by the Holy See requires the consent of the Federal Republic of Germany;[332] with respect to the Protestant military bishop, the state relies on the EKD to actively inquire about state objections to its candidate.[333]

*471.* The *Reichskonkordat* requires Roman Catholic bishops to take an oath of loyalty to the secular power. This has also been referred to above (in paragraph 362). Before bishops take possession of their dioceses, they are to take an oath of loyalty either to the governor of the *Reich* in the competent *Land* (which now is the minister president or equivalent in the *Länder*) or to the President of the *Reich* (the federal president), according to the following formula:

> Before God and on the Holy Gospels I swear and promise as becomes a bishop, loyalty to the German *Reich* and to the *Land* of … I swear and promise to respect the in accordance with the constitution legally constituted government and to cause the clerics of my Diocese to respect it. In my dutiful care for the welfare and the interests of the German polity I will in the performance of the office transferred to me, strive for averting all detrimental acts which might endanger it.[334]

*472.* Religious communities operate a number – and sometimes, a broad variety – of commissions or advisory groups into which they appoint relevant people. The EKD habitually calls for membership to these bodies, influential people also from leading political parties and other fields of society. Here, political opinions have a chance to influence the will and view of the religious community. In some religious communities, politicians are also called to leading organs of the community. For example, the Synod of the EKD consists of 126 church members, of whom 106 are elected by the Synods of the member churches. The remaining twenty members of the EKD Synod are called to that body by the Council of the EKD for a variety of reasons; one of the criteria relates to political party affiliation, as it relates to include their views and knowledge of the process of forming the will of the church.[335]

*473.* There is a steady exchange of views between the political and the religious spheres. Sermons often relate to political issues. Leaders of religious communities are present in the media, taking part in talk shows and giving interviews on general political issues. In general, representatives of the religious communities are well accepted in the political sphere and in the media. One must see, however, that the influence of religion in politics has diminished in recent years.

---

332. Article 27 Reichskonkordat.
333. Article 11, s. 1 MilSeelsV.
334. Article 16 Reichskonkordat.
335. Evangelische Kirche in Deutschland (ed.), 'Synode der EKD', https://www.ekd.de/synode-der-ekd-10772.htm, 9 Nov. 2023.

## Chapter 3. Interaction Between Religions and State on a Political and Legal Level

*474.* Regular meetings between officials of religious communities and the governments take place in order to exchange views. This has been explicitly agreed upon in the Treaty of Loccum; the *Land* Government and the church managements agreed to have regular meetings to deepen their relations. They will at all times make themselves available to discuss questions concerning their mutual relationship.[336] This is also stated in the treaty between Saxony-Anhalt and the Jewish Community in that *Land*, which says that the *Land* Government and the Land Association shall regularly and when needed meet to discuss questions that are relevant to their relationship to each other or other questions that are of mutual interest.[337]

*475.* Parliamentary hearings on bills of law and other issues are a somewhat formal way of religious influence into general politics. Religious communities are invited to these hearings when questions are at stake that relate to them. This is not only the case for institutional religious matters but also for general questions, especially when public issues of an ethical nature must be addressed. Religious communities are also invited to parliamentary *enquête* commissions on topics of ethical relevance, such as stem-cell research. The German Ethics Council[338] includes, among others, leading representatives from religious communities. The Council works on a variety of ethical questions; its statements have no legally binding force on lawmakers but do have considerable factual relevance in the political process.

*476.* The usual way that a draft law is produced is within parliament or, more often, within the competent government ministry. Once a first draft has been completed, various stakeholders in society are included in the process of discussing the draft law. This lobbying process also includes religious communities whenever their interests are at stake. Religious communities are invited, or at least permitted, to express their views. An example of this is explicitly stated in the treaty between the LSA and the Jewish Community in Saxony-Anhalt, which says that in intended lawmaking and manifestos in fields directly concerning the interests of the Jewish Community in Saxony-Anhalt, the *Land* Government must suitably involve the Land Association.[339]

*477.* The most important Muslim organizations and individual Muslims who are representative of the variety of Muslim life in Germany have shown active participation in the *Deutsche Islam Konferenz* (German Islam Conference). As indicated

336. Article 2, s. 1 Loccumer Vertrag.
337. Article 2, s. 1 JüdGemStVtr LSA.
338. German Ethics Council (ed.), https://www.ethikrat.org/, 9 Nov. 2023; *see* German Ethics Council Act (Gesetz zur Einrichtung des Deutschen Ethikrats), BGBl. 2008 I, 1385.
339. Article 2, ss 1, 2 JüdGemStVtr LSA.

above, this Conference was established by the German federal minister of the interior in 2006 to discuss issues of Muslim life in Germany.[340] It is meant to improve the integration of the Muslim population in Germany and has produced recommendations, *inter alia*, for a common value basis for the building of mosques, introduction of Muslim religious instruction in public schools and improved reporting in the media. Muslim organizations actively participate in inter-religious dialogues. Several inter-religious initiatives have been subsidized by public funds.

340. Deutsche Islam Konferenz (ed.), 'Deutsche Islam Konferenz', https://www.deutsche-islam-konferenz.de/DE/Startseite/startseite_node.html, 9 Nov. 2023.

**477–477 Part V, Ch. 3, Interaction Between Religions and State on a Political**

# Part VI. Labour Law Within Religious Communities

## Chapter 1. Scope of Application of Labour Law

### §1. Factual Situation

*478.* The large churches in the Federal Republic of Germany together employ about 1.8 million persons. While in practice, the employers are very often small or medium-sized institutions such as hospitals or religious orders, individual parishes or dioceses, the charitable institutions '*Caritas*' on the Catholic and '*Diakonisches Werk*' on the Protestant side in their manifold subunits, all of them taken together, form the second largest employer after the state institutions in Germany. This is evidence of the importance of their position as employers.

*479.* The Evangelical Church and the Roman Catholic Church, as well as many other religious communities, see themselves as a community under God. The churches reflect and actively live common ideals and convictions about what is true and what is right. Church work, in its very substance, is regarded by those churches not just as individual work for changeable goals. It is common work for a common and religiously defined good. These churches therefore usually do not speak of employers and employees in respect of the work in their institutions but use other terms such as service-giver and service-taker; this also is to express the special nature of church services as a service community. It is of decisive impact to the existence of a church for it to be able to determine who shares in this common life. Service within the church, that is, the professional work in the church and in its charitable services, is determined by the assignment of the church to give witness to the gospel in words and deeds.

*480.* Therefore, acceptance and non-acceptance of views, teachings, and ways of life, conduct and behaviour of each of the members and staff of the religious community are of core relevance to each other member and staff within the community and for the religious community as an institution. The same fundamental principles apply in the field of collective labour law as do in the field of individual labour law. Furthermore, the success of religious activity depends at its very core on the credibility of the religious community in its words and in its deeds. Maintaining the credibility of the religious community is a core issue of the exercise of its freedom of religion. Any compromising of the teaching required by the religious community by any of its employees falls back on the community itself. This is even more the case when an employee compromising these teachings holds an important and publicly visible position within the religious community and among its employees, but it also applies to any other staff member of the religious community.

*481.* It is important to note that the various churches and religious communities have a variety of different rules on these issues.[341] Some of them have undergone important amendments in answering to developments in society and mirroring changes in the theological teaching of their religious community.

## §2. Individual Labour Law

### I. General Principles

*482.* For the large majority of employees in the service of a religious community, normal state labour law applies. It is, however, modified in many circumstances on the basis of the religious community's right to self-determination and its particular religious context. Freedom of religion demands that the special conditions that result from the religious duties of the religious communities must be taken into consideration when examining their labour status.

*483.* A specific expression of this is that employees of religious communities or their organizations owe a particular obligation of loyalty to their employer. It is the religious community itself that, within the constitutional framework of the notion of *ordre public*, good faith, and prohibition of arbitrary action, determines the contents of these obligations. The religious communities' right to self-determination allows them, within the limits of the law that applies to all, to regulate internal working conditions according to their own terms and to make specific duties obligatory for their employees. Which basic duties of the religious community are important as part of the terms of employment are decided according to the organized religious community's own acknowledged standards. In cases of dispute, the labour courts have to respect the standards of the religious community in assessing the contractual obligation of loyalty insofar as the Basic Law recognizes the right of the religious community to determine the matter internally. It is thus normally left to the organized religious community to decide what is required for the credibility of the religious community and its teaching, what the specific duties are, what constitutes essential principles of faith and morality, and what is to be considered contrary to these norms. In the case of a violation of such an obligation of loyalty by the employee, the public labour courts are the final judges of whether termination of employment is justified or not.[342] As a result of their religious mandate, religious

341. *See*, as an example, for the dioceses of the Roman Catholic Church in Germany: Grundordnung des kirchlichen Dienstes (Directive of the Ecclesiastical Service (GrO)), 22 Nov. 2022, available at Deutsche Bischofskonferenz (ed.), https://www.dbk.de/themen/kirche-staat-und-recht/kirchliches-arbeitsrecht/grundordnung/, 9 Nov. 2023.

342. Cf. BVerfG 4 Jun. 1985, BVerfGE 70, 138 et seq.

communities have the right to give notice to an employee when the employee, in his or her public way of life or publicly expressed opinions, acts contrary to the teachings of the specific religious community. These basic principles are implemented in applying the general secular labour law by the state courts; in interpreting and applying the secular general labour law, these courts have to take due account of the self-understanding of the religious communities in balancing the rights and obligations of the employees and the employers.

*484.* Upon being employed, the employee, in his or her individual labour contract with the religious employer, signs a promise of loyalty to the teaching and moral standards of his or her employer. This is the individual basis on which the labour relationship rests and from which individual rights and duties result. If problems arise in this relationship, this may result finally in the termination of the labour contract by the employer.

*485.* In its landmark decision of 4 June 1985, the *Rommelfanger* case, already dealt with above (paragraphs 405 et seq.) in the context of general church autonomy, the Federal Constitutional Court underscored far-reaching self-determination rights of religious organizations in the field of labour law.[343] The ruling has been upheld by the European Commission of Human Rights.[344] In this case, a Catholic hospital had dismissed two assistant physicians who had actively and publicly in the weekly journal *Stern* criticized the Roman Catholic teaching related to abortion. They had at least indirectly criticized this position as 'clerically conservative' and 'inhuman' and insisted on these statements in a television interview.[345] In the same ruling, the Federal Constitutional Court also decided a case in which an institution of the Catholic Salesians of Don Bosco had dismissed an employee who had left the Roman Catholic Church by formal statement before the state authorities. This clerk had been responsible for cash-keeping, settlement of accounts, establishment of the budget, and the annual statement of accounts. While the European Commission of Human Rights based its decision on the freedom of speech of the religious employer guaranteed in Article 10 ECHR, the Federal Constitutional Court argued on the grounds of freedom of religion as guaranteed in Article 4 GG and the right to self-determination of religious communities provided for in Article 140 GG in conjunction with Article 137 section 3 WRV. The Federal Constitutional Court decided that the constitutional guarantee of the churches' right to self-determination entitles religious communities to decide which services should exist in their institutions, in which legal form they are to be performed, and which are the loyalty obligations of their employees.

*486.* Religious charitable institutions are a part of the religious community as an institution. It is left to the religious communities and their autonomous decision in which form and institutional linkage within the framework of secular law they

343. BVerfG 4 Jun. 1985, BVerfGE 70, 138 et seq.
344. ECHR, *Rommelfanger v. Federal Republic of Germany*, 6 Sep. 1989, appl. no. 12242/86.
345. BVerfG 4 Jun. 1985, BVerfGE 70, 138 et seq.

intend to establish and operate their institutions.[346] Religion is not only about internal belief and liturgical worship. Religion is expressed in activity within and for the world. It is the conviction of the Evangelical Church, as well as the Roman Catholic Church, that social and cultural engagement in the secular world is a form of worship to which all Christians are called. The religious communities act in the secular sphere, as in the case of employment, for religious reasons. Termination of contract by the religious employer because of gross misconduct in view of the religious teaching of the employing community is regarded as an act based on the freedom of religion of the religious employer. Therefore, the right to self-determination entitles the religious communities to organize their activities, including the developing and keeping of an internal organizational structure, the choice of their employees and the providing of the religious principles that should be the basis of all their activities.

*487.* If the religious communities were denied the right to make membership obligations a condition of employment, the ability of the religious communities to carry out their missions in accordance with their beliefs and doctrines would be undermined. This would constitute an interference with the religious communities' internal affairs. The religious communities would suffer a violation of their right to freedom of religion or belief and would encounter profound difficulties in carrying out their affairs in ways that are consistent with their teachings. The religious communities' ability to preach their message and carry out their missions with authenticity and without compromise would be subjected to the vicissitudes of the beliefs and practices of individual employees or secular powers. While any individual who does not share these religious convictions can continue to do so and thus conserve his or her religious identity, the religious community as an institution loses its identity when it has to upkeep employment and thus community with those whom it regards incompatible with its teaching. Employees who do not conform to the religious teaching or the ethos of their employer can find other employment. The religious communities, however, cannot find other teachings or ethos. These rules have long been the standing court practice. They have been explicitly formulated and applied by the Federal Constitutional Court.[347]

## II. Secular Labour Law and Its Application on Religious Communities

*488.* Religious communities make use of private autonomy in establishing and regulating a labour relationship. State labour law applies to such labour relations; however, religious communities' right to self-determination remains essential. This enables religious communities, within the limitations set by the law that applies to all, to organize the personnel structure service of the church according to its self-understanding and to attribute binding force to the specific obligations of their employees. The basic commitments of the religious community that can be of

346. BVerfG 4 Jun. 1985, BVerfGE 70, 138, 162.
347. BVerfG 4 Jun. 1985, BVerfGE 70, 138 et seq.

importance as a matter of the employment relationship are to be determined according to the standards acknowledged by the official, formally organized religious community (i.e., the formal entity as opposed to a spiritual understanding of a religious community). The opinion of an individual religious institution that may be affected, the forming of which may be influenced by a variety of motives, is of no relevance for the state authorities in establishing these basic commitments; the opinion of any larger group of members of the religious community or that of certain individual employees which may adhere to specific tendencies is equally of no relevance. When assessing contractual loyalty obligations in controversial cases, the labour courts have to apply the standards provided by the religious community as far as the constitution acknowledges the right of the religious communities to decide on these standards by themselves. It is left to the official, formally organized religious communities to decide with binding force what the credibility of the religious community and of its teaching requires, what the specific assignments of the religious community are, what proximity to those means, what the 'essential principles of the belief and moral teaching' are and what has to be regarded as a – possibly severe – violation of those principles. Also, the decision about whether and how a gradation of loyalty obligations should take place among the staff that is active within the community service remains a matter that, in principle, falls under the right to self-determination of the religious community. In case there is a violation of loyalty obligations, the additional question of whether this violation justifies termination of the employment contract is to be decided according to the employment protection provisions of §1 KSchG (Protection Against Unfair Dismissal Act (*Kündigungsschutzgesetz*)) and §626 BGB (Civil Code). These provisions fall – being laws that apply to all in the sense of Article 137 section 3 WRV in conjunction with Article 140 GG – under the comprehensive competence of the labour courts.[348]

*489.* The German Civil Code (BGB) provides the pertinent provision for termination of labour contracts:

§626 BGB Termination without notice for a compelling reason

(1) The service relationship may be terminated by either party to the contract for a compelling reason without observing a period of notice if facts are given on the basis of which, having considered all circumstances of the individual case and weighed the interests of both parties to the contract against each other, the party giving notice cannot reasonably be required to continue the service relationship until the end of the notice period or the agreed end of the service relationship.
(2) Notice of termination may only be given within two weeks. The period of time commences upon the point in time at which the person entitled to give notice obtains knowledge of the facts relevant for the notice of termination. On demand, the party giving notice must notify the other party, without undue delay in writing, of the reason for terminating the service relationship.

348. *Ibid.*

*490.* The German Employment Protection Act (KSchG) provides for protection of the employee against unjustified dismissal:

§1 KSchG Socially unjustified terminations

Termination of a labour relationship vis-à-vis an employee whose labour relationship has existed within the same plant or enterprise without interruption for more than six months is legally invalid when it is socially unjustified.

A termination is socially unjustified when it is not conditioned by reasons that lie within the person or within the conduct of the employee or by compelling operational needs which are contrary to a continuation of the employment of the employee in this plant. …

*491.* §§138 and 242 BGB provide for further detailed protection against unjustified terminations:

§138 Legal transaction offending common decency; usury

(1) A legal transaction that offends common decency is void.
(2) In particular, a legal transaction is void by which a person, by exploiting the predicament, inexperience, lack of sound judgment or considerable weakness of will of another, causes a promise to be made to them or to a third party, in exchange for an act of performance, for pecuniary advantages that are clearly disproportionate to the performance, or causes such pecuniary advantages to be granted.

§242 Performance in good faith

An obligor has a duty to perform according to the requirements of good faith, taking customary practice into consideration.

*492.* These provisions of German labour law have to be seen together with the relevant German provisions of constitutional law. They are applied by German courts in this context and in a consistent and predictable manner. German constitutional law provides for the guarantee of self-determination (autonomy) of religious communities in Article 4 GG and Article 140 GG in conjunction with Article 137 section 3 WRV. This guarantee of religious self-determination is enjoyed by all religious communities. The right to self-determination carries a limitation clause. Self-determination is guaranteed 'within the limits of the law that applies to all'. In interpreting the scope of self-determination, the religious community's conception of itself is of special importance, particularly when deciding on loyalty obligations of employees.[349]

349. BVerfG 13 Dec. 1983, BVerfGE 66, 1, 22; BVerfG 4 Jun. 1985, BVerfGE 70, 138, 167; BVerfG 14 May 1986, BVerfGE 72, 278, 189.

*493.* All this is in line with the relevant anti-discrimination law. According to §§1 and 2 of the General Equal Treatment Law (AGG), no one may be discriminated against because of reasons of race, ethnicity, gender, religion or belief, disability, age or sexual orientation in the field of profession and employment, social security or education, or access to social benefits, health services or goods and services open to the public including housing facilities. There is no discrimination when the requirements of §9 AGG are met: A different treatment because of religion or belief is allowed in view of the employment by a religious community regardless of its legal form, by an organization attached to it or by an association which has as its objective the common care for a religion or a belief if a specific religion or belief is a justified professional requirement in view of its right to self-determination or the kind of activity while respecting the self-understanding of the community. The prohibition of unequal treatment because of religion or belief does not prejudice the right of these communities and organizations to demand from their employees loyal and honest behaviour in the sense of their respective self-understanding.

*494.* This provision is based on Article 4 Council Directive 2000/78/EC of 27 November 2000, establishing a general framework for equal treatment in employment and occupation. Pursuant to this provision, Member States may provide that a difference of treatment which is based on a characteristic related to any of the grounds referred to in Article 1 of the Directive shall not constitute discrimination where, by reason of the nature of the particular occupational activities concerned or of the context in which they are carried out, such a characteristic constitutes a genuine and determining occupational requirement, provided that the objective is legitimate and the requirement is proportionate. Member States may maintain national legislation in force at the date of adoption of that Directive or provide for future legislation incorporating national practices existing at the date of adoption of the Directive pursuant to which, in the case of occupational activities within churches and other public or private organizations the ethos of which is based on religion or belief, a difference of treatment based on a person's religion or belief shall not constitute discrimination where, by reason of the nature of these activities or of the context in which they are carried out, a person's religion or belief constitutes a genuine, legitimate and justified occupational requirement, having regard to the organization's ethos. This difference of treatment shall be implemented taking account of Member States' constitutional provisions and principles, as well as the general principles of Community law, and should not justify discrimination on another ground. Provided that its provisions are otherwise complied with, the Directive shall thus not prejudice the right of churches and other public or private organizations, the ethos of which is based on religion or belief, acting in conformity with national constitutions and laws, to require individuals working for them to act in good faith and with loyalty to the organization's ethos.

*495.* The ECJ has acknowledged a rather far-reaching competence of the state courts to decide whether a person's religion or belief constitutes a genuine, legitimate and justified occupational requirement having regard to the organization's ethos.[350] It is a matter of ongoing debate whether this approach is consistent with German constitutional law, but also with European Union law.

## III. Individual Churches

### A. The Evangelical Church

*496.* The principles of labour law outlined above apply to the example of the EKD. Pluralism is a core principle within the EKD. The EKD unites a community of twenty Lutheran, Reformed, and United regional churches in Germany with about 19,100,000 individual members. German Protestant Church structures are based on federal principles at all levels. Each local congregation is responsible for Christian life in its own area, while each regional church has its own special characteristics and retains its independence. Without in any way diminishing this autonomy, the EKD carries out joint tasks with which its members have entrusted it.

*497.* In carrying out its tasks to give guidelines for its member churches, the EKD has promulgated the 2005 Directive concerning the requirements of civil law employment in the EKD and the *Diakonisches Werk* of the EKD (*Loyalitätsrichtlinie* EKD). It has been amended in 2016.[351] According to its §2, the service of the church is determined by the assignment to give witness to the Gospel in words and in deeds. All women and men who are active in an employment relationship in the church and Diaconia contribute to that this assignment can be fulfilled. This assignment is the basis of the rights and duties of employers and employees. They together form a service community. According to §3 of the Directive, employment in the Evangelical Church and its Diaconia requires, in principle, membership in a member church of the EKD or in a church that is connected with it in church unity. Exceptions can be made for services that do not belong to preaching, spiritual care, teaching or governing the church, and other employees cannot be found. In these cases, persons can be employed who should belong to another member church of the Alliance of Christian Churches (*Arbeitsgemeinschaft Christlicher Kirchen* (ACK)) or the Association of Evangelical-Free Churches; if compatible with the assignment of the Church, it is also possible to employ people who do not belong to any Christian church. In such cases, each individual employment has to be examined, taking into account the size of the institution and the number of its staff, its tasks and its special surroundings.

*498.* Employees take over responsibility for the credible fulfilment of the ecclesiastical and diaconical tasks. They therefore have to act loyal to the Evangelical Church (§4 of the Directive). When a church employee does not comply with a requirement outlined in the Directive, the employer shall engage in eliminating the shortcoming through counselling and conversation. The last means can be summary

350. EuGH, 17 Apr. 2018 – C-414/16 (Egenberger); EuGH, 11 Sep. 2018 – C-68/17 (Chefarzt).
351. Loyalitätsrichtlinie, https://www.kirchenrecht-ekd.de/pdf/36983.pdf, 26 Apr. 2024.

dismissal if the shortcoming cannot be eliminated by other means. A reason for summary dismissal is especially conduct that signifies gross disregard for the Evangelical Church or its rules and, thus, an impairment of the credibility of the ecclesiastical service (§5 of the Directive).

*499.* The EKD itself has, again, rules of employment that are framed to match specific needs. The service contract regulation of the EKD as amended in 2020 (DVO.EKD),[352] which applies to the staff directly employed by the EKD, itself stipulates in its §2: 'Church service is determined by the assignment to teach the Gospel of Jesus Christ in words and deeds. The diaconical service is an expression of the life and the essence of the Evangelical Church.' The employees have to act in accordance with this assignment in their work and in their private lives. Employment practice of the EKD itself is consistent. Only members of the Evangelical Church, and in a few exceptions also members of other Christian Churches, are employed. The Labour Contract Directives of the Diaconical Work of the EKD (AVR-RL Diakonie), which is a separate institution linked with the EKD and other Protestant Churches, are guidelines and orientation for about 600,000 salaried staff in diaconical institutions and services. It has been amended as of 1 May 2023.[353] In some Diaconical Works and Associations, different rules apply. According to §1 of the Labour Contract Directives, the relevant institutions are obliged by the task to give witness to the Gospel of Jesus Christ. The diaconical service is an expression of the essence and the life of the Evangelical Church. All persons working in a diaconical institution form a service community. It is expected of these service community members that their conduct inside and outside of the service be in accordance with the responsibility of the neighbour. The diaconical service is performed in the name of Jesus Christ. Anyone who is prepared to carry out this service for other motivations is an employee with the same rights and duties; however, she or he must acknowledge the evangelical foundation of the diaconical work.

*500.* Churches differ in what they believe is appropriate in respect of membership and incompatibility. There is considerable plurality even among the member churches of the EKD. Differences sometimes may seem less visible to outsiders; however, as a matter of deep religious beliefs, these principles are of high theological importance to believers and the churches. They form part of the very essence of the religious life of a church. Some examples are outlined in the following.

352. Dienstvertragsordnung der Evangelischen Kirche in Deutschland, https://www.kirchenrecht-ekd.de/document/20785, 9 Nov. 2023.

353. Arbeitsvertragsrichtlinien für Einrichtungen, die der Diakonie Deutschland angeschlossen sind, beschlossen von der Arbeitsrechtlichen Kommission der Diakonie Deutschland Stand: 1 May 2023, https://www.diakonie-wissen.de/documents/4999827/13352553/958_AVR-DD_2023-05-01_mit-Inhaltsverzeichnis.pdf/62fc3643-9e8a-4418-83e2-e94c349598ec, 9 Nov. 2023.

*B. The Catholic Church*

*501.* Similar principles apply within the Catholic Church. Following its own specific teaching, however, some differences exist in detail. The Roman Catholic bishops have adopted for their respective dioceses a Basic Ordinance of the Clerical Service within Clerical Employment (GrO).[354] It has been substantially amended and modernized in 2022. The regulation is based on the task and teaching of the church. It applies to the individual as well as to the collective labour law relations within the church and its institutions. It does not apply to clerics and members of religious orders for whom special rules exist.

*502.* Article 2(2) GrO states that all those active in institutions of the Catholic Church contribute together by their work so that the institution can fulfil its share in the mission of the church (service community), regardless of their labour law position.

*503.* The regulation explicitly states the loyalty obligations of employees in the institutions of the church. Catholic staff members are expected to accept and observe the principles of the Catholic faith and moral teaching within their work.

*504.* Employers and employees assume joint responsibility for the credible fulfilment of the mission in the facility. The requirements relate primarily to conduct in the line of duty. Off-duty conduct is only legally significant if it is publicly perceptible, violates the fundamental values of the Catholic Church, and thereby impairs its credibility. The core area of private life, in particular relationship life and intimacy, remains exempt from legal assessments. This does not affect special ecclesiastical requirements for clerics, candidates for the ordained ministry, members of religious orders, and persons in the novitiate and postulancy.

*505.* Activities hostile to the Church which, according to the specific circumstances, are objectively likely to impair the credibility of the Church may be punished by law. Activities hostile to the church include actions that are publicly perceptible and are directed against the church or its value system. These include, in particular, the public advocacy of fundamental principles of the Catholic Church (e.g., the propagation of abortion or xenophobia), the denigration of Catholic beliefs, rites or customs, the propagation of religious and ideological convictions that are in contradiction to Catholic beliefs, during working hours or in the context of work, including the promotion of other religious or religious worldview communities. In the case of Catholic employees, leaving the Catholic Church usually leads to a termination of the legal relationship on which the employment is based. In these cases, termination may be waived by way of exception if serious reasons for the individual case make it appear inappropriate.

---

354. Grundordnung des kirchlichen Dienstes 5., völlig überarbeitete Neuauflage, 22 Nov. 2022, Basic Ordinance of the Clerical Service within Clerical Employment (GrO), available at Sekretariat der Deutschen Bischofskonferenz (ed.), https://www.dbk.de/themen/kirche-staat-und-recht/kirchliches-arbeitsrecht/grundordnung/, 9 Nov. 2023.

§3. COLLECTIVE LABOUR LAW

*506.* In the sphere of collective labour law, the religious communities are also in a special position because of their specific religious needs as protected by the freedom of religion and, consequently, the right to self-determination. The state is, in principle, not allowed to intervene in the internal organizational structures and set up of the religious communities also in the field of collective labour law.[355]

*507.* The great churches in Germany have developed the so-called Third Way in this area. This option is called the 'Third Way' in order to distinguish the special collective labour law applicable within church-maintained institutions from one-sided determination of labour conditions by the church employer (the so-called First Way) and also from establishing labour conditions by way of collective bargaining with trade unions (the so-called Second Way). The relevant churches understand their vocation, especially in the area of charity, as part of one undivided, religiously based commitment. This, in principle, makes it impossible for them to accept a legal structure of labour relations, which is based on the idea of an antagonistic, fundamental opposition between employer and employee. The 'Third Way', in contrast to that antagonistic approach, is a model for labour relations based on co-determination and common goals of employers and employees while not ignoring possible differences in interests. The 'Third Way' provides ample instruments for protecting the interests and the rights of the employees. They have, through their representatives, an intensive say in establishing and observing the rules of employment. They can turn to state labour courts if they are dissatisfied with the solution found in case of conflict.

*508.* The Catholic Church, along with most of the Protestant churches as well as the Central Council of Jews in Germany, therefore, rejects the conclusion of agreements through collective bargaining with trade unions for their institutions. Within the church structure, there is no right to strike, just as there is no possibility by way of an internal church decision of locking out employees. The Federal Constitutional Court has held that representatives of trade unions who are not staff of the respective institution have no right to enter without specific permission into charitable institutions of religious communities for the purpose of informing, recruiting new members and attending to trade union members.[356] It has based this decision on the assumption that there is no specific law allowing for such activities in institutions of religious communities, while there is one in respect of secular institutions. It must be assumed, however, that freedom of religion or belief and the right to self-determination of religious communities exclude outsiders from being active in the premises of religious communities without special permission.

*509.* Most of the twenty member churches of the EKD and the EKD itself frame the labour law in their institutions together with the staff members in the framework of the 'Third Way'. For this purpose, labour law commissions have been instituted

355. *See* BVerfG 25 Mar. 1980, BVerfGE 53, 366, 400.
356. BVerfG 17 Feb. 1981, BVerfGE 57, 220 et seq.

in which the representatives of employers and employees have an equal number of seats. These labour law commissions decide on the amount of pay, vacation and other working conditions. The main principles of the 'Third Way' in the Protestant churches are laid out in a Church Directive on Employment Relations.[357] Fundamental principles here are the equality of both sides, employers and employees, in numbers and weight, readiness for cooperation in trust and partnership even in controversial situations, and a neutral and binding conciliation. For this conciliation, there is a conciliation commission that is also characterized by an equal number of representatives of both sides, but in addition to that, it is presided over by a neutral chairperson who has been commonly elected.

*510.* In contrast to that, the Evangelical Church in Berlin-Brandenburg-schlesische Oberlausitz[358] and the Evangelical-Lutheran Church in North Germany (*Nordkirche*)[359] have concluded collective labour agreements with trade unions. These collective labour agreements are modified to meet the special requirements of the churches; they especially exclude industrial actions on the side of trade unions and employers, such as strikes and lock-outs.

*511.* The German Catholic bishops have described the principles of the participation of the church employees in shaping their working conditions in the Basic Ordinance of the Clerical Service within Clerical Employment (GrO).[360] This regulation underlines that industrial actions such as strikes and lock-outs are contrary to the character of the church service. The Catholic Church in Germany does not conclude collective labour agreements with trade unions. The services of the church are conducted in a service community with which antagonistic labour relations would be incompatible. The Catholic Church has established commissions for the regulation of the labour contract law as an expression of the service community in which employers and employees are equally represented.[361] The decisions of those commissions need the approval of the bishop of the respective diocese.

*512.* The structures of the religious communities are not subject to the general state co-determination laws.[362] In general secular collective labour law, works councils in businesses have far-reaching powers concerning the working conditions of

357. Richtlinie gemäß Art. 9 Buchstabe b) der Grundordnung für ein Kirchengesetz über das Verfahren zur Regelung der Arbeitsverhältnisse der Mitarbeiter im kirchlichen Dienst (Arbeitsrechts-Regelungsgesetz – ARRG) of 8 Oct. 1976, https://www.kirchenrecht-ekd.de/document/3153, 9 Nov. 2023.
358. Evangelische Kirche Berlin-Brandenburg-schlesische Oberlausitz (in and around Berlin).
359. Created by a fusion of the Northelbian Evangelical-Lutheran Church (basically Hamburg and Schleswig-Holstein), the Evangelical-Lutheran Land Church of Mecklenburg and the Pomeranian Evangelical Church on 27 May 2012. *See* Evangelisch-Lutherische Kirche in Norddeutschland, 'Nordkirche', https://www.nordkirche.de/, 9 Nov. 2023.
360. 'Grundordnung des kirchlichen Dienstes', 5., völlig überarbeitete Neuauflage 22 Nov. 2022, https://www.dbk.de/themen/kirche-staat-und-recht/kirchliches-arbeitsrecht/grundordnung/, 9 Nov. 2023.
361. Kommissionen zur Ordnung des Arbeitsvertragsrechtes (KODA).
362. §118 Works Council Constitution Act (BetrVG); §1, s. 4 Act on Co-determination of Employees (MitbestG).

employees. Pursuant to §1 Works Council Constitution Act (BetrVG), works councils will be elected in works that regularly have at least five permanent employees with voting rights, three of whom are eligible. This would apply to many institutions maintained by religious communities. However, §118 section 1 BetrVG stipulates that the law does not apply to enterprises and works that directly or predominantly serve political, labour association, denominational, charitable, educational, scientific or artistic purposes or purposes of reporting or expression of opinion to which Article 5 section 1 clause 2 of the Basic Law is applicable[363] when the character of the enterprise or works conflicts with this. Certain provisions of the law are completely barred in view of such enterprises and works,[364] others[365] are applicable only insofar as they serve to compensate or minimize economic disadvantages of employees because of changes in operations. Furthermore, §118 section 2 BetrVG provides that the law does not apply at all to religious communities and their charitable and educational institutions, regardless of their legal form. Also, the Staff Representation Acts of the Federal Republic and of the *Länder* do not apply to religious communities.

*513.* The Federal Labour Court has upheld the general principle that there is no right to strike for employees within institutions of religious communities that have adopted the 'Third Way' in their labour law.[366] This is because and as long as there are conciliation commissions with representatives of employees and trade unions for these institutions.

*514.* The respective laws of the Protestant Churches have instituted representative bodies for their employees[367] that are equivalent to the works councils and staff councils of the secular laws. These representative bodies have far-reaching rights of information and co-decision in matters such as dismissals or the restructuring of the institution.

*515.* Also, employees elect representatives into bodies of co-determination within the institutions of the Catholic Church.[368]

363. That is freedom of the press and freedom of reporting by means of broadcasts and films.
364. §§106–110 BetrVG, concerning the creation and the rights of economic committees in enterprises with more than one hundred permanent employees.
365. §§111–113 BetrVG, concerning rights and procedures in cases of changes in operations.
366. BAG 20 Nov. 2012, 1 AZR 179/11.
367. *See*, e.g., Kirchengesetz über Mitarbeitervertretungen in der Evangelischen Kirche in Deutschland (MVG-EKD) (Ecclesiastical Act on Employee Representation in the Evangelical Church in Germany), 2019, https://www.kirchenrecht-ekir.de/document/31071, 9 Nov. 2023.
368. Grundordnung des kirchlichen Dienstes (GrO) (Basic Ordinance of the Ecclesiastical Service (GrO)), available at Deutsche Bischofskonferenz (ed.), https://www.dbk.de/themen/kirche-staat-und-recht/kirchliches-arbeitsrecht/grundordnung/, 9 Nov. 2023.

§4. THE SOCIAL SECURITY SYSTEM

## I. General Principles

*516.* People who work as employees in religious establishments such as religiously run hospitals, kindergartens, etc., form part of the general social security system, like everybody else.

*517.* The greater religious communities, such as the Catholic Church, the Protestant Church and other religious communities, have established specific social security provisions for their priests and special personnel. Such personnel that are regarded as public officials (though not state officials) are included in pension systems similar to state officials, but these systems are run by those religious communities themselves. For certain specific religious people, such as members of religious orders, special agreements have been concluded between the state and those relevant religious communities to include them in the general social security systems.

## II. Employment Promotion

*518.* The Social Code III (Employment Promotion – SGB III) provides in its §26 section 1 number 5 that persons who are not statutory members of clerical brotherhoods or similar religious confraternities and who receive out-of-school training for service in such a brotherhood or similar religious confraternity are compulsorily insured in the general unemployment insurance. Exempt from such insurance are, pursuant to §27 section 1 SGB III, clerics of religious communities that have been recognized as corporations under public law if, in case of illness, they are entitled under the legal provisions or principles applicable to civil servants to continued payment of remuneration and allowances; teachers employed as their main occupation in private approved schools, if in case of illness, they are entitled under the legal provisions or principles applicable to civil servants to continued payment of remuneration and allowances; statutory members of clerical brotherhoods, deaconesses and similar persons if they engage in sick nursing, education or other non-profit work on predominantly religious or moral grounds and do not receive more than their free board and lodging or a small sum by way of remuneration that merely suffices to cover their direct needs in terms of accommodation, food, clothing and the like.

## III. Health Insurance

*519.* In relation to health insurance, §5 SGB V provides that persons subject to compulsory insurance are workers, employees and those engaged in their vocational training, employed for a wage; persons also shall be deemed employees engaged in their vocational training who are in out-of-school training as not-regular members of clerical brotherhoods or similar religious confraternities for service in such a brotherhood or similar religious confraternity.

*520.* §6 SGB V provides for exemptions from compulsory health insurance in the field of religion. Clerics of religious societies recognized as corporations under public law are exempt from insurance if, in case of illness, they are entitled under the legal provisions or principles applicable to civil servants to continued payment of remuneration and allowances. The same applies to statutory members of clerical brotherhoods, deaconesses and similar persons if they engage in sick nursing, education or other non-profit work on predominantly religious or moral grounds and do not receive more than their free board and lodging or a small sum by way of remuneration that merely suffices to cover their direct needs in terms of accommodation, food, clothing and the like. Finally, also exempt from compulsory insurance are surviving dependants of the persons referred to if they derive their pension rights only from the insurance of these persons and, in case of illness, are entitled under the legal provisions or principles applicable to civil servants to allowances.

*521.* For persons undergoing out-of-school training as non-statutory members of clerical brotherhoods or similar religious confraternities for service in such a brotherhood or similar religious confraternity, the clerical brotherhood or similar religious confraternity bear the contributions as is stated in §251 SGB V.

## IV. Pensions Insurance

*522.* Within the national pension insurance system, members of clerical brotherhoods, deaconesses and members of similar confraternities during their service for the community and during their out-of-school training are subject to compulsory insurance as is provided for in §1 SGB VI. §5 SGB VI concerns the exemption from compulsory pension insurance. It reads as follows:

> §5 SGB VI Exemption from Insurance
>
> (1) Exempt from insurance are:
> (…)
> 2. other employees of corporations, institutions or foundations under public law, their associations, including the head associations or their working groups, if, in accordance with the legal provisions or principles applicable to civil servants, they are entitled to expectancies of support in the event of reduced ability to work and in old age as well as for surviving dependants and the fulfillment this guarantee is ensured,
> 3. employees in the sense of number 2, if, in accordance with canonical regulations, they are entitled to expectancies of support in the sense of number 2, and the fulfillment of this guarantee is ensured, as well as statutory members of clerical brotherhoods, deaconesses and members of similar confraternities, if, in accordance with the regulations of the

confraternity, they are entitled to the support usual in that confraternity in the event of reduced ability to work and in old age and the fulfillment of this guarantee is ensured,

in this employment and other employment, to which the guarantee of an expectancy of support is extended.

(…)

(4) Exempt from insurance are persons who:

1. after the end of the month in which the standard retirement age has been reached draw an old-age pension,
2. in accordance with the legal provisions or principles applicable to civil servants or the corresponding canonical regulations or in accordance with the regulations of an occupational pension scheme receive support or the old-age support usual in a confraternity in the sense of section 1, sentence 1, number 3, after reaching an age limit

(…).

*523.* Exemption from compulsory pension insurance is also granted pursuant to §6 SGB VI for teachers or educators employed at non-public schools or institutions, including religiously maintained ones, if they are, in accordance with principles applicable to civil servants or corresponding canon law provisions, entitled to expectancies of support in the event of reduced ability to work and in old age, as well as to support for surviving dependants, and it is ensured that the guarantee will be implemented.

*524.* According to the general principles of the compulsory pension insurance system, the contributions payable are calculated on the basis of defined contributory earnings. These are in relation to members of clerical brotherhoods, deaconesses and members of similar confraternities the benefits in cash and remuneration in kind which they receive personally, but with members that on termination of their training are not entitled to the support usual in the community, or for whom the guarantee is not ensured at least 40% of the reference value.

*525.* The payment of contributions is regulated in §168 SGB VI. The contributions in the case of members of clerical brotherhoods, deaconesses and members of similar confraternities are borne by the brotherhoods or confraternities if the monthly wage does not exceed 40% of the monthly reference value, otherwise half each by the members and the brotherhoods or confraternities. Special provisions apply to supplement payments for clerics and religious according to §206 SGB VI. Clerics and other staff of the religious societies recognized as corporations under public law, members of clerical brotherhoods, deaconesses and members of comparable charitable communities recognized as expellees and who exercised prior to their expulsion employment or a qualifying activity, may, if they have not reassumed similar employment or activity in the inland, on application for the times of exemption from insurance, but backdated to a maximum of 1 January 1943, pay voluntary contributions unless these times are already covered by contributions.

*526.* This does not apply if the times of exemption from insurance are eligible in terms of a pension from public service or employment with a right to support in accordance with the legal provisions or principles applicable to civil servants or corresponding canonical regulations or are recognized as eligible when the pensionable event takes place. The subsequent payment is only permissible if the general waiting time has been completed or if compulsory contributions have been paid for at least twenty-four calendar months after taking up residence in the inland.

## V. Accident Insurance

*527.* The national accident insurance system provides special benefits for persons who engage in voluntary honorary work. Under certain conditions, these persons are insured by an act of law and without having to pay insurance contributions in case of accidents that they suffer in the course of their honorary work. According to §2 SGB VII, those persons are insured by act of law who work on an honorary basis for religious communities that are corporations under public law or for their institutions or for organizations of private law on behalf of them or with their explicit approval, in special cases with their written consent or who take part in training events for such activities.

*528.* Exempt from compulsory accident insurance are statutory members of clerical brotherhoods, deaconesses and members of similar confraternities if they are entitled to expectancy in accordance with the rules of the community to the support usual in this community, and it is ensured that the guarantee will be implemented.

## Chapter 2. Religious Ministers and Labour Law

*529.* For priests and ministers, the Roman Catholic Church and the great Protestant churches have adopted separate service laws that mirror public civil service law to a large extent, considering the special context.

*530.* Religious communities can exempt their clergy from state labour law. The secular law respects that these relationships are structured as spiritual relationships not subject to secular law. The courts have accepted that the officers of the Salvation Army are not employees of the church but form part of a spiritual relationship according to the rules of the Salvation Army.[369]

*531.* The Federal Constitutional Court has held that the compulsory retiring of a Protestant pastor and the assessment of the pension are no 'acts of state power'; they are matters of the relevant Protestant church. The organization of the law of church service and office are matters of self-determination of the religious community and are exempt from state judicial review unless the religious community submits the matters voluntarily under such review.[370]

369. BGH 28 Mar. 2003, BGHZ 154, 306 et seq.
370. BVerfG (K) 9 Dec. 2008, *Neue Juristische Wochenschrift* 62 (2009): 1195 et seq.

## Chapter 3. Other Church Employees and Labour Law

*532.* As public corporations, the churches are considered to be entitled to confer public office. This means that they are able to have employees who are considered to be civil servants; reciprocally, church administrations are structured along the same lines as their state counterparts. The churches frame their own civil service law along the same lines as the public civil service law, even in respect of salaries and benefits.

*533.* Priests in the military chaplaincy are, as a matter of principle, regarded as state civil servants, and they are paid by the state. Teachers in public schools teaching religion are also paid by the state. The same holds true for professors of theology in state universities. All of them share the specific status of their secular colleagues. If they have the status of a civil servant, they enjoy all the benefits of state civil servants and have the same duties. The state, however, has no power to determine in any way their religious work. The state's supervisory power over its civil servants, being military chaplains, teachers of religious instruction in public schools or professors of theology in state universities refers to the secular status; it ends at the borderline to religious issues.

# Part VII. Religious Communities and Protections of the Individual

*534.* The basic principles of (indirect) horizontal application of fundamental rights also apply to the relationship between religious communities and individuals. In general, there is no direct application of fundamental rights that would obligate religious communities. Only religious communities that are corporations under public law are bound to observe fundamental rights when they make use of sovereign powers transferred to them by the state, such as the right to levy church tax.[371]

*535.* In view of individuals who are not members of the specific religious community, these communities relate to them, as do private associations with any other individual. This can be of relevance, for example, in the case of the bell ringing of churches or the Muezzin-call of mosques: while there is a right to manifest the belief in such a way based on freedom of religion or belief, individuals have the right not to be disturbed; both rights will be balanced appropriately as to give as much space as possible to both of them. General rules for this balancing process are specified in the relevant laws such as emission laws on the production and avoidance of noise or in the general construction laws.

*536.* In view of their own members – and more intensively so in view of their staff, clerics, officials or employees – these basic principles of horizontal application of fundamental rights also apply. However, the special status of each of the individuals will add further aspects and reasons to the process of balancing the rights at stake. The laws that are applicable in the various issues, such as labour laws, family law, or procedure laws elaborate on these relations and also have to be interpreted and applied in the light of the relevant fundamental rights.

*537.* Religious communities that have the status of public law corporations have to observe specific obligations and enjoy specific rights that follow from this status also in view of individuals. For example, this applies in cases that relate to the status of public property objects in relation to the general public or in cases that relate to the public service status of their officials.

*538.* The following chapters, therefore, give examples of the relationship between religious communities and individuals in many areas of relevance, but they do not exhaust all the issues that arise in practice.

371. BVerfG (K) 19 Aug. 2002, *Deutsches Verwaltungsblatt* 117 (2002): 1624 et seq.

## Chapter 1. Protection of Privacy

### §1. General Principles

*539.* Religious communities can oblige their members to behave in their private lives in specific ways. They can, as a matter of principle, make compliance with their moral and spiritual principles a condition of membership and labour relations. The state also cannot interfere with merely religious sanctions that may be imposed by a religious community as a reaction to specific behaviour, such as exclusion from sacraments.

*540.* However, religious communities may not impose sanctions that would contradict criminal or any other state law. No religious community, therefore, may use bodily force or deprivation of personal freedom of movement to enforce their internal rules.

### §2. Data Protection

*541.* General data protection law respects the special needs of religious communities, at least to a certain extent. As in all Member States of the European Union, the General Data Protection Regulation (GDPR) applies directly within Germany. Article 91 GDPR provides for a special status of religious communities by respecting existing data protection rules of churches and religious associations: Where in a Member State, churches and religious associations or communities apply, at the time of entry into force of the regulation, comprehensive rules relating to the protection of natural persons with regard to processing, such rules may continue to apply, provided that they are brought into line with the regulation. Churches and religious associations which apply comprehensive rules in accordance with paragraph 1 of this Article shall be subject to the supervision of an independent supervisory authority, which may be specific, provided that it fulfils the conditions laid down in the regulation. By these rules, the regulation pursues the goal of (165) No Prejudice of the Status of Churches and Religious Associations.[372]

372. General Data Protection Regulation, Recital 165.

## Chapter 2. Freedom to Marry

*542.* The federal constitution protects marriage and family in its Article 6 section 1: 'Marriage and family shall enjoy the special protection of the state.' This includes the individual freedom to marry and not to marry. Marriage (and the family) is also protected as an institution.

*543.* The constitutional protection of marriage and family does not exclude religious communities from requiring their clergy not to get married.

*544.* Fundamental rights protection of marriage does not oblige religions to perform marriage rites for a divorced person under religious marriage rules when they want to marry again.

*545.* The right to marry is also not violated when a religious community makes it a condition for their employees to keep loyal to the marriage standards of that community. Thus, in general, a religious community can give notice to an employee who remarries after having been divorced if this is contrary to the teaching of the religious community. This strict approach has been rather softened, however, by a ruling of the ECJ. The Court has held that is constitutes an unfair practice to give notice to a head physician in a Catholic hospital for having remarried after he had had a divorce.[373] Subsequently, the German Catholic Church has amended its rules on labour relations accordingly.[374]

*546.* Religious marriage is, as a matter of principle, an entirely non-state issue. Only civil marriage is recognized under state law. Exceptions to this rule occur in private international law. The preconditions for the conclusion of marriage are subject for each fiancée to the law of the state of which he or she is a citizen. If a precondition of this is not met, German law applies according to Article 13 subsection 2 of the Introductory Act to the Civil Code if: (1) the habitual residence of one of the persons engaged to be married is within the country or one of them is a German national; (2) the persons engaged to be married have taken reasonable steps to fulfil the requirement; and (3) it is incompatible with the freedom of marriage to refuse the conclusion of the marriage; in particular, the previous marriage of a person engaged to be married shall not be held against him or her, if it is nullified by a decision issued or recognized here, or the spouse of the person engaged to be married has been declared dead.

*547.* Marriage, as far as its relevance in secular law is concerned, may in domestic territory only be concluded in the form prescribed in Germany. The religious

373. EuGH, 11 Sep. 2018 – C-68/17 (Chefarzt).

374. Basic Ordinance of the Ecclesiastical Service, 5th ed., 2022 (Grundordnung des kirchlichen Dienstes, 5., völlig überarbeitete Neuauflage, 22. Nov. 2022), https://www.dbk.de/themen/kirche-staat-und-recht/kirchliches-arbeitsrecht/grundordnung/, 9 Nov. 2023.

communities do not have any functions in this process. Marriage concluded in Germany only in religious forms is not registered with state authorities and has no consequences in secular law. A marriage between two persons engaged to be married, neither of whom is a German national, may, however, be celebrated before a person properly authorized by the government of the state of which one of the persons engaged to be married is a national, according to the formalities prescribed by the law of that state; a certified copy of the registration of the marriage in the Register of Births, Deaths and Marriages, kept by the person properly authorized therefore, furnishes conclusive evidence of the marriage celebrated in that manner. This makes it possible that marriage between foreign fiancées can be concluded by a priest properly empowered by the foreign government, if this is possible in their home countries.[375]

*548.* In order to fight child marriage performed by some religious groups, such child marriages have been declared invalid. Article 13 subsection 3 number 1 of the Introductory Act to the Civil Code had been introduced providing: the nubility of a person engaged to be married is governed, according to paragraph 1, by foreign law, the marriage is, according to German law, invalid, if the person engaged to be married has not completed his or her 16th year at the time when the marriage was celebrated. This provision, however, has been declared unconstitutional by the Federal Constitutional Court because it does not provide for adequate rules regarding the factual consequences of the invalidity of the marriage, such as maintenance and property. The provision is valid only until 30 June 2024.[376]

375. §13 Introductory Act to the Civil Code (EGBGB).
376. BVerfG 1 Feb. 2023, – 1 BvL 7/18 – nn. 1–194.

## Chapter 3. Freedom of Expression

*549.* Religious communities are free to demand special respect from their employees for their spiritual and moral teaching. This has been clearly stated by the Federal Constitutional Court in the *Rommelfanger* case, which has been repeatedly and extensively been referred to above (paragraphs 405 et seq., 485).[377]

*550.* When members of a religious community make statements against the teaching of the community, they can be excluded from the community.

377. BVerfG 4 Jun. 1985, BVerfGE 70, 138 et seq.

## Chapter 4. Due Process Norms and Religious Groups

*551.* The Federal Constitutional Court, as has been stated above (paragraph 531) in the context of the labour law status of ministers and priests, has held that the compulsory retiring of a Protestant pastor and the assessment of the pension are no 'acts of state power'; they are matters of the relevant Protestant Church. The organization of the law of church service and office are matters of the self-determination of the religious community and are exempt from state judicial review unless the religious community submits the matters voluntarily under such review.[378] There also is no review of internal procedures of religious communities as to whether and how elections of persons in religious offices are conducted.[379] The constitutional complaint to the Federal Constitutional Court against a ruling of a disciplinary court of a Roman Catholic diocese is inadmissible;[380] the same holds true for the organizational decision of a religious community to split a parish.[381]

378. BVerfG (K) 9 Dec. 2008, *Neue Juristische Wochenschrift* 62 (2009): 1195 et seq.; *see also* BVerfG 27 Jan. 2004, 2 BvR 1978/00; BVerfG (K) 18 Sep. 1998, *Neue Juristische Wochenschrift* 52 (1999): 349 et seq.; BVerfG (K) 18 Sep. 1998, *Neue Juristische Wochenschrift* 52 (1999): 350; BVerfG 17 May 1965, BVerfGE 18, 385, 387 et seq.
379. BVerfG (K) 18 Sep. 1998, *Neue Juristische Wochenschrift* 52 (1999): 350.
380. BVerfG 30 Mar. 1984, *Die Öffentliche Verwaltung* 47 (1984): 974 et seq.
381. BVerfG 17 May 1965, BVerfGE 18, 385 et seq.

## Chapter 5. Professional Secrecy

*552.* The confessional secret of clergy is intensely protected. This protection is not only limited to information received under confession in a narrow spiritual definition such as the Roman Catholic confession but also applies to any information gathered during spiritual care given to anyone. It is also regarded as following directly from freedom of religion or belief as guaranteed by Article 4 GG, which is stronger than the mere protection of freedom of profession as provided for in Article 12 GG. Clergy are not obliged to report under any circumstances what they have learned in performing spiritual care (e.g., §139 section 2 Criminal Code – StGB, §53 Criminal Procedure Code – StPO, §383 Civil Procedure Code – ZPO, etc.). §139 subsection 2 Criminal Code guarantees that a cleric is not obliged to report what has been confided to him in his capacity as a spiritual adviser. Under these circumstances, they are also not obliged to inform of planned crimes. As an example, §53 Criminal Procedure Code provides: '(1) The following persons may also refuse to testify: 1. clergy, concerning that information which was confided to them or which became known to them in their capacity as spiritual advisers.' Clergy may also refuse to give evidence according to §62 Federal Criminal Investigation Office Act (BKAG).[382] Evidence in view of potential dangers to public safety or public order secured by technical means such as interception may not be used unless the cleric him- or herself is the source of the danger to public safety (§62 subsections 1 and 4 BKAG).[383] According to §97 Criminal Procedure Code governing the prosecution, the following objects are not subject to seizure: (1) written correspondence between the accused and those persons who, under section 52 or section 53(1) sentence 1 numbers 1 to 3b of the Criminal Procedure Code, may refuse to testify; (2) notes made by the persons referred to in section 53(1) sentence 1 numbers 1 to 3b of the Criminal Procedure Code concerning confidential information confided to them by the accused or concerning other circumstances covered by the right to refuse to testify; (3) other objects, including the findings of medical examinations, which are covered by the right of the persons referred to in section 53(1) sentence 1 numbers 1 to 3b of the Criminal Procedure Code to refuse to testify. These restrictions only apply if these objects are in the custody of a person entitled to refuse to testify. These rules apply to clerics. The restrictions on seizure do not apply if certain facts give rise to the suspicion that the person entitled to refuse to testify participated in the offence or in handling stolen data, aiding after the fact, obstructing prosecution or punishment, or handling stolen goods, or if the objects concerned were derived from an offence or have been used or are intended for use in committing an offence or if they emanate from an offence. According to §1005 subsection 5 Criminal Procedure Code, interception of non-public speech of clerics in their cure of souls activity is prohibited even in serious cases of crime.

---

382. *See also* for example, §9a s. 3 Police Act Rhineland-Palatinate (POG RLP).
383. *See also* for example, §29, ss 4, 31 and s. 4 POG RLP.

*553.* Police authorities may not search premises of a recognized addict guidance centre of a religious community and seize patient's documents. The Federal Constitutional Court has held contrary action to be a violation of the right to free development of one's personality seen together with human dignity (Article 2 section 1 in conjunction with Article 1 section 1 GG) and has left open whether it also violated other fundamental rights, namely the freedom of religion or belief.[384]

384. BVerfG 24 May 1977, BVerfGE 44, 353 et seq.

## Chapter 6. Medical Deontology

*554.* Medical treatment in German law is regarded as depending on the personal decision of the patient. Treatment against the will of a patient is a crime according to §223 Criminal Code: Bodily Injury. Thus, a Jehovah's Witness who willingly rejects a necessary blood transfusion must not be forced to receive such treatment against his or her religious convictions. However, in a case decided by the Higher Regional Court Munich in 2002, a pregnant Jehovah's Witness faced difficulties with her pregnancy in a general hospital and became unconscious.[385] The guardianship court was called upon by the hospital, and her husband agreed to a blood transfusion against her previously declared will in order to save her life. The treatment caused damages to the woman's health, for which she claimed compensation. The court held the blood transfusion to be legal, stating that the medical doctor treating the woman also had a right to the integrity of his conscience and must not be compelled to act like a machine, only following the patient's will and seeing her die while being able to help; should the woman insist in her not being treated with a blood transfusion she should not have gone to a general hospital but to a hospital maintained by or following the teaching of Jehovah's Witnesses.

*555.* If parents reject a blood transfusion that is needed by their child, the family courts substitute this decision with a ruling allowing the treatment. This is general court practice in order to protect the life of the child, which in these cases takes precedence over the religious will of his or her parents.[386]

*556.* The Federal Constitutional Court has rejected a constitutional complaint of the widow of a Jehovah's Witness who had deceased after an accident because he refused a blood transfusion. The courts had denied the right of the widow to receive a widow's pension because it was not the accident that had caused the death of the spouse but the refusal to receive a blood transfusion.[387]

*557.* Circumcision of the male child as described above (paragraph) is allowed pursuant to §1631d Civil Code. In the first six months after the birth of the child, persons designated for this purpose by a religious society may also perform circumcisions if they are specially trained for this purpose and, without being doctors, are comparably qualified to perform circumcision. Circumcision of the female child is prohibited.

*558.* Medical treatment is regulated. Religious healing, ghost healing, or spiritual healing is not recognized as medical treatment. Physicians need an approbation, which requires studies and examinations in medicine. Those who want to exercise the art of healing without being approbated as a physician need a special

385. OLG Munich 31 January, OLGR 2002, 438 et seq.
386. OLG Celle 21 Feb. 1994, *Neue Juristische Wochenschrift* 48 (1995): 792 et seq.; BayObLG München 25 Sep. 1975, *Neue Juristische Wochenschrift* 29 (1976): 2017 et seq.; OLG Hamm 10 Oct. 1967, *Neue Juristische Wochenschrift* 21 (1968): 212 et seq.
387. BVerfG (K) 9 Mar. 2005, *Zeitschrift für das gesamte Familienrecht* 53 (2006): 764.

permit according to the Act on Non-Academic Medical Practitioners (HPG).[388] The art of healing, in the meaning of that law, is defined as every professionally or commercially exercised activity to diagnose, heal or allay diseases, sufferings or bodily injury of human beings. Such activity is already exercised when such impression is made on the one who is seeking help. Practising without such permit is a punishable crime. Thus, religious healing, ghost healing, or spiritual healing must not be exercised in a commercial or professional way.

*559.* Hospitals that are maintained by religious communities are free to decide on the scope of medical treatment based on their religious beliefs and within the requirements of professional medical standards. Thus, Roman Catholic hospitals are free not to perform abortions.[389] This rule would probably also apply when hospitals or homes for the elderly deny access to persons who offer assistance with suicide.

388. *See also* BVerfG 10 May 1988, BVerfGE 78, 179 et seq.
389. *See*, as one of many examples: Basic order of Catholic hospitals in North Rhine-Westphalia (Grundordnung für katholische Krankenhäuser in Nordrhein-Westfalen as of 1 Oct. 1996, as amended, KA 1996, no. 198, 5.203, KA 1999, no. 117, 5.147, KA 2001, no. 80, 5.138), available at Diözesane Arbeitsgemeinschaft der Mitarbeitervertretungen im Bistum Aachen (DiAg MAV) (ed.), file:///C:/Users/gerha/Downloads/2001_NRW_Grundordnung-katholische-krankenhaeuser.pdf, 9 Nov. 2023: 'Aims and activities of the hospital have to follow the faith and moral teachings of the Church. The hospital does under no circumstances perform abortions' (under B.; translation by the author).

## Chapter 7. Non-discrimination

*560.* The Basic Law also provides explicit rules on equal treatment in relation to religions in Article 3 section 3 and Article 33 section 3 GG. No person shall be favoured or disfavoured because of sex, parentage, race, language, homeland and origin, faith, or religious or political opinions. Neither the enjoyment of civil and political rights, eligibility for public office, nor rights acquired in the public service are dependent upon religious affiliation. No one may be disadvantaged by reason of adherence or non-adherence to a particular religious denomination or philosophical creed. According to Article 136 WRV in conjunction with Article 140 GG, civil and political rights and duties are neither dependent upon nor restricted by the exercise of religious freedom. Enjoyment of civil and political rights and eligibility for public office are independent of religious affiliation.

*561.* As stated above (paragraphs 430 et seq., 493), §§1 and 2 of the General Equal Treatment Law (AGG)[390] prohibit any discrimination because of reasons of race, ethnicity, gender, religion or belief, disability, age or sexual orientation in the field of profession and employment, social security or education, or access to social benefits, health services or goods and services open to the public including housing facilities. There is no discrimination when the requirements of §9 AGG are met: A different treatment because of religion or belief is allowed in view of the employment by a religious community regardless of its legal form, by an organization attached to it or by an association which has as its objective the common care for a religion or a belief if a specific religion or belief is a justified professional requirement in view of its right to self-determination or the kind of activity while respecting the self-understanding of the community. The prohibition of unequal treatment because of religion or belief does not prejudice the right of these communities and organizations to demand from their employees a loyal and honest behaviour in the sense of their respective self-understanding.

390. Cf. Part 4, Ch. I, §2, s. 4, B, nn. 416 et seq.

# Chapter 8. Penal Law and Religion

## §1. Religious Peace

*562.* Religion enjoys considerable protection in German criminal and procedural law. According to §130 StGB, a person inciting hatred against a religious group in specifically defined ways is punishable by up to three years imprisonment or a fine:

> §130 StGB Incitement of masses
>
> (1) Whoever, in a manner suited to causing a disturbance of the public peace,
> 1. incites hatred against a national, racial, religious group or a group defined by their ethnic origin, against sections of the population or individuals on account of their belonging to one of the aforementioned groups or sections of the population, or calls for violent or arbitrary measures against them or
> 2. violates the human dignity of others by insulting, maliciously maligning or defaming one of the aforementioned groups, sections of the population or individuals on account of their belonging to one of the aforementioned groups or sections of the population
>
> incurs a penalty of imprisonment for a term of between three months and five years.
>
> (2) Whoever
> 1. disseminates content (section 11 (3)) or makes it available to the public, or offers, supplies or makes available to a person under 18 years of age content (section 11 (3)) which
>    a) incites hatred against one of the groups referred to in subsection (1) no. 1, sections of the population or individuals on account of their belonging to one of the groups referred to in subsection (1) no. 1, or sections of the population,
>    b) calls for violent or arbitrary measures against one of the persons or bodies of persons referred to in letter (a) or
>    c) attacks the human dignity of one of the persons or bodies of persons referred to in letter (a) by insulting, maliciously maligning or defaming them, or
> 2. produces, purchases, supplies, stocks, offers, advertises or undertakes to import or export content (section 11 (3)) as referred to in no. 1 (a) to (c) in order to use it within the meaning of no. 1 or to facilitate such use by another
>
> incurs a penalty of imprisonment for a term not exceeding three years or a fine.
>
> (3) Whoever publicly or in a meeting approves of, denies or downplays an act committed under the rule of National Socialism of the kind indicated in section 6 (1) of the Code of Crimes against International Law in a manner suited to causing a disturbance of the public peace incurs a penalty of imprisonment for a term not exceeding five years or a fine.

(4) Whoever publicly or in a meeting disturbs the public peace in a manner which violates the dignity of the victims by approving of, glorifying or justifying National Socialist tyranny and arbitrary rule incurs a penalty of imprisonment for a term not exceeding three years or a fine.
(5) Subsection (2) also applies to content (section 11 (3)) as referred to in subsections (3) or (4).
(6) In the cases under subsection (2) no. 1, also in conjunction with subsection (5), the attempt is punishable.
(7) In the cases under subsection (2), also in conjunction with subsections (5) and (6), and in the cases under subsections (3) and (4), section 86 (4) applies accordingly.

§86(4) StGB provides:

(4) Subsections (1) and (2) do not apply if the act serves civic information, to prevent unconstitutional activities, to promote the arts or science, research or teaching, reporting about current or historical events, or similar purposes.

*563.* Also punishable is a person who attacks the contents of religious or philosophical beliefs in a way that threatens to disturb public peace:

§ 166 StGB: Revilement of religious faiths and religious and ideological communities

(1) Whoever publicly or by disseminating content (section 11 (3)) reviles the religion or ideology of others in a manner suited to causing a disturbance of the public peace incurs a penalty of imprisonment for a term not exceeding three years or a fine.
(2) Whoever publicly or by disseminating content (section 11 (3)) reviles a church or other religious or ideological community in Germany or its institutions or customs in a manner suited to causing a disturbance of the public peace incurs the same penalty.

*564.* The same applies to a person who interrupts the worship of a religious community existing in Germany or commits vituperating mischief in a place dedicated to worship by such a community. The ceremonies of philosophical, non-religious communities are equally protected. Interrupting funeral ceremonies as well as disturbing the peace of the dead is equally punishable (§§166–168 StGB):

§167 StGB Disturbing of exercise of religion

(1) Whoever
   1. intentionally and seriously disturbs a religious service or an act of religious worship of a church or other religious community in Germany or
   2. commits defamatory mischief in a place which is dedicated to the religious worship of such a religious community

incurs a penalty of imprisonment for a term not exceeding three years or a fine.

(2) The ceremonies of an ideological community in Germany are equivalent to a religious service.

§167a StGB Disturbing of funeral

Whoever intentionally or knowingly disturbs a funeral incurs a penalty of imprisonment for a term not exceeding three years or a fine. §168 StGB Disturbing of peace of dead

(1) Whoever, without being authorised to do so, takes the body or parts of the body of a deceased person, of a dead foetus or parts thereof, or the ashes of a deceased person from the custody of the person entitled thereto, or whoever commits defamatory mischief on them incurs a penalty of imprisonment for a term not exceeding three years or a fine.

(2) Whoever destroys or damages the place where a body is laid out, a burial site or a public memorial for the dead, or whoever commits defamatory mischief on them incurs the same penalty.

(3) The attempt is punishable.

## §2. Religious Property

*565.* Religious property is under special protection of the criminal law:

§243 StGB Aggravated theft

(1) In especially serious cases of theft, the penalty is imprisonment for a term of between three months and 10 years. An especially serious case typically occurs where the offender

(…)

4. steals property which is dedicated to the exercise of religion or used for religious worship from a church or other building or space used for religious veneration,

(…)

(2) In the cases under subsection (1) sentence 2 nos. 1 to 6, an especially serious case is ruled out if the property is of minor value. §304 StGB Criminal damage to objects of public interest

(1) Whoever unlawfully damages or destroys objects of veneration of a religious community in Germany or property dedicated to religious worship, or tombstones, public monuments, natural monuments, or objects of art, science or craft which are kept in public collections or are publicly exhibited, or objects which serve a public interest or add to the ambience of public roads and ways, squares or parks incurs a penalty of imprisonment for a term not exceeding three years or a fine.

(2) Whoever, without being authorised to do so, substantially and permanently alters the appearance of an object referred to in subsection (1) incurs the same penalty.
(3) The attempt is punishable. §306a StGB Aggravated arson
(1) Whoever sets fire to or by setting fire to them destroys, in whole or in part,
(...)
2. a church or other building which serves the practice of religion,
(...)
incurs a penalty of imprisonment for a term of at least one year.
(...)
(3) In less serious cases under subsections (1) and (2), the penalty is imprisonment for a term of between six months and five years.

## §3. Religious Titles, Garments and Emblems

*566.* A person who, without being authorized, uses titles, ranks, uniforms or ensigns of a public law religious community is liable to punishment of up to one year's imprisonment or a fine. The destruction or suppression of official documents of a public law religious community is punishable by up to two years imprisonment or a fine; in severe cases, this rises to up to five years of imprisonment (§§132a and 133 StGB):

§132a StGB Abuse of titles, professional designations and symbols

(1) Whoever, without being authorised to do so,
1. uses domestic or foreign titles of office, academic degrees, honorific titles or public honours,
2. uses the professional designation of 'physician', 'dentist', 'psychological psychotherapist', 'child or youth psychotherapist', 'psychotherapist', 'veterinarian', 'pharmacist', 'lawyer' (Rechtsanwalt), 'patent attorney', 'certified accountant', 'sworn auditor', 'tax consultant' (Steuerberater) or 'tax representative' (Steuerbevollmächtigter),
3. uses the title of 'publicly appointed expert' or
4. wears domestic or foreign uniforms, official dress or official insignia

incurs a penalty of imprisonment for a term not exceeding one year or a fine.
(2) Designations, academic degrees, titles, honours, uniforms, official dress or official insignia which are easy to confuse with those referred to in subsection (1) are equivalent to those referred to in subsection (1).
(3) Subsections (1) and (2) also apply to official titles, titles, honours, official dress and official insignia of the churches and other religious communities under public law.
(4) Objects to which an offence under subsection (1) no. 4, either alone or in conjunction with subsections (2) or (3), relates may be confiscated.

§133 StGB Destruction of material in official custody

(1) Whoever destroys, damages, renders unusable or removes from official access any papers or other movable items which have been put in official custody or which have been officially placed in their or another's custody incurs a penalty of imprisonment for a term not exceeding two years or a fine.
(2) The same applies to papers or other movable items in the official custody of a church or another religious community under public law or which have been placed in official custody with the offender or another.
(3) Whoever commits the act in relation to an object which has been entrusted to or made available to them in their capacity as a public official or a person entrusted with special public service functions incurs a penalty of imprisonment for a term not exceeding five years or a fine.

## §4. Confessional Secret

*567.* The confessional secret is broadly protected. Clergy are not obliged to report under any circumstances what they have learned in performing spiritual care (e.g., §139 section 2 StGB, §53 Criminal Procedure Code; *see also* §383 Civil Procedure Code, etc.). Under these circumstances, they are also not obliged to inform of planned crimes (§139 section 2 Criminal Code):

§139 StGB Exemption from punishment for failure to report planned crimes

( … )
Clergy are not obliged to report what has been confided to them in their capacity as spiritual advisers. ( … )

## §5. Position of Religious Communities

*568.* Special rules apply for religious communities in regard of application for criminal prosecution in cases of insult or bodily harm inflicted on their office holders. In such cases, the religious community can apply in addition to the person harmed:

§194 StGB Request to prosecute

( … )
Insults committed against public officials, persons entrusted with special public service functions or soldiers in the Federal Armed Forces in the discharge of their duties or in connection with their duties may also be prosecuted upon the request of their superior. Offences directed against an authority or other

agency which performs duties of public administration are prosecuted upon the request of the head of the authority or the head of the supervisory authority. The same applies accordingly to office holders and offices of the churches and other religious communities under public law. ( … )

§230 StGB Request to prosecute

(1) Causing intentional bodily harm under section 223 and negligent bodily harm under section 229 are prosecuted only upon request, unless the prosecuting authority deems there to be a special public interest in prosecution which calls for ex officio intervention. ( … )
(2) Acts committed against public officials, persons entrusted with special public service functions or soldiers in the Federal Armed Forces in the discharge of their duties or in connection with their duties are also prosecuted upon the request of their superior. The same applies to office holders in the churches and other religious communities under public law.

## §6. Special Duties of Religious Office Holders

*569.* Office holders of religious communities can be subject to special obligations or intensified punishment:

§355 StGB Breach of tax secrecy

(1) Whoever, without being authorised to do so, discloses or uses
   1. the personal data of another which became known to them in their capacity as a public official
      a) in administrative proceedings, an audit procedure or judicial proceedings in tax matters,
      b) in criminal proceedings on account of a tax offence or in regulatory fines proceedings on account of a breach of tax regulations,
      c) in the context of further processing under section 29c (1) sentence 1 no. 4, 5 or 6 of the Fiscal Code or on another official occasion, in particular by means of a communication by a revenue authority or through the legally required submission of a tax assessment notice or a certificate concerning the findings made on taxation or
   2. the business or trade secret of another which became known to them in their capacity as a public official in one of the proceedings listed in no. 1

   incurs a penalty of imprisonment for a term not exceeding two years or a fine. The personal data of another or business or trade secrets of another are deemed to have become known to the offender in the capacity as a public official in one of the proceedings referred to in sentence 1 no. 1 if they result from data to which the offender had access and which the offender retrieved without being authorised to do so. Information concerning identified or identifiable deceased natural persons or relating to committees, associations with or without legal capacity, or assets are equal to the personal data of another.

(2) The following are equal to a public official within the meaning of subsection (1):

(…)
office holders in the churches and other religious communities under public law.

(3) The act is prosecuted only upon request by the official superior or the victim. In the case of offences by officially consulted experts, the head of the authority whose proceedings have been affected is entitled to file a request in addition to the victim.

## §7. Administrative Misdemeanours

*570.* Not only is the criminal law in special ways relevant to religions, but also the law on administrative misdemeanours. The Administrative Offences Act (OWiG) provides special protection for official costumes and insignia of religious communities against misuse:

§126 OWiG Abuse of Vocational Clothing or Badges

(1) Whoever, without authorisation, wears
   1. vocational clothing or a badge which are state-recognised or approved in the Federal Republic being designed for persons engaged in nursing or welfare work, or
   2. vocational clothing or a badge of a religious association

   recognised by a church or another religious association under public law shall be deemed to have committed a regulatory offence.

(2) Working clothes and badges which so closely resemble those designated in subsection (1) that they may be mistaken for them, shall be deemed equal to those.

(3) The regulatory offence may be sanctioned by a regulatory fine.

## §8. Crimes Against International Law

*571.* The Code of Crimes against Public International Law (*Völkerstrafgesetzbuch*) protects religion and religions against genocide and against crimes against humanity as well as against prohibited methods of warfare:

§9. CCAIL GENOCIDE

*572.*

(1) Whoever with the intent of destroying as such, in whole or in part, a national, racial, religious or ethnic group
1. kills a member of the group,
2. causes serious bodily or mental harm to a member of the group, especially of the kind referred to in section 226 of the Criminal Code,
3. inflicts on the group conditions of life calculated to bring about their physical destruction in whole or in part,
4. imposes measures intended to prevent births within the group,
5. forcibly transfers a child of the group to another group

shall be punished with imprisonment for life.

(2) In less serious cases referred to under subsection (1), numbers 2 to 5, the punishment shall be imprisonment for not less than five years.

§10. CCAIL CRIMES AGAINST HUMANITY

*573.*

(1) Whoever, as part of a widespread or systematic attack directed against any civilian population,

( … )

10. persecutes an identifiable group or collectivity by depriving such group or collectivity of fundamental human rights, or by substantially restricting the same, on political, racial, national, ethnic, cultural or religious, gender or other grounds that are recognized as impermissible under the general rules of international law

shall be punished, ( … )

in the cases referred to under numbers 8 to 10, with imprisonment for not less than three years.

( … )

(3) Where the perpetrator causes the death of a person through an offence pursuant to subsection (1), numbers 3 to 10, the punishment shall be imprisonment for life or for not less than ten years in cases under subsection (1), numbers 3 to 7, and imprisonment for not less than five years in cases under subsection (1), numbers 8 to 10.

(4) In less serious cases under subsection (3), the punishment for an offence pursuant to subsection (1), numbers 3 to 7, shall be imprisonment for not less than five years, and for an offence pursuant to subsection (1), numbers 8 to 10, imprisonment for not less than three years.

( … )

### §11. CCAIL War Crimes Consisting of the Use of Prohibited Methods of Warfare

*574.*

(1) Whoever in connection with an international armed conflict or with an armed conflict not of an international character

(…)

2. directs an attack by military means against civilian objects, so long as these objects are protected as such by international humanitarian law, namely buildings dedicated to religion, education, art, science or charitable purposes, historic monuments, hospitals and places where the sick and wounded are collected, or against undefended towns, villages, dwellings or buildings, or against demilitarized zones, or against works and installations containing dangerous forces,

(…)

shall be punished with imprisonment for not less than three years. In less serious cases under number 2 the punishment shall be imprisonment for not less than one year.

(2) Where the perpetrator causes the death or serious injury of a civilian (section 226 of the Criminal Code) or of a person who is to be protected under international humanitarian law through an offence pursuant to subsection (1), numbers 1 to 6, he shall be punished with imprisonment for not less than five years. Where the perpetrator intentionally causes death, the punishment shall be imprisonment for life or for not less than ten years.

(…)

# Part VIII. Church Financing

## Chapter 1. Direct Financing of Religious Communities

### §1. Protection of Property

*575.* The property of religious communities is guaranteed in specific ways. Article 140 GG in conjunction with Article 138 WRV states:

(1) Rights of religious societies to public subsidies on the basis of a law, contract or special grant shall be redeemed by legislation of the *Länder*. The principles governing such redemption shall be established by the *Reich*.
(2) Property rights and other rights of religious societies or associations in their institutions, foundations, and other assets intended for purposes of worship, education or charity shall be guaranteed.

These provisions take preference over the general guarantee of property rights pursuant to Article 14 GG, which also covers the rights of religious communities:

(1) Property and the right of inheritance shall be guaranteed. Their content and limits shall be defined by the laws.
(2) Property entails obligations. Its use shall also serve the public good.
(3) Expropriation shall only be permissible for the public good. It may only be ordered by or pursuant to a law that determines the nature and extent of compensation. Such compensation shall be determined by establishing an equitable balance between the public interest and the interests of those affected. In case of dispute concerning the amount of compensation, recourse may be had to the ordinary courts.

### §2. State Subsidies in General

*576.* As a result of repeated expropriation of church property in the past, the churches in Germany now have only a relatively small amount of property. As compensation for this secularization following the *Reichsdeputationshauptschluss* of 1803, a series of government decisions guaranteed funds for the churches. They are guaranteed by Article 138 section 1 WRV in conjunction with Article 140 GG. This provision also envisages the ending of those payments which are necessarily linked to the payment of compensation; this so far has not been pursued on grounds of impracticality. Here are, however, official negotiations going on between the state and the relevant churches aiming at redeeming these ancient subsidies. It is still an open question whether and how these negotiations will lead to a valid solution to the situation.

*577.* In addition, other subsidies granted by the state are often related to long-standing claims of the churches; an important example is the fact that local authorities must discharge their public duty to contribute to the maintenance of church buildings. Likewise, on the basis of contractual terms, there are some obligatory contributions to be made by the state to the church, such as subsidies to the salaries of church officials.

## §3. Church Tax

### I. Basic Facts

*578.* Approximately 80% of the entire church budget is covered by the church tax, guaranteed by Article 137 section 6 WRV in conjunction with Article 140 GG. On the basis of the civil tax lists, in accordance with the law of the *Länder*, the religious communities that are public law corporations are allowed to levy taxes. The large churches have made ample use of this opportunity, but smaller religious communities with the status of public corporations, such as the Jewish communities, have also done so. The church tax is a tax levied by the religious communities; it is not a state tax. The church tax was instituted from the beginning of the nineteenth century onwards in order to relieve the national budget of its obligations to the churches, which were in turn based on the secularization of church property.

### II. Taxable Persons

*579.* Only members of the particular religious community authorized to levy the church tax are obliged to pay. No religious community may levy taxes on other persons than their own members. Any member who does not want to pay the church tax must be able to leave the religious community.[391] It does not matter whether the member has already reached the age of religious maturity.[392]

*580.* There is no church tax on legal persons; only natural persons are taxable. This follows from the fact that only members of religious communities can be taxed and legal persons cannot be members of religious communities.

391. BVerfG 31 Mar. 1971, BVerfGE 30, 415 et seq.
392. BVerfG 30 Nov. 1983, *Neue Juristische Wochenschrift* 37 (1984): 969.

## III. Objection to Church Tax

*581.* Those desiring to be free of the tax may achieve that result by leaving the religious community. Withdrawal from the religious community is effected by de-registering with the proper state officials and simply means that one has, according to the state classification, officially ended one's membership in the particular religious community in question. However, most Protestant churches see the withdrawal as a withdrawal from their particular church as well. The Catholic Church, as a general rule, views the withdrawal as a serious violation of the person's obligations to the church without bringing into question the theological dimension of church membership.

## IV. Tax Rate

*582.* The rate of the church tax is usually between 8% and 9% of the individual's wage and income tax liability. Other tax standards may also be used. The percentage is calculated taking the wage and income tax liability as the basis of calculation and is then paid in addition to the amount of the wage or income tax.

*583.* In some, but not all, churches, amounts of church tax owed that exceed a certain maximum level are cut, and the exceeding part does not have to be paid (*Kappungsgrenze*). This is a response to the situation of tax law options in which taxpayers have to pay a very high income tax, and the 8% to 9% church tax may amount to exceedingly high church tax dues.

## V. Administration of the Church Tax

*584.* Upon application of qualified religious communities, the church tax may be collected by the state on behalf of the religious community along with the normal state wage and income tax. The *Länder* require a certain minimum number of members of the relevant religious community to collect the church tax for them; the minimum amount varies from *Land* to *Land*. In doing so, the state offers a service to the religious community; the church tax remains a tax of the religious community only and does not become a state tax. The state hands over the income of the church tax to the relevant religious community. For this service, the religious community has to remunerate the state. This emolument varies from *Land* to *Land*. In Rhineland-Palatinate, it amounts to 4% of the church tax income; in Baden-Wuerttemberg, it is 3% of the church tax income. Certain religious communities do not make use of this service and collect the tax themselves.

## VI. Example: North Rhine-Westphalia

*585.* The (*Land*) Act on Collection of Church Taxes in the *Land* North Rhine-Westphalia (KiStG NRW) provides the details on the church tax for the *Land* North

Rhine-Westphalia. It is representative of the various laws on church tax in the German *Länder*. According to this law, the Catholic Church and the Protestant Church levy church taxes in the *Land* North Rhine-Westphalia on the basis of their own tax regulations. Church taxes may be levied in accordance with tax regulations as diocesan church tax or *Land* church tax, as local church tax, and simultaneously as diocesan church tax or *Land* church tax and local church tax. The tax regulations are issued by the Dioceses of the Catholic Church and the Protestant *Land* churches.

*586.* The corporation competent in accordance with the tax regulations determines the amount of the church taxes to be levied.

*587.* All members of the Catholic Church and the Protestant Church who are residents or have their habitual place of residence in the *Land* North Rhine-Westphalia are liable to church tax. Liability to pay church tax terminates with resignation from the church declared in accordance with the valid state provisions on the expiry of the calendar month in which the declaration of resignation from the church has become effective.

*588.* Church taxes may be levied as a supplement to income tax and wage tax, also with setting minimum amounts. It can also be levied in accordance with income on the basis of a special tariff (church tax on income). Furthermore, the church tax may be levied as a supplement to property tax (church tax on property), as a supplement to the real property tax assessment amounts (church tax on real property), as general church dues, and finally, as special church dues by church taxpayers whose spouses are not liable to church tax.

*589.* Prior to calculating the church tax as a supplement to income and wage tax, the proper income tax and wage tax are ascertained in accordance with general income tax law.

*590.* If the liability to pay church tax does not pertain during the whole calendar year, for each calendar month in which the liability to pay church tax pertains, in general, one-twelfth of the amount is levied, which would result in an annual tax liability if the liability to pay church tax were to pertain for the whole year.

*591.* If spouses belong to different churches entitled to levy taxes (inter-confessional marriages) and if the conditions apply for a joint income tax declaration, both churches levy the church tax in the form of a supplement to income and wage tax from both spouses. In this case, the church tax for each individual spouse is based on half the income or wage tax that both spouses owe to the state. The spouses then are jointly and severally liable. If the conditions do not apply for a joint income tax assessment, or if the spouses are taxed separately or specially, the church tax is levied from the income of each spouse in accordance with his or her church affiliation and with the tax assessment basis applying to them personally.

*592.* If only one spouse belongs to a church entitled to levy taxes (inter-faith marriage), the church entitled to levy taxes levies the church tax in accordance with the tax assessment basis relating to that person.

*593.* If such spouses are taxable together for income tax, the church tax of the spouse liable to pay tax is proportionally calculated in the shape of the supplement to income tax. The church tax is calculated in accordance with the part of the joint income tax incurred by the spouse liable to pay tax if the joint tax in the ratio of the income tax amounts that would emerge on the income of each spouse is distributed between the spouses.

*594.* Provisions about interest, delay penalties, criminal and administrative fines, and criminal and administrative fine procedures are not applicable to the church tax.

*595.* The churches are competent for respite and abatement of the church taxes. They may transfer these powers to the finance offices or the municipalities.

*596.* Upon application of the Dioceses of the Catholic Church or upon application of the Protestant *Land* churches, the ministry competent for the *Land* finance administration assigns to finance offices the administration of church taxes on income and assets and of the special church dues. If the church tax on income is levied because of a special tariff or as special church dues, the obligation to transfer only pertains with regard to taxpayers liable to income or wage tax. In other cases – with the exception of general church dues – the administration of church tax may be assigned to the finance offices.

*597.* Undertaking of administration is effected for an emolument that is to be agreed.

*598.* Where church tax on income is administrated by the state finance offices, employers whose establishments are in the *Land* are obliged to collect the church tax from all Catholic and Protestant employees with residence or habitual place of residence within the *Land* in the amount of the relevant tax rate for the place of the establishment and to pay it to the finance office competent for the employer.

*599.* Upon application of Dioceses of the Catholic Church or of Protestant *Land* churches whose area wholly or partly lies outside the *Land*, the ministry competent for the *Land* finance administration, in agreement with the ministry competent for church matters, may order the collection and payment of church tax using the wage deduction procedure also for those employees who are liable to pay tax to these churches who do not have their residence or habitual place of residence in the *Land* but are paid by an establishment in the *Land*. If the tax rates at the place of residence are lower than at the establishment, the application shall only be approved if it is ensured that too much collected church tax will be refunded. If another tax rate applies to the residence or habitual place of residence of employees than to the place of the establishment, the finance office of the establishment may, upon application, permit the employer to collect and pay the church tax of these employees in accordance with the tax rate applicable at the residence or habitual place of residence. The decision of the finance office requires the consent of the Diocese of the Catholic Church and the Protestant *Land* Church in whose area the employer maintains the establishment for its effectiveness.

*600.* The church tax on real property may, upon application of the corporation competent in accordance with the Ordinance on Dues, be administrated by the municipalities (municipal associations).

*601.* Administration is also, in this case, carried out for an emolument that is to be agreed upon.

*602.* If the church tax is administrated by the churches themselves, the church tax, including additional payment, will upon application be collected by the finance offices in accordance with the provisions of the Ordinance on Dues or by the municipal law enforcement authorities where these collect the base tax, in accordance with the provisions of the administrative executory procedure.

*603.* The competent *Land* or municipal authorities, upon request, provide the churches with the documents required for taxation and for church financial equalization.

*604.* The taxpayer is entitled to file an objection to the collection of church tax as an out-of-court legal recourse, which has to be submitted within a period of one month from announcement of the tax notice to the agency stated in the Ordinance on Taxes. If the tax is collected by means of wage deduction, the objection is admissible until the expiry of the calendar month following the wage payment period in which the deduction has been effected. Recourse to the state Finance Courts is available.

*605.* The same rules apply *mutatis mutandis* to religious communities, which have the rights of a corporation under public law.

*606.* The obligation to transfer the administration of church taxes to the finance offices applies in this case if the religious community entitled to levy taxes has at least 40,000 members in the *Land*;[393] the religious community entitled to levy taxes collects the church tax in accordance with the same tax rates as the churches entitled to levy taxes, and – where there are religious communities with the same confession in the *Land* – these all collect taxes in accordance with uniform principles.

*607.* The church tax regulations and resolutions require state recognition.

393. This minimum number applies for the Land North Rhine-Westphalia; it is different in other Länder.

## VII. Church Due

*608.* Because of the links with state taxes, tax exemptions also affect the churches' own church tax. It is estimated that about one-third of all church members pay no church tax because they are not liable to income tax. In some cases, the churches attempt to make up for it by demanding an alternative contribution to the church, which is independent of income tax. This is usually called church due (*Kirchgeld*). It applies often in cases of married couples who are liable to joint assessment of husband and wife for income or wage tax and in which one of the spouses earns the money but is not a member of a church and therefore is not liable to church tax, and the other spouse is a member of a church, but has no or little income and therefore pays no or very little church tax. The latter spouse is then liable to pay the church due because in fact he or she does have enough means to support his or her church.

## VIII. Case Law

*609.* Quite a number of court decisions have been taken in respect of the church tax as provided for in Article 140 GG in conjunction with Article 137 section 6 WRV.[394]

*610.* The Federal Constitutional Court has repeatedly ruled that the church tax can be levied on the members of the specific religious community only.

*611.* Whoever does not want to pay the church tax can leave the church by way of a statement declared before a state authority. This follows from the right not to believe and not to support a specific religious community, which is entailed in the freedom of religion or belief.

*612.* It does amount to a limitation on this right that a former member of a religious community who has left the church in this way can be obligated to pay church tax until the end of the month following his or her declaration of secession.[395] This has been upheld by ruling that the well-functioning of the tax levy system is a constitutional value and that a relatively short time of further duty to pay the tax is not a disproportionate burden for the one concerned.

---

394. BVerfG 14 Dec. 1965, BVerfGE 19, 206 et seq.; BVerfG 14 Dec. 1965, BVerfGE 19, 242 et seq.; BVerfG 14 Dec. 1965, BVerfGE 19, 248 et seq.; BVerfG 14 Dec. 1965, BVerfGE 19, 253 et seq.; BVerfG 14 Dec. 1965, BVerfGE 19, 268 et seq.; BVerfG 14 Dec. 1965, BVerfGE 19, 226, 228; BVerfG 14 Dec. 1965, BVerfGE 19, 282 et seq.; BVerfG 14 Dec. 1965, BVerfGE 19, 288; BVerfG 20 Apr. 1966, BVerfGE 20, 40; BVerfG 31 Mar. 1971, BVerfGE 30, 415 et seq.; BVerfG 8 Feb. 1977, BVerfGE 44, 37 et seq.; BVerfG 8 Feb. 1977, BVerfGE 44, 59 et seq.; BVerfG 17 Feb. 1977, BVerfGE 44, 103 et seq.; BVerfG 23 Oct. 1978, BVerfGE 49, 375 et seq.; BVerfG 7 Oct. 1980, BVerfGE 55, 32 et seq.; BVerfG 23 Oct. 1986, BVerfGE 73, 388 et seq.; BVerfG 23 Mar. 1994, BVerfGE 90, 226 et seq.

395. BVerfG 8 Feb. 1977, BVerfGE 44, 59 et seq.

*613.* From the system of church tax collection by the state tax authorities follows the employer's duty to transfer the church tax of its employees together with the general wage tax to the state tax authorities. The Federal Constitutional Court has seen this to be in conformity with the rights of the employer because the church tax system is based in Article 140 GG in conjunction with Article 137 section 7 WRV and thus amounts to a limitation to the rights of others prescribed by the constitution.[396] The administration, the payover, and also the liability of the employer for this payment foreseen by the church tax laws has been held constitutional by the Federal Constitutional Court because it amounted to a normal duty of private persons vis-à-vis the state.[397] This system also means that the membership of an employee in a religious community who is entitled to levy taxes and makes use of the state tax collection service is printed on his or her wage tax card. The Federal Constitutional Court has held that this does not violate constitutional rights of the employee.[398]

The European Court of Human Rights has upheld the German church tax system in its decision *Wasmuth v. Germany*.[399] Mr Wasmuth had argued that the obligation to indicate the membership or non-membership in a religious community for church tax reasons would violate his right not to disclose his adherence to a religion. The European Court of Human Rights held that there are prevailing public interests necessary in a democratic society that put a legitimate limit to this right in the present case.

*614.* The Federal Constitutional Court upheld in 1994 the general practice by which the amount of unemployment aid in the general public unemployment insurance system is calculated, taking into account the 'normal' deductions from the gross income of an employee regardless of whether the individual unemployed belongs to a qualified religious community or not.[400] This means that the average amount paid in church taxes is a negative factor in the calculation of the amount of unemployment aid. The Federal Constitutional Court has held that this practice violates neither freedom of religion or belief nor the guarantee of property because the authorities are allowed to generalize to a certain extent to facilitate administration. However, this would not apply anymore if no longer a clear majority of the employees belonged to a religious community with the right to levy taxes. The legislator is required to monitor the development, especially in light of the fact that in the east of Germany, a large part of the employees do not belong to any religious community.

396. BVerfG (K) 27 Aug. 1987, *Höchstrichterliche Finanzrechtsprechung* 27 (1988): 583.
397. BVerfG 17 Feb. 1977, BVerfGE 44, 103 et seq.
398. BVerfG 23 Oct. 1978, BVerfGE 49, 375 et seq.
399. ECHR, *Wasmuth v. Germany*, 17 Feb. 2011, appl. no. 12884/03.
400. BVerfG 23 Mar. 1994, BVerfGE 90, 226 et seq.

§4. STATE SUBSIDIES

*615.* There are quite a number of religious activities that are sponsored directly or indirectly by public funds.[401] However, state funds or subsidies only contribute a small part to the church's finances.

*616.* A considerable part of state subsidies results from historical state commitments, such as the compensation for the secularization following the 1803 *Reichsdeputationshauptschluss*. In addition, other subsidies granted by the state are often related to long-standing claims of the churches; an example is the fact that the local authorities must discharge their public duty to contribute to the maintenance of church buildings. These very often have their basis in the general public use of church towers as outlook for fire protection or later as general clock towers for the local community. The Federal Administrative Court ruled in 2009 that local subsidies for churches that had been contracted before the 1919 Weimar Constitution took effect remain valid. They are subject to change according to general rules of administrative law when the basic general circumstances undergo a substantive change. Accordingly, since no such substantive change had occurred, the Federal Administrative Court has upheld the maintenance obligations in the West German *Länder*.[402] However, the same court ruled in 2008 that the subsidies by municipalities in the former DDR have ceased to exist because they have not explicitly been upheld by the 1990 unification treaty.[403] This highly debatable decision amounts to the greatest expropriation of the churches since the 1803 *Reichsdeputationshauptschluss*.

*617.* Teachers of religion in public schools are paid by the state. Also, military chaplains are paid by the state, as is the case for professors of theology in state universities.

*618.* Further, many churches receive allocations from the state for activities in the same way as other publicly funded activities: it is part of the idea of state neutrality that church activities are not to be put in a worse position than that of, say, state-funded local athletic clubs.

*619.* Few religious buildings are – for historical reasons – still property of the state. This is the background of the case of the St. Salvator Church in Munich that the Federal Constitutional Court decided in 1998 between two competing religious

---

401. *See* Gerhard Robbers, 'Förderung der Kirchen durch den Staat', in *Handbuch des Staatskirchenrechts der Bundesrepublik Deutschland*, Joseph Listl & Dietrich Pirson eds, vol. 1, 2nd edn (Berlin: Duncker & Humblot, 1994), 867; Ute Mager, ‚Förderung von Kirchen und anderen Religionsgemeinschaften durch den Staat', in: *Handbuch des Staatskirchenrechts*, Dietrich Pirson et al. eds, 3rd edn (Berlin: Duncker & Humblot, 2020), 2767, nn. 1 et seq.

402. BVerwG 5 Feb. 2009, *Neue Zeitschrift für Verwaltungsrecht-Rechtsprechungsreport* 22 (2009), 590 et seq.

403. BVerwG 11 Dec. 2008, *Thüringer Verwaltungsblätter 2009*, 102–105.

communities.[404] Originally a Roman Catholic Church, the St. Salvator Church was secularized in the course of the 1803 *Reichsdeputationshauptschluss* and became property of the Bavarian state. The then Bavarian King Ludwig I decreed in 1828 that the 'Greek-Orthodox Cult' was permitted to use the church free of charge, in conformity with the decree that the church was since 1833 under the canon law jurisdiction of the Greek-Orthodox Autocephaly Church of Greece. The complainant was the parish of the Autocephaly Church of Greece, a registered association which had since 1924 been using the St. Salvator Church. The priest had been sent by the Metropolitan of Germany, which had been erected by the Ecumenical Patriarchy. In 1976, conflicts arose between the parish and the Metropolitan, in the course of which the Metropolitan ordered the parish priest not to make use of the church any more. The parish then had its cantor ordained as priest of the 'Church of the true Orthodox Christians of Greece and of the Diaspora', a split-off from the Autocephaly Church of Greece since the 1920s; after that, priests of that split-off church served as priests in the St. Salvator Church. The Bavarian government ended the right of the complainant to use the church building and ordered the priest to hand over the premises. The Federal Constitutional Court decided that this was in conformity with the Constitution. The use permit's original purpose was the use by the Autocephaly Church of Greece; it had to be left to the autonomous decision of that church to determine which unit was one of her parishes. In ending the right of use by the split-off parish, state authorities followed the original will and purpose of the decree in conformity with state neutrality, and they did not interfere with any right to church property protected by Article 138 section 2 WRV in conjunction with Article 140 GG.

## §5. Examples of Facts and Figures

*620.* It is difficult to give reliable data on the annual amount of funds that are allocated for religious purposes because there are numerous sources and recipients of funding. In 2022, church taxes and equivalent membership contributions amounted to EUR 6,242,000,000 for the Protestant Churches (EKD),[405] while the Catholic Church had an overall income of EUR 6,850,000,000,[406] forming a total of EUR 13,100,000,000.

*621.* The most important source of income is the church tax. It is paid by church members who are taxable for income and wage tax. The total income of the EKD and its member Churches amounted in 2022 to EUR 29.29 billion.[407] 45.9% of these

404. BVerfG 13 Oct. 1998, BVerfGE 99, 100 et seq.; *see also* the interim order by the Federal Constitutional Court in BVerfG 13 Feb. 1997, *Neue Zeitschrift für Verwaltungsrecht* 16 (1997): 782 et seq. and BVerfG 30 Nov. 1983, *Neue Juristische Wochenschrift* 37 (1984): 968 et seq.
405. Evangelische Kirche in Deutschland (ed.), 'Kirchensteuerstatistik 2022 Statistischer Bericht', ttps://www.ekd.de/ekd_de/ds_doc/Steuerstatistik_Bericht_2022.pdf.
406. https://www.domradio.de/artikel/ein-paar-fragen-und-antworten-zur-kirchensteuer, 9 Nov. 2023.
407. The Protestant Church and the Money (Die evangelische Kirche und das Geld), https://www.ekd.de/ekd_de/ds_doc/Faltblatt_Kirche_und_Geld.pdf, 9 Nov. 2023.

funds result from church tax and donations, 26.2% from subsidies, 8.2% from church services, 7.2% from church properties, and 12.4% from various other sources. By paying for the maintenance of kindergartens, schools, homes for the elderly, and other social services, religious communities render services to society which otherwise the state or the individual users would have to provide for.

## Chapter 2. Indirect Financing of Religious Communities

*622.* Religious communities receive a certain number of tax exemptions and exemptions from state fees. Many of them have historical reasons found in the expropriations of the churches (and also the Jewish communities) in the past. Other exemptions find their reason in the idea that religious communities contribute actively to public life and should thus be supported, as are other entities and participants in public life.

*623.* The church tax and charitable donations to the religious communities may be deducted from the taxable income, §10 section 1 number 4, §10b section 1 Income Tax Code (EStG); this applies equally to donations to non-profit organizations. From the taxable income, donations to religious communities of up to 20% of the total income can be deducted.

*624.* The existing exemptions from taxes and fees are extremely detailed and spread in manifold laws. There is no statistical data on how much those benefits would amount as benefits for religious communities.

*625.* Religious communities are exempt from corporate income tax as far as they perform religious and charitable functions, §5 section 1 number 9 Corporate Income Tax Act (KStG). This also applies to the inheritance and gift tax, §13 section 1 numbers 16, 17 Inheritance and Gift Tax Act (ErbStG), the tax on real property, §3 section 1 numbers 4, 5 Real Property Tax Act (GrStG) and to the local business tax, §3 number 6 Local Business Tax Act (GewStG).

*626.* Religious and charitable acts performed by religious communities are not subject to value added tax, §4 Turnover Tax Act (UStG).

*627.* Religious communities that are public law corporations are exempt in very specific and various ways from certain court fees according to varying provisions of various *Länder*, for example, §7 section 1 number 1 Legal Expenses Act Baden-Württemberg (LJKG BW). The same applies to a number of administrative fees.[408]

408. For example, §8, s. 1, no. 5 Act on Administrative Fees of North Rhine-Westphalia (GebG NRW), §1, s. 1, no. 1 Act on Fee Exemption, Forbearance and Acceptilation of Judicial Costs (GerGebBefrG NRW).

# Part IX. Education

## Chapter 1. Religious Education in Public and Private Schools

### §1. Religious Education in Public Schools

#### I. General Principles of Public Education

*628.* There is a general school-attendance requirement based on the right and obligation of the state to care for the upbringing of the children pursuant to Article 7 section 1 GG: 'The entire school system shall be under the supervision of the state.' This task of the state is regarded as being an original right of the state on equal footing with the right of the parents to raise their children.[409]

*629.* As a general rule, all children over the age of 6 (with more specific rules relating to when the school year begins) must attend school. The obligation to attend school ends at the age of 18. The child must attend school full-time for nine years and thereafter must at least attend school for another three years part-time or must attend vocational school. The precise content of the rules on this subject depends on which *Land* the child lives in. There are no school fees for attendance at public schools.

*630.* General education in public schools, that is, schools run and maintained by the state, must be religiously neutral. There may be no mission or proselytism; religions must be treated equally. The Christian values and traditions, however, may be visible as one of the characteristics of the general culture in which the state and public education are based.

*631.* Homeschooling for religious reasons is in general not an option, while permission for homeschooling can be given by the authorities for a variety of reasons. The Federal Constitutional Court has upheld the prohibition of homeschooling in a case in which parents had objected to sending their child to compulsory schooling because they wanted to keep their child from religious influences that they deemed harmful. The Federal Constitutional Court has argued that the interference with the religious and parental rights caused by compulsory schooling was justified by legitimate public interests. These interests are the prevention of religiously or philosophically motivated parallel societies and the pursuit of integration of minorities. Parents

409. BVerfG 16 Oct. 1979, BVerfGE 52, 223, 236.

have enough influence on their children in and outside of school. The interference with religious and parental rights, however, is justified only if due regard is taken by the school to the deviating religious convictions at stake. The school must ensure by strictly observing state neutrality and tolerance that no unreasonable conflicts of religion or conscience arise and any indoctrination of the pupils is also avoided in the field of sexual education.[410]

*632.* Crucifixes in public schools have been a matter of intense public debate related to a decision of the Federal Constitutional Court in 1995.[411] Crucifixes were – and still are – exhibited in public primary schools in Bavaria, while the situation varies among the other *Länder*. The Federal Constitutional Court, in a much-debated decision, has held by a majority of five to three judges that crucifixes must not be exhibited in public primary schools in Bavaria. It has been argued that while the individual does not have a right not to be confronted with manifestations of religion, worship activities or religious symbols in general, different principles apply in areas that are organized by the state, such as public schools. Here, the state must guarantee a space for the free development of the individual's personality in the field of religion or belief, protected from assaults and disturbances by adherents of other beliefs or competing religious groups.[412] The state must remain neutral in terms of religion or belief; it must not identify with specific religious communities and has to treat religions equally.[413] In classes of public primary schools crucifixes, as the Federal Constitutional Court stated, cause a situation in which pupils are forced to learn 'under the cross' as 'the symbol of the missionary spreading of Christianity' without being able to avoid this confrontation.[414] The Federal Constitutional Court held that crucifixes also violated the right of parents to raise their children in the religion or belief they preferred. It furthermore rejected the idea that positive religious freedom of other pupils – and parents – could support the exhibition of crucifixes in schools because human rights are, at their core, also rights of minorities and serve to protect them against majority decisions. The dissenting opinion argued that because the constitution leaves school matters in the competence of the *Länder*, regional differences must be taken into account that allow for the exhibition of crucifixes where the majority culture so wishes. In the public debate about the decision, it was argued that the Federal Constitutional Court had misinterpreted the meaning of the cross, that it is in fact a symbol that stands for tolerance, the basic culture of the country, and respect for the existence of transcendence as referred to in the preamble of the Basic Law. It was also argued that the Federal Constitutional Court had not sufficiently respected the educational needs of the other pupils and had underestimated the duty of the public school to actively create an atmosphere of tolerance in the field of religion or belief.[415] While

410. BVerfG 29 Apr. 2003, *Deutsches Verwaltungsblatt* 118 (2003): 999 et seq.
411. BVerfG 16 May 1995, BVerfGE 93, 1 et seq.
412. *See also* BVerfG 17 Dec. 1975, BVerfGE 41, 29, 49.
413. *See also* BVerfG 31 Mar. 1971, BVerfGE 30, 415, 422; BVerfG 16 Oct. 1968, BVerfGE 24, 236, 246.
414. BVerfG 16 May 1995, BVerfGE 93, 1, 21.
415. Martin Heckel, 'Das Kreuz im öffentlichen Raum – zum "Kruzifix-Beschluss" des BVerfG', *Deutsches Verwaltungsblatt* 111 (1996): 453–482; Juliane Kokott, 'Laizismus und Religionsfreiheit im

the Federal Constitutional Court's decision declared the law under scrutiny void, the Bavarian legislature soon afterwards introduced a new law which states that:

> In view of the historical and cultural characteristic of Bavaria, a cross shall be exhibited in every classroom. This expresses the wish to realize the highest educational aims of the constitution on the basis of Christian and occidental values in conformity with freedom of faith. If the legal guardians object to the exhibition of crosses with serious and understandable reasons, the head of the schools shall try to bring about an amicable agreement. If an amicable agreement cannot be reached, the head of the school shall make, after informing the school office, a decision in the individual case which respects the freedom of faith of the objecting person and achieves a just balance of the religious and belief convictions of all those concerned in the class; in doing so, the will of the majority also shall be taken into account as far as possible.[416]

*633.* This solution explicitly stated in the Bavarian amendment law could also have been reached by the Federal Constitutional Court by way of 'constitutional-conform interpretation' of the previous law in view of the standing practice of the Court because the pre-existing law was in fact open to a non-discriminatory interpretation. Some litigation has taken place since about the new law, but no final decision of the Federal Constitutional Court has been taken.[417] In a case in which a teacher has objected to having to teach in classrooms with a crucifix, the Bavarian Administrative Court of Appeals has held that the crucifix has to be taken off while the teacher is teaching and has declared this to be an individual case.[418] The Federal Administrative Court has held that the new law provides sufficient means of avoiding a discriminatory situation for dissenters if no over-strict requirements are made in view of the reasoning of the objection.[419]

*634.* In public schools, pupils are allowed to wear religious symbols such as the Muslim headscarf, the Christian cross or the Jewish Kipa.

*635.* The same applies in most of the federal *Länder* for teachers. Some *Länder*, however, have started to forbid teachers in public schools from exhibiting religious symbols in class to varying extents, as has been stated in detail above (paragraphs 175 et seq.). This highly controversial issue relates predominantly, though not exclusively, to the Muslim women's headscarf.

---

öffentlichen Raum', *Der Staat* 44 (2006): 343–365; Hans Maier (ed.), *Das Kreuz im Widerspruch* (Freiburg/Breisgau: Herder, 1996); Ulf Häußler, 'Schulkreuze im säkularen Staat', *Zeitschrift für evangelisches Kirchenrecht* 43 (1998): 461–492.

416. Bavarian Law of 23 Dec. 1995 (Bayer. GVBl., 850) amending Art. 7, s. 3 Bavarian Education and Instruction Act (Bayerisches Erziehungs- und Unterrichtsgesetz).
417. BayVerfGH Bavaria 1 Aug. 1997, *Neue Juristische Wochenschrift* 1997, 3157; BVerfG 27 Oct. 1997, *Neue Juristische Wochenschrift* 52 (1999): 1020 et seq.; VG Augsburg, Au 2 K 07/347 of 14 Aug. 2008.
418. BayVerwGH Bavaria 21 Dec. 2001, VGHE BY 55, 52 et seq.
419. BVerwG 21 Apr. 1999, BVerwGE 109, 40 et seq.

*636.* School prayers and religious services in public schools are permissible but have become rather rare. Limitations on the freedom of religion or belief can be based on manifestations of religion or belief by others. This is the basic reason for the possibility of the school prayer. Public schools in Germany can offer prayers at school or religious services. No one is obligated to take part, and everybody can opt out. Nevertheless, a pupil objected to these school prayers and services and stated that actively opting out of this would harm him in his freedom not to believe and not to manifest a religion. The Federal Constitutional Court has upheld the possibility of school prayer (and services).[420] It has been held that public schools in Germany may offer the possibility to pupils to freely manifest their religion through prayers or services. There always has to be an atmosphere of tolerance towards anyone in the school, including especially those who form a minority or who opt out of such services. The teachers in public schools have to actively create and uphold this atmosphere of tolerance. In the case that this atmosphere of tolerance cannot be upheld in practice, school prayers or services would be illegal.

*637.* The Federal Constitutional Court has also decided that public schools in Germany can be based on Christian culture and tradition.[421] Some of the *Länder* explicitly make this statement in their law; others do not. However, any such reference to Christianity is strictly limited to the existing culture coined by Christian influences. It must never be a missionary activity in favour of Christianity or any specific religion or non-religion. Germany is a neutral state in respect to religion or belief. It can be argued that this is based on Christian tradition and culture by fact and that history amounts to a structural limitation on freedom of religion or belief for other creeds. However, the main reason for allowing school prayers and services is that state authorities have to give space for manifestations of religion or belief when they oblige their citizens to perform certain duties, such as attending school. In this case, the right not to believe or manifest a belief collides with the positive right to actively manifest one's religion or belief. The solution found is allowing school prayer and opting out of it in an actively upheld atmosphere of tolerance.

*638.* There was a very controversial public debate in the 1970s about compulsory education in public schools on sexual matters. The Federal Constitutional Court has held that such compulsory sex education is constitutional if certain conditions are met:[422] this education must be open to different moral value conceptions, and it must be considerate of the parents' natural right to educate their children as well as of their religious and belief convictions; the school has to refrain from any attempt to indoctrinate the children. If these conditions are met, sex education does not require the consent of parents or children; parents, however, have a right to be informed in good time about the contents and method of sex education in school.

---

420. *See* BVerfG 6 Nov. 1968, BVerfGE 24, 289; BVerfG 16 Oct. 1979, BVerfGE 52, 223 et seq.
421. BVerfG 17 Dec. 1975, BVerfGE 41, 29 et seq.; BVerfG 14 Dec. 1975, BVerfGE 41, 65 et seq.; BVerfG 17 Dec. 1975, BVerfGE 41, 88 et seq.
422. BVerfG 21 Dec. 1977, BVerfGE 47, 46 et seq.

*639.* Opting out of co-educative sports for religious reasons is possible. The Federal Administrative Court held in 1993 that freedom of religion or belief guarantees this right.[423] A 12-year-old Muslim girl had objected to compulsory sports education that was taught to girls and boys because these classes involved sports dress that violated the religious norms stated by the Koran. The court argued that the legitimate aims of education could also be achieved without such compulsory co-educative teaching. The issue remains controversial in the public debate and also among the state courts. A decision of the lower Administrative Court of Augsburg in 2008 denied the right to opt out of co-educative swimming for a Muslim girl of 8 years because the Koran would distinguish between girls and women, and no religious norm existed in the Koran that prohibited children from taking part in co-educative swimming.[424]

## II. Religious Instruction in Public Schools

*640.* According to Article 7 section 3 GG, religious instruction shall form part of the regular curriculum in state schools, with the exception of non-denominational schools. Without prejudice to the state's right of supervision, religious instruction shall be given in accordance with the tenets of the religious community concerned. Teachers may not be obliged against their will to give religious instruction. The system of religious instruction in state schools, as provided for by Article 7 section 2 GG, is, in general, well accepted. However, there always has also been some criticism against this system.

*641.* Religious instruction in state schools, as outlined in Article 7 section 3 GG, is a common task of state and religious communities. Both partners work together in providing this educational service to the pupils.

*642.* The general system of religious education in public schools is a confessional teaching. It is Catholic religious education for Catholic pupils, Protestant religious education for Protestant pupils, Christ-Catholic religious education for Christ-Catholic pupils, Jewish religious education for Jewish pupils, Christian-Orthodox religious education for Christian-Orthodox pupils, etc. Since Catholicism and Protestantism are the main religions in Germany, Catholic religious education and Protestant religious education prevail in terms of numbers.

*643.* As a matter of practice, the curricula of religious instruction, notwithstanding their character of being confessional, include information about relevant other religions. This information thus is given from a confessional perspective. In practice, this information, as a matter of principle, is objective. One can also say from a legal point of view that this information has to be objective because religious instruction remains a state competence, and there is a right of pupils to objective information.

423. BVerwG 25 Aug. 1993, BVerwGE 94, 82 et seq.
424. VG Augsburg, Au 3 E 08.1613 of 17 Dec. 2008.

*644.* Quite a number of religious communities make use of this system. Minority religions also teach religious instruction in the general system.[425] This is the case for Jewish religious teaching for Jews, Christian-Orthodox religious teaching for Christian-Orthodox, etc. Religious instruction is not limited to traditional or Christian religious communities.

*645.* Religious community, in the meaning of Article 7 section 3 GG and thus able to cooperate in this system of religious instruction, is not any religious group or organization. Only those religious organizations qualify as a religious community that have a minimum amount of organizational structure and a common set of beliefs. The Federal Labour Court has defined a religious community as an association the members or adherents of which profess a common notion about the meaning and living of a life as human beings on the basis of common religious convictions.[426] The self-understanding of the individual religious organization is an important factor in assessing whether it meets these conditions; however, it is the state that finally decides on this question.[427] Because the teaching of the religious community defines the curriculum and the status of the teachers and, not the least, influences the school career of the pupils, the religious organization must have organizational structures to define such teaching and must also guarantee a minimum duration of itself as a functioning institution.

*646.* The status as a corporation under public law is not required to qualify as a religious community in the meaning of Article 7 section 3 GG and to cooperate in the system of religious instruction in public schools.[428]

*647.* Belief communities, that is, associations whose purpose is to foster a philosophical creed (*Weltanschauungsgemeinschaften*), are also entitled to participate in this system of 'religious' instruction.[429] This follows from Article 140 GG in conjunction with Article 137 section 3 WRV, according to which associations whose purpose is to foster a philosophical creed shall have the same status as religious societies.

*648.* The exception of non-confessional schools stipulated in Article 7 section 3 GG provides the competence of the state to run a particular type of state school as an exception. Non-confessional schools are such schools that operate as merely

425. Cf. Claudia M. Corlazzoli, *Religionsunterricht von kleineren Religionsgemeinschaften an öffentlichen Schulen in Deutschland*, Schriften zum Staatskirchenrecht, vol. 43 (Frankfurt: Peter Lang, 2008); Markus Ogorek, 'Religionsunterricht', in: *Handbuch des Staatskirchenrechts*, Dietrich Pirson et al. eds, 3rd edn (Berlin: Duncker & Humblot, 2020) 1799, n. 50.
426. BAG 22 Mar. 1995, BAGE 79, 319 et seq.; BVerwG 23 Feb. 2005, BVerwGE 123, 49 et seq.
427. BVerfG 5 Feb. 1991, BVerfGE 83, 341, 353.
428. Stefan Mückl, 'Freiheit kirchlichen Wirkens', in *Freiheitsrechte*, *Handbuch des Staatsrechts der Bundesrepublik Deutschland*, Josef Isensee & Paul Kirchhof eds, 3rd edn (Heidelberg: C.F. Müller, 2009), §161, n. 36; Gerhard Robbers in *Kommentar zum Grundgesetz*, Hermann von Mangoldt, Friedrich Klein & Christian Starck eds, 7th edn (Munich: Vahlen, 2018) Art. 7, n. 151.
429. BVerwG 7 Aug. 1996, *Neue Juristische Wochenschrift* 50 (1997): 1796 – in relation to the Land Berlin.

secular schools, explicitly without a religious background. In such schools, the guarantee of religious instruction does not apply. However, from a constitutional point of view, these schools remain entitled to provide such instruction. The Basic Law refers to non-confessional schools as an exception. Therefore, the state is not allowed to make this type of school the general system and consequently makes religious instruction in public schools an exception.[430]

*649.* The curriculum of religious education in public schools is prepared in cooperation between the relevant religious community and the state educational authorities. The relevant religious community decides on the religious content of the curriculum independently and without interference from state authorities. State authorities, however, can supervise this curriculum with respect to the state educational aims as laid out in the constitution. Thus, no curriculum in religious instruction may be contrary to the basic values of the Constitution, such as human dignity, freedom, equality, etc.

*650.* State's supervision covers the curriculum as well as the factual day-to-day presentation of the subject which also must keep in line with the basic constitutional values and aims of education.

*651.* The relevant religious communities supervise the religious contents of the curriculum as well as the teaching of the teacher. This follows from the constitutional provision that religious instruction shall be given in accordance with the tenets of the religious community concerned.[431]

*652.* The teachings of various religions in the world are presented to the pupils in public schools also in other courses such as language, philosophy, geography, etc. This is not a matter of religious instruction as provided for in Article 7 sections 2 and 3 GG, but a matter of general education.

*653.* Article 141 GG is the basis for an exception to the general system of religious instruction in public schools as provided for in Article 7 section 3 GG. Article 141 GG reads: 'The first clause of section 3 of Article 7 shall not apply in any *Land* in which *Land* law otherwise provided on 1 January 1949.' Often, it is referred to as the 'Bremer Clause'. This rule applies not only to the *Länder* of Berlin and Bremen but also to certain types of schools in other federal *Länder* where and for which specific provisions were in force on 1 January 1949.

*654.* In the *Land* Berlin, religious education in public schools is a matter of the religious communities themselves. The *Land* Berlin, according to the school law and treaties concluded between the *Land* Berlin and certain religious communities,

---

430. Christoph Link, 'Religionsunterricht', in *Handbuch des Staatskirchenrechts*, Joseph Listl & Dietrich Pirson eds, vol. 2, 2nd edn (Berlin: Duncker & Humblot, 1995), 467; Gerhard Robbers, in *Kommentar zum Grundgesetz*, Hermann von Mangoldt, Friedrich Klein & Christian Starck eds, 7th edn (Munich: Vahlen, 2018), Art. 7, n. 129.

431. *See also* §20 Schooling Act of the Land Saxony-Anhalt (SchulG LSA).

allows these religious communities to teach their religion within the general curriculum of the public schools. The *Land* Berlin allocates a certain amount of funds for this religious education to the religious communities. Berlin has also introduced compulsory courses in ethics with no possibility of opting out. The Federal Constitutional Court held in 2007 that the obligation to attend the courses in ethics without the possibility of opting out does not violate the freedom of religion of pupils nor educational rights of their parents; as stated in this ruling, the state may introduce such a duty in pursuance of its legitimate aim to foster tolerance and integration of the population and to counteract the development of parallel societies.[432]

*655.* In Bremen, the law establishes a non-confessional 'instruction in biblical history on a general Christian basis' as an ordinary subject. It mirrors attempts in the nineteenth century to overcome inner Protestant frictions.[433]

*656.* There has been intense debate about whether the exception of Article 141 GG should apply to the new German *Länder* after the reunification of Germany in 1990. The Federal Constitutional Court has left the question open. The majority opinion in constitutional law literature denies the application of the provision to these *Länder*.[434] While other *Land* law existed in these *Länder* on 1 January 1949, it is argued that these *Länder* ceased to exist in the Soviet Occupation Zone which later became the DDR; the *Länder* were newly introduced by the law of 22 July 1990. Most important is, however, that the basic concept of Article 141 was and is to uphold old and special traditions that existed in certain regions, but not to uphold specific Communist law newly introduced as a breach of tradition in and after 1949.

*657.* Most of the new *Länder* in Eastern Germany have introduced religious instruction as an ordinary subject on the basis of Article 7 section 3 GG. However, this has predominantly been structured as an alternative option, as an alternative to instruction in ethics.[435] Pupils can choose between these two alternatives; there, thus, is – in a legal sense – no priority of religious instruction to then opt out of it in order to choose ethical instruction instead. This minor development has generally been accepted as taking account of the widespread atheism in the new *Länder*.

*658.* In the *Land* Brandenburg, some further special rules apply. Brandenburg has introduced a highly controversial subject called 'Life Shaping, Ethics, Religious Knowledge' (*Lebensgestaltung, Ethik, Religionskunde* (LER)). Litigation

432. BVerfG (K) 15 Mar. 2007, BVerfGK 10, 423 et seq.

433. Christoph Link, 'Religionsunterricht', in *Handbuch des Staatskirchenrechts*, Joseph Listl & Dietrich Pirson eds, vol. 2, 2nd edn (Berlin: Duncker & Humblot, 1995), 484 et seq.; Gerhard Robbers, in *Kommentar zum Grundgesetz*, Hermann von Mangoldt, Friedrich Klein & Christian Starck eds, 7th edn (Munich: Vahlen, 2018), Art. 7, n. 122.

434. *See* Axel von Campenhausen & Heinrich de Wall, *Religionsverfassungsrecht*, 5th edn (Munich: C.H. Beck, 2022), 257.

435. Article 105 Constitution of the Free State of Saxony (SächsVerf); §§18–20 Schooling Act Saxony (SächsSchulG); Art. 25, s. 1 Constitution of the Free State of Thuringia (Thüring.Verf); §19, s. 2 SchulG Sachsen-Anhalt.

before the Federal Constitutional Court ended in a compromise: Today, the Brandenburg school law provides that those pupils who participate in religious instruction provided by the churches instead of LER can opt out of LER.[436] Pupils can participate in the religious instruction courses of the Catholic and the Protestant Churches and the life-shaping courses of the Humanist Union.

*659.* Religious instruction, as provided for in Article 7 section 3 GG, is an institutional guarantee of the subject as such. It is furthermore a subjective right of the pupils, their parents and the religious communities.

*660.* No one is obligated to take part in religious instruction. As is made explicit in Article 7 section 2 GG, parents or legal guardians have the right to control the participation of their children in religious education. In principle, when the child reaches the age of 12 years, the parental decision is not allowed to conflict with the child's. Upon reaching 14 years of age, the child may decide for him- or herself. In Bavaria and in the Saarland, the age is 18 years.[437]

*661.* Pupils who opt out of religious instruction usually have to take part in classes of ethics. Most of the *Länder* have made provisions for such a substitute or alternative instruction in ethics.[438] The subject of this instruction is based on 'the generally accepted principles of morals'.[439]

*662.* Pupils who do not belong to the denomination or religion of the specific religious instruction may take part in that religious instruction if the teaching of that denomination or religion so provides.[440] This follows from the principle of confessionality of the religious instruction. The definition of confessionality therefore is up to the religious communities.

*663.* Since religious instruction in the general system is a confessional teaching, there is no individual right of pupils who do not belong to the specific religious community to take part in these courses. Thus, a Protestant pupil does not have a right to opt for instruction in the Catholic religion, and a non-believer has no right to participate in one of the religious instruction courses. It is up to the relevant religious communities to decide whom they admit to the courses for which they are

436. BVerfG 11 Dec. 2001, BVerfGE 104, 305 et seq.; BVerfG 21 Oct. 2002, BVerfGE 106, 210 et seq.; §11, s. 3 School Act Brandenburg (BbgSchulG).

437. §5 Act on the Religious Upbringing of the Child of 15 Jul. 1921(RelKErzG); Art. 29, s. 2, cl. 3 Constitution of the Saarland (SLVerf); Art. 46, s. 4, cl. 2 Bavarian Education and Schooling Act (BayEUG).

438. Article 137, s. 2 Bavarian Constitution (BayVerf); Art. 35, s. 2 Constitution of Rhineland-Palatinate (RLPVerf); Art. 29, s. 2 SLVerf; §128 Lower Saxon School Act (NdsSchG); §100a, s. 1 Schooling Act Baden-Württemberg (SchG BW); §7, s. 4 Hamburg Schooling Act (HambSG); §8, s. 4 Hesse Schooling Act (HessSG); §7, s. 2 Schooling Act Mecklenburg Western Pommerania (SchulG M-V); §32 Schooling Act North Rhine-Westphalia (SchulG NRW); §19, s. 1 Schooling Act Saxony (SächsSchulG); §19, s. 2 Schooling Act Saxony-Anhalt (SchulG LSA); Art. 25, s. 2 Constitution of Thuringia (ThürVerf).

439. For example, Art. 137, s. 2 BayVerf.

440. BVerfG 25 Feb. 1987, BVerfGE 74, 244, 252, 254.

responsible. The state must accept this decision of the relevant religious community. Thus, the Roman Catholic Church decides whether it wants to admit a pupil of another faith or none to these courses, and the same principles apply to all other religious communities for their courses.[441]

*664.* Religious education, according to the requirements of Article 7 section 3 GG, is to be a standard subject in public schools.[442] This means that religious instruction shall form part of the regular curriculum. The German term used: '*ordentliches Lehrfach*' can also be translated as 'ordinary subject'.

*665.* It is the state that provides religious instruction in state schools as laid out to be the general system by Article 7 section 3 GG, not the religious communities. The state has to provide this instruction; it is state instruction. The state also has to provide the necessary means for this instruction; it is the state that pays the teachers.[443]

*666.* From the term 'standard subject', it follows that religious instruction must be an independent subject of its own. It is not permissible to integrate religious instruction into other subjects such as history, political education or languages.[444] It is also not permissible to discriminate against religious instruction by pushing the lessons to early hours before the normal start of the teaching day or at the far end of it.

*667.* It is therefore not permissible to put religious instruction into the position of simply a minor or a mere optional subject.[445] Religious instruction is an obligatory subject for the pupils belonging to that specific religious community with an opting out right.

*668.* Religious instruction has to be provided with an adequate minimum of teaching hours per week. The exact amount follows from a balancing of the requirement of meaningful teaching in relation to the needs of other subjects; differences as to the kind of school (primary school, secondary school, vocational school) and the year of schooling are allowed.[446]

*669.* The notion of standard subject also requires treating religious instruction in the same way as other normal subjects regarding the marks achieved by the pupil and the relevance of the marks for being moved into the higher grade.[447]

441. *Ibid.*
442. Gerhard Robbers, in *Kommentar zum Grundgesetz*, Hermann von Mangoldt, Friedrich Klein & Christian Starck eds, 7th edn (Munich: Vahlen, 2018), Art. 7, nn. 130 et seq.
443. *Ibid.*, n. 130.
444. *Ibid.*, n. 140.
445. *Ibid.*, nn. 136 et seq.
446. *Ibid.*, n. 141.
447. *Ibid.*, n. 142.

*670.* Teachers of religion, whether they be state officials or provided for by the religious community, have a seat and decision-making voice in the school's teacher's conference.[448]

*671.* The qualification as a standard subject allows a minimum number of pupils required to provide religious instruction. A minimum requirement of five to twelve pupils taking part in the instruction has been regarded to be constitutional.[449] The school has to take up appropriate organizational means to make it possible that such a minimum number of participating pupils can be reached, for example, by organizing joint teaching with several classes or neighbouring schools.

*672.* The teachers of religious instruction are selected and appointed by the state in cooperation with the churches. The teacher needs the consent of the relevant religious community to teach that specific religion, called *missio canonica* for the Roman Catholic Church and *vocatio* in respect of the Protestant Churches. If that consent is withdrawn, the teacher may not teach that religious instruction any more. Those teachers who are public officials – as is the case for the large majority of teachers in public schools – do not lose their status or work but have to be allocated to other teaching subjects.

*673.* It is possible that the religious community provides for teachers such as priests or other personnel to teach religious instruction in public schools on the basis of special treaties between the school authorities and the religious community. Usually, the religious community then receives a lump sum of payment for this service; the teachers are then paid according to the rules of the religious community by the religious community itself.

*674.* No teacher may be obligated against his or her will to teach religious instruction. If the teacher refuses to teach that subject, no disadvantage may follow from that for him or her.

*675.* A question not yet adequately settled in the whole of Germany relates to the religious instruction for Muslim schoolchildren. Courses in Islamic confessional religious instruction are offered in public schools in Berlin, Hamburg, Lower Saxony and Hessen. Rhineland-Palatinate, Saarland, North Rhine-Westphalia and Baden-Wurttemberg offer Islamic confessional religious instruction in various

---

448. *Ibid.*, n. 143.

449. Christoph Link, 'Religionsunterricht', in *Handbuch des Staatskirchenrechts*, Joseph Listl & Dietrich Pirson eds, vol. 2, 2nd edn (Berlin: Duncker & Humblot, 1995), 484; Gerhard Robbers, in *Kommentar zum Grundgesetz*, Hermann von Mangoldt, Friedrich Klein & Christian Starck eds, 7th edn (Munich: Vahlen, 2018), Art. 7, n. 144.

forms of experimental model instruction. Islamic religious instruction is state performed in Bavaria, Bremen, Hessen and Schleswig-Holstein. Various Muslim groups take part in these classes.[450]

*676.* Separation of state and religion is the basic notion that stands behind the general system of religious instruction in state schools. The German system of religious instruction, notwithstanding its character of cooperation between state and religious communities, is a clear expression of strict separation between state and religion. Religious freedom urges religious instruction within the public school system. When the state introduces a duty to attend a school for young people, it must give the opportunity to public schools that pupils can follow their religious convictions and practices. As has been stated above, all children from the age of 6 years are obligated to attend school for basically 12 years.[451] The state thus takes the competence to decide on how the citizens are to spend their time. Therefore, the state has to care for adequate time also to meet the religious needs of the citizens affected. This state obligation is based on the overall idea that fundamental rights are not only rights against intrusion of the state into the sphere of the individual but also constitute positive rights for state action. Religious instruction in state schools, therefore, is a right of the children following from their right to freedom of religion. Moreover, the children have a right to education following from Article 7 section 1 GG, Article 3 section 1 GG, Article 12 section 1 GG and explicit provisions in many *Land* constitutions.[452] This, in turn, obligates the state to take care of religious education as far as the state's competences reach in this field. The parental right to raise their children in their own religion and according to their own educational convictions is guaranteed in Article 6 section 2 GG. The parents – and accordingly the legal guardians – of the child therefore have an own right that the state school adequately takes their religious and educational convictions into consideration. The state, finally, has its own competence to educate the young generation. This follows from Article 7 section 1 GG.[453] This state's competence is independent of the parental right to raise and educate their children. It is the state's obligation to adequately balance these sometimes conflicting rights and interests.

*677.* Public education is based on the idea that the state is obliged to educate the young generation. Not the least, this is done with the objective of integrating the population, holding them together and unifying the pluralistic or sometimes antagonistic society. Equally, education aims at developing the young individual's own identity and his or her ability to self-determination. Education is a process touching the whole personality of a young human being and developing it. Education does not mean only conveying certain specific knowledge of facts and specific technical

450. Mediendienst Integration (ed.), *Factsheet. Islamischer Religionsunterricht an Schulen in Deutschland (Factsheet. Islamic Religious Instruction in Germany),* 2023, https://mediendienst-integration.de/fileadmin/Dateien/Factsheet_MEDIENDIENST_Islamischer_Religionsunterricht_2023.pdf, 9 Nov. 2023.
451. For example, §§7, 57 Schooling Act Rhineland-Palatinate (SchulG RLP); cf. also BVerfG 29 Apr. 2003, *Deutsches Verwaltungsblatt* 118 (2003): 999 et seq.
452. For example, Art. 29, s. 1 Constitution of Brandenburg (BbgVerf).
453. BVerfG 16 May 1995, BVerfGE 93, 1, 21.

abilities. Education means forming a personality which is also able to integrate into a culture. This holistic understanding of education also covers and includes religion. To form a personality also means to open the field of religious convictions and ideas to him or her. The religious side of a personality cannot be formed only by confronting a young boy or girl with different ideas, leaving the decision completely to him- or herself at a later age. Forming a personality within religious life means conveying a set of truths and deeply rooted convictions. Religion means to rely on certain truths. This can be compared to language: Spanish is not taught to a Spanish child in Spain – its mother tongue – by showing it all the different, major languages in the world in order to enable the child to one day choose between all of what may fit most to its conviction. What is taught is Spanish; otherwise, the child will never be able to speak at all.

*678.* This is a dilemma for the neutral state. The neutral state cannot implement religious truth but has to be open to different religious ideas. Being responsible – alongside the parents – for forming the personality of the young person, the state also has responsibility for the religious side of this personality. Rejecting religion completely, pushing it aside to the evening hours or the Sundays, and ignoring the thrust for truth would discriminate against religion. This again would mean a contradiction to state neutrality. More than that, rejecting religion would mean failing in the task of forming the whole personality of the child.

*679.* The solution of the dilemma is that the state organizes the possibility of religious instruction within public schools, while leaving the contents of that instruction to the relevant churches. They decide on the curriculum; they decide on truth. The state sees to it that it happens, and churches see to how it happens. The state is obliged only to make religious instruction adequately possible and to guarantee that no one is forced against his or her will to follow these courses. If this is guaranteed, the cooperationist approach is an exact expression of the separation of state and church.

## §2. Religious Instruction in Private Schools

*680.* Private schools are allowed and meant to contribute their specific educational, religious, and philosophical approach to the general state school system. Private schools have the freedom to organize – within the general law – according to their own convictions. This is an expression of pluralism and an important contribution to it.

*681.* Schools that are operated by the two great churches in Germany usually offer religious instruction in their own confession, but also – as a matter of fact, not because of a legal obligation – in the other confession. This means that schools run by the Roman Catholic Church would have classes in the Catholic religion, but also classes in Protestant religion. Some of them also offer courses in general ethics. As a matter of experiment, individual Christian schools also offer courses in Islam religion for Muslim pupils.

*682*. While there is a general right to opt out of confessional religious instruction, schools run by religious communities in general expect their pupils to attend a class of religious instruction and ask them to leave the school and attend a state-run school if they object to participating in religious instruction.

## Chapter 2. Religious Schools

*683.* There is a fundamental right to found and to operate private schools guaranteed by Article 7 section 4 GG. Also religious communities and belief communities (*Weltanschauungsgemeinschaften*) enjoy this right. For them, this also follows from the right to freedom of religion or belief.

*684.* The large churches operate a significant number of private schools. The entire school system of Germany, however, exists on the basis of Article 7 section 1 GG and is thus under the supervision of the state; compared with the number of state schools, churches, or other private schools or educational establishments form a small minority. The school system in Germany remains largely state-run. There are a certain number of private schools which are often run by religious communities, groups representing particular philosophies, or groups with some particular pedagogic or commercial motivation. Private schools can be officially recognized as alternative schools. If such recognition is granted, the private school may be attended instead of a state school.[454] The approval must be given when private schools are not inferior to the state schools in terms of their educational aims, their facilities, or the professional training of their teaching staff, and when segregation of pupils according to the means of their parents will not be encouraged thereby. Approval must be withheld if the economic and legal position of the teaching staff is not adequately assured. The majority of schools maintained by religious communities are recognized by the state authorities as replacing public schools. Viewed as a whole, both the structure of the school system and the content of the material taught are strongly influenced by the state. Since the *Länder* are competent in matters concerning the school system, significant differences do exist between the *Länder* in detailed questions.

*685.* Concerning the financing of private schools, the churches, as do other organizations running private schools, receive public funding. The general basis of legitimization of such public funding for private schools is found in Article 7 sections 4 and 5 GG. The Federal Constitutional Court has ruled that the state is obligated to subsidize private schools to a certain degree because the state requires them to fulfil certain standards while prohibiting school fees that encourage segregation of pupils according to the means of their parents. Since these quality standards can thus be met only when funding is provided, the state has to do so.[455]

*686.* The large churches operate a considerable number of kindergartens for children between about 3 and 7 years of age. There is no requirement that a child be sent to preschool. The period prior to reaching the age at which school attendance becomes compulsory is subject to little state regulation. At this stage, the services available consist largely of kindergartens run by a church or the local communities.

454. Article 7, s. 4 GG.
455. BVerfG 8 Apr. 1987, BVerfGE 75, 40, 61 et seq.; BVerfG 9 Mar. 1994, BVerfGE 90, 107 et seq.

*687.* In 2022, there are 5,895 private schools in Germany, while there are 34,590 state run schools. 3,757 of these private schools are for general education. There are also 2,138 private vocational schools. In 2021–2022, 1,024,797 pupils attended a religious or non-religious private school.[456]

*688.* The Catholic Church runs about 9,445 *Kindergartens* with 633,023 children. The Protestant Church runs 9,278 *Kindergartens* (in 2022) with about 540,000 children.[457]

---

456. Verband Deutscher Privatschulverbände (ed.), *Statistische Daten über die Schulen in freier Trägerschaft in Deutschland (Statistical Data on the Independent Schools in Germany)*, https://privatschulen.de/wp-content/uploads/2023/01/2022_Privatschulstatistiken_21_22.pdf#new_tab, 9 Nov. 2023.

457. Statista (ed.), *Anzahl der Kindertagesstätten von evangelischen und katholischen Trägern sowie darin betreute Kinder in Deutschland im Jahr 2022 (Number of Protestant and Catholic Kindergartens and Children Therein in Germany in the Year 2022)*, https://de.statista.com/statistik/daten/studie/1282288/umfrage/kinder-und-kindertagesstaetten-in-kirchlichen-traegern/, 9 Nov. 2023; EKD (ed.) *Evangelische Kindertagesstätten (Protestant Kindergartens)*, https://www.ekd.de/Evangelische-Kindertagesstaetten-14493.htm, 9 Nov. 2023.

## Chapter 3. Theological Faculties and Religious Universities

*689.* The university system in Germany is predominantly, although not exclusively, maintained by the state. Universities are usually state universities with a status of autonomy in matters of arts and sciences, research and teaching. Article 5 section 3 GG also guarantees for state universities: 'Arts and sciences, research and teaching shall be free.'

*690.* At numerous state universities, there are theological faculties of a specific confession. Theological faculties at state universities are state institutions which also serve matters of the relevant religious community. They are one of the common matters (*res mixtae*) of state and religious communities. These theological faculties have their roots in history; legally, they rest upon constitutional provisions, general law and treaties between the state and the specific religious communities. Based upon a variety of differently fashioned state-church agreements, the churches have a more or less determinative influence upon the appointment of professors and on the curriculum and examinations. In this area, the Catholic Church enjoys a greater area of control than the Protestant Church.

*691.* The origins of theological faculties in the state university system go back to the care of the German secular power for religious affairs since the beginning of universities in Germany in the fourteenth century. Since the times of the Protestant reformation, both the Protestant as well as the Roman Catholic churches regained influence on the education of their clerics. The *Kulturkampf* in the latter half of the nineteenth century, again, brought a strong grip of the state on the study of theology. In Prussia, the law of 11 May 1873 established conditions for admittance to church offices as to the necessary education. The law also put pressure on Catholic Church educational institutions in favour of state faculties.[458] When the anti-church laws of the *Kulturkampf* were gradually repealed, the requirements of successful secondary school examination (*Abitur*) and a minimum of three years of theological studies remained in existence as state conditions for church office. Church seminaries could be founded only in those dioceses in which a state faculty for Catholic theology did not exist; this meant a factual pressure to study theology at the state faculty. The Protestant Churches for long did not establish their own theological institutions and also did not care very much for influence on the chairs and curricula because of their traditional proximity to the Protestant states. It was predominantly the Catholic Church that tried to gain influence on state faculties for Catholic theology during the nineteenth and early twentieth centuries, leading to compromises that became treaty law after the 1919 revolution.[459]

---

458. Axel Freiherr von Campenhausen & Heinrich de Wall, *Religionsverfassungsrecht*, 5th edn (Munich: C.H. Beck, 2022), 272 et seq.
459. *Ibid.*

*692.* The existence of the theological faculties in state universities is guaranteed by the constitutions of several of the *Länder*.[460] The Federal Republic has no competence in the matter, except perhaps the highly theoretical possibility to establish theological faculties within the (federal) universities of the armed forces.

*693.* The professors at the theological faculties at state universities are state officials, as are the other professors at state universities. The state appoints the professors and supervises them within their general right to freedom of art, sciences, research, and teaching as laid out in Article 5 section 3 GG. Nevertheless, theological faculties and the professors within these faculties serve the purpose of the relevant church and therefore enjoy a special status within the state universities. Professors must be members of the relevant religious community. They must be accepted by this religious community as professors at the faculty. The involvement of the religious communities varies according to the historical development of the matter.

*694.* In relation to the Roman Catholic theological faculties at state universities, the Roman Catholic Church has the right to make a statement about the candidate for a professorship (the '*nihil obstat*') with binding effect. The church can exclude the candidate by withholding the '*missio canonica*'.

*695.* The Roman Catholic Church can object to a person who is already a professor at the Roman Catholic state theological faculty for reasons of a serious violation of the requirements of teaching and lifestyle by the professor. This intervention has the consequence that the university teacher may not act as a church-authorized teacher, researcher or examiner any more. The state then has to remove that person from the staff of the Roman Catholic theological faculty at the state university and provide for someone else.[461] Minority opinion holds that the removal of the person from the faculty is not a necessary consequence,[462] but state practice acts according to the majority opinion.

*696.* The person removed from the Roman Catholic theological faculty at the state university – being a state official with all the rights attached to that status – remains a state official at the state university and does not lose his or her right to teach, research, and examine, and the relevant pay and alimentation. The state has to provide him or her with adequate working opportunities within the university but outside of the theological faculty. This solution is a compromise between the needs,

460. Article 10 Constitution of Baden-Württemberg (Verf BW); Art. 150 BayVerf; Art. 60, s. 2 Constitution of Hesse (HessVerf); Art. 9, s. 3 Constitution of Mecklenburg-Western Pommerania (Verf M-V); Art. 39, s. 3 Verf RLP.

461. Axel Freiherr von Campenhausen & Heinrich de Wall, *Religionsverfassungsrecht*, 5th edn (Munich: C.H. Beck, 2022), 278.

462. Ernst-Wolfgang Böckenförde, 'Der Fall Küng und das Staatskirchenrecht', *Neue Juristische Wochenschrift* 34 (1981): 2101.

freedoms and rights of the professor, the state and the Roman Catholic Church. In practice, it has served the peaceful settlement of controversial issues.

*697.* Famous cases of this kind have been the removal of Hans Küng from his chair at the Roman Catholic theological Faculty of the University of Tübingen in 1979. More recent cases are that of Prof. August Jilek of Regensburg in 2004[463] and Prof. Werner Tzscheetzsch of Freiburg in 2009.[464]

*698.* The Treaty between the Free State of Prussia and the Holy See of 14 June 1929, which is still relevant for the Roman Catholic theological faculty of the Universities of Bonn and Münster, provides accordingly:[465] Before anyone is to be employed or licensed to practice the teaching profession at a Catholic theological faculty, the competent bishop shall be heard as to whether he has to raise reasoned demurs to the teaching or the moral conduct of the person proposed. A person against whom such objections are raised shall not be employed or licensed. The designation prior to employment … , i.e., offering of the chair in question by the Minister of Science, Art and National Education, shall take place in confidential form and subject to a hearing of the Diocesan Bishop. At the same time, the bishop will be notified and asked for his statement, for which he will be given a sufficient period. In the statement, objections to the teachings and the moral conduct of the person proposed shall be pointed out; how far the bishop may go in this explication shall be entrusted to his dutiful discretion. The designation shall not be published until the bishop has declared to the minister that he has no demurs to the teachings or the moral conduct of the person designated. If a teacher being a member of a Catholic theological faculty in his teaching or writings offends the Catholic doctrine or commits a serious or vexing breach of the requirements of the priestly moral conduct, the competent bishop shall be entitled to inform the Minister of Science, Art and National Education of this. In such a case, the minister shall take remedial measures irrespective of the rights of the person concerned emerging from employment in the civil service and, in particular, shall find a replacement in line with the teaching requirement.

*699.* Protestant theological faculties at state universities have equivalent functions compared to the Roman Catholic ones. Their professors also are state officials with a confessional, church related office. For historical reasons, the older treaties between the state and the Protestant churches only provide for a counselling statement of the Protestant Church as to the religious qualification of a candidate for a professorship. Similarly, these treaties do not provide for an intervention of the Church because of misconduct of a university teacher.

---

463. Spiegel Online (ed.) 'Regensburger Bischof entlässt kritischen Professor', http://www.spiegel.de/unispiegel/studium/0,1518,321619,00.html, 9 Nov. 2023.

464. Domradio (ed.), 'Nihil obstat auf Anfrage', http://www.domradio.de/aktuell/artikel_49819.html, 9 Nov. 2023.

465. Final Protocol in re Art. 12, s. 1, cl. 2 of the Preußenkonkordat.

*700.* However, since these offices are confessional offices, state neutrality prohibits religious decisions of the state, and equal treatment with the Roman Catholic Church is necessary; only the church can decide on the religious qualification of a professor. The church also must be free in view of the religious training of its future staff. The majority opinion therefore holds that the older treaties between the state and Protestant churches must be interpreted in the sense of the equivalent concordatarian provisions with the Roman Catholic Church.[466] The counselling statements about professors are taken as being binding for the state. The new treaties between the Protestant churches and the *Länder* provided accordingly. The Treaty of the Free State of Thuringia with the Protestant churches in Thuringia of 15 March 1994 (ThEvKirchStV) states in its Article 3 section 2:

> Prior to appointing a professor, and before the permanent appointment of either a university lecturer of a special branch of Protestant Theology or Pedagogics of Religion at a university of the Free State of Thuringia, the churches shall be given the opportunity to express their views. If reservations relating to church doctrine and confession are expressed and substantiated in detail, the Land Government will take this statement into consideration.

*701.* Since this provision has not been tested in practice yet, it still remains open to broader interpretation. The matter is stated even more clearly in the treaty between the *Land* Mecklenburg-Western Pomerania and the Evangelical-Lutheran *Land* Church of Mecklenburg and the Pomeranian Evangelical *Land* Church (The Treaty of Güstrow) of 20 January 1994. Its Article 4 provides that the scholarly care for Protestant theology is a task of universities and will be guaranteed by the evangelical-theological faculties at the universities of Greifswald and Rostock. The appointment of a full-time university lecturer at an evangelical-theological faculty requires, in relation to the teaching and confession of the appointee, the consent of the relevant *Land* Church. The *Land* government shall give the church the opportunity to express its view. Against an explicit church statement, it will neither begin with the appointment nor make the appointment. Furthermore, the provision continues that in decisions about curricula and examination rules for an evangelical-theological faculty, the relevant *Land* church will be involved with the aim of mutual consent.

*702.* Cases of Protestant Church interventions against university staff have occurred and have been solved accordingly. A professor for Protestant theology at the University of Göttingen in the *Land* Lower Saxony had publicly renounced from important parts of belief and confession of Christendom. His chair was changed in

466. Axel Freiherr von Campenhausen & Heinrich de Wall, *Religionsverfassungsrecht*, 5th edn (Munich: C.H. Beck, 2022), 277; contrary opinion Wolfgang Huber, 'Lehrbeanstandung in der Kirche der Lehrfreiheit', in *Zur Praxis des Kirchenrechts*, *Das Recht der Kirche*, Gerhard Rau, Hans-Richard Reuter & Klaus Schlaich eds, vol. 3 (Gütersloh: Kaiser, 1994), 118.

its public function, and his permit to examine students of theology and religious teaching was withdrawn. The courts have upheld that decision.[467]

*703.* There must be reasons provided for this system of religious higher education beyond mere historical developments. Also, the positive constitutional law of the *Länder* only gives reasons for the system to be legal, not necessarily to be legitimate. However, legitimacy is found in the principles of state neutrality and basic state responsibility for higher education. State universities also provide higher education for other professions than religious offices; for example, they provide programmes for medical doctors, lawyers, or management personnel. It is not the hospitals, law firms or industries that usually run university institutions to educate their forthcoming staff. It would amount to discrimination against the religions if the state did not provide equivalent services for the religions. This already would violate state neutrality between the non-religious and the religious spheres. However, religious neutrality prohibits the state from influencing the religious part of such education; this part must be left to the relevant religious community. In addition to such reasoning on the level of principles, it is in line with the basic idea of university to include also theology and religious teaching within the holistic approach of science, research, teaching, and arts. Also, theology would lose if it were pushed or taken aside in isolation from other fields of knowledge. Religion and the secular would be driven apart while they are part of the same world.

*704.* The European-wide reform of university studies into programmes of Bachelor's and Master's also raises questions for the study of theology at state universities.[468] State neutrality and treaties between state and religious communities require that the secular power does not act without the consent of the religion in fields of common competency (*res mixtae*). These principles prohibit that the state structure programmes, such as the Bachelor's, as programmes that qualify for office in a religion without the consent of that religion. In the process of accrediting programmes of theology, the relevant church must be involved in a way similar to that of the appointment of teaching staff.

*705.* State-church treaties also provide for further higher education institutions and their links with religious needs beyond theological faculties. For example, the treaty between the *Land* Mecklenburg-Western Pomerania and the Evangelical-Lutheran *Land* Church of Mecklenburg and the Pomeranian Evangelical *Land* Church (The Treaty of Güstrow) of 20 January 1994 in its Article 4 section 7 guarantees that in the city of Greifswald, there will be an institute for Protestant church music.

*706.* According to the concordat between Bavaria and the Holy See, the Free State of Bavaria maintains chairs for Catholic theology and Catholic religious instruction at the universities Erlangen-Nuremberg and Bayreuth in the faculties for

467. OVG Lüneburg 14 Feb. 2000, *Neue Zeitschrift für Verwaltungsrecht* 19 (2000): 954 et seq.
468. Joachim E. Christoph, 'Zur Akkreditierung theologischer Studiengänge', *Zeitschrift für evangelisches Kirchenrecht* 49 (2004), 253 et seq.

education. Bavaria will further maintain chairs for (general) philosophy, societal sciences and pedagogics in the universities of Augsburg, Munich (*Ludwig-Maximilians-Universität*), Passau, Regensburg, Würzburg, and Bamberg. To these chairs, rules equivalent to those applicable to the faculties of Catholic theology apply.[469] The Catholic bishops in Bavaria have declared, however, not to make use of these veto-rights any more.[470]

*707.* The large churches also maintain their own theological and philosophical faculties with the rights of universities. The Catholic Church has its own university in Eichstätt, which also has a significant number of non-theological faculties. There are also a large number of church-run colleges offering an education that is more vocationally orientated than that of a university. The dioceses, furthermore, operate their priest seminaries for the advanced studies of clerics.

*708.* Christian-Orthodox theology can be studied at the University of Munich, where an 'Education Facility for Orthodox Theology' is operating in close cooperation with the Catholic and Protestant faculties of theology.[471]

*709.* As of 2021, there are seven university institutes for Islamic theology in Germany (Osnabrück, Münster, Tübingen, Frankfurt am Main, Giessen, Erlangen-Nuremberg and Berlin), and further Islamic chairs have been established at the Universities of Hamburg and Paderborn. Since January 2020, DITIB has been offering the two-year, mainly German-language training programme 'Religious Officers for Mosque Communities'. The trainees are to be prepared for the practical tasks of imams, preachers and community educators. The prerequisite for participation is, among other things, a bachelor's degree in Islamic theology. Other Muslim communities also train imams.[472] Jewish studies have a centre in the College of Jewish Studies (*Hochschule für Jüdische Studien* (HfJS)) in Heidelberg.[473] Sponsored by the Central Council of the Jews in Germany (*Zentralrat der Juden in Deutschland*), it shares responsibility for the development of the Jewish community in Germany and the general society of Europe, as well as furthering the comprehensive study of Jewish religion, history and culture. It provides training for teachers of Jewish religion in public schools and cooperates with the state university Heidelberg. The HfJS offers ten professorships in a range of different academic areas. As such, it represents the central place for Jewish studies in Europe. Furthermore, there is the

469. Article 3, s. 4 BayKonk.
470. Erklärung der Freisinger Bischofskonferenz, *Frühjahrsvollversammlung der bayerischen Bischöfe in Waldsassen am 30. und 31. Januar 2013 (Declaration of the Bishops Conference of Freising, Spring Plenary Assembly of the Bavarian Bishops in Waldsassen on 30 and 31 January 2013),* https://www.erzbistum-muenchen.de/news/bistum/Erklaerung-der-Freisinger-Bischofskonferenz-24772.news, 9 Nov. 2023.
471. Ausbildungseinrichtung für Orthodoxe Theologie der Ludwig-Maximilians-Universität München (ed.), 'Portrait' http://www.orththeol.uni-muenchen.de/ueber_uns/portraet/index.html, 9 Nov. 2023.
472. Mediendienst Integration (ed.), *Factsheet. Imamausbildung in Deutschland (Factsheet. Imam Courses in Germany),* 2021, https://mediendienst-integration.de/fileadmin/Dateien/Factsheet_Imamausbildung_Mediendienst_Integration.pdf, 9 Nov. 2023.
473. Hochschule für jüdische Studien (ed.), www.hfjs.eu/index.en.html.

Jewish Liberal Abraham Geiger Kolleg for the training of rabbis and cantors at the University of Potsdam[474] and the Jewish Orthodox Rabbi Seminary at Berlin of the Yeshiva-Beis-Zion of the Lauder Foundation.[475]

474. http://www.abraham-geiger-kolleg.de, 9 Nov. 2023.
475. http://www.lauderyeshurun.de/de/yeshivas-beis-zion, 9 Nov. 2023.

# Part X. Matrimonial and Family Law

## Chapter 1. Legal Position of Religious Marriage

*710.* Contrary to the position in some other European countries, the religious communities in Germany have no competence in the areas of marriage and family law. Marriage, according to the German legal system, is a wholly civil affair: it takes place in the registrar's office.

*711.* As has been stated above (in paragraph 547), a different form, especially a religious marriage with legal effect, may be contracted only between foreigners before a body recognized by their home country as having the right to conduct a marriage. In this case, the person conducting the marriage can be a priest.

*712.* For German nationals, a religious wedding in Germany has no civil legal effect. However, everyone is free to have a religious wedding service. A constitutionally questionable rule stated that a religious wedding is not to precede a civil marriage; however, sanctions for the violation of this rule did not exist. This rule was repealed in 2006 taking effect on 1 January 2009.[476]

*713.* Marriage issues cannot be submitted under private arbitration according to §1030 Civil Procedure Code (ZPO). This private arbitration, otherwise, can be submitted to state courts to gain civil law effect. This is not possible for matters of marriage law. Therefore, decisions of religious courts such as those maintained by the Catholic Church based in canon law or possibly those that might be established on the grounds of Sharia law cannot acquire civil law effects in these matters.

*714.* When legally married persons come to Germany, the marriage is recognized under international private law. This also applies to plural marriage. The marriages of a man with several women under Muslim law abroad are recognized as valid marriages. Social benefits such as widow pensions are shared among the widows.[477]

---

476. BGBl. 2007 I, 122.
477. BSG 30 Aug. 2000, BSGE 87, 88 et seq.

## Chapter 2. Legal Position of Religious Family Law

*715.* Family law of religions does not have a legal position in German family law. While anyone is, as a matter of principle, free to live his or her family life according to religious norms, German state law on family is prevalent to religious family law.

*716.* Family issues are exempt from arbitration law; family matters cannot be submitted under arbitration courts according to §1030 ZPO. Therefore, as is the case for marriage issues, decisions of religious courts cannot acquire civil law effects in matters of family law.

*717.* However, religious family law relevant to foreign law can have effects in Germany through the rules of international private law.

# Part XI. Religion and Culture

## Chapter 1. Religion and Art

### §1. Religious Monuments

*718.* Religious communities in Germany own a considerable amount of cultural monuments. The law on cultural monuments – which, for the most part, is a matter in the competence of the *Länder* – is rather strict throughout Germany. Owners of cultural monuments in general are strongly restricted in the way they use their property. Changes in appearance need the consent of the respective state authorities. In general, a cultural monument is only to be restored or repaired, its appearance or substance changed or impaired, equipped with fittings, writings or signs or advertising, removed from an environment, destroyed or disposed of with the approval of the monument conservation authority. This can lead to difficult situations if, for example, a religious community adopts changes in its liturgy for theological reasons and wants to change the appearance of its place of worship – which is a cultural monument – accordingly, while the state authorities want to preserve the traditional appearance of the place.[478]

*719.* An example of the relationship between religious communities and the state authorities in dealing with issues of cultural monuments is the Act to Protect and Care for Cultural Monuments in the Free State of Saxony (SächsDSchG). According to its §18 (Cultural Monuments Serving the Practice of Religion), the monument protection authorities must, as a matter of priority, adhere to the concerns of religious service, which are to be determined by the superior church authority or the appropriate agency of the religious community in question in respect of cultural monuments serving the practice of religion. Decisions and measures of the monument protection authorities with cultural monuments owned by a church must be taken in agreement with the superior church authorities or the appropriate agency of the religious community in question.

*720.* In the case that a cultural monument is to be restored or repaired, its appearance or substance changed or impaired, equipped with fittings, writings or signs or advertising, removed from an environment, destroyed or disposed of, this decision

478. Cf. Burkhard Kämper & Hans-Werner Thönnes (eds), 'Denkmalschutz und Denkmalpflege im kirchlichen Bereich', *Essener Gespräche* 41 (Münster: Aschendorff, 2007).

does not need the approval of the monument conservation authority if the monument is owned by the churches and used for religious services where the churches issue their own provisions to protect these cultural monuments in agreement with the highest monument protection authority. Prior to implementation of such projects, agreement must be reached with the competent superior *Land* authority. If no agreement can be reached either with it or with the higher monument protection authority, the highest monument protection authority will decide, in agreement with the highest church authority.

*721.* While in general cultural monument law an expropriation is possible, this does not apply to cultural monuments owned by a religious community and to other cultural monuments serving the practice of religion. Article 138 section 2 WRV, in conjunction with Article 140 GG, guarantees that the property rights and other rights of religious societies or associations in their institutions, foundations, and other assets intended for purposes of worship, education, or charity shall be guaranteed. This guarantee also applies in the case of monument preservation.

*722.* The federal Act to Protect German Cultural Assets against Removal from the Country (KultGSchG) provides that cultural assets owned by the Churches or against religious communities, which are public law corporations, enjoy a special regime of protection. In this regime, the religious institutions decide to a far-reaching extent themselves on the status of the cultural assets and their protection against being transferred abroad. The churches and religious communities recognized as corporations under public law may register works of art and other cultural assets which they own within the meaning of this act for inclusion in the 'List of cultural assets valuable to the nation' (§§9 and 7(4) KultGSchG). The highest *Land* authority shall decide on inclusion.

## §2. Religion in the Arts

*723.* Religions are key factors of culture. It is obvious that Christianity has a dominant function in the development of culture in Germany.[479] The Jewish contribution is of utmost importance; it has been widely disrupted by the Nazi rule between 1933 and 1945 and is gradually reappearing. Also, the Muslim impact on the genesis of occidental culture is considerable; Muslim immigration to Germany renews this impact.

*724.* The great churches use about 20% of their income for cultural purposes, that is, about EUR 3.5 to 4.8 billion per year.[480] The churches thus spend about the same amount of money in this field as the *Länder* and the local communities.

479. *See* Deutscher Bundestag (ed.), 'Schlussbericht der Enquete-Kommission "Kultur in Deutschland"', BT-Drs. 16/7000 143 et seq., https://dserver.bundestag.de/btd/16/070/1607000.pdf, 9 Nov. 2023.
480. *Ibid.*, 145.

*725.* Religions have some special rights in copyright law. Parts of works, works of speech and small works of music that are protected by a copyright may be reproduced and publicized in collections used for religious purposes without the special permission of the author; however, an appropriate remuneration has to be paid.[481]

*726.* The Federal Constitutional Court has held that the public performance of a work of art in a ceremony of a public law religious community without permission of the author is in line with the constitution. However, the author must have a right to receive an appropriate remuneration.[482]

481. §46 Copyright Act (UrhG).
482. BVerfG 25 Oct. 1978, BVerfGE 49, 382 et seq.

## Chapter 2. Religion and Media

*727.* It is part of the specific position of the religious communities that they have – in terms of the law – a special public mandate. This public mandate is secured by state-church treaties and has its foundations in the religious freedom enjoyed by the religious communities. This accordingly allows them – in the framework of the public democratic process – to have a say and a right to information in the matters and affairs of public life. On the basis of their public mandate, religious institutions have designated time slots on public television and radio; one of the most well-known and popular programmes of this kind is the 'Word for Sunday' (*Wort zum Sonntag*) broadcast by the ARD, the public law German first channel, on Saturday nights; it is created in the responsibility of the Catholic and Protestant churches.[483] Sunday services are broadcast by public law TV companies on Sunday mornings and attract as many viewers as people attend the services in the churches. The churches are active in the media of whichever nature.[484] Religions dispose of on airtime on radio channels and make ample use of broadcasting.

*728.* Religious communities are also given a representative position on the supervisory boards of public institutions where a particular societal representation is necessary. The Protestant and Roman Catholic Church's position is relevant to the broadcasting commissions of public broadcasting corporations such as ZDF, ARD and *Land*-based broadcasting corporations, the supervisory commissions for the private television and radio stations, and also appraisal and classification boards in order to identify and restrain scripts and films that are deemed harmful to young viewers and listeners. Mirroring their historical and cultural impact, the Jewish communities usually are also represented in these bodies. As the first *Land* of the Federal Republic of Germany, Bremen has introduced a provision into its media law which stipulates that one member of the media council must represent the Muslims living in Bremen and one must represent the Alevits living in Bremen (§50 section 1 numbers 24, 25 Bremisches Landesmediengesetz [BremLMG] of 12 January 2021).[485] The Muslims are represented in – for example – the Television Council (Fernsehrat) of the nationwide television broadcaster ZDF.[486]

*729.* The German broadcasting system combines public broadcasting institutions and private broadcasting enterprises. Basically, the *Länder* are competent to govern broadcasting and do so by way of general laws and agreements among each other to coordinate and cooperate in this field of the media. The federation has the

483. Arbeitsgemeinschaft der öffentlich-rechtlichen Rundfunkanstalten Deutschlands zusammengeschlossenen Landesrundfunkanstalten (ARD) (ed.), 'Das Wort zum Sonntag' https://www.daserste.de/information/wissen-kultur/wort-zum-sonntag/index.html, 9 Nov. 2023.

484. *See*, e.g., Katholische Fernseharbeit (ed.), https://fernsehen.katholisch.de/default.aspx, 9 Nov. 2023.

485. Bremisches Landesmediengesetz (BremLMG) of 12 Jan. 2021, Brem. GBl. 2021, 42, available online at https://www.transparenz.bremen.de/metainformationen/bremisches-landesmediengesetz-bremlmg-in-der-fassung-der-bekanntmachung-vom-12-januar-2021-175379?asl=bremen203_tpgesetz.c.55340.de&template=20_gp_ifg_meta_detail_d, 9 Nov. 2023.

486. https://www.zdf.de/zdfunternehmen/zdf-fernsehrat-mitglieder-100.html, 9 Nov. 2023.

power to maintain broadcasting abroad as an expression of foreign relations and policy. According to §5 of the Act on the '*Deutsche Welle*' (DWG), the programme of the institution must not one-sidedly support a political party or other political association, a religious community, a profession or other interest association; it must respect the moral, religious and philosophical convictions of the listeners and viewers. The Broadcasting Council of the *Deutsche Welle* is composed of seventeen members; the Protestant Church, the Catholic Church, and the Central Council of the Jews in Germany have the right to nominate one member of the Broadcasting Council each.

*730.* The State Media Treaty between the *Länder* outlines the general principles of broadcasting in Germany in its Article 3.[487] It is representative of the manifold special provisions on federal and *Länder* levels. The *Land* broadcasting corporations combined in the ARD, ZDF and all broadcasters of nationwide television must in their programmes respect and protect the dignity of man. They are to contribute to strengthening respect for life, freedom and physical integrity for the faiths and opinions of others and must not contravene the diminishing of discrimination against people with disabilities. The moral and religious convictions of the population must be respected. Advertisements must not violate human dignity or discriminate on the basis of gender, race or ethnic origin, nationality, religion or belief, disability, age or sexual orientation. Product placements are prohibited in religious programmes. Advertisements of a political, ideological or religious nature are prohibited. Free contributions in the service of the public, including appeals for donations for charitable purposes, however, are not prohibited.[488] Broadcasts of religious services must not be interrupted by advertisements or teleshopping.[489] Advertisements on (the public law) German Television Channel I (ARD) and ZDF must not be broadcast on Sundays or on legal holidays, which are observed throughout the country.

*731.* The provisions on private broadcasting require that programmes are subject to the requirements of the constitutional order. Broadcasts must respect human dignity as well as the moral, religious and ideological convictions of others. The Protestant churches, the Catholic Church, and the Jewish communities must, upon request, be conceded suitable time for the transmission of religious programmes; the broadcaster may demand reimbursement of prime costs.[490]

*732.* The system for promoting German films and movies provides public subsidies for film and movie productions. It includes religious communities in the decision-making board: The Administrative Council is composed of twenty-nine members, including one member each nominated by the Protestant Church and the

487. State Media Treaty (Medienstaatsvertrag (MStV) in der Fassung des Dritten Staatsvertrags zur Änderung medienrechtlicher Staatsverträge (Dritter Medienänderungsstaatsvertrag)) of 21 Oct. to 2 Nov. 2022, valid since 1 Jul. 2023.
488. Note: The first and fourth clause correspond to §10, s. 8 DWG.
489. Note: Similar provisions are contained in §10, s. 9 DWG.
490. Note: The content of the first subsection corresponds to that of §19, s. 1 LMG RLP, although the latter also affords this right to on-air time to other religious communities.

Catholic Church. The Act on Measures to Promote German Film (FFG) does not allow public funding for films that violate *inter alia* religious feelings.

*733.* Religious advertising in some fields is somewhat restricted, as is political advertising: According to §26 federal Ordinance on the Operation of Transport Enterprises in Local Public Passenger Transport (BOKraft), third-party advertising on taxis and hired cars is only permissible on the side doors of the vehicle; political and religious advertising on taxis is prohibited. The reason behind this seems to be that taxis are part of the general public transport system and have a duty to transport anyone; if there is religious or political advertising on the car, the passenger could feel offended, annoyed or otherwise kept from making use of the service to which he or she has a right. Furthermore, taxis have to line up in public taxi-providing places; sensitive advertisements could lead to situations in which potential passengers might object to taking the first taxi available in the queue, which may incite struggle and unrest among the taxi drivers.

*734.* Religious communities operate or are linked with a great variety of print media. Bible TV (Bibel TV) is a Christian broadcast enterprise operated by an ecumenical circle of associates, including Protestant, Catholic and free church companies, as well as missionary societies and media organizations. It broadcasts religious programmes and services.[491]

*735.* For the protection of children and young people against dangers to their bodily, mental, and spiritual well-being, a body monitors media with texts, pictures or tunes as well as endangering places and events.[492] Endangering media has to be indexed and may not be sold to children and young people. Media are endangering, especially when they are immoral or brutalizing, inciting violence, crime or racial hatred. Media may not be indexed just because of their religious, philosophical, political or social content. The monitoring and indexing body is composed of a variety of personalities from society and government. The competent ministry has to appoint members of the body also from among the churches, the Jewish Cult Communities, and other religious communities that are corporations under public law; the representative of the Council of the EKD at the seat of the German government, the Secretariat of the Bishop's Conference, and the Central Council of the Jews in Germany are entitled to suggest suitable persons.

*736.* Also, according to the Youth Protection Act, children and young people have to be excluded from attending events or places that can have endangering effects on them, meaning that those effects are immoral or brutalizing, incite violence, crime or racial hatred.

491. Bibel TV (ed.), https://www.bibeltv.de/home/, 9 Nov. 2023.
492. Cf. Youth Protection Act (JuSchG).

## Chapter 3. Religion and Civil Society

*737.* Whether the religious communities in Germany are a part of society or whether they form a specific, third area which is distinct from the state as well as from the society is a matter of some academic controversy in Germany. While the Roman Catholic Church seems to insist that it is neither part of the state nor of society, there are a variety of views within the Protestant Churches on this matter. The Federal Constitutional Court has held that the churches face the state as a part of society.[493] It did so, however, in decisions pointing out that religious communities with the status of corporations under public law do not form part of the state and enjoy full freedom of religion. The decision, therefore, does not finally answer the specific relationship between society and religious communities. This question, anyway, is of predominantly theoretical, perhaps theological, relevance. In the field of law, it seems to be more important to identify the specific position of religious communities, their rights and duties in specific circumstances and cases.

*738.* There are a number of public institutions in which religious communities are represented. However, these public institutions are not state institutions. They form part of a sphere of public existence that is not integrated into the state. Examples are the bodies supervising public television and radio broadcasting referred to above. These supervisory bodies comprise representatives of groups of society such as trade unions and employer's associations, consumer protection groups, political parties, state government and normally also the Catholic Church, the Protestant Church and the Jewish Faith Communities.[494]

*739.* The same holds true for the bodies deciding on youth protection, such as the body deciding on the age of young people from which a specific movie may be shown in public cinemas and the bodies deciding on whether certain publications have to be regarded as pornographic, etc.[495]

493. BVerfG 19 Dec. 2000, BVerfGE 102, 370, 387; BVerfG 25 Mar. 1980, BVerfGE 53, 366, 387; BVerfG 4 Jun. 1985, BVerfGE 70, 138, 160.

494. For example, §17 et seq. Treaty on the North-German Broadcasting Corporation (NDR-StV); North-German Broadcasting Council (*Norddeutscher Rundfunkrat*), Norddeutscher Runfunk (ed.), https://www.ndr.de/der_ndr/unternehmen/rundfunkrat/index.html, 9 Nov. 2023.

495. §19, s. 2 JuSchG.

## Chapter 4. Religion and Public Debate

*740.* There is no special representation of religious communities in the realm of politics, in parliament or in any equivalent bodies. No seats are reserved for them.

*741.* Members and personnel of religious communities, as has been stated above, can run for parliament and equivalent bodies and exercise political functions as everyone else. There are no restrictions from the point of view of the state. Some religious communities have introduced internal restrictions for their personnel concerning political offices. For example, the Catholic Church does not want its priests to run for public office in parliaments, etc. However, if any particular priest nevertheless wants to do so, the state will and must not hinder that priest from doing so.

*742.* In public debate, religion and religion are, in general, a topic that is widely debated. In general, religion has been viewed positively in the media. Religious issues are reported on by the great newspapers. The public does take notice of developments within the religious communities. The leaders of religious communities are personalities of public interest with an impact on public opinion. This holds especially true for the Catholic and Protestant Church and for the Jewish community. Issues of integration of Muslim immigrants are closely linked with the religious question in the public debate.

*743.* The scandal of sexual child abuse has somewhat changed the atmosphere in the media in view of religion. Criticism has centred primarily on the Catholic Church, while incidents of sexual child abuse have occurred in many fields of society and religious communities. The Catholic Church has concluded a Joint Declaration with the Independent Commissioner for Child Sexual Abuse Issues on an independent investigation of sexual abuse in the Catholic Church in Germany.[496] In each diocese, an independent commission has been installed to investigate the matter. A further independent commission decides on monetary payments in acknowledgement of the suffering. This does not depend on any statutory prescription. The victim does not have to prove the abuse; plausibility suffices.

496. Gemeinsame Erklärung über verbindliche Kriterien und Standards für eine unabhängige Aufarbeitung von sexuellem Missbrauch in der katholischen Kirche in Deutschland des Unabhängigen Beauftragten für Fragen des sexuellen Kindesmissbrauchs und der Deutschen Bischofskonferenz (Joint Declaration with the Independent Commissioner for Child Sexual Abuse Issues on Binding Criteria and Standards for an Independent Investigation of Sexual Abuse in the Catholic Church in Germany by the Independent Commissioner for Child Sexual Abuse Issues and the German Bishops' Conference), 2020, https://www.dbk.de/fileadmin/redaktion/diverse_downloads/presse_2020/2020-074a-Gemeinsame-Erklaerung-UBSKM-Dt.-Bischofskonferenz.pdf, 9 Nov. 2023.

# Part XII. Religious Assistance in Public Institutions

## Chapter 1. General Principles

*744.* Insofar as the need for religious services and religious assistance in the armed forces, hospitals, penal institutions or other public institutions is concerned, the various religious institutions are free to undertake such activities. Article 141 WRV, in conjunction with Article 140 GG, provides: 'To the extent that a need exists for religious services and pastoral work in the army, in hospitals, in prisons, or in other public institutions, religious societies shall be permitted to provide them, but without compulsion of any kind.'

*745.* Religious communities have a right to give religious assistance in hospitals and to prisoners. Religious activities within the police and the military forces are governed by treaties. Military chaplains are sent from the churches for a specific time. For the duration of their service, they are given the status of state officials; a contractual status is also possible. Their overall superior in matters of their state position is the Head of the Federal Defence Ministry. German military chaplains have the status of normal state officials without a uniform or military rank. As part of the state administration, there is an Evangelical Church office for the Defence Forces for Protestant military chaplains and, for the Catholics, a Catholic military bishop's office. Their sphere of duties is considered to be part of both church and state administration. In church matters, they are subordinate to their respective military bishop, acting for his church, and in matters of public administration, to the Federal Defence Minister. A military rabbinate was installed in 2020, equivalently structured like the Protestant and Catholic military chaplaincies.

## Chapter 2. Institutions

### §1. Cure of Souls in Hospitals

*746.* Cure of souls in hospitals is currently only governed in the shape of basic intra-church (Protestant and Catholic) rules and guidelines.[497]

*747.* The national health insurance system takes account of religious issues. According to §2 subsection 3 Social Code V, the religious needs of the insured parties shall be accommodated. This reiterates the general principle of the right to cure of souls in hospitals. It also enlarges the scope of consideration for religious affiliation: Preferences of the patient as to whether to consult a Protestant hospital, a Catholic hospital, a hospital of other or of no religious affiliation should if at all possible, be followed. Furthermore, this means that religious norms on food or prayer times must be respected in all institutions of the national health insurance system.

*748.* The hospital may ask incoming patients about their religious affiliation if this question is asked, together with the information about the patient's right not to answer this question.[498] The question is justified by the general offer of cure of souls in the hospital, which is in the general interest of patients and their relatives. The service of cure of souls could not be provided for those interested if such questions may not be asked.

### §2. Cure of Souls in the Police Forces

*749.* The spiritual care in the federal police is structured by agreements.[499] An example of the state-church treaties in police cure of souls in the *Länder* is the Agreement on the Church Service to Police Officials (Police Cure of Souls) in the Saarland (PolSeels Saarland). Special ministers are mandated by the churches for the service within the police forces. They do service within the police for a limited amount of time and are paid by the state.

### §3. Cure of Souls in Prisons

*750.* Based on special treaties, there is an extensive cure of souls in prisons. About 300 Protestant and a similar number of Catholic ministers are working in

497. Cf. for example, Ordinance for the Cure of Souls in Hospitals in the Protestant Church in Hesse and Nassau (KSVO Hessen-Nassau) and §7 of the Model Rules for the Internal Structure and Organization of Catholic Hospitals in Hesse, Rhineland-Palatinate and the Saarland (MusterO kath-Krankenhäuser Hessen u.a.).
498. BVerfG 25 Oct. 1977, BVerfGE 46, 266 et seq.
499. Cf. Agreement on Protestant Cure of Souls in the Federal Border Police (EvSeelsBGS) and the Agreement on Catholic Cure of Souls in the Federal Border Police (KathSeelsBGS).

prisons.[500] Individual agreements relate to Imams who visit prisons when this is required in individual cases.[501]

## §4. MILITARY CHAPLAINCY

*751.* The Federal Republic of Germany and the EKD have concluded the state-church Treaty in the Special Field of Military Chaplaincy (MilSeelsV).[502] According to its preamble, the Federal Republic of Germany and the Protestant Church in Germany have agreed to conclude the treaty in the endeavour to ensure free religious activity and the exercise of cure of souls in the federal armed forces, conscious of the joint responsibility for this task. The treaty provides that a permanent Protestant military chaplaincy will be established for the federal armed forces (Article 1). Military chaplaincy, as a part of the church's work, is exercised on behalf and under the supervision of the church. The state takes care of the organizational construction of military chaplaincy and bears its costs (Article 2). In general, according to Article 3 of the treaty, military chaplaincy is carried out by clerics charged with this task on a full-time basis (military chaplains). One military chaplain is appointed for every one thousand five hundred Protestant soldiers. In special cases, clerics in the service of the member churches of the EKD may be entrusted with tasks of military chaplaincy part-time. The important structural provision of Article 4 provides that the task of the military chaplains is to serve in word, sacrament and cure of souls. In this service, the military chaplains are independent within the framework of the ecclesiastical system. As holder of an ecclesiastical office, the military chaplain remains bound to his or her EKD member church concerning confession and doctrine.

*752.* Soldiers are afforded the opportunity to participate in church life within the bounds of the possibilities of service (Article 5).

*753.* According to Article 6, military chaplaincy is carried out in personnel cure of souls areas, but the churches can also establish military parishes. Soldiers, civil servants and employees active in the federal armed forces who are to follow the troops in case of defence, and the wives and children under parental authority of soldiers and civil servants and employees mentioned, form part of these cure of souls areas if they belong to their households at the post. Persons who have declared their resignation from the church with legal effect cease to form part of such cure of souls areas or military parishes. Article 8 provides that the members of the personnel cure of souls areas are members of the local parishes where the personnel cure of souls areas are formed. Members of military parishes do not belong to local parishes.

---

500. *See* Evangelische Konferenz für Gefängnisseelsorge in Deutschland (ed.), https://www.gefaengnisseelsorge.de/, 9 Nov. 2023; and Konferenz der Katholischen Seelsorge bei den Justizvollzugsanstalten in der Bundesrepublik Deutschland (ed.), https://gefaengnisseelsorge.net/organisation, 9 Nov. 2023.
501. These remain largely unpublished.
502. Cf. Art. 1 Act on Military Chaplaincy (MilSeelsG).

*754.* The ecclesiastical management of military chaplaincy lies with the Military Bishop, as is provided by Article 10. Article 11 further provides that the Military Bishop is nominated by the Council of the Protestant Church in Germany. Prior to nomination, the Council of the Protestant Church in Germany contacts the Federal Government to ensure that from the state point of view, no weighty demurs are raised against the cleric designated for the office of the Military Bishop. The Council of the Protestant Church in Germany may remove the Military Bishop from office for important ecclesiastical reasons. It has to inform the Federal Government in advance of such an intention and, at the same time, must communicate the person envisaged as the new holder of that office to it. The Military Bishop is, pursuant to Article 12, competent for all ecclesiastical matters in connection with military chaplaincy, in particular, and, *inter alia*, for the installation of military chaplains in their ecclesiastical office in military chaplaincy; the highest ecclesiastical supervision of military chaplains with the exception of discipline related to teachings and disciplinary power, which remains with the member churches, the visitation of the personnel cure of souls areas and the military parishes; the issuance of a field liturgy; and, finally and so far of no practical application, the cure of souls for Protestant prisoners-of-war.

*755.* To exercise the central administrative duties of Protestant military chaplaincy, at the seat of the Federal Ministry of Defence, a 'Protestant Ecclesiastical Office for the Federal Armed Forces' directly subordinated to the Federal Minister of Defence is established (Article 14). A General Military Superintendent is appointed, according to Article 15, as head of the Protestant Ecclesiastical Office for the Federal Armed Forces at the proposal of the Military Bishop. The General Military Superintendent is subordinate to the Military Bishop. However, as far as he or she exercises state administrative duties connected with military chaplaincy, the General Military Superintendent is subordinate to the Federal Minister of Defence.

*756.* Military chaplains have a clerical assignment in fulfilment of which they shall be independent of state directives (Article 16). They do not have a military rank, and they do not wear a military uniform. Military chaplains are appointed as temporary civil servants, which is their normal status; if they are to be permanently employed for managerial tasks in military chaplaincy, they are appointed as permanent civil servants (Article 19). Proposals to nominate and promote or transfer military chaplains require the approval of the Military Bishop according to Article 20. Also, prior to other important decisions in personnel matters of military chaplains, the Federal Minister of Defence shall obtain a statement from the Military Bishop.

*757.* The important provision of Article 22 provides for a split structure of military chaplaincy, which is an expression of the separation of state and religious communities: '(1) In ecclesiastical matters, military chaplains are subordinate to the leadership and supervision of the Military Bishop as well as the supervision of the General Military Superintendent and the remainder of military chaplains entrusted by the Military Bishop with the supervision.' However, '(2) for military chaplains as federal civil servants, the highest authority is the Federal Minister of Defence, and the direct superior is the General Military Superintendent'.

*758.* For Catholic military clerics, the Act on Military Chaplaincy provides that the public-service-law provisions of the agreement with the EKD shall be applied analogously to the Catholic military clerics.[503]

*759.* Military chaplaincy for Jewish is provided for by the Act on Jewish Military Chaplaincy together with the Treaty between the Federal Republic of Germany and the Central Council of the Jews in Germany on the Jewish military chaplaincy.[504]

## §5. Special Questions

*760.* Subject to negotiations in individual cases, Imams may be allowed into prisons, healthcare institutions and the police to provide care for Muslim religious needs. There are about 4,000 Muslims in the armed forces.[505] A military 'chaplaincy' equivalent to other religions has not been institutionalized as of yet. The debate on Muslim military chaplaincy is ongoing.

503. Article 2 MilSeelsG.

504. Gesetz über die jüdische Militärseelsorge vom 10. Juli 2020; Vertrag vom 20. Dezember 2019 zwischen der Bundesrepublik Deutschland und dem Zentralrat der Juden in Deutschland – Körperschaft des Öffentlichen Rechts – zur Regelung der jüdischen Militärseelsorge.

505. https://www.dw.com/de/muslime-in-der-bundeswehr-soldaten-ohne-milit%C3%A4r-seelsorge/a-54303770, 9 Nov. 2023.

# Part XIII. Religions in the Social Field

## Chapter 1. Basic Principles and Activities

*761.* It is predominantly the great churches that cooperate with state institutions and other organizations in maintaining a social system in Germany. The churches do so while preserving their special missions and identities. They contribute personal engagement and specific approaches as well as substantial amounts of funds. This system of cooperation is an expression of separation of state and religious communities. The great churches and other religious communities operate social institutions as an expression of practising religion. This is part of freedom of religion as guaranteed by the German constitution in its Articles 4 and 140 in conjunction with Article 137 section 3 WRV. The German Federal Constitutional Court and other German courts have consistently ruled that acting in conformity with one's religion in all aspects of life forms part of freedom of religion.[506] While religious freedom is, to a large extent, a matter of individual conscience, it also implies, *inter alia*, freedom to manifest one's religion, alone and in private, or in community with others, in public and within the circle of those whose faith one shares.

*762.* This cooperative system of social care and culture is a key factor of pluralism. The state ensures that different religions and non-religious institutions can share in the common task of caring for the people, each one of them offering its specific values and convictions. This also has an impact on the labour law policy: if it were no longer possible for a religious community to employ in their institutions only those who respect and act in line with its teachings, the whole system of pluralist social care and culture would come into question. It would be difficult for free institutions of social service or culture to remain involved in the system. By tendency, the whole sector would be left exclusively to the state. Pluralism would be lost.

*763.* One also has to see that the German social state, as defined by Article 20 section 1 GG, relies to a vast extent on the cooperation between the state and free institutions, among them the churches. Churches operate a large amount of hospitals, homes for the elderly, nursery homes, and also kindergartens, schools, and academic institutions. While there is no monopoly of the great churches in the social field, the social state in Germany would hardly be able to function in practice without the activity of the large Churches. If the Churches were not allowed to operate

506. BVerfG 19 Oct. 1971, BVerfGE 32, 98, 106; BVerfG 17 Dec. 1975, BVerfGE 41, 29, 49.

in this sector according to their own beliefs and teachings, including the autonomous religious decision about religious requirements of employment, the German social state in its pluralist structure would be endangered.

*764.* Equivalent principles would apply to other free institutions of social care. In the field of social welfare, several other organizations have a share, among them youth associations, trade union organizations, the Red Cross, the *Paritätische Wohlfahrtsverband*, and Jewish Cult Communities. Some of them engage in social care for religious reasons, others for political or humanitarian ideals. While the religious grounding accounts for a specific status of religious communities, also all other of these institutions have a specific ethos. The ethos of religious communities as well as that of secular institutions would be lost if they cannot further insist that their employees comply with this ethos.

*765.* Religious charitable work is an expression of the principle of subsidiarity based on the principle of the social state in Article 20 section 1 GG: the state only takes care of a field of necessary activity when a smaller entity such as a religious community or a private institution cannot properly fulfil the task with its own means. The state acknowledges and promotes societal and other non-governmental initiatives in supporting people in need. This principle of subsidiarity is mentioned in Article 23 section 1 GG. It finds an expression in and is characteristic of, for example, §3 Social Code (SGB) VIII – children and youth care. This provision characterizes youth care by a multitude of institutions of different value orientations and by a multitude of contents, methods, and forms of work. Youth care is provided by the institutions of free youth care and by institutions of public youth care. This is seen as an important expression of the idea of a pluralistic society that leaves space for different approaches and convictions.

*766.* The two great churches maintain travellers' aid service points (*Bahnhofsmission*) at railway stations and seamen's missions in seaports. There are over one hundred travellers' aid service points in Germany with some 2,000 staff; they are financed predominantly by the churches and receive subsidies from state authorities and the railway company.[507]

*767.* The German Caritas Union (*Deutscher Caritasverband*) is the welfare organization of the Roman Catholic Church in Germany. It is the largest German welfare association. Caritas has 24,952 centres and institutions in Germany where people can get professional support and guidance to help them cope with and overcome their problems. These services are intended for all people who are socially disadvantaged, regardless of skin colour, religion or nationality. People who are unemployed, have AIDS, have a substance addiction, are homeless, in prison, or mentally ill, or people who have immigrated from other countries all utilize the services Caritas offers in its day centres and part-residential and residential care centres. These services are utilized by families, children, young adults, people with

507. Konferenz für Kirchliche Bahnhofsmission in Deutschland (KKBM) (ed.), https://www.bahnhofsmission.de/index.php?id=3, 9 Nov. 2023.

disabilities, and the elderly. In all, Caritas helps about 12 million people every year. In its nursing homes, playschools, day nurseries, hospitals, health clinics and health and advice centres, people receive advice, care, assistance and counsel. They come to youth and disability centres, women's shelters and advice centres for families, women, people in debt, addicts and immigrants to get support and guidance. More and more people living under the poverty level are also coming to Caritas' soup kitchens for food and 'clothes closets' for clothing. Caritas is organized in local Caritas associations and local special branch institutions in which concrete help and assistance for people in need are rendered. In September 2020, the German Caritas Union comprised twenty-seven diocese Caritas associations and about 25,000 individual institutions and services.[508] The Caritas associations employ about 695,900 people in regular occupation, and about 500,000 people engage themselves on an honorary basis in these services.[509] The Caritas Union maintains 488 hospitals and more than 1,650 social healthcare units.[510] In the field of care for disabled people, there are 848 centres for rehabilitation and homes as well as 821 day centres and schools for disabled children and young people. Many more institutions and services could be added.

*768.* There are also a multitude of professional institutions, especially in the field of healthcare and homing, that belong to the Roman Catholic Church by way of their statutes but do not form part of the Caritas associations. They are, while closely linked with the Roman Catholic Church, independent enterprises.

*769.* The diaconate is the social work of the Protestant Churches. The *Diakonisches Werk* (Diaconate Work) of the EKD is organized as a charitable association, the members of which are the EKD, the member churches of the EKD, some independent churches with their diaconate works, and a number of specialized associations of various services. The diaconate works in about 31,000 independent units of different sizes and legal forms with more than 1,175,000 care places, which does not include assistance in cases of natural disasters and catastrophes. The diaconate employs more than 627,000 full and part-time staff. Some 700,000 people are active in the diaconate on an honorary basis.[511]

*770.* Brot für die Welt (Bread for the World) is a special entity within the diaconate that is especially known for its collections to combat hunger worldwide and to render help in cases of natural disasters and catastrophes. In the year 2022, *Brot*

---

508. Caritas Deutschland, https://www.caritas.de/diecaritas/uebersicht, 26 Apr. 2024.
509. Deutscher Caritasverband e.V. (ed.), *Caritas Deutschland*, https://www.caritas.de/diecaritas/uebersicht, 26 Apr. 2024; https://www.caritas-im-norden.de/engagement/ehrenamt/ehrenamt, 26 Apr. 2024.
510. These and the following data originate from Deutscher Caritasverband e.V. (ed.), file:///C:/Users/gerha/Downloads/Einrichtungsstatistik_DCV_Erhebung_2020_12_31.pdf, 26 Apr. 2024.
511. Diakonie Bundesverband (ed.), https://www.diakonie.de/freiwilliges-engagement/, 9 Nov. 2023.

*für die Welt* has collected EUR 75.6 million in donations; substantial contributions from the churches and the state are added.[512]

*771*. Misereor, the German Catholic bishop's organization for development cooperation, was founded in 1958 as an agency 'against hunger and disease in the world'. It has received an income from donations, church funds, and public subsidies of EUR 241.5 million in 2022; donations amounted to EUR 61.7 million.[513] A great variety of other organizations maintained or mandated by religious communities are active in the field of social assistance.

*772*. Hospitals run by religious communities, which in some parts of Germany make up the majority of the available hospital beds, are part of the publicly run financing systems for hospitals.

*773*. The hospitals and health institutions of the great churches are integrated into the general national health insurance system. Pluralism of religious affiliation is a key factor also in this system. Accordingly, §2 subsection 3 Social Code (SGB) V provides that in selecting the service provider, their diversity shall be observed.

*774*. Furthermore, a substantial amount of prevention and rehabilitation, as well as nursing service facilities are maintained by the big churches and by religious communities.[514] The Jewish communities maintain a considerable number of social care institutions.

*775*. Muslim social care is gradually developing. Concerning childcare, there has been significant development in the past years: more and more Muslim kindergartens and daycare centres for children are opening. Most of these are located in those cities of the *Länder* with large Muslim populations (such as Hamburg, Frankfurt, Cologne, Mainz and Karlsruhe, to name a few).

512. Diakonisches Werk der Evangelischen Kirche in Deutschland e. V. (ed), https://www.brot-fuer-die-welt.de/fileadmin/mediapool/40_Ueber-uns/Finanzen-Transparenz/Jahresbericht_2022/BfdW_Jahresbericht-2022_Online.pdf, 9 Nov. 2023.

513. Bischöfliches Hilfswerk Misereor e. V. (ed.), https://www.misereor.de/ueber-uns/jahresbericht, 9 Nov. 2023.

514. *See*, e.g., §111b SGB V.

## Chapter 2. Kindergartens

*776.* Religious communities operate numerous kindergartens, as has been referred to above. Kindergartens are part of the general educational system as well as part of the social system. §22 section 3 Social Code (SGB) VIII – children and youth care defines as a comprehensive task of kindergartens: 'upbringing, education, and care'.

*777.* Catholic as well as Evangelical and Jewish kindergartens have a clear religious assignment. Not all, but many of the parents do expect from a religious kindergarten a child-appropriate religious education which provides strength to the child and compensates for their own uncertainties. These parents are also ready to take over religious practices such as prayers, religious customs on holy days, and rituals into their daily lives.

*778.* Religious kindergartens are a part of the religious communities as institutions. It is left to the religious communities and their autonomous decision in which form and institutional linkage within the framework of secular law they intend to establish and operate their institutions.[515]

*779.* The system of cooperation between state and religion in the field of kindergartens is an expression of separation of state and religious communities in that religion is part of many children's upbringing and education. While religious education entails questions and decisions of truth, this cannot be done by the religiously neutral state but must be left to religious institutions. This is one of the reasons why the German state cooperates with the religious communities also in the field of kindergartens. This system of cooperation enables an offer to those who wish a religious upbringing of their children also in conformity with Articles 4 and 6 GG, Article 2 of the Protocol to the Convention for the Protection of Human Rights and Fundamental Freedoms and Article 14 of the Convention on the Rights of the Child. However, the system does not burden the religiously neutral state with having to teach religious truth itself. This is left to religions and the free choice of parents.

*780.* This cooperative system of youth care is an expression of pluralism. The state secures that different religions and non-religious institutions can share in the common task of upbringing the new generation, each one of them offering its specific values and convictions. The religious character of kindergartens maintained by religious communities requires freedom of choice of staff. If it were not possible for a religious community to employ in their kindergartens only those who act in line with and respect its teachings, the whole system of pluralist children and youth care would become impossible. Free institutions of youth care could no longer be involved in the system. The whole sector of youth care would be left exclusively to the state. Pluralism would be lost.

515. BVerfG 4 Jun. 1985, BVerfGE 70, 138, 162.

*781.* When providing services by their kindergartens, the religious communities do not take over a state task. While Articles 6 and 7 GG attribute to the state a genuine state task in raising and educating the children, the care for children also is a genuine task of religious communities that is based on Article 4 sections 1 and 2, Article 137 section 3 WRV in conjunction with Article 140 GG, always with due respect to the right of parents to raise and educate their children as guaranteed by Article 6 GG.

*782.* In the whole of Germany there were in 2022 9,445 kindergartens maintained by the Catholic Church with 633,023 children and 9,278 kindergartens maintained by the Protestant churches.[516]

516. https://de.statista.com/statistik/daten/studie/1282288/umfrage/kinder-und-kindertagesstaetten-in-kirchlichen-traegern/, 9 Nov. 2023.

# Part XIV. Sunday and Religious Holiday Protection

*783.* Article 139 WRV, in conjunction with Article 140 GG, gives special recognition and protection to Sundays and religious holidays: Sundays and holidays recognized by the state are protected by law as days of rest from work and of spiritual improvement. The constitutions of the *Länder* have some special language for Sunday protection that mirrors the general approach to religion in that specific *Land*.[517] Holiday Acts of the *Länder* and a few federal provisions lay out details of such protection. The Sunday is – already by way of federal constitutional law – protected in all *Länder*; the number of recognized religious holidays and the scope of their protection varies from *Land* to *Land*.

*784.* However, there is no guarantee that specific individual religious holidays would continue to enjoy state protection or that a certain number of religious holidays should be protected. When the Protestant Repentance Day was abolished as a day of rest in Lower Saxony and in other *Länder* to compensate indirectly for higher costs of the reformed general national health insurance system, the Federal Constitutional Court held that Article 140 GG in conjunction with Article 139 WRV only obliges the legislature to protect an appropriate number of religious holidays. Also, there is no individual right following from freedom of religion or belief as guaranteed by Article 4 GG that specific religious holidays should be protected as days of rest. Moreover, the abolition of the Protestant church holiday only did not constitute any discrimination on religious reasons of Protestants against members of other denominations or non-believers and thus did not violate Article 3 section 3 GG in the eyes of the Federal Constitutional Court.[518]

*785.* Religious holidays that are legally recognized are defined in state law. Legally recognized holidays and legally protected holidays enjoy special protection. On Sundays and on recognized holidays, working activities are prohibited that can be publicly noticed and that are suitable to disturb the peace of the holiday unless the law does not provide otherwise. During the normal time of the main religious services, certain activities are also prohibited, such as any avoidable noisy

517. For example, Art. 3, s. 1 Verf BW; Art. 147 BayVerf; Art. 35, s. 1 VvB; Art. 14, s. 1 BbgVerf; Art. 55, s. 3 BremVerf.
518. BVerfG 18 Sep. 1995, *Neue Juristische Wochenschrift* 48 (1995): 3378 et seq.

activities near churches and other places of worship that can disturb the service. Furthermore, public entertainment events are prohibited during this time except sports events and events of culture, arts or education that normally take place at such times. Not prohibited are a number of activities such as public transport, gardening work performed by the owners of the garden and their relatives, and a number of urgent, unavoidable activities. Further exceptions are possible, such as the opening of shops. Exceptions also apply for those activities that are necessarily performed on such days of rest, like the work of the priest or clergy, emergency services, hospitals and homes for the elderly, police, certain agricultural activities, and work for the leisure time needs of the population.

*786.* Beyond the Sunday, the following religious holidays are legally recognized holidays in most German *Länder*: Epiphany, Maundy Thursday, Good Friday, Easter Sunday, Easter Monday, Ascension Day, Pentecostal Monday, Corpus Christi, Reformation Day, All Saints' Day, Day of Prayer and Repentance, First Christmas Day, Second Christmas Day. The only religiously orientated holiday protected merely on a local community basis is the *Augsburger Friedensfest* on 8 August, commemorating the Peace of Westphalia of 1648 that ended the Thirty Year's War and finally recognized the Lutheran (Augsburg) confession; the day is a holiday only in the city of Augsburg.

*787.* Jewish religious holidays enjoy explicit and specific protection in some of the German *Länder*: Bavaria, Bremen, and North Rhine-Westphalia. In Bavaria, for example, the following Jewish holidays are protected: Passover (first two and last two days), the Shavuot (two days), Succot (first two and last two days), Rosh Hashanah (two days), Yom Kippur (one day). During the normal time of the main Jewish religious services, certain activities are prohibited, such as public assemblies or any avoidable noisy activities near synagogues and other places of Jewish worship that can disturb the service. Jewish pupils are free from classes on those days. Jewish employees are free from work except in certain cases, such as those works that are allowed on holidays or are necessary to uphold the business (section 6 Bavarian Holiday Act (FeiertG Bayern)).

*788.* There are also so-called quiet days. Such quiet days enjoy special protection. On quiet days, public entertainment events are allowed only when they do not contradict the serious character of these days. Sports events are allowed, however, except on Good Friday and – for example, in Bavaria – on the Day of Prayer and Repentance. On Good Friday, in bars and restaurants any music performances are prohibited.[519] Religious holidays protected as quiet days almost everywhere, or at least in many parts of Germany, are Ash Wednesday, Maundy Thursday, Good Friday, Good Saturday, Easter Sunday, Pentecostal Sunday, All Saints' Day, Eternity Sunday, and Christmas Eve.

*789.* Those religious holidays that are not explicitly protected by the holiday laws enjoy protection through freedom of religion or belief: believers of the specific

519. §3 FeiertG Bayern.

faith have a right to free time from employment to attend the services if that is feasible, taking into account the needs of the employer.[520] Some laws explicitly regulate the free time of pupils and teachers in schools to attend services of their religious community. The range of protection differs in detail between the various *Länder*. However, if there is no legally defined specific protection, a fair balance has to be struck between the religious needs of the believers and the needs of his or her employer or institution in deciding about free time.

*790.* Muslim religious holidays have not been explicitly or specially protected in the same way as Christian and Jewish religious holidays. However, the agreements of the *Land* Hamburg with Muslim communities explicitly protect Id-ul-Adha (or Kurban Bayrami), the Ramadan festivity of breaking the fast (Id-ul-Fitr or Ramazan Bayrami), and Aschura; for the Alevis Asure, Hizir, Nevruz, Hidirellez, Sivas, Haci Bektas Veli, and the day of Hüseyin are protected.[521] As has been stated above, those religious holidays that are not explicitly protected by the holiday laws enjoy protection through freedom of religion or belief. This also applies to Muslim religious holidays. Believers have a right to free time from employment to attend the services if that is feasible, taking into account the needs of the employer. Some laws explicitly regulate the free time of pupils and teachers in schools to attend services of their religious community. The range of protection differs in detail between the various *Länder*. If there is no legally defined specific protection, a fair balance has to be struck between the religious needs of the believers and the needs of his or her employer or institution in deciding about free time in the individual case.

520. For example, §7, s. 1 Schleswig-Holstein Holiday Act (SFTG); §8 Bremen Holiday Act (FeiertG Bremen).

521. For example, Art. 3 Treaty between the Free and Hanseatic City of Hamburg, the DITIB Land Association Hamburg, SCHURA – Council of Islamic Communities in Hamburg and the Organization of Islamic Culture Centres (*Vertrag zwischen der Freien und Hansestadt Hamburg, dem DITIB-Landesverband Hamburg, SCHURA – Rat der Islamischen Gemeinschaften in Hamburg und dem Verband der Islamischen Kulturzentren*), available at https://www.buergerschaft-hh.de/ParlDok/dokument/38534/1-vertrag-zwischen-der-freien-und-hansestadt-hamburg-dem-ditib-landesverband-hamburg-schura-%E2%80%93-rat-der-islamischen-gemeinschaften-in-hamburg.pdf, 9 Nov. 2023; Art. 3 Treaty between the Free and Hanseatic City of Hamburg and the Alevi Community in Germany (*Vertrag zwischen der Freien und Hansestadt Hamburg und der Alevitischen Gemeinde Deutschland e.V.*), available at https://www.buergerschaft-hh.de/ParlDok/dokument/38534/1-vertrag-zwischen-der-freien-und-hansestadt-hamburg-dem-ditib-landesverband-hamburg-schura-%E2%80%93-rat-der-islamischen-gemeinschaften-in-hamburg.pdf, 9 Nov. 2023.

# Part XV. The Burial System

*791.* The two big churches in Germany are intensely integrated into the general public burial system. The burial system is a matter of the law of the *Länder*. It thus differs in detail throughout Germany. All over Germany, however, religious communities that are corporations under public law are allowed to run cemeteries.

*792.* An example of burial law is the Act on the Bodies, Burials and Cemetery System in the *Land* Mecklenburg-Western Pomerania – Burials Act (BestattG M-V). This law mirrors the way in which the burial system is structured throughout Germany. In the case of cremation, the urn shall be buried with the ashes in a cemetery or in a suitable form in a church. Bearers of cemeteries may only be communities such as religious communities that are corporations under public law. The municipalities have to establish and maintain cemeteries (municipal cemeteries). This does, however, not apply if a church cemetery exists in the municipality or the municipality ensures by agreement that the cemetery of another bearer can be used. This also applies *mutatis mutandis* to mortuaries.

*793.* On church cemeteries, it must be made possible to bury all persons deceased in the municipality if the municipality does not maintain its own cemetery and has not concluded an agreement with another bearer of a cemetery. In such cases, the municipality contributes towards those costs of the cemetery that cannot be covered by fees for use.

*794.* If the bearer of a church cemetery levies fees for use in the shape of public-law fees, these fees are collected on application by the mayors of urban districts, the mayors of independent municipalities and the supervisors of the offices in execution assistance in accordance with the provisions stipulated in respect of state administrative execution. The cost of execution assistance not covered by payments from the debtor has to be refunded to the law enforcement authority by the bearer of the church cemetery.

*795.* The bearer of the cemetery governs the order, use and formation, as well as the exercise of commercial activities by means of cemetery rules. The bearer is obligated to keep a record of burials.

*796.* The establishment or expansion of cemeteries requires the approval that the chief administrative officers or the mayors of urban districts give in agreement with the competent water authorities.

*797.* Muslim burial traditions have caused some changes in the German burial law. Some of the *Länder* have amended their respective laws and repealed the former obligation to have a coffin when burying a dead body that has not been cremated.[522] Also, the minimum time between death and burial can be shortened in some *Länder* to meet Muslim requirements.[523] In many cemeteries, also in those operated by Christian churches, areas for Muslims have been set aside where it is possible to bury in the direction of Mecca. Ablution facilities are usually available. Some *Länder* provide for unlimited burial time. In a number of *Länder*, problems remain, and most first-generation Muslims who die in Germany are still buried abroad in their or their ancestor's countries of origin.

522. For example, §1, s. 4 Ordinance relating to burials in Hamburg (HambBestVO); similar provisions apply in: Bremen, Hesse, Lower Saxony, North Rhine-Westphalia, Schleswig-Holstein, and the Saarland.
523. For example, §17, s. 1, cl. 2 Act on Corpses of Bremen (LeichenG Bremen) and §7, s. 2 Burial Act North Rhine-Westphalia (BestG NRW).

# Part XVI. Data Law

## Chapter 1. Registration of Residents

*798.* The system of public registration of individuals is governed by the federal Registration Law Framework Act (MRRG) and the registration laws of the *Länder*. The authorities of the *Länder* who are competent for registration have to register each person resident in their area of competence in order to be able to determine and prove their identity and places of residence. They issue information from registration registers, assist in the implementation of tasks of other authorities or other public bodies and transmit data where legally appropriate. In carrying out their tasks, the registration authorities maintain registration registers. These contain data collected from those affected, from authorities and other public bodies or which otherwise become officially known.

*799.* In carrying out their tasks, the registration authorities store data on residents in the registration register, including their legal affiliation to a religious society (§2 MRRG).

*800.* If the registration register is incorrect or incomplete, the registration authority must correct or supplement it ex officio. The authorities or other public bodies, including religious communities with public law status, will be informed as to which incorrect or incomplete data have been transmitted in regular data transmission.

*801.* Religious communities do not have to inform the registration authorities about incorrect data. However, they may notify the registration authorities in the event of the existence of such indications.

*802.* The registration authority may, according to §19 section 1 MRRG, transmit to a public-law religious society the following data on its members if these data are needed to carry out its competence or tasks lying in its competence: (1) last names, (2) previous names, (3) first names, (4) doctor's degree, (5) religious names, artistic names, (6) date and place of birth, (7) gender, (8) nationalities, (9) present and last previous address, main and secondary residence, if moving in from abroad the last previous address in the inland as well, (10) date of moving in and out, (11) civil status, restricted to the statement of whether married, leading a life partnership or not; in addition concerning married persons or life partners: date of marriage or establishment of the life partnership, (12) number of minor children, (13) transmission barriers, (14) date and place of death.

*803.* The registration authority may, according to §19 section 2 MRRG, transmit from family members of the members who do not belong to the same or to any public-law religious society the following data: (1) last names, (2) first names, (3) date of birth, (4) affiliation to a public-law religious society, (5) transmission barriers, and (6) date of death. Family members for this purpose are the spouse, minor-age children and the parents of minor-age children. It may be determined by virtue of a *Land* statute that more of the data may be transmitted. The person affected may require his or her data not to be transmitted, and he or she will be informed of this on registering; this does not apply if it has been determined by virtue of *Land* law that for purposes of the law on levying taxes of the respective public-law religious society data are to be transmitted thereto.

*804.* Data transmissions to public-law religious communities are only permissible if it is ensured that the data recipient has taken sufficient data protection precautions.

*805.* The registration laws of the *Länder* provide further details. An example is the Registration Act of the *Land* Saxony-Anhalt (MG LSA). According to this law, the registration authorities, in carrying out their tasks, store certain specified data on residents in the registration register, including the legal affiliation to a religious society and for the issuance of a wage tax card certain fiscal data: tax class, tax-free allowances, religious affiliation of the spouse, legal status and allocation of the children, first and last names, as well as address of the foster and step-parents (§22 MG LSA).

*806.* If a resident has registered with a registration authority, the latter shall instruct the previously competent registration authority and the registration authorities competent for other residences of this without delay, not later than within a week, by transmitting certain enumerated data on the resident, including his or her affiliation to a public-law religious society (§28 MG LSA).

*807.* The registration authority may transmit to a public-law religious society, in order to carry out its tasks, the following data on its members from the registration register: (1) classification aid, (2) first and last names, (3) previous names, (4) doctor's degree, (5) religious names, artistic names, (6) date and place of birth, (7) gender, (8) nationalities, (9) present and last previous and future addresses, main and secondary residence, date of moving in and out, (10) civil status, restricted to the statement of whether married or not; additionally with married persons: date of conclusion of marriage, (11) number of minor-age children, (12) transmission barriers, and (13) date and place of death. It must be ensured in the transmission that the third party to whom the data are transmitted has taken sufficient data protection precautions (§30 MG LSA).

*808.* The Ministry of the Interior is empowered to permit or prescribe regular data transmission from the registration authority to public bodies, public-law religious societies and the search service by means of an ordinance if the transmissions are necessary in order to carry out tasks for which the third party, to which is transmitted, is competent. In the ordinance, the reason for and purpose of the transmission, the data to be transmitted, and the third party to which it is transmitted must be established; in addition, the form and procedure of transmission may be regulated (§32 MG LSA).

## Chapter 2. Census and Religious Affiliation

*809.* No person is required to disclose his or her religious convictions. The authorities have the right to inquire into a person's membership in a religious society only to the extent that rights or duties depend upon it or that a statistical survey mandated by a law so requires (Article 136 section 3 WRV in conjunction with Article 140 GG). Data about the religious affiliation collected by way of such a survey may not be transmitted to local communities for purposes of regional or urban planning; however, statistical data on religious affiliation may be publicized as long as they are completely anonymous.[524]

524. BVerfG 15 Dec. 1983, BVerfGE 65, 1 et seq.

# Part XVII. The Law on Aliens

*810.* While freedom of religion or belief as such does not constitute a right of foreigners to enter the Federal Republic of Germany, it does have to be taken into account when deciding on a permit to enter the country. The Federal Constitutional Court had held that it violated the constitution when the husband and wife Mun, the leaders of the Mun community, were prohibited from entering the country without taking due regard to the religious importance of the contacts between the believers and the leaders or the founder of the religion.[525] The visit of the religious leaders had a specific religious purpose because, according to the self-understanding of the religious community, the contact of believers with the founder of the religion had religious meaning.

*811.* The Federal Act on the Residence, Professional Activity, and Integration of Foreigners on Federal Territory (Residence Act (AufenthG)) also refers to issues of religion and religious affiliation. According to its §47, political activity of a foreigner is prohibited if it endangers the free democratic basic order or the security of the Federal Republic of Germany or contradicts the codified norms of international public law, or if it supports, advocates or aims at evoking or is suitable to evoke the use of violence for the achievement of political, religious or other interests.

*812.* It is important to note that, pursuant to §60 Residence Act, a foreign person must not be deported into a state in which his or her life or liberty is endangered because of his or her race, religion, nationality, membership to a specific social group, or political conviction. These are also reasons for receiving political asylum according to §3 Asylum Act (AsylG). A person also has the right to political asylum if the reasons for granting political asylum have occurred only after he or she has come into the Federal Republic of Germany and also when the person has created these reasons voluntarily. This can apply to cases of religious conversion in Germany that would expose the person to religious persecution in his or her country of origin. In order to establish the validity of such reasons, the German authorities sometimes interrogate the applicant on the credibility of his or her religious convictions. They have done so by asking about religious facts and the knowledge of the applicant in matters of his or her new religion. They try to establish whether the conversion is credible or is a mere pretext. It has to be noted that only the so-called

525. BVerfG (K) 24 Oct. 2006, BVerfGK 9, 371 et seq.

religious minimum of existence is protected; this religious minimum of existence is guaranteed if the persons can meet and manifest their religion in private without being subjected to persecution.[526]

*813.* The religious minimum of existence forms part of the irrevocable core of privacy, which the religious person needs as a moral person. In defining the extent of this religious minimum, the specific, absolutely indispensable requirements of manifestation of religion or belief according to the general practice have to be taken into account. For Yazidi, this can be, according to the Federal Constitutional Court, the cohesion of family life; when there is strong pressure to assimilation, such religious minimum can be endangered and violated.[527]

*814.* The Federal Constitutional Court has held it possible that a Sikh can be granted political asylum in Germany because of religious persecution in India.[528] Likewise, religious persecution of Ahmadiyya in Pakistan can constitute a valid reason for the right to political asylum.[529]

*815.* Extradition to a foreign country in criminal matters is inadmissible if serious reasons exist for the presumption that the persecutee, in the event of his or her extradition, would be persecuted or punished because of his or her race, religion, nationality, membership of a specific social group or his or her political views or that his or her situation would be made worse for one of these reasons.[530]

526. OVG Saxony, A 2 B 817/05 of 27 Mar. 2007; VG Düsseldorf, 5 K 1068/07.A of 6 Jun. 2007.
527. BVerfG 10 Nov. 1989, BVerfGE 81, 58 et seq.
528. BVerfG (K), 2 BvR 1819/07 of 22 Nov. 2008.
529. BVerfG 1 Jul. 1987, BVerfGE 76, 143 et seq.; BVerfG (K), 2 BvR 1171/86 of 6 Nov. 1987.
530. §6, s. 2 Act on International Mutual Assistance in Criminal Matters (IRG).

# Part XVIII. The Law on Foundations

*816.* Foundations are legal entities that have property that is dedicated to a specific purpose. The Foundation Act of Rhineland-Palatinate (LStiftG RLP) can serve as an example for church foundations in Germany, although some principles and provisions differ in detail. The Foundation Act of Rhineland-Palatinate distinguishes between civil law foundations and public law foundations. Furthermore, there are private foundations, that pursue primarily private interests, and there are public foundations. Public foundations are those private law foundations that pursue primarily non-profit, charitable, or church aims in the meaning of tax law. Public foundations are also public law foundations. The Act explicitly defines church foundations as being foundations of civil or public law that perform church functions and are established or recognized as church foundations. Church foundations are also private or public law foundations that perform functions of a Jewish community or of another religious or belief community of public law and that have been established or recognized as a foundation assigned to those.

*817.* The state foundation authority keeps the register of public foundations having legal capacity that have their seat in the *Land*. The competent church can apply for registration of church foundations in that register. The respectively competent state ministry is the foundation authority for foundations that are dedicated primarily to religion, science and research, teaching and education, arts or care of monuments. However, if the minister or other staff of the ministry is a member of an organ of the foundation, the foundation authority is the *Land* Supervising and Service Authority.

*818.* If a church foundation is terminated and no person or institution of accession has been determined, the property of the foundation accrues to the respective church.

*819.* A foundation established by a church has to be recognized by the foundation authority upon application as having legal capacity if the permanent and persistent fulfilment of the purpose of the foundation seems to be guaranteed to the church authority, the purpose of the foundation does not endanger the public weal, and it meets the pertinent formal requirements. If the church foundation has not been established by the church, recognition of its legal capacity requires the prior consent of the respective religious community. Changes in the purpose of the church foundation, amendments to its statutes, mergers with other foundations or termination of the foundation have to be recognized by the state foundation authority if the respective religious community has given its prior approval. It is important to note that church foundations are not subject to state foundation supervision. This can be rather far-reaching because the state foundation authority supervises other foundations in terms of their proper budget and can demand to remove members of the organs of a foundation because of gross violations of duty or because of incompetence. No church foundation is subject to such supervision because of the autonomy rights of religious communities.

# Selected Bibliography

von Campenhausen, Axel Freiherr & Heinrich de Wall. *Religionsverfassungsrecht*. 5th edn. Munich: C.H. Beck, 2022.

Classen, Claus Dieter. *Religionsrecht*. 3rd edn. Tübingen: Mohr Siebeck, 2021.

Czermak, Gerhard. *Religions- und Weltanschauungsrecht*. Berlin: Springer, 2008.

European Consortium for Church-State Research (ed.). (Yearly reports on state-religion topics in Europe, including reports on Germany).

Listl, Joseph & Dietrich Pirson (eds). *Handbuch des Staatskirchenrechts der Bundesrepublik Deutschland*. 2nd edn. Berlin: Duncker & Humblot, 1994 and 1995.

Pirson, Dietrich, et al. (eds). *Handbuch des Staatskirchenrechts der Bundesrepublik Deutschland*. 3rd edn. Berlin: Duncker & Humblot, 2021.

Robbers, Gerhard (ed.). *State and Church in the European Union*. 3rd edn. Baden-Baden: Nomos, 2019.

Robbers, Gerhard & Durham Cole (eds). *Encyclopedia of Law and Religion*. 5 volumes, Leiden: Brill 2016.

Unruh, Peter. *Religionsverfassungsrecht*. 5th edn. Baden-Baden: Nomos, 2023.

# Selected Bibliography

# Index

*The numbers here refer to paragraph numbers.*


Accidence insurance, 527, 528
*Advocatio dei*, 52
Alien, 125, 675
Alternative service, 134, 169, 170, 239
Associate, 190
Association, 38, 43, 67, 168, 188, 191, 192, 209 et seq., 215 et seq., 244, 281 et seq., 286, 290, 291, 296, 298, 325, 390, 493, 512, 561, 570, 619, 645, 729, 767, 769, 774
Atheism, 28, 80, 657
Atheist, 50, 122, 206, 332, 380, 382
Autonomy, 14, 44 et seq., 215, 225, 248, 264, 303 et seq., 312, 408, 411, 413, 429, 438, 492 et seq., 496, 689, 819

Belief, 4, 33, 38, 43, 44, 47, 49, 61, 64, 65, 69, 79, 83, 85, 89, 91, 92, 94 et seq., 111 et seq., 121, 121, 124, 126, 130, 136, 139, 141, 144, 145, 152 et seq., 159, 167 et seq., 189 et seq., 194 et seq., 207, 218, 229, 230, 237, 324, 325, 332, 378, 396, 398, 402, 410, 413, 416, 417, 428 et seq., 435, 508, 535, 552, 553, 561, 611, 614, 632, 636 et seq., 683, 702, 784, 789, 790, 810, 813, 816
Bhagwan, 171
Blood transfusion, 112, 128, 554 et seq.
Broadcasting, 274, 382, 388, 449, 727 et seq., 738
Burial laws, 252
Burial system, 791, 792

Cemeteries, 67, 68, 237, 252, 386, 791 et seq.
Charitable work, 363, 765
Children, 57, 69, 101, 103 et seq., 111, 112, 128, 140, 179, 229, 268, 271, 366, 381, 388, 556, 72, 575, 629, 631, 632, 638, 639, 660, 675, 676 et seq., 686, 688, 735, 736, 753, 767, 775, 777, 779 et seq., 802 et seq.
Christian, 19, 29, 41, 42, 48, 50, 53, 69, 70, 76, 77, 86, 88, 92, 111, 113, 118, 156, 168, 178, 179, 190, 195, 204, 227, 249, 277, 285, 294, 332, 353, 381, 427, 444, 446, 449, 454 et seq., 463, 496, 497, 630 et seq., 637, 644 et seq., 655, 659, 664, 671, 681, 695, 708, 723, 734, 790, 797
Church bell, 237
Church due, 588, 596, 608
Church of Scientology, 119, 411
Church tax, 47, 115, 229, 230, 288, 312, 328, 335, 377, 534, 578 et seq., 582 et seq., 602, 604, 606, 607, 608 et seq., 621, 623
Circumcision (male), 113
Civil servant, 233, 234, 236, 250, 253, 355, 358, 378, 382, 388, 517, 520, 522, 523, 526, 532, 533, 753, 756, 757
Civilian service, 130 et seq., 404
Clergy, 36, 46, 68, 357, 530, 543, 552, 785
Co-determination, 515
Co-educative physical education, 126
Co-educative sport, 639
Collective labour law, 480, 501, 506, 507, 512
Collective religious freedom, 189
Concordat, 333, 346 et seq., 357, 365, 370 et seq., 470, 715
Confessional secret, 552, 567
Conscience, 35, 38, 41, 43, 55, 62, 64, 65, 89 et seq., 101, 130, 134, 138, 145, 169, 194, 407, 554, 631, 761

## Index


Conscientious objection, 74, 89, 131 et seq., 170, 239, 240, 404
Cooperate, 269, 301, 645, 646, 658, 729, 761
Cooperation, 67, 75, 142, 344, 359, 376, 385, 388, 392, 447, 458, 459, 648, 672, 675, 676, 708, 761, 763, 779
Corporative freedom of religion or belief, 189
Criminal, 89, 131, 152, 153, 170, 196, 218, 219, 540, 552, 562, 565, 568 et seq., 594, 815
Crucifix, 633
*Cuius regio, eius religio*, 33
Cultural monument, 392, 718 et seq.
Culture, 1, 8, 88, 383, 387, 388, 421, 422, 444, 630, 632, 637, 675, 677, 709, 723, 762, 767, 785

Data protection, 272, 303, 541, 804, 807
Define religion, 116
Democracy, 77, 218, 369, 376, 426, 441, 442, 462
Democratic, 70, 95, 96, 150, 178, 179, 336, 338, 348, 376, 407, 408, 410, 412, 435, 440, 443, 454, 462, 464, 727, 811
Democratic process, 95, 440, 443, 464, 727
*Deutscher Bund,* 41, 723
Disciplinary measures, 235
Drugs, 122

Education, 1, 44, 46, 56 et seq., 67 et seq., 95, 101, 111, 122, 126, 178, 179, 353, 363, 382, 388, 422, 444, 493, 518, 520, 561, 574, 575, 630, 631, 638, 639, 642, 644, 648 et seq., 654, 660, 664, 666, 675, 676, 677, 684, 687, 691, 703 et seq., 721, 767, 776 et seq., 785, 817
*Einheitsvertrag,* 391
Election, 30, 329, 372, 390, 440, 454, 464
Eligibility, 56, 59, 200, 202, 442, 560
Employment, 46, 131, 177, 233, 329, 406, 428, 478, 483 et seq., 505, 525, 526, 561, 698, 762, 763, 767, 780, 789 et seq.
Employment Promotion, 518
Equal treatment, 35, 59, 84, 172, 200, 204, 205, 335, 378, 380, 418, 428, 493, 494, 560, 700
Equality, 77, 81, 84, 99, 155, 200, 202, 330, 426, 509, 648

European Convention on Human Rights, 400, 406
European Union, 220, 347, 360, 414 et seq., 425 et seq., 430, 458, 459

Family, 104, 107, 112, 152, 229, 536, 542, 543, 710, 715 et seq., 767, 803, 813
Federalism, 1
Financing, 75, 388, 595 et seq., 602, 606, 685, 772
Food requirements, 143
Forum internum, 114, 201
Foundation, 73, 209, 249, 257, 264, 363, 499, 816 et seq.
Free press, 96
Freedom of association, 67, 191, 325
Freedom of expression, 406
Freedom of opinion, 441
Freedom of religion or belief, 4, 6, 18, 33, 35, 44, 47, 49, 50, 55, 61, 64, 85, 89 et seq., 115, 118, 121, 124 et seq., 139, 141, 144, 145 et seq., 152 et seq., 159, 167 et seq., 188 et seq., 194 et seq., 207, 218, 229, 230, 237, 309, 324, 325, 329, 371, 376, 394, 398, 401, 402, 405 et seq., 426, 431, 435, 441, 480, 506, 508, 535, 552, 553, 611, 614, 636, 637, 639, 654, 676, 683, 737, 761, 784, 789, 790, 810
Freedom of speech, 405, 441
Full treaty, 389, 391
Fundamental rights, 1, 15, 17, 18, 41, 95 et seq., 142, 144, 146, 148 et seq., 158, 159, 161, 166, 176, 189 et seq., 308, 319, 325 et seq., 397, 415, 417, 419, 431, 434, 436, 534, 536, 553, 676

German Democratic Republic, 3, 19, 50, 168, 370, 463, 656

Health insurance, 226, 234, 519, 520, 747, 773, 784
Holocaust, 445
Holy Roman Empire, 30, 33, 45, 204
Holy See, 46, 75, 333, 340, 341, 343 et seq., 356 et seq., 363, 365, 370, 372 et seq., 469, 470, 698, 706
Horizontal application of fundamental rights, 144, 327 et seq., 534, 536
Horizontal effect, 329
Hospital, 128, 131, 405, 554, 559, 747, 748, 772

Human Rights, 171, 309, 310, 347, 400 et seq., 779

Immigration, 2, 23, 24, 27, 175, 723
Incompatibility, 451, 500
Insolvency, 246, 316
Institution, 81, 99, 131, 209, 233, 296, 306, 336, 360, 406, 411, 450, 466, 480, 502, 503, 508, 514, 542, 645, 729, 789, 790, 818
Institutional guarantee, 47, 56, 67, 96, 324, 436, 659
International law, 11, 12, 75, 337, 339 et seq., 344, 346, 395 et seq., 413, 546, 571, 573
International treaties, 12, 75, 357, 394, 399
*Invocatio dei*, 52
Islam, 20, 86, 298, 300, 301, 444, 461, 477, 654, 675 et seq., 681, 709
Islam Conference, 461, 477

Jewish, 4, 23, 29, 35, 48, 49, 53, 75, 76, 86, 139, 176, 201, 254, 258, 268, 274, 277, 278, 294, 332, 383 et seq., 445, 449, 460, 474, 476, 578, 622, 634, 642, 644, 709, 723, 728, 731, 735, 738, 742, 764, 787, 790, 816
Jews, 4, 32, 35, 42, 48, 49, 156, 168, 294, 392, 445, 454, 460, 644, 709, 729, 735
Josephinism, 36
Judiciary, 1, 5, 119

*Kirchenkampf,* 48, 333
*Kulturkampf,* 46, 691

Labour law, 144, 233, 318, 422, 480, 482, 483, 492 et seq., 501, 502 et seq., 530, 536, 551
*Länder,* 1, 6, 13, 14, 16 et seq., 22, 38, 41, 44, 56, 58, 62 et seq., 110, 119, 150, 176 et seq., 180, 196, 200, 202, 218, 219, 228 et seq., 237, 252, 260, 264, 265, 271, 278, 283, 284, 287, 294, 300, 333, 335, 339 et seq., 344 et seq., 353, 359, 361, 362, 366, 370, 373, 376, 379 et seq., 393, 433 et seq., 444, 447 et seq., 457, 457, 458, 469 et seq., 474, 476, 512, 575, 578, 584, 585, 587, 596, 598, 599, 603, 606, 616 et seq., 627 et seq., 635, 637, 647, 651, 653 et seq., 661, 675 et seq., 684, 692, 698 et seq., 718, 720, 722, 724 et seq., 749 et seq., 791, 792, 797, 798, 803, 805, 817
Legal guardians, 101, 111, 268, 632, 660, 676
Legal person, 86, 189, 191, 192, 194, 265, 325, 580
Liaison office, 458
Limitations, 5, 44, 67, 112, 145 et seq., 153, 156 et seq., 166 et seq., 197, 307 et seq., 319, 357, 373, 378, 402, 413, 417
Local communities, 212, 237, 260, 265, 304, 438, 616, 724, 786, 809
Loyalty obligation, 411, 412, 492 et seq., 503

Manifestation, 33, 47, 95, 124, 168, 190, 324, 409, 813
Marriage, 46, 104, 152, 195, 202, 229, 368, 542 et seq., 592, 710 et seq., 767, 802, 807
Martin Luther, 31, 33
Maturity, 101, 102, 110 et seq., 579
Media, 28, 226, 268, 382, 388, 405, 412, 422, 460, 473, 477, 727, 729, 734, 735, 742
Medical treatment, 89, 112, 128, 558, 559
Membership, 26, 56, 64, 65, 98, 140, 210, 227, 234, 348, 390, 406, 472, 497, 500, 539, 581, 613, 620, 809, 812, 815
Middle Age, 30
Military chaplaincy, 47, 75, 340, 356, 533, 751 et seq.
Military service, 55, 74, 91, 92, 130, 132, 134, 169, 170, 239, 240, 357, 404
Military service, suspension of compulsory, 130, 169, 239
Minister, 13, 477, 698, 817
Muezzin–call, 187, 535
Municipalities, 14, 67, 438, 439, 595, 600, 792 et seq.
Muslim, 24, 28, 53, 76, 82, 83, 114, 125, 126, 141, 142, 144, 172 et seq., 202, 222, 298 et seq., 332, 393, 444, 449, 454, 461, 477, 634, 635, 639, 654, 675 et seq., 681, 709, 714, 723, 728, 742, 760, 775, 790, 797
Muslim headscarf, 125, 172, 173, 202, 634
Muslim ritual prayer, 185

Name, 30, 190, 197, 212, 229, 332, 333, 361, 454, 469, 499

## Index


National Socialism, 4, 19, 48, 61, 139, 201, 348
Natural law, 8
Neutrality, 35, 79 et seq., 93, 99, 172, 176 et seq., 200, 233, 293, 309, 320, 321, 336, 379, 390, 408, 418, 425, 442, 444, 509, 617, 619, 630 et seq., 637, 678, 700, 703, 704, 779
Non-discrimination, 178, 179, 200, 202
Non-profit association, 209, 211, 212, 217

Oath of office, 60, 61, 136, 202
Object, 131, 134, 139, 170, 237, 329, 565, 575, 632, 682, 695, 733
Objection, 74, 92, 127, 130 et seq., 170, 240, 404, 604, 633
Occupation, 428, 466, 494, 518, 767
Official costumes and insignia, 570
Official liability, 250
Orthodox Christian, 25, 619

Parents, 101, 103, 106, 111, 112, 140, 178, 179 et seq., 268, 366, 556, 631, 632, 638, 654, 659, 660, 676, 678, 777, 779, 781, 803, 805
Parity, 79, 84, 200, 204, 334, 335, 342, 343, 378, 389
Parliament, 63, 333, 343, 395, 450, 454, 476, 740, 741
Parochial right, 251
Penal law, 182
Pension insurance, 522 et seq.
Philosophical communities, 67, 75, 78, 99, 203, 206, 223, 294, 332, 380, 425, 427
Pluralism, 79, 99, 332, 336, 407 et seq., 680, 762, 780
Police, 1, 182, 237, 340, 745, 749, 760, 785
Political clause, 361, 373, 469
Political parties, 46, 233, 348, 412, 452 et seq., 464, 472, 729, 738
Practice of religion, 4, 55, 64, 91, 93, 122, 123, 381, 565, 719, 721
Preamble, 51 et seq., 62, 63, 349, 370, 376, 379, 383, 392, 427, 632, 751
Priests, 318, 356, 357, 450, 517, 529, 551, 619, 673, 741
Prison, 46, 124, 152, 153, 168, 767
Prisoner, 124, 168
Privacy, 813
Private schools, 179, 314, 422, 683 et seq., 687
Property, 24, 30, 33, 40, 50, 95, 96, 219, 237, 254, 261, 330, 351, 352, 363, 386, 463, 537, 565, 575 et seq., 588, 600, 614, 619, 621, 625, 718, 721, 816, 818
Proportionality, 119, 165, 166
Proselytism, 124, 630
Protestant, 19 et seq., 28, 29, 32 et seq., 44 et seq., 75, 86, 107, 133, 134, 196, 202, 274, 277, 294, 306, 319, 321, 339, 376, 378, 379, 444, 446, 447, 454, 457, 459, 462 et se., 469, 470, 496, 508, 509, 514, 517, 529, 531, 551, 581, 585, 587, 596 et seq., 620, 642, 654, 658, 663, 681, 688, 690, 691, 699 et seq., 727, 728 et seq., 734, 737, 738, 745 et seq., 754, 755, 784
Public assignment, 376, 379, 440, 446 et seq.
Public debate, 167, 178, 427, 440, 444, 462, 632, 638, 639, 742
Public law corporations, 193, 225, 231 et seq., 237, 238, 241, 245 et seq., 294, 296, 305, 320, 322, 326, 328, 443, 537, 578, 627
Public mandate, 449, 727
Public office, 56, 59, 64, 77, 200, 202, 243, 250, 329, 358, 442, 450, 451, 466, 532, 560, 741
Public property, 50, 237, 463, 537
Public sphere, 75, 87, 115, 197, 445

Reformation, 31, 32, 33, 786
Registration, 207, 214, 229, 238, 251, 271, 284, 411, 798 et seq., 817
*Reichsdeputationshauptschluss,* 40, 45, 576, 616, 619
*Reichskonkordat,* 75, 333, 335, 348 et seq., 355, 358, 365 et seq., 376, 469 et seq.
Religious community, 43, 57, 65, 67, 69, 74, 75, 80, 98, 115, 124, 128, 140, 141, 168, 171, 188, 195 et seq., 205, 209, 218, 227 et seq., 233 et seq., 244, 253, 261, 279, 283 et seq., 293 et seq., 303 et seq., 311 et seq., 317 et seq., 326, 328, 335, 346, 347, 378, 381, 386, 390, 391, 405, et seq., 430 et seq., 443, 448, 467, 472, 483, 492, 493, 508, 531, 535, 539, 540, 545, 550, 551, 553, 561, 564, 568, 575, 579, 581, 584, 606, 609 et seq., 640, 645, 646, 648, 651, 663, 667, 670, 672 et seq., 690, 693,

718, 719, 726, 729, 762, 774, 780, 789, 790, 810, 819
Religious holiday, 111, 144, 386, 783 et seq.
Religious instruction, 47, 57, 71, 75, 104, 110, 115, 178, 202, 253, 298, 301, 353, 367, 375, 381, 477, 533, 640, 643 et seq., 657 et seq., 676, 679 et seq., 706
Religious Peace of Augsburg, 33, 35
Reunification, 3, 50, 68, 370, 373, 379, 462, 463, 616, 656
Right to strike, 508
Ritual slaughter, 141, 142
Roman-Catholic, 19, 33, 35, 45 et seq., 107, 197, 277, 306, 333, 334, 479, 481, 501, 551, 559, 619, 663, 767, 768

School, 46, 47, 57, 69 et seq., 74, 75, 83, 90, 104, 110, 111, 115, 174 et seq., 180 et seq., 202, 298, 301, 306, 314, 333, 349, 353, 354, 360, 366, 375, 381, 386, 388, 422, 477, 518 et seq., 533, 621, 629 et seq., 645 et seq., 652 et seq., 658, 664, 665, 668, 670 et seq., 679 et seq., 691, 709, 763, 767, 789 et seq.
Second World War, 49, 62, 168, 346, 349, 370, 376, 446, 447
Sect-commissioner, 196
Self-determination, 47, 80, 128, 177, 203, 215, 246, 248, 303 et seq., 329, 378, 406, 408, 430, 468, 482, 483, 492, 506, 508, 531, 551, 561, 677
Separate, 22, 149, 529
Separation, 47, 77, 78, 82, 334, 676, 679, 757, 761, 779
Social care, 762, 764, 775
Social security, 493, 516, 517, 561
Socialism, 50, 463
State court, 107, 118, 246, 313, 317, 318, 321 et seq., 483, 639, 713
State of defence, 158
State warning, 171
Status, 4, 32 et seq., 56, 66, 67, 74, 76, 80, 84, 86, 167, 193, 196, 200, 205 et seq., 217, 223 et seq., 229, 232, 233, 235, 237, 247, 249, 250, 253, 258, 262, 263, 267, 269, 273 et seq., 283 et seq., 294 et seq., 303, 305, 312, 316 et seq., 326, 328 et seq., 349, 351, 358, 378, 380, 424, 426, 443, 467, 482, 533, 536, 537, 541, 551, 578, 645, 646, 647, 672, 689, 693, 696, 737, 745, 756, 764, 800, 802, 805, 807
Subsidies, 46, 56, 67, 265, 267, 335, 352, 382, 386, 388, 390, 575, 576, 577, 616, 621, 732, 766
Sunday, 56, 156, 727, 783, 786 et seq.

Tax, 47, 115, 229 et seq., 253 et seq., 275, 312, 328, 335, 377, 534, 569, 575, 578, 579 et seq., 621, 622 et seq., 805, 816
Tax law, 253, 583, 589, 613, 816
The right not to believe, 115
Theological faculties, 67, 68, 75, 335, 364, 374, 378, 422, 689 et seq., 699, 701, 705 et seq.
Third Way, 507, 509, 513
Tobacco Case, 168
Tolerance, 4, 70, 79, 83, 90, 99, 115, 418, 444, 631, 632, 637, 654
Tolerate, 237
Trade unions, 329, 442, 507 et seq.
Treaty, 35, 75, 233, 298, 331, 333 et seq., 342 et seq., 349, 357, 370, 376 et seq., 386 et seq., 423, 447, 468, 474, 476, 691, 701, 705, 751

Universities, 67, 68, 74, 75, 174, 304, 314, 335, 364, 374, 378, 533, 689 et seq., 699 et seq.
Urban planning, 122, 245, 809

Vollvertrag, 389, 391

Weimar Republic, 47, 56, 145, 348
*Weltanschauungsgemeinschaften,* 75, 206, 237, 287, 294, 647
World War I, 47

Youth welfare, 267

## Index

www.ingramcontent.com/pod-product-compliance
Lightning Source LLC
Chambersburg PA
CBHW070242030525
26096CB00033B/1218
* 9 7 8 9 4 0 3 5 3 9 4 8 5 *